UNDERSTANDING
US/UK GOVERNMENT
AND POLITICS

MANCHESTER
UNIVERSITY PRESS

UNDERSTANDING POLITICS

Series editor **DUNCAN WATTS**

Following the review of the national curriculum for
16–19 year olds, UK examining boards introduced
new specifications, first used in 2001 and 2002.
A-level courses are now divided into A/S level for the
first year of sixth-form studies, and the more difficult
A2 level thereafter. The **Understanding Politics**
series comprehensively covers the politics syllabuses
of all the major examination boards, featuring a
dedicated A/S-level textbook and four books
aimed at A2 students. The books are written in an
accessible, user-friendly and jargon-free manner
and will be essential to students sitting these
examinations.

Already published

Understanding political ideas and movements
Kevin Harrison and Tony Boyd

**Understanding British and European political
issues**
Neil McNaughton

**Understanding American government and
politics**
Duncan Watts

**Understanding A/S level government and
politics**
Chris Wilson

Understanding US/UK government and politics

A comparative guide

DUNCAN WATTS

Manchester University Press
Manchester and New York

distributed exclusively in the USA by Palgrave

Published by Manchester University Press
Oxford Road, Manchester M13 9NR, UK
and Room 400, 175 Fifth Avenue, New York, NY 10010, USA
www.manchesteruniversitypress.co.uk

Distributed exclusively in the USA by
Palgrave, 175 Fifth Avenue, New York,
NY 10010, USA

Distributed exclusively in Canada by
UBC Press, University of British Columbia, 2029 West Mall,
Vancouver, BC, Canada V6T 1Z2

British Library Cataloguing-in-Publication Data
A catalogue record for this book is available from the British Library

Library of Congress Cataloging-in-Publication Data applied for

ISBN 0 7190 6721 9   *paperback*

First published 2003

11   10   09   08   07   06   05   04   03   10   9   8   7   6   5   4   3   2   1

Typeset by Northern Phototypesetting Co. Ltd, Bolton
Printed in Great Britain
by CPI, Bath

Contents

Political leaders of the post-1945 era

Britain			United States		
Prime minister	*Party*	*Term*	*President*	*Party*	*Term*
C. Attlee	Labour	1945–51	F. Roosevelt	Democrat	1945
W. Churchill	Conservative	1951–55	H. Truman	Democrat	1945–53
A. Eden	Conservative	1955–57	D. Eisenhower	Republican	1953–61
H. Macmillan	Conservative	1957–63	J. Kennedy	Democrat	1961–63
A. Douglas-Home	Conservative	1963–64	L. Johnson	Democrat	1963–69
H. Wilson	Labour	1964–70	R. Nixon	Republican	1969–74
E. Heath	Conservative	1970–74	G. Ford	Republican	1974–77
H. Wilson	Labour	1974–76	J. Carter	Democrat	1977–81
J. Callaghan	Labour	1976–79	R. Reagan	Republican	1981–89
M. Thatcher	Conservative	1979–90	G. Bush	Republican	1989–93
J. Major	Conservative	1990–97	W. Clinton	Democrat	1993–2001
T. Blair	Labour	1997–	G. W. Bush	Republican	2001–

Political systems are shaped by the societies in which they function. For this reason, it is helpful to know something about the historical, geographical, social and economic settings against which they operate, and to understand something of the values and ideas which have mattered and continue to matter to those who inhabit any individual country.

In this introduction, we examine the background factors that help to shape the way in which political life and processes operate in Britain and America. In particular, we examine similarities and differences in the political culture of the two countries, for some commentators have attempted to identify broadly shared attitudes, belief systems and values that characterise the people of a country. Inevitably, this is to some extent an impressionistic topic and analysts tend to fall back on generalisations about national characteristics.

People's beliefs and values are based on the different experiences to which they are exposed throughout their lives. Growing up in Birmingham (Alabama) is different from growing up in rural Wyoming or New England, just as growing up in Birmingham (West Midlands) is different from growing up in Cornwall or the Lake District. Growing up in Birmingham on either side of the Atlantic is also very different, even if they are both large conurbations with a substantial ethnic mix. These different experiences reflect regional differences and affect what people believe and care about. Further differences derive from such matters as class, ethnicity, gender, language and religion.

The term 'culture' refers to the way of life of a people, the sum of their inherited and cherished ideas, knowledge and values, which together constitute the shared bases of social action. In assessing the attitudes and way of life of a people, it is easy to fall back on generalisations as a shorthand means of describing what they are like. Sometimes, these are related to ideas

*   Strictly speaking, Great Britain is comprised of England, Wales and Scotland, and the United Kingdom is made up of Great Britain and Northern Ireland. Throughout this book, however, we use 'Britain' and 'United Kingdom' interchangeably. Similarly, US, the USA and America are all used to mean the United States of America.

about national or group character. When in the 1960s the Beach Boys referred to 'California girls', the image they intended to convey was of a sun-tanned, lithe, fun-loving and easy-going category of young women. This is a stereotype, but many members of their audience probably had a clear impression of what such girls were like. However, generalisations such as these have obvious limitations and are insufficient for those who want to analyse the culture of a country. They want a more reliable tool and so turn to survey research. They find out the responses of a selected sample of the population to a series of questions about beliefs and actions, and then assess the overall findings.

Political culture is culture in its political aspect. It emphasises those patterns of thought and behaviour associated with politics in different societies, ones that are widely shared and define the relationship of citizens to their government and to each other in matters affecting politics and public affairs. Citizens of any country or major ethnic or religious community tend to have a common or core political culture, a set of long-term ideas and traditions which are passed on from one generation to the next. The survey work of Almond and Verba[1] led to the publication of *The Civic Culture* in 1963, a landmark study in the field of political culture. Based on lengthy inter-

> **political culture**
> The widely held underlying political beliefs and values which most citizens of a country share about the conduct of government, the relationship of citizens to those who rule over them and to one another.

views conducted in five countries, the researchers pointed to considerable variations in the political beliefs of the societies they explored.

The impressions and survey work of commentators and academics are of interest to those who wish to study politics. They enable us to make comparisons about the approaches which characterise the inhabitants of other democracies. For instance, the French are more willing to resort to social upheaval and 'man the barricades' when conflict between groups arises. In contrast, the British are more willing to compromise, having a long tradition of progress by evolution rather than revolution. Such conclusions can be helpful, but they have their limitations. Their findings about a particular country cannot be regarded as applicable for all people and for all time.

Research inevitably focuses on what the majority of the people appear to think and feel. However, some of the surveys carried out since the 1960s have pointed to the differences in the political beliefs of individuals within the same society. They have also shown that political culture is not an unchanging landscape, a fixed background against which the political process operates. Attitudes can evolve and change over time, for there are in society often a number of forces at work that serve to modify popular attitudes, among them migration and the emergence in a number of liberal democracies of a substantial underclass. Both can be a cause of greater diversity in popular attitudes, because immigrants and those alienated from majority lifestyles may have a looser attachment with prevailing cultural norms. In the words of one author, 'culture moves'.[2]

The process by which people acquire their central tenets and values, and gain knowledge about politics, is known as **political socialisation**. It derives from learning and social experience, and is strongly influenced by people with whom individuals have contact from early childhood through to adulthood. Political socialisation ensures that important values are passed on from one generation to the next and that the latest influx of immigrants comprehend, accept and approve the existing political system, and the procedures and institutions through which it operates. Political socialisation is for this reason overwhelmingly conservative in its effects, having a tendency to ensure that people conserve the best of the past.

> **political socialisation**
> The process by which individuals acquire their particular political ideas, their knowledge, feelings and judgements about the political world.

In any society, the political culture will have several strands which are only partially compatible. Different elements of the public draw more or less strongly from these several strands. Because of this, **public opinion** will vary on and across the issues of the day. Public opinion is the distribution of citizen opinion on matters of public concern or interest. As Heywood explains, 'political culture differs from public opinion in that it is fashioned out of long-term values rather than simply people's reactions to specific policies and problems'.[3]

> **public opinion**
> The cluster of attitudes and beliefs held by people about a variety of issues, in our case those concerning politics and policy issues. There can be no single public opinion. There are rather several opinions held by members of the public.

Political culture in Britain

Britain has a long history of independent existence as a more or less united nation. It has a strong commitment to democracy, with its representative institutions of government, based on regular and free elections, in addition to strong liberal values about individual rights and responsibilities. It was the first parliamentary democracy in Europe, so that many of the other countries modelled their institutions, party system and methods on the British experience. In particular, the Westminster model was exported to many of the colonies and territories of the old Empire, when countries became independent.

The British have traditionally preferred to use parliamentary channels rather than the anti-parliamentary politics of street demonstrations, direct action and terrorist violence. People generally accept the main institutions of state and the idea that issues should be resolved through the ballot box and not by the bullet and the bomb, even if at various times individuals and groups in parts of Ireland have not subscribed to that preference. People have been willing to place trust in the political elite that rules them, so that social deference (respect for or compliance with the wishes of those in authority) has often been mentioned as a source of British conformity and acquiescence in the status quo.

Continuity is another key element in British political life. It affects not just the hereditary monarchy and House of Lords, which until 1999 had a large hereditary element, but other institutions that also have a long history. As we have seen, the country has not been a prey to the internal turmoil, revolutionary dissent or occupation by a foreign power which many of our continental neighbours have experienced. Relatively free from upheaval, the British have enjoyed a stable political system, in which the past presses heavily on present practice. Evolutionary rather than revolutionary change has been preferred. The British have a preference for pragmatism over ideology and doctrine. As the country lacks a written constitution, ideas and institutions relating to government have evolved over the years, being modified as change becomes desirable or necessary. When politicians do suggest something which is very different to what voters are used to, such proposals are regarded with suspicion. Constitutional and parliamentary reformers invariably find that many individuals and groups are resistant to new thinking.

Britain's island position has affected its attitudes, with important historical, economic and political consequences. The sea has helped to protect the country from invasion, but has also strengthened the development of a common language and national identity. It has made people reluctant to throw in their lot with the European Community/Union, for Britain is separated from the continent by geography, language and culture. In many respects it has stronger bonds with the United States, with ties of historical development, defence interests, language and entertainment. To the island Britain, trade was always important and a spur to colonial expansion – it developed a British Empire, now the Commonwealth, so that in foreign policy it has links with Europe (since joining the Community in 1973), the Commonwealth and the USA.

Political unity, stability and a tradition of independence have long been regarded as characteristics of the British political system. So too has consensus – the preference for agreement, cooperation and moderation. The majority of British people have long preferred cooperation to confrontation and party politicians, once in office, have acknowledged this and for much of the time avoided confrontationalism. A political consensus prevailed in the postwar era through to the late 1970s, but the procedural consensus – broad agreement about the means of conducting political debate – has a much longer history.

British governments usually command a parliamentary majority following their election victory. This provides them with a legitimate right to govern.

The British appear to favour strong government by leaders of united parties and often punish divided parties at election time. Defenders of the First Past The Post electoral system have traditionally emphasised the importance of effective and stable government by a single party, in preference to any notions of fairness to small parties. Other than after a result which has been particularly distorted and harsh on the Liberals or some other third party, there has been until relatively recently been little demand for change in the way we elect our MPs.

Many people like to be led by politicians who know what they are doing and who lead parties which are broadly in agreement about what needs to be done and the manner and timing of doing it. Leaders such as Margaret Thatcher and Tony Blair have both been seen as 'strong leaders', prepared to ignore the dissident voices of some of their backbenchers and even carry out unpopular social policies. In both cases, too, they have relished the roles of war leader and statesperson on the global stage. Such has been the power of British administrations in the postwar era that writers have claimed we have an 'elective dictatorship'. British government has a reputation among commentators for being powerful and centralised, so that opposition in the House of Commons can be ignored – particularly if the majority is a large one. Ministers can use the government majority to push through fundamental changes in British life, if it is their will so to do.

Yet alongside the preference for strong government, there is also an attitude of tolerance towards the expression of alternative and minority opinions, with a clear recognition of the right – duty – of the Opposition to oppose. The existence of an official Opposition party in the House symbolises a commitment to free speech and the rights of personal liberty. Individual freedom is a much-cherished value. Whenever suggestions are made which appear to make an inroad into that attachment, there tends to be an outcry that is not just confined to civil libertarians. In a more dangerous age, people have had to get used to more security checks at airports, but issues such as alleged tapping of telephones, proposals for greater police surveillance, speed cameras to control the way we drive, the abandonment of juries in some court trials and the possible introduction of ID cards cause much resentment, if not actual resistance. British people do not like having to prove who they are and the idea of carrying 'papers' goes 'against the grain'. Neither do they like unnecessary regulations which deny them access or tell them how something should be done.

In spite of the growth of a less deferential, more questioning attitude (see box on p. 6) and a willingness on occasion to resort to direct action, there is still no great desire on the part of the majority for radical change. There remains a broad – if declining – acceptance of the institutions of government and a preference for democratic methods. Madgwick has described the way in which 'the British people stumble on, resilient, tolerant, hopeful (in a Micawber fashion), confused, but with a remarkable capacity for putting up with discontent for fear or worse, and defying the political scientist to penetrate the secret of the ambivalent political attitudes which have sustained their stable democracy'.[4]

Homogeneity, consensus and deference

Back in the 1960s, Punnett wrote of British society as being marked by three particular characteristics: homogeneity (sameness), consensus (broad agreement) and deference (social respect for one's superiors).[5] They were long-established features of the British way of life. All of them have been under strain since he wrote his first edition.

Ethnic homogeneity is no longer the force that it was, for British society is now more culturally diverse than ever before. It has been – sometimes painfully – transformed into a multicultural society, with London and several towns and cities being areas of high-density immigration. It still lacks the problems which characterise many other countries where linguistic, religious or racial cleavages are more apparent. However, conflicts based on such divisions are often difficult to resolve, more so than those based on class and economic disparities. People have a chance of escaping from a depressed region, poor living conditions or a particular social class. It is more difficult to escape from a group into which you were born – even should you wish to do so – especially if your skin colour is distinctive.

Consensus in society about shared ideas and values has been shaken in recent years as well. Broad agreement on policy goals was a feature of government in the 1950s to 1970s. It was replaced after 1979 by the more ideological approach of the Thatcher years, when the Prime Minister provided a more distinctive and many would say harsher approach to social and economic policy. Consensus on procedural matters has also been under strain. The vast majority still accept that grievances can be addressed through peaceful, parliamentary channels, but a minority has been more willing to employ direct action to achieve its ends. Strikes have been much less common than they were in the 1960s and 1970s, but (sometimes politically motivated) protests and riots have been more in evidence in recent decades.

Deference too has been a declining feature of British life. Walter Bagehot drew attention to deference in his classic study of the English Constitution, written in 1867, noting the respect of the people for law and order and their near-reverence liking for the monarchy.[6] It is a rather out-of-date concept which dates back to the social respect with which some members of the working class looked up to those above them on the class ladder. They regarded the traditional rulers of the country as people 'born to rule', having had the right background, education and upbringing. Working-class Conservatism was often explained in terms of deference, voters seeing the sort of people who once led the party as superior in their governing abilities. These days have long disappeared. In a more educated age, people are likely to value others according to their contribution rather than their social status, and journalistic attitudes to figures of authority have also served to undermine respect. In any case, it is less easy to look up to Conservative leaders who – in several recent cases – have had a similar background to one's own.

Political culture in the USA

A sense of unity, despite diversity

America is a multi-lingual, multi-racial society of great social diversity. Yet many of the immigrants and their descendants have taken on board many traditional American values such as a commitment to liberty and equality. There are forces which bring Americans together and give them a sense of common identity. Part of this sense of national unity can be explained by the pursuit of the **American Dream** via which all may prosper in a land of opportunity. The Dream is much referred to in literature and films. It is in Bill Clinton's words, 'the dream that we were all raised on'. It is based on a powerful but simple idea, that if you work hard and play by the rules you should have the chance to go as far as your God-given talents will take you. Americans are valued according to what they make of their chances in life. They should use their enterprise and initiative to make the best of themselves. If they do, 'there is gold in that there mountain'.

> **American Dream**
> The widespread belief that by hard work and individual enterprise even the most poor and lowly Americans can achieve economic success, a better way of life and enhanced social status, in a land of immense opportunity. According to the Dream, there are no insurmountable barriers which prevent Americans from fulfilling their potential, even if many individuals and groups do not do so.

Adversity, a sense of common danger, has also helped to unify Americans. War and the threat of war often serve to bind a nation. In World War Two, Americans of all creeds and backgrounds could recognise the contribution made by people very different from themselves. The same is true of September 2001 and thereafter. The attacks on the World Trade Center, which destroyed the well-known image of the New York skyline and killed nearly 4000 people, had the effect of bringing New Yorkers and their fellow Americans together. They were determined to hunt down the perpetrators of the outrage and to show the world that their spirits could not be crushed.

Finally, shared values, a common culture, the prevalence of the mass media and intermarriage serve to blur the differences between different groups. Most Americans can accept and embrace American values. They share a common attachment for certain ideals and processes, and it is to those that we now turn.

Common values

Political culture in the USA derives from some of the ideas which inspired the pioneers who made the country and the Founding Fathers who wrote its constitution. It includes faith in democracy and representative government, the ideas of popular sovereignty, limited government, the rule of law, equality, liberty, opportunity, support for the free-market system, freedom of speech and individual rights. But of course, at different stages in history, the existing political culture and the process of political socialisation serve some individuals and groups better than others. Until the 1960s, the prevailing political culture suggested that women and ethnic minorities were not full members of the political community. Not surprisingly, these two groups sought to change the political culture. They wanted to see ideas of equality and opportunity applied to them as much as to other groups. Since then, there has been a 'rights culture', as activists sought to demand the rights they regarded as their due.

American political culture is tied up with **American exceptionalism**, the view that American society and culture are exceptional in comparison with other advanced industrial democracies. In a sense this is true of all societies and cultures, but supporters of this view suggest that there are several features peculiar to US politics and society that distinguish the country from other Western democracies. It was the Frenchman **Alexis de Tocqueville**, who first wrote of 'American exceptionalism', back in 1835.[7] He saw the United States as 'a

> **Alexis de Tocqueville**
> (1805–59)
> A liberal French aristocrat, writer and politician, who visited the United States as a young man, was impressed and wrote his *Democracy in America*.

society uniquely different from the more traditional societies and status-bound nations of the Old World'. It was 'qualitively different in its organising principles and political and religious institutions from . . . other western societies', some of its distinguishing features being a relatively high level of social egalitarianism and social mobility, enthusiasm for religion, love of country, and ethnic and racial diversity.

One of its characteristics is a strong belief in **liberal individualism** dating back to the ideas of the English political philosopher John Locke (1632–1704), who wrote of people's inalienable natural rights. By contrast, the culture of the Old World has emphasised ideas of hierarchy and nationality. What Hames and Rae refer to as **messianism** is another.[8] Americans tend to see themselves as the 'Last, Best, Hope of Mankind', a theme apparent in foreign policy where some are isolationists who reject the rest of the world as beyond redemption while others are idealists who want to save the world and make it better (i.e. adopt American values and goals).

Sometimes, the different values identified conflict with each other. If liberal individualism is one element of the American outlook, stressing as it does freedom from overbearing governmental interference, so too is the republican strand another. As we see below, it is associated with the idea of political involvement by a concerned and interested citizenry, what Welch describes as 'a marked tilt towards participation'.[9] At times, the dislike of central government and fear of 'governmental encroachment' is more influential than the commitment to the ideal and practice of participation.

What are the key elements of American political culture?

As we have pointed out, analyses of political culture are inevitably replete with generalisations which must be regarded with a degree of scepticism. There is and can be no definitive listing of shared political values and the ones suggested in any contribution often tend to overlap with each other. At times, they have been ignored or at least denied in regard to certain social groups. Nonetheless, we can point to a number of shared interests and concerns.

1 Liberalism

A recognition of the dignity and worth of the individual and a tendency to view politics in individualistic terms. Classical liberals believed in government by consent, limited government, and the protection of private property and opportunity. They also stressed the importance of individual rights, some of which were regarded as 'inalienable'. Americans have great faith in the common sense of the average citizen and believe that all individuals have rights as well as responsibilities. Everyone should have the chance to fulfil their destiny, and no individual or group should be denied recognition of their worth or dignity. Individual liberties must be respected and people's opportunities for economic advance unimpeded. By contrast, collectivist policies and solutions (those based around the idea of the state – on behalf of its citizens – acknowledging society's collective responsibility to care about those in need) have never been embraced. (see the section on socialism on pp. 15, 188–91).

The word 'liberal' derives from the Latin *liber*, meaning 'free' or 'generous', from which we can detect an attachment to qualities such liberty and tolerance. The Americans have a strong attachment to liberty, as symbolised by the statue erected in its name. The War of Independence was fought in its name, and the Constitution, like the American Revolution, proclaims this commitment. The late Clinton Rossiter, a renowned American political scientist, saw liberty as the pre-eminent value in US political culture: 'We have always been a nation obsessed with liberty. Liberty over authority, freedom over responsibility, rights over duties – these are our historic preferences'.[10]

2 Equality

The words in the Declaration of Independence are clear enough: 'We hold these truths to be self-evident, that all men are created equal . . . '. As a relatively young nation, the USA lacks the feudal past which was a feature of many European countries. There has always been a strong belief in social equality, and although there are sharp inequalities of income and wealth, the divisions are not associated with a class system as they have been in Britain. The equality Americans favour is not equality of outcome, but rather of worth. They do not want a society in which all are reduced to the same level, for this would conflict with their belief in the opportunities they value in the American Dream. They do believe that every American is entitled to equal consideration, equal protection under the law and equal rights, even if at times there has been considerable reluctance to acknowledge that this applies to both black and white inhabitants.

Equality is more about prospects of advancement than about result. No one should be limited by his or her social background, ethnicity, gender or religion. All should have the chance to climb the ladder of success and share in the American Dream, in a land of opportunity. Even those of humble origins can still rise to greatness, so that Bill Clinton, the lad from Hope (Arkansas) could reach the White House.

3 Democracy

A belief in government by the people, according to majority will. Today, this might be seen as similar to liberalism with its emphasis on personal freedom and rights, but at the time the American Constitution was written in 1787 there was far more support for liberalism (as set out in the writings of John Locke) than for democracy, seen as rule by majorities and mobs.

Liberalism and democracy have roots in an older classical republican tradition. This dates back to the days of Ancient Rome and in particular to the writings of the Roman consul and writer Cicero. The speeches and writings of the Founding Fathers often employed republican imagery and symbols, and statues of George Washington have often shown him wearing Roman costume. The Ancient Romans believed in the idea of a self-governing republic ultimately ruled by a knowledgeable and involved citizenry. In this sense, the term 'republic' refers to a form of government that derives its powers directly or indirectly from the people. In a representative democracy, Americans could select representatives to govern and lay down the rules by which society operates. For the Founding Fathers, 'republic' seemed preferable to 'democracy', with its overtones of demagogy, mass rule and the mob.

Such fears have long disappeared and there has throughout much American history been a strong consensus in support of democracy and the values that underpin it, including:

- **A deep interest in the exercise of power**, who has it, how it was acquired and how those who exercise it can be removed.

- **A general acceptance of majority rule**, but also respect for minority rights so that minorities can have the opportunity to become tomorrow's majority. Pluralism in society, involving the existence and acceptance of distinctive groups and political toleration, has been important as the country has become more ethnically and religiously diverse, and people have adopted new lifestyle arrangements.

- **A firm commitment to popular sovereignty**, the idea that ultimate power resides in the people themselves

- **Strong support for the rule of law**, with government being based upon a body of law applied equally and with just procedures. The principle of fairness applies, with all individuals entitled to the same rights and level of protection, and expected to abide by the same codes of behaviour. No one is above the law, for in the words of Chief Justice Marshall: 'the government of the United States has been emphatically termed a government of laws, not of men'.

- **A dislike and distrust of government and a fear of the tyrannical rule and exercise of excessive authority that can accompany it**, not surprising in a land whose pioneers tamed the wilderness, created new frontiers and tried to build themselves a better future. Americans have always had a wariness about those who exercise power over them – a distrust which has roots in Lockean liberalism, but was primarily based upon the experiences of the colonists in their dealings with King George III. This suspicion of government and things associated with it may be a factor in the low turnouts in many elections.

- **A liking for politicians who seem to articulate the thoughts and feelings of the common man.** Populists who have railed against the special interests, the East Coast establishment or communists have often found a ready response. Anti-politicians such as **Ross Perot** and those who blend religion and politics in the fashion of **Jesse Jackson** have at times found themselves backed by a surge of popular enthusiasm.

Ross Perot

A billionaire Texan businessmen who had created and managed a highly successful computer firm; in 1992 he made known his interest in running for the presidency. Lacking any party label, he was able to get his name on the ballot paper in every state as a representative of his own creation, the 'United We Stand America' movement. Campaigning on the need to cut the deficit in national finances, he recruited campaign professionals and a mass of volunteer workers, and attracted a high profile on television. In the November election, although he failed to win in any single state, he did very well, attracting some 19 per cent of the popular vote. He stood again in 1996, as the candidate for the newly created Reform Party. This time, he made little impact.

Jesse Jackson

In the movement for civil rights, the black church played an influential role in communicating ideas and information. Black ministers such as Dr Martin Luther King and Jesse Jackson became nationally recognised figures. Jackson was a Democratic presidential candidate in 1984 and 1988. He has never held elective office, but has maintained a high profile – largely as a result of media visibility. An effective orator, he is on the left of the party and has shown a strong interest in the rights of minority groups and in issues of peace and war. He was highly critical of the Florida election result in 2000, alleging that numerous irregularities and examples of intimidation of potential black voters meant that the outcome was deeply flawed.

**THE GROWING DISTRUST OF GOVERNMENT AND POLITICIANS
IN THE UNITED STATES**

In the middle of the twentieth century, Americans viewed government much more positively than today. According to the National Opinion Research Center, more than three quarters of US people felt that national government was a beneficial influence which improved conditions in the country. Since then, many things have happened to undermine their confidence, among them the war in Vietnam, the Watergate scandal and the resignation of President Nixon, the Iran Contra affair, and the impeachment and trial of President Clinton. In addition, a series of cases involving the ethics of elected officials at national, state and local level have taken their toll. Political scandals have been a virus infecting political life for a long time, probably throughout American history, but the combination of recent abuses of power and personal indiscretions has fuelled a belief that politicians cannot be trusted and contributed to an increase in cynicism. At the approach of the new millennium, the number of Americans who expressed 'confidence in Washington to do what is right', was down from 76 per cent in 1964 to 29 per cent. Nearly two-thirds claimed to feel 'distant and unconnected' with government'.

Many Americans are indifferent to what goes on in Washington. It seems remote from their experience and – many might add – the policies which emerge from the capital are often wasteful, ineffective and ill-judged. Such anti-government feeling is widely held, even if its intensity varies considerably. At the one end of the spectrum are moderates who are wary of over-bearing Washingtonian attitudes and too much interference. At the other, there are strong devotees of states rights who much resent the intrusion of central government and who wish to see far more decision-making conducted at state or local level.

The anti-government message was evident in the 'Harry and Louise' TV ads used to attack the health reform plans of President Clinton in the early–mid-1990s. It is also apparent in the lobbying of those who fight any attempt at governmental interference in the constitutional right of all Americans to bear arms (see also p. 49).

War in Vietnam

Began under Kennedy and escalated under Johnson, waged to prevent communist North Vietnam from taking over the South, and by so doing to contain the spread of communism in Southeast Asia. This was America's first defeat in war. Vietnam was deeply divisive in American society. As the administration talked peace at the same time as intensifying the bombing of the North there was a credibility problem. Americans did not know what to believe.

4 Others

Other features could be mentioned, such as love of God and of their country, eternal optimism and idealism. Americans tend to be very religious. **Religion** (see also p. 22) matters in American life, in a way that it does not in most of Europe. There is a high rate of religious observance, especially among older

Watergate – Nixon resignation

The collective name for a series of abuses of power which began with a break-in at the national headquarters of the Democratic Party in the Watergate Building, Washington DC, in June 1972, as part of an attempt by the White House to find out the Democrats' election plans and thereby assist the chances of a Republican victory. As the story unfolded, many revelations were made, not least concerning the behaviour of the Nixon administration. Several Cabinet members ended up in jail, for a variety of offences. Eventually, the finger pointed to the President himself, who had clearly been deeply involved in the burglary and the cover-up which followed. It became apparent that he had been taping conversations in the Oval Office. When parts of the tapes were released on the demand of the Supreme Court, his position became untenable and with talk of him being impeached (see below), he resigned in August 1974 – the first President to so do.

Iran–Contra affair

'Irangate' concerned the illegal selling of arms to Iran in return for the release of American hostages detained in the Middle East, during the Reagan administration. The proceeds of the sales were channelled to the Contras, rebel forces who were seeking to overthrow a left-wing government in Nicaragua which the American government was hoping to desta-bilise. The President had publicly denounced the sale of weapons to states sponsoring terrorism, but his reputation remained reasonably intact even if the behaviour of some of his supporters was highly damaging.

Clinton and his impeachment

Impeachment is the process by which Congress can remove officers of the national government, including the President. The House votes on a series of charges and a trial is then conducted in the Senate. After a series of investigations into tales of presidential dissembling and sexual/financial misconduct, Bill Clinton was impeached by the House but later acquitted in the Senate. He was said to have lied under oath, obstructed justice and failed to respond to the questions posed by the House Judiciary Committee, in the case concerning Monica Lewinsky, widely known as Monicagate. Rumours of financial, political and sexual misconduct had swirled around him during his entire public life, and they continued to do so during his eight years in the White House.

Americans. Polling evidence suggests that they are more likely than citizens in other Western countries to consider religion important in their lives, to believe in Heaven, Hell and the Day of Judgement, to pray and to attend church. Religion is a defining feature of the political culture and has shaped the character of aspects of political life. The Declaration of Independence affirms that all men are 'endowed by their Creator' with certain rights and ends with a recognition of the 'firm reliance on the protection of divine Providence' necessary to make the Declaration a success. Religious faith – the Christian faith – has been and remains all-important. Candidates for office routinely acknowledge the Almighty in their speeches and discuss issues such as abortion, gay rights and foreign policy in moralistic terms. In the 2000 election, both George W. Bush and his Democrat opponent, Al Gore, frequently referred to their status as 'born again' Christians, and many other candidates were keen to parade details of their personal faith. Every President from Jimmy Carter onwards has claimed to have been 'born again'.

Religious groups operate at all levels of the political system, seeking to ensure that those who would attain political power share their beliefs. Religion has shaped and informed the character of political movements such as the one which campaigned for civil rights, and more recently the **religious right**.

Today, there are many more faiths in the USA than ever before, part of a remarkable upsurge in religious feeling. Religious toleration is a long-standing tradition, extending to groups with all manner of idiosyncrasies and eccentricities. It applies to the growing number of Islamic supporters, some of whom have been associated

> **religious right**
> The term is used to cover a broad movement of conservatives who advance moral and social values. It first attracted attention as the Moral Majority, but later became known as the Christian Coalition. Highly active in the Republican Party, it seeks to take America back to its 'true heritage' and to 'restore the godly principles that made the nation great'. Most of its members emphasise that they have been 'born again' (in other words, their religious life has been dramatically altered by a conversion experience which has made them see issues very differently). They tend to be fundamentalist (accepting the literal truth of the Bible), and are unquestioning in accepting Christian doctrines.

with more radical black political attitudes. Adherence to the Muslim faith poses a challenge to some traditional attitudes and values, the more so since the attack on the twin towers which placed many American Muslims in an uncomfortable and unenviable position. But as yet America has been spared the kind of religious tension which has bedevilled many other parts of the globe.

Intense admiration for and love of country is another American quality. Americans also tend to be very patriotic and to support emblems which help them to identify with their country. They acknowledge their Constitution, their anthem, their flag and other symbols of their nationhood. In particular, they respect the office of President, if not the behaviour of individual Presidents. The figure in the White House operates as a focal point of their national loyalty and especially in times of crisis he speaks up for the interests of all Americans. He and they possess the same vision. They want to build a better world for themselves and their families. They want a share in the American Dream. That Dream encompasses many of the values listed above – individualism, limited government, liberty and equal opportunities among them. It is in essence the belief that the United States of America is a land of opportunity for those prepared to work hard, get ahead and make a fortune. Americans are valued as individuals, according to what they make of their chances in life.

Given the commitment to the American Dream and the ideas that underpin it, it is no surprise that **socialism** has never taken root in the United States. Indeed, for Seymour Lipset and Gary Marks, its absence is a cornerstone of American exceptionalism.[11] They point out that opinion polls in America continue to reveal a people whose attitudes are different to those of people in Europe and Canada. Americans do not favour an active role for government in the economy or a desire for large welfare programmes. They favour private efforts in business and welfare and rely more on philanthropic giving. The two writers point to the absence of those conditions that the left has always seen as a prerequisite for the development of any 'mass allegiance' to socialism, but draw attention to the diversity of explanations given for the failure of American socialism (see also pp. 190–1 for a more detailed analysis):

> **socialism**
> Socialists share in common a belief that unrestrained capitalism is responsible for a variety of social evils, including the exploitation of working people, the widespread existence of poverty and unemployment, gross inequality of wealth and the pursuit of greed and selfishness. Socialists would prefer to see a social system based on cooperative values and emphasise the values of community rather than of individualism. They also believe strongly in the need for a more equal and just society, based on brotherhood and a sense of social solidarity.

> Explanations for [socialism]'s weakness are as numerous as socialists were few. Some . . . attribute the weakness of socialism to the failures of socialist organisations and leaders. Another school ascribes socialism's bankruptcy to its incompatibility with America's core values, while still others cite the American Constitution as the decisive factor.

In their analyses of the development of socialism, Karl Marx and Friedrich Engels contributed a Marxist perspective to the debate on the failure of American socialism. Marx had assumed that the working class was destined to organise revolutionary socialist parties in every capitalist society. He and Engels had, however, noted the respects in which the United States differed from other European societies. Above all, it was a new nation and society, a democratic country lacking many of the institutions and traditions of previously feudal societies. It had a 'modern and purely bourgeois culture'. After Marx's death in 1883, Engels gave more thought to the non-emergence of socialist movements on a mass scale. He attributed the 'backwardness' of the American workers to the absence of a feudal past. In his view, 'Americans [were] born conservatives – just because America is so purely bourgeois, so entirely without a feudal past and proud of its purely bourgeois organisation'.[12]

Political ideas, institutions and values in Britain and the United States: similarities and differences

The political culture in Britain has a number of elements in common with that in the United States, as well as substantial differences. The most obvious similarity is a common commitment to the democratic process, with overwhelming support for the political institutions of either country and a wide measure of consensus about the framework in which politics should operate. It has been written that part of the confusion about American political parties is that all Democrats are republicans, and all Republicans are democrats. There are few monarchists in the United States, just as there are few who would question the merits of the democratic form. So too in Britain: monarchy is still preferred by the majority of people, even if they want it in a modernised form. Attachment to democracy is not in question, so that Malcolm Shaw has described the two countries as 'the world's two great democracies'.[13]

In the same way, both countries share a common commitment to individual liberty. At times it may be overridden, often because of perceived threats to national security, but in terms of respect for basic rights both rate highly in the **Humana** scale. There is a common commitment to the **rule of law**, majority rule and tolerance for those who disagree, although in the USA such toleration has not always extended to groups on the political Left.

There is also the same preference for gradual political and social change, even if at times there is a sudden move forward in a particular area of policy. When changes are introduced, they tend to be accepted by the party which once opposed them, so that there is substantial continuity of policy and an unwillingness to 'rock the boat' without good reason. Broad policy consensus was characteristic of both countries in the early decades after World War II. But even when the Conservatives under Margaret Thatcher and the Republicans under Ronald Reagan shifted the centre of political gravity sharply to the Right, within a few years the main opposition party modified its stance to accept the changed situation. The Democrats were reinvented as the New Democrats and Labour became New

> **rule of law**
> Government based on the idea of the supremacy of law which must be applied equally and through just procedures. The law governs the actions of individual citizens to one another and also controls the conduct of the state towards them. Nobody is above the law, regardless of their status or position. In the United States, freedom from arbitrary action by government is written into the Constitution. The 5th Amendment requires that no person shall be deprived of 'life, liberty and property', without 'due process of law'.

> **Humana**
> Professor Charles Humana, once of Amnesty International, irregularly produces a World Human Rights Guide. It is an evaluative comparison of the state of human rights in more than 100 countries. It offers a human rights rating, derived from 40 criteria. The UK scores well on press freedom and balanced broadcasting, the US on support for political rights and civil liberties.

Labour. In both cases, some old attitudes were cast aside and policies discarded, in a bid to regain voters who had deserted them and to gain future electoral success.

There are differences in the political culture, not so much affecting thinking about the preferred form of government but more about some of the values that matter most. In Britain, liberty has rated more highly than equality. Even the Labour Party has now abandoned equality of outcome as an end objective and settled instead for equality of opportunity. From Neil Kinnock onwards, it has emphasised that liberty has the priority over equality and is to be regarded as a central tenet of party thinking, though some on the Left would

> **Clause Four**
> The original Clause Four of the 1918 Constitution committed the party to public ownership (nationalisation) of the means of production, distribution and exchange. There had been previous attempts to revise it, but Tony Blair succeeded in effecting change, in 1995. The 'new' version does not include a commitment to public ownership. It actually give prominence to enterprise, competition and the free market, with references to a just society and our duty to care for each other.

not share such a view. The new **Clause Four** stresses equality of opportunity and talks of enabling people 'to realise our true potential [and] the enterprise of the market and the rigour of competition'. In America, egalitarianism has a longer history, but it is interpreted more in terms of equal rights and equal participation than equality of reward or result. Equality of opportunity is again the preferred goal.

American talk of equality is seen in the attitude of people towards social class. Class barriers and differences of status based upon a class hierarchy are not recognised in American society, as they have traditionally been in Britain. In his study of 'Politics and Society', Alford found that 'status differentiation' was far more clearly apparent in Britain than in Australia, Canada or New Zealand.[14] Others too have noted a British preoccupation with class consciousness and the surviving existence of social snobbery. This runs counter to American ideas, for as Warner *et al* point out: 'In the bright glow and warm presence of the American Dream all men are born free and equal. Everyone in the American Dream has the right, and often the duty, to try to succeed and to do his best to reach the top'.[15] In the same way, deference may have lost much of its impact in Britain, but it never was a powerful force in the United States, for the whole idea of looking up to and respecting 'social superiors' is anathema.

Partly because of this difference in outlook, there has in the past been a difference of attitude towards government in both countries. Traditionally, the British have been willing to trust the men who led them, especially in the days when those politicians came from 'the 'natural rulers' of the people. Such faith cannot now be taken for granted, for distrust of the actions of government and diminished esteem for politicians have become common features in many democracies. Many people have become disillusioned by the differences in promise and fulfilment, and have become cynical about the intentions and probity of those who run their country.

According to Parry, the British are now less trusting and more cynical than Austrians, Germans and the Swiss, but more trusting and less cynical than the Italians or the Americans.[16] Yet more recent research suggests that the number of British people who trust government to put the needs of the nation above the interests of party 'just about always/most of the time' has steadily fallen from 39 per cent in 1974 to 22 per cent in 1996, and 75 per cent now trust the government 'only some of the time/almost never', a figure which is actually lower than that recorded for America (22 per cent).[17]

THE CIVIC CULTURE

The Almond and Verba findings

The first major study of political culture was that conducted by Almond and Verba in 1963.[18] Based on lengthy interviews in five countries – Italy, Mexico, West Germany (as it existed before unification), the United Kingdom and the United States) – the authors tried to identify the political culture in which a liberal democracy may best develop. They classified political cultures into three types, according to the relationship between individuals and the political order. These were parochial, subject and participant cultures. In parochial culture, which exist in areas populated by remote tribes, the people have little to do with the process of decision-making by central government. In subject cultures, people see themselves as subjects of the government, as applies in any dictatorship. In participatory cultures, people see themselves as citizens who play a role in the political system, both contributing to it and being affected by it. Almond and Verba argued that the ideal form was a 'civic culture' in which all three elements were present, so that 'citizens are sufficiently active in politics to express their preferences to rulers, but not so involved as to refuse to accept decisions with which they disagree. Thus the civic culture resolves the tension within democracy between popular control and effective governance'.

Some results adapted from the Almond and Verba findings:

	Britain (%)	United States (%)
Proud of government/institutions	46	85
Proud of economic system	10	23
Believe national government improves conditions	77	76
Believe the ordinary man should be active in community	39	51

The writers concluded that Britain came near to the ideal, as did the United States to a lesser degree. In Britain, with its 'deferential civic culture' the strong 'subject' role meant that people had a positive view of the effects of government action. They were proud of and attached to their governing institutions, and good at using them effectively. This

In the United States, the distrust of government is much more long-standing, even if the fears about behaviour and motives of politicians are similar. American distrust of those in authority stems partly from their more egalitarian attitudes, but also from a feeling that those who rule may have some worthy motives but are also out to advance their own self-interest and so need to be viewed with suspicion. It was Ronald Reagan who expressed the view that 'government is the problem', rather than the solution. He was reflecting an old American view that government is at best an uncomfortable necessity, at worst a menace and that Americans needed to be left alone to pursue their ideas and enterprises.

supplemented the more 'participant' role, providing a mix which worked well. The Americans scored well on several counts, especially pride in their system of government. They had a more 'participant' culture than the British, wanting to be more involved in political life. This might not prove so stable in the long term, given the constant pressure of extensive citizen involvement and demands. But it was recognised that people in either country possessed reasonable influence over their government but often chose not to exercise it, thereby allowing governments to act with considerable freedom of manoeuvre.

Since the research was conducted in 1963, both democracies have undergone changes. As Almond and Verba noted in their 1980 update, some of the attitudes and problems of the 1960s and 1970s had left their mark on the political cultures. Britain has become less deferential, and in both countries people have become more sceptical of government, their trust in its essential benevolence having seriously declined. Moreover, they have been less willing to turn out and vote in elections. In a controversial study which challenges the original Almond and Verba research, Putnam suggests that the willingness of Americans to engage in political life has diminished in recent decades.[19] He is at odds too with the views expressed by de Tocqueville back in 1835.

De Tocqueville v Putnam

De Tocqueville observed that 'Americans of all ages, all stations in life, and all types of disposition are forever forming associations'.[20] He portrayed them as belonging to 'the most democratic country in the world', extolling their involvement in groups which helped them pursue 'the objects of common desires'. Putnam doubts whether this still applies and argues that there is now a 'degree of social disengagement and civic disconnectedness' which has damaging consequences for political life. He believes that social participation is declining in the USA, observing that today more people spend time watching *Friends* than making them! More seriously, he points to fewer people engaged in volunteer work (there may be more pressure groups but average membership is only 10 per cent of its 1962 level and members tend to take a less active role), attending church or public meetings, voting in elections and trusting government.

Americans are more individualistic and wary of state intervention, whereas the British have been more willing to accept the role of government in our national life. In twentieth-century Britain, the state, on behalf of its citizens, came to acknowledge the collective responsibility of everyone to care about those in need (collectivism). After 1945, the Labour Party introduced a comprehensive programme of social welfare based upon the idea of a massive extension of governmental involvement in the nation's social and economic life. Many party enthusiasts felt that this was socialism in action. In America, with its individualist ethos and commitment to the American Dream, socialism has never taken root. Nor have the collectivist ideas associated with it, so that policies based on an extension of governmental control have been quickly denounced as 'socialistic'.

In our study of Britain and the United States, we are dealing with two very different countries: one old, one young; one relatively small, one large; one without and one with strong regional differences and attachments. They also differ greatly in their international stature. Britain is a once great power,

The social and economic background in Britain and the United States: some relevant and distinguishing characteristics		
	Britain	*United States*
History	Old country, invaded in distant past by a series of races who came and went, each leaving some aspect of their lifestyle on the island. Not successfully invaded since 1066; long, stable history, largely unbroken by serious internal conflict, except for Civil War in the seventeenth century.	Developed as a result of long series of migrations. Crossing of Columbus in 1492 first of a series of voyages of exploration and discovery which ultimately led to settlement of continent. Colonisation only began in the early seventeenth century, so essentially a young country. Colonists revolted, declaring their independence from Britain in 1776, so just over 200 years of independent nationhood, with a Civil War in the mid-nineteenth century.
Size and geographical position	Relatively small: 93,000 sq. miles. Distance from south coast to north of Scotland just over 600 miles. Offshore island of European continent.	Vast landmass: 3,794,083 sq. miles. Bordered by Canada in north and Mexico in south, with Pacific Ocean to west and Atlantic to east. Geographically isolated, faces little anger of invasion or conquest. Fourth largest country in world.

whose influence in the world has waned over the last fifty years; it might continue to 'punch above its weight in world affairs', but its ability to shape events has been markedly reduced. America is a 'Super Power', the leader of the free world and the most powerful nation in the world.

Yet the countries are linked by a common language and a number of common ideals and values. The colonial link of the past is an obvious bond and so is the democratic path they have taken. In both cases, there has been continuity of free and representative government, a preference for gradual rather than revolutionary change and a commitment to individual freedom. Theirs' has been a 'special relationship'. It is not a relationship of equals, nor can it be so. Some Americans might even be unsure who the 'special relationship' is with – Israel, Germany or some other country. But when world crises develop, as over the attacks on the twin towers, the bonds soon become apparent. As John Major put it: 'It is, I think, a product of history and the long relationship of trust between like-minded democracies with a common language and similar – but not identical – interests in the world'.[21]

	Britain	United States
Sectional/regional differences	Lacks serious regional, sectional divisions, although Scots and Welsh have long made claims about a distinctive Scottish and Welsh identity (now recognised with the creation of the Scottish Parliament and Welsh National Assembly. Some regional feelings, especially in north-east of England. Broadly, the further from London people are, the more complaints there are about the 'remoteness' of Westminster, which 'doesn't care'. Northern Ireland is distinctive. The majority Protestant population stresses its 'Britishness' and wishes to remain part of the UK. Many members of the large Catholic minority emphasise their preference to belong to a united Ireland.	Obvious regional differences, traditionally between rural, agricultural South and more industrial North. South always distinctive, especially over issue of slavery; its secession led to Civil War. South also distinctive in religion. No other region has such a cohesive identity as South, but West tends to be more isolationist (further from W. Europe), as well as less inclined to favour Washington's intervention in state affairs. East is more cosmopolitan than elsewhere, with diversity of ethnic groups in cities. New England, in the north-east, wealthy, liberal and parochial.

	Britain	United States
Population size and density	Just over 59m in UK (57.5m in Britain) in 2001, compared with 56m in 1991. Densely populated, with 245 people per square mile.	Approximately 283m today, compared with 240m in 1990. Much less densely populated: 79.6 people per square mile.
Composition of population	No such thing as pure British stock. Blood and culture of successive invaders (e.g. Romans and Angles) mingled with that of native British inhabitants. Composition also affected by various migrations of Jews, Irish, etc. Substantial post-war immigration from New Commonwealth and recent influx of asylum seekers. Black, Asian and other ethnic minority population now 6–7 per cent of total. More than half their number born in Britain.	A nation of immigrants; all Americans other than native American Indians are immigrants or descendants of them. Came broadly in three waves: north-western Europeans and Africans (brought as slaves) before the Civil War, Southern and Eastern Europeans in late nineteenth century/early twentieth century and Hispanics (Latinos) and Asians since World War Two. Country often seen as a melting pot, with mixture of cultures, ideas and peoples. African-Americans traditionally largest minority group, now equalled by Hispanics; with Asians, make up nearly 30% of population.
Religion and religious observance[i]	Not generally a divisive factor, except in Northern Ireland. Proportion who attend church has been diminishing for years. In most families, not a key issue for discussion. Traditionally a Christian country: majority are nominally Protestant, but some cities have sizeable Catholic population. 40m describe themselves as nominally Christian. Most Christians are not active worshippers, attending only for family occasions or in times of crisis. Influx of Hindus, Sikhs and Muslims has changed character of religious observance and deep fundamentalism (interpretation of every word in the scriptures as basically true) of some Muslims has opened up a new divide.	Strong Protestant leanings in Bible Belt of South where religious fundamentalism is widespread. Protestantism is creed of most Americans (58%), though Roman Catholics (26%) outnumber any single Protestant group. Religion matters in family life, society and politics, there being many varieties and shades of religious belief. God features strongly in public speeches, and 60 per cent of the population attend a church service regularly, at least every month. Politically, religion has been a catalyst for social change (e.g. Civil Rights movement of 1950s/1960s). Influence of Christian Coalition (the Religious Right) very important in Republican Party, affecting stand taken on abortion and school prayer.

	Britain	United States
Where people live	Highly urbanised: 90 per cent live in urban areas, though trend away from city centres to outer suburbs. Vast majority live in England (49.75m); Scotland, Wales and N. Ireland have around 5, 3 and 1.5m respectively.	Traditionally, most populous area was North-east; last few decades have seen move away from frost belt to sun belt, South and South-west gaining significantly. Twentieth century saw the development of an urban society, but now trend away from urban centres to suburban areas. 75 per cent live in urban areas.
Resources	Oil, coal and gas reserves, agriculture and forestry.	Endowed with considerable resources, ranging from coal to special metals. Rich in farmland.
Impact of industrialisation and present employment	Industrialisation has had significant impact on landscape. Engineering traditionally largest single industry. However, several millions of jobs lost with passing of old industries (coal, iron and steel, shipbuilding). Development of new industries.	North more industrialised. Now less reliance on traditional industries and more development of new ones.
Income, wealth and social class.	Significant discrepancies in ownership of income and wealth between those at top and those at bottom of social ladder. Class structure traditionally fairly rigid, though more opportunities for class mobility in recent decades with spread of educational opportunities. Substantial minority experiences relative poverty, including many members of ethnic minorities.	Income levels vary dramatically, in country which encourages enterprise and initiative. Some 10% below official poverty line, including many African-Americans, Hispanics and Native Americans. Class not seen as important, many seeing themselves as 'working Americans', irrespective of income and wealth. No strong notion of class solidarity.

Note: Figures for religious observance taken from Gallup polls, 1999 and 2000. Others from Statesmen's Yearbook, 2002.

REFERENCES

1   G. Almond and S. Verba, *The Civic Culture*, Princeton University Press, 1963.
2   T. Rochon, *Culture Moves: Ideas, Activism and Changing Values*, Princeton University Press, 1998.
3   A. Heywood, Politics, Macmillan, 1997
4   P Madgwick, *A New Introduction to British Politics*, Thornes, 1994.
5   R. Punnett, *British Government and Politics*, Gower, 1974.
6   W. Bagehot, *The English Constitution*, 1867. re-issued Fontana, 1963.
7   A. de Tocqueville, *Democracy in America*, vol. 2, re-issued by Alfred Knopf, 1948.
8   T. Hames and N. Rae, *Governing America*, Manchester University Press, 1996.
9   S. Welch, in G. Peele *et al.* (eds) *Developments in American Politics 4*, Palgrave, 2002.
10   C. Rossiter, *Conservatism in America*, Vintage, 1962.
11   S. Lipset and G. Marks, *Why Socialism Failed in the United States: It Didn't Happen Here*, W Norton, 2000.
12   Letter quoted as note 9 above.
13   M. Shaw, *Anglo-American Democracy*, Routledge and Kegan, 1968.
14   R. Alford, *Party and Society*, Murray, 1964.
15   W. Warner, M. Meeker and K. Eells, *Social Class in America*, Harper and Row, 1960
16   G. Parry, G. Moyser and N. Day, *Political Participation and Democracy in Britain*, Cambridge University Press, 1992.
17   *Political Action Study*, 1974 and *British Social Attitudes*, 1986–96, cited by J. Curtice and R. Jowell, 'Trust in the Political System', in R. Jowell *et al. British Social Attitudes: the 14th Report*, Ashgate, 1997.
18   As note 1 above.
19   R. Putnam, *Bowling Alone: The Collapse and Revival of American Community*, Simon & Schuster, 2000.
20   As note 7 above.
21   J. Major, *The Autobiography*, Harper Collins, 1999.

USEFUL WEB SITES

For the UK

www.data-archive.ac.uk UK Data Archive (University of Essex). Evidence on British social attitudes and public opinion.

www.natcen.ac.uk National Centre for Social Research.

www.statistics.gov.uk Office for National Statistics. Useful source of up-to-date information on social/economic features.

For the USA

www.census.gov US Census Bureau. Variety of statistics about social composition and lifestyles.

www.icpsr.umich.edu/GSS General Social Survey. Mass of polling evidence.

www.umich.edu/nes National Election Studies. More evidence from the polls.

Constitutions

2

Constitutions describe the fundamental rules according to which states are governed, be they embodied in the law, customs or conventions. They set out how decisions are made, how power is distributed among the institutions of government, the limits of governmental authority and the methods of election and appointment of those who exercise power. Constitutions also define the relationship between the state and the individual and usually include a listing of the rights of the citizen.

There are wide variations between different types of constitution and even between different constitutions of the same type. In essence, the British Constitution can be described as unwritten, unitary, parliamentary, monarchical and flexible, whereas the American one can be seen as written, federal, presidential, republican and rigid. There are qualifications to be made to this categorisation, as we shall see in this chapter.

POINTS TO CONSIDER

➤ What is a constitution?

➤ How important are constitutions?

➤ What advantages are there in having a codified constitution?

➤ How important are conventions within the British and American constitutions?

➤ What are the underlying principles of the British and American constitutions? How do they differ?

➤ How easy is it to amend the British and American constitutions?

➤ Is the American Constitution a perfect and timeless document?

➤ Why is there more talk of constitutional reform in Britain than in the United States?

General developments concerning constitutions

In recent decades, there has been a revival of interest in constitutions and constitutional matters, following a period in which study of them was often seen as dull and arid. This renewal of interest was in part associated with the collapse of dictatorial regimes in countries such as Portugal and Spain in the 1970s, and those formerly under Soviet control in Central and Eastern Europe, following the fall of the Berlin Wall in 1989. Other countries ranging from Canada to Sweden have also opted for new constitutional arrangements, in these cases to bring their original documents up-to-date to make them more in tune with the reality of their present systems of government.

Elsewhere, increased discussion of constitutional issues indicates that peoples ranging from the Australians to the Indians are seeing the need to revamp their constitutional arrangements, because of a mood of growing disillusionment with existing political systems and those who operate them. As Heywood points out, 'political conflict has increasingly been expressed in terms of calls for constitutional reform . . . conflicts assume a constitutional dimension only when those demanding change seek to redraw, and not merely re-adjust, the rules of the political game. Constitutional change is therefore about the re-apportionment of both power and political authority'. This has been true of the United Kingdom, but in the United States there has not been the same zeal for reform.[1]

What are constitutions?

Every country has a constitution of some kind, but the term is used in two different but related ways. There are many definitions of a constitution, such as that provided by the Oxford English Dictionary: 'the system or body of fundamental principles according to which a nation state or body politic is constituted and governed'. For our purposes, a working definition is: 'an agreed set of rules prescribing the organisation of the government of a country'. In other words, the constitution is concerned with the way in which decisions are made, and how powers are distributed among the various organs of government, be they central or local. It usually determines the boundaries of governmental authority, and the methods of election/appointment of those who are in power.

In a more precise and narrower sense, the 'constitution' refers to a single authoritative document which sets out the rules governing the composition, powers and methods of operation of the main institutions of government and the general principles applicable to their relations to citizens. There are many examples of such documents, for almost every country currently possesses one. The oldest one is the American Constitution, the writing of which intro-

duced 'the age of constitutions'. The view that
came to be adopted was that expressed by the
radical **Thomas Paine**, in *The Rights of Man*:
'Government without a Constitution is power
without Right'.[2]

Britain does not have such a written statement
describing the framework and functions of the
organs of government and declaring the
principles governing the operation of such institutions. Yet it obviously has institutions and rules
determining their creation and operation, and
the British Constitution consists of these. In Britain institutions have
developed through the ages, sometimes as a result of deliberate choice,
sometimes as the result of political forces. In addition, there have evolved a
number of conventional rules and practices which have helped to attune the
operation of the Constitution to changing conditions.

> **Thomas Paine** (1737–1809)
> A radical pamphleteer at the
> time of the American and
> French revolutions, he also
> wrote several fiery books,
> notably *Common Sense* (1776),
> a work which had fuelled the
> hot flames of revolution in the
> months leading to the War of
> Independence, *The Rights of
> Man* (1791–92) and *The Age of
> Reason* (1794–95).

Characteristics of the two constitutions

Age

Britain and the United States both have old constitutions, the one being the
oldest in the world, the other being the oldest *written* constitution in the
world. In both countries, constitutional development has been continuous and
largely unbroken. There have been serious interruptions to this – the English
Civil War and Protectorate, and the American Civil War – but in neither case
has the breach with tradition resulted in permanent change to the broad
pattern of evolution. As far as the form of government was concerned, the
status quo before the upheaval was in both cases restored. Few other countries
have constitutions which have stood the test of time in this way. Many continental examples have been relatively short-lived, with France having
seventeen since 1789, and Germany and Russia finding it necessary to rewrite
their constitutional arrangements on several occasions.

The British Constitution comprises an accumulation over many centuries of
traditions, customs, conventions, precedents and Acts of Parliament. It is old
by any standards, for its origins can be traced back at least to the period
following the Norman Conquest. No group of men ever sat down to agree on
what it should contain. Rather, it has been 'hammered out . . . on the anvil of
experience', progress being based on empiricism, a practical response to
prevailing need. Constitutional developments have come about gradually.
Although many of the institutions have a long history, the role they play is
constantly changing, which is why two writers were able to refer to the British
habit of placing 'new wine in old bottles'.[3]

In the case of America, its framers (the Founding Fathers) met at the Philadelphia Convention in 1787 in order to negotiate agreement on a replacement for the Articles of Confederation. The delegates at the Convention were a mix of older, experienced men and younger persons, some of whom were learned students of political philosophy. The more youthful element had matured politically during the revolutionary period and, being less tied to state loyalties than some of the older men whose attitudes had been formed before the war, they were able to think beyond the protection of state interests to embrace a wider national picture. They were nationalists intent upon building a nation, and this nation would require a constitution which was appropriate for its needs.

The debate was primarily between the federalists who favoured a strong national government, and the anti-federalists who favoured strong state government for they believed that this would be closer to the people. The outcome was a compromise between these two positions, often labelled dual federalism (see p. 164). As part of that compromise, the federalists gained much of what they wanted when it came to determining the form which the institutions of government would take.

Written v unwritten constitution

Written constitutions are important in states which have been subjected to internal dissension and upheaval over a long period. The American Constitution followed in the aftermath of the War of Independence, just as the Japanese and West German documents were devised after World War Two following the trauma associated with a major military defeat. They can provide no necessary guarantee of the enforcement of the principles for which they stand, but their existence serves as a reminder to citizens and those who rule of the need to abide by acceptable rules of behaviour involving an orderly approach to the conduct of affairs As such, they are a useful means of introducing a new political era after the failure or rejection of the older order.

Most constitutions are written down and embodied in a formal document. The American one is much briefer than many, having some 7000 words, expressed in seven long articles, and a mere ten pages. It establishes underlying principles, a broad framework for government. Few democratic countries today have unwritten constitutions. Apart from the United Kingdom, only Israel and New Zealand lack formal documents. Even among those countries usually classified as 'undemocratic' it is usual for there to be a clear statement of constitutional provisions.

It is misleading to seek an absolutely clear distinction between written and unwritten constitutions, and the differences between constitutions overseas and Britain's unwritten one are easily exaggerated. Countries with written documents may find that other information becomes necessary. No single document could ever describe all the rules and principles of government, certainly not in an intelligible manner. They need to be supplemented and interpreted by other documents or in court judgements which are recorded. In the United States, such key institutions as congressional committees, primary elections and the bureaucracy have gradually evolved to fill in the gaps in constitutional arrangements and to adapt the political system to changing conditions.

Much depends upon the meaning of the terms 'written' and 'unwritten'. Most of the British Constitution is written down somewhere, so that it is technically not 'unwritten'. This is why back in 1962 Wheare could suggest that rather than an unwritten constitution, Britain had no written constitution.[4] It is largely because of its ancient origins that the British Constitution is so unsystematic. No attempt has been made to collate it together, and codify the various rules and conventions that are part of it. It is probably more useful to distinguish between:

- codified constitutions such as that of the United States, in which all the main provisions are brought together in a single authoritative document; and
- uncodified constitutions such as that of the United Kingdom, which exist where there are constitutional rules many of which are written down but have not been collated.

Sources

In the American case, the major source of the Constitution is the document itself and those developments which have been included in the Constitution as a result of the passage of amendments (for example, the 13th Amendment guaranteeing the freeing of the slaves, and their constitutional rights). However, there are other sources which show that the web of constitutional arrangements goes beyond the formal ones above. Certain statutes have had a constitutional impact (such as the laws creating the executive departments and fixing the jurisdiction of federal courts). In addition, judicial decisions have been significant, rather more so than in Britain, for judges have been called upon to decide what the Constitution means at any given moment. Their decision can change over time, so that segregation was seen as acceptable in 1896 but unacceptable in 1954.

In the United Kingdom, there are many sources which can be consulted in order to locate the elusive British Constitution. These include:

- major constitutional documents – e.g. Magna Carta 1215;
- major texts by eminent experts on the Constitution – e.g. Bagehot's *The English Constitution* 1867;

- major statutes – e.g. the Human Rights Act 1998;
- case (judge-made) law – e.g. Spycatcher Case 1987;
- common law, based on custom and precedent – e.g. ancient law such as the powers of the Crown (the Royal Prerogative);
- constitutional conventions – e.g. that the choice of Prime Minister should be made from the House of Commons;
- European Union Law – e.g. primary legislation as is to be found in the Treaty of Rome and the other treaties, and secondary law as is to be found in EU regulations.

Most of the British Constitution is written down in various statutes, documents and commentaries, the unwritten part comprising the common law of the land in so far as it relates to the relations between government and citizens, and conventions, those customary rules followed in governing the country and which are recognised as constitutional modes of procedure. Membership of the European Union, with its acceptance of the Rome Treaty and Union regulations provides a significant written element to our constitutional arrangements.

Conventions have greater importance in Britain than in the United States, if only because there were significant gaps in British arrangements which required some resolution. Americans have in any case a reputation for being more legalistic, so that at times in their history they have wanted to see things clearly stated and codified in law. But in America, conventions are not totally unknown. It is a convention that electors in the **Electoral College** will cast their vote for the presidential candidate to whom they were pledged on polling day in November. Normally this is the case, but on occasion this has not happened. Electors have switched their allegiance (as in 1988 when a Democrat voted for Lloyd Bentsen, the vice-presidential nominee rather than Michael Dukakis, the candidate for the presidency) or withheld their vote to make a protest (as in 2000 when a Gore-supporting Democrat from the District of Columbia cast a blank vote to make a point about the city's lack of representation in Congress).

As in Britain, when American conventions are flouted, they can be turned into law. Just as the Parliament Act gave legal recognition to the convention that the House of Lords would not reject a money bill (once the convention had been ignored), so too the Americans passed an amendment to limit the period for which a President

Electoral College
A system under which a body is elected with the expressed purpose of itself electing a higher body. The best example is that of the United States, by which the Founding Fathers provided for the people of each state to elect a number of electors equal to the number of senators and representatives for that state. In nearly all states, the presidential candidate winning the plurality vote in that state receives all its electoral college votes. In usual times, the electoral college is a purely formal body which in effect confirms the decision already made by the voters in the November presidential election.

could serve in office. Until 1940, it had been assumed that Presidents would withdraw after two terms. Franklin Roosevelt had not done so, standing for a third and then a fourth term. The **22nd Amendment** (1947) restored the situation to what had always been assumed.

Flexible v rigid constitution

Flexible constitutions are rare. They can be altered via the law-making process without much difficulty, as in Britain. Being unwritten in a formal sense, the British Constitution can be easily amended. Even drastic changes can be made by passing an Act of Parliament, though there is a developing custom that fundamental

> **22nd Amendment**
> Proposed in 1947 and adopted in 1951, the amendment limits a President's tenure in office to two whole terms, although if he is Vice-President he may take over as President and complete the term of the outgoing President before starting the two terms won in his own right.

Advantages and disadvantages of the differing arrangements in the two countries

America's written constitution has a number of **advantages**:

- It provides a clearer statement of the position of what is and is not constitutional. It is convenient to have a written document to which reference can be made. There are areas of constitutional uncertainty in Britain, such as the role and powers of the monarch in the event of a hung parliament (for example could a demand for a **dissolution** ever be refused?).

- American citizens are in a position to be more aware of their rights and freedoms than are the people of Britain. They can quote their constitution in defence of their liberties, especially its Bill of Rights (see chapter 3). Until recently, the British position has been notably unclear and it will still be some time before we see how British courts interpret the clauses of the now-incorporated European Convention.

- The American document may have an educational value, helping to curb the behaviour of those in government office. They will not wish their actions to be found in breach of the Constitution, and the

> **dissolution of parliament**
> The termination of a parliament. The Prime Minister dissolves parliament by calling a general election.

knowledge that there is a reference point for those who are dissatisfied with the conduct of policy should help to keep them in line. The educative value of the constitution is wider than this, however. It serves as a statement of beliefs and values, and therefore helps to inform people about the ideas to which the majority of the population hold dear. In Britain, it has traditionally been easier for politicians to get away with actions which curb essential liberties, although the recent use of judicial review and the passage of the Human Rights Act has served to concentrate their minds.

- Finally, the American Constitution is more difficult to amend, for the key provisions are entrenched. Presidents cannot tamper with them at a whim, merely because of their inconvenience, as Franklin Roosevelt found out when he tried to 'pack the court' in the

changes would probably require a referendum if they have not already been submitted to the electorate in a general election.

Rigid constitutions are difficult to amend, the intention being that there is a delay sufficient to allow full discussion of any proposed change. The process of amendment is normally outlined in the constitution itself. The US Constitution is usually described as 'rigid', in that it can only be amended after prolonged deliberation. Article V reads:

> The Congress, whenever two thirds of both houses shall deem it necessary, shall propose amendments to this Constitution, or, on the application of the legislatures of two thirds of the several States, shall convene a convention for proposing amendments, which in either case shall be valid to all intents and purposes as part of this Constitution, when ratified by the legislatures of three fourths of the several states, or by conventions in three fourths thereof, as one or other mode of ratification may be proposed by Congress.

1930s, when it was proving obstructive to New Deal legislation. In Britain, ministers can devise new constitutional arrangements to the advantage of the governing party (such as electoral systems and plans for a revived House of Lords).

Yet against the case above, many **disadvantages** can be detected:

- Constitutions can be inflexible and rigid, incapable of being easily adapted to the needs of the day. Whereas the British Constitution is adaptable and has evolved according to circumstances, a formal document can be difficult to amend, and therefore may act as a barrier to much-needed social change. Several US Presidents have been attracted to the idea of gun control as a means of combating American crime, but they have run into fierce opposition from the National Rifle Association, which reminds people of the statement in the Constitution in Article Two of the Bill of Rights, guaranteeing citizens the right to bear arms. The Supreme Court was similarly able to restrict some of the New Deal legislation on the grounds that it was a breach of the Constitution, restricting states rights and giving too much power to the President.

- The existence of a written constitution does not necessarily provide a clear protection for people's rights. The US experience proves this, for the 15th Amendment passed in 1870 provides that: 'The right of citizens to vote shall not be denied or abridged by the US or by any states on account of race, colour or previous condition of servitude ... Congress shall have the power to enforce this by appropriate legislation.' Yet in many states, blacks were excluded from exercising their democratic right to vote until the 1960s on grounds of illiteracy or by such devices as **poll taxes**. For instance, the Puerto Ricans of New York were long excluded by a literacy test, though of course they may have been perfectly literate in Spanish. Rights clearly depend on other things, such as the tradition of liberty in a country.

poll tax
A tax levied per head of adult population.

Because it is not codified in a single document, it is easy to suggest that the British Constitution is more flexible than the American one. It is not difficult to pass a law or adapt a convention. Yet by virtue of its brevity and the generality of its language, the American one has required interpretation and supplementation, and has been relatively flexible. Twenty-seven amendments have been passed and as we have already seen judges have been able to give their verdict on what the Constitution actually means in practice, adapting their conclusions to the social and political climate of the day. The contrast between British experience and that of other countries with written constitutions is much greater than it is with the United States.

Constitutional principles

Support for democracy and the rule of law

Both constitutions include implicit or explicit constitutional principles. Implicitly, both countries are committed to democracy. Their institutional arrangements enable free political activity to take place, and regulation of the clashes of interest which arise within any society. But as Benn and Peters suggest, 'democracy is not merely a set of political institutions like universal suffrage . . . and decisions by majority procedure, but also a set of principles which such institutions tend to realise'.[5] Ideals and institutions are closely connected, for the more deep-rooted are the values of broad consensus, compromise, consent, discussion and tolerance among the population, the more likely it is that the institutions and procedures of government will give expression to them. The American philosopher John Dewey, was a leading exponent of the democratic ideal.[6] He saw such a system as a superior in form and purpose to other systems, for in his view it embodies the principle that each individual possesses intrinsic worth and dignity.

The rule of law is a core liberal-democratic principle with deep roots in Western civilisation. As stated by two British constitutional experts, Wade and Philips, it means that 'the exercise of powers of government shall be conditioned by law and that the subject shall not be exposed to the arbitrary will of the ruler'.[7] It does not by itself explain what it means to live in a free society, but it acts as an important restraint upon the power of government and as an assurance to individuals that there can be certainty about the law and its application. The phrase is sometimes used emotively with a meaning best suited to support a particular argument that is being advanced, but a certain vagueness of definition does nothing to undermine the importance of the moral ideas implicit in its use. It implies that there is a standard of impartiality, fairness and equality against which all governmental actions can be evaluated, and that no individual stands above the law. Rulers, like those over whom they rule, are answerable to it.

In Britain, there is widespread support for the rule of law and for the individual rights which it seeks to protect. It is seen as a cardinal feature of the British Constitution, deeply rooted in common law. In the USA, the principle is not specifically mentioned in the Constitution, yet it is one of the most important legacies of the Founding Fathers. The rule of law is implicit in a number of constitutional provisions in the American Constitution. Under Article IV, the 'Citizens of each State shall be entitled to the Privileges and immunities of Citizens in the several states. In the Bill of Rights, the Fifth Amendment requires 'due process of law' and 'just compensation' whenever government initiates adverse actions against a citizen.

Monarchy v republic

One of the most obvious differences between the two countries is the fact that one is a monarchy and the other a republic. Many American tourists now seem to admire the British Royal Family, and the colour, pageantry and quaintness that are associated with it. But when the colonists broke away from the British Crown in the War of Independence and subsequently devised a new constitution, they were not tempted to follow the British example. The difference is very visible, but yet not of crucial significance. The British monarchy is a constitutional one, in which the Queen 'reigns but does not rule'. She is Head of State and as such exercises a number of ceremonial functions. So too do elected Presidents in republics, but in the American case the President combines the role of figurehead with the more important, politically active position of being Chief of the Executive. The distinction between constitutional monarchies and republics is much less than in the days when monarchs exercised real power.

Unitary v federal

The British Constitution is a unitary rather than a federal one. Parliament at Westminster makes laws for all parts of the United Kingdom, whereas under federal arrangements the power to make laws is divided between central and state authority. In bygone days, royal authority was extended to the component parts of Scotland, Wales and Northern Ireland, either by conquest (in the case of Wales) or by agreed union (subsequently regretted by a section of the population) in the cases of Scotland and Northern Ireland. It was a long time before recognition was given to their separate identities within the context of the United Kingdom, even if sectional sentiment in the three non-English countries has always been present and a growing factor in recent decades.

Power may be – has been – devolved to other layers of government, both local – throughout the United Kingdom – and national, in the case of Scotland, Wales and Northern Ireland. But such bodies have only the powers granted to them, powers which may be taken away. In the words of Malcolm Shaw: 'In Britain, sovereign authority, whether exercised by King or Parliament, has always meant central authority. If Parliament is supreme, this supremacy must apply throughout the nation'.[8]

Unlike the British, Americans have always been used to the idea of living separately (in the days of the colonies), in powerful independent states (in the days of the Articles of Confederation) or in states which shared power with Washington (ever since the federal union was created by the Founding Fathers). Although they have long accepted that many decisions are taken beyond their states, their attachment to state government remains in several cases stronger than their liking for the federal government. The official motto of Illinois still recognises their divided loyalties: 'State Sovereignty, National Union'.

Not so long ago, there were signs that such was the increasing power of Washington in the federal relationship that states' rights were being ignored or overridden. Examination questions in Britain of the 1970s went as far as to ask whether the United States was becoming a unitary country. Since the 1980s there has been a reversal of the drift towards increased central control. Today, few would question the value of the states as useful and viable political entities with in many cases a marked capacity for innovation.

In Britain, the devolution introduced in Scotland and Wales by the Blair administration has meant that a form of decentralised government is common to both Britain and America. If in broad historical terms America now has stronger central power than was ever imagined by the Founding Fathers, so Britain has a greater degree of self-government than ever before, a process not yet perhaps completed (see pp. 159–63). Writers in Britain often debate whether or not Britain is moving in the direction of federalism with a form of 'Home Rule All Round', and it does seem that Britain has moved towards a kind of 'federal devolution'. The two systems of government have in a sense drawn closer together, but the fact remains that one is unitary, the other federal and as such this is a major constitutional distinction.

Parliamentary v presidential government, a fusion or a separation of powers?

Apart from the respective arrangements affecting the relationship between the centre and the regions and localities in the two countries, there are also significant difference in the relationship between the different branches of government in Britain and America. The British have a system of parliamentary government, in which the **Executive** is chosen from the **Legislature** and is dependent upon it for support. Thus the Cabinet is chosen from the

House of Commons and responsible to it. The Americans have presidential government, in which the Executive is separately elected and in theory equal to the Legislature.

Andrew Heywood explains the distinction well:

> A Parliamentary system of government is one in which the government governs in and through the assembly, thereby 'fusing' the legislative and executive branches. Although they are formally distinct, the assembly and the executive (usually seen as the government) are bound together in a way that violates the doctrine of the separation of powers, setting Parliamentary systems clearly apart from Presidential ones.[9]

Most liberal democracies – ranging from Australia to Sweden, from India to New Zealand – have some kind of parliamentary government, often of a Westminster type. Historically, Britain had an era of legislative supremacy over the Executive. The situation evolved into one in which there was a relatively even balance between the two branches. The suggestion is that we have now moved towards executive supremacy. The Executive tends to dominate the Legislature, because the party and electoral systems usually produce a strong majority government, what Lord Hailsham called 'an elective dictatorship'.[10]

Executive
The branch of government responsible for implementing or carrying out public policy and the laws of the state. The Executive is today much involved in formulating policy and laws.

Legislature
The branch of government that makes law through the formal enactment of legislation.

Parliamentary government appears to imply that government is checked by the power of Parliament, which examines, criticises and checks its activities via such methods as Question Time and the use of select committees. Ministers are individually and collectively responsible to Parliament, and should resign if the administration has been defeated on a Vote of Confidence (as happened with the Callaghan Government in 1979).

The term suggests that Parliament has real power. This may have been an accurate description in the mid-nineteenth century, when there was much cross-voting and governments were often brought down by an adverse vote in the House of Commons. That rarely happens today, for power has passed to the executive branch, and in a crisis (such as the Westland affair in 1986) all Tory MPs supported the Government. Such is the strength of party discipline today. Also, it is very difficult for Parliament to control the executive, because government is so vast and complex. MPs are so inadequately equipped and lacking in time that they cannot monitor its work really effectively.

Presidential government does not refer to the fact that America has a President rather than a monarch as head of state. As Heywood explains: 'A presidential system is characterised by a constitutional and political separation of powers between the legislative and executive branches of government'. A presidential system is one in which the Executive is elected separately from the Legislature, is outside of and in theory equal to it. The President is chosen by the people rather than from the legislative branch, and acts as Head of the Government as well as ceremonial Head of State.

In America there is a separation of powers; in Britain there is a fusion of power. In America, heads of departments and other executive bodies do not sit in Congress, and neither can congressmen possess executive office; in Britain, government ministers always sit in Parliament, the majority of them in the elected House of Commons – via the principle of ministerial responsibility, both individually as heads of their departments and collectively as members of the Cabinet, they are answerable to the House. Of course, the key member of the Executive in America – the President – is answerable as well, but in his case his responsibility is directly to the people rather than to the Legislature.

In Britain, Parliament is sovereign, so that the government can only continue in office as long as it has the support of the House of Commons. The Prime Minister and his or her colleagues have to attend the House and defend and answer for their actions. Parliament is the supreme law-making body; it has no rivals. Its position in the Constitution is in theory of paramount importance, even if in reality we live in an age often described as an elective dictatorship, with power having passed from the Legislature to the Executive. American experience is different, and the Legislature is not constitutionally supreme. The Legislature and Executive are in theory constitutional equals, even though at different times Congress may have seemed to be stronger than the Presidency and at others the White House dominant over Capitol Hill.

In both countries, there is a recognition of the desirability of an independent judiciary. Judges are appointed for life, and politicians do not involved in the proceedings or judgements of actual cases before the courts. However, ministers may bring about changes in court procedure and amend the law to affect sentences passed on categories of defendant. Michael Howard, as Conservative Home Secretary, imposed minimum prison sentences for burglars and hard-drug dealers, as well as automatic life sentences on rapists and other violent offenders who commit a second offence. His Labour successor, Jack Straw, made inroads into the principle of trial by jury. In America, although Congress may pass new laws affecting the courts, ultimately judges decide on the constitutional acceptability of any legal changes. Indeed, they are the final arbiters of what is meant by the principle of a separation of powers.

American constitutional arrangements have resulted in a diffusion of authority. It was always intended that no part of the constitution should develop excessive powers at the expense of the others. In Britain, constitutional sovereignty lay in theory with parliament, but there has been a significant drift of power from the legislature to the executive, resulting in a concentration rather than a diffusion of power.

The sovereignty of parliament v the sovereignty of the people

If the British Constitution provides for the sovereignty of parliament, the American one stresses the sovereignty of the people – popular sovereignty. The opening words of the American document establish this clearly: 'We the People of the United States . . . do ordain and establish this Constitution'. They echo the ideas associated with the French writer and philosopher Jean Jacques Rousseau, who argued that the best form of government was one that reflected the general will of the people, which was the sum total of those interests that all citizens had in common.

In America, ultimate power rests with the people and has done so ever since the republic was established. The elective principle is well established at every level of authority in the United States, with more than one million posts being subject to such popular control. Britain was an established country long before it was an established democracy and the notion of power resting with the people has been slower to take root. In the final analysis, the people do have the ultimate say because they can 'throw the rascals out' in a general election. Governments are aware of the need to secure re-election and this induces caution as they create and develop their policies. But it is a representative democracy which has been slow to adopt any methods of direct democracy, such as the use of initiatives and referendums. The emphasis has always been on politicians making the decisions and the voters giving their general verdict at periodic intervals.

The ease of constitutional change

The flexibility of the unwritten British Constitution makes constitutional change relatively easy to accomplish. Amending it is no different in essence to passing a law relating to homosexuality or the health service, for example, although there is a growing practice that divisive constitutional issues might be put before the relevant electorate in a pre-legislative or post-legislative referendum. Many such changes to the Constitution have been carried out in recent years, as we shall see in the next section. Few have aroused much diffi-culty in their passage, although reform of the House of Lords continues to be a thorny issue.

In America, the constitution has been amended on 27 occasions by the passage of a constitutional amendment (a complicated process as the experience of the Equal Rights Amendment shows), but there is another way by which change can

---

Passing a US constitutional amendment

Any proposal requires approval by a two-thirds majority in both houses of Congress, in the same session, or the approval of a special national constitutional convention convened by two-thirds of the state legislatures. (No such convention has ever been summoned.) Any amendment passed by Congress or a special convention must in addition be ratified by three-quarters of the state legislatures or by ratifying conventions in three-quarters of the states. In 26 cases, constitutional amendment has been brought about by Congressional action and state legislature ratification. The 21st Amendment, which repealed the 18th and therefore ended the experiment of prohibition) was proposed by Congress, but ratified by state conventions.

When campaigning groups such as the National Organisation for Women (NOW) urged the passage of an Equal Rights Amendment to introduce equality of rights under the law irrespective of gender, the amendment was approved by the necessary two-thirds majority in both chambers of Congress, in 1972. But not enough states were willing to ratify the measure. The original deadline (March 1979) was extended by more than three years, but by the end of June 1982 only 35 states had given their support. Three more would have provided the necessary three-quarters majority for a constitutional amendment. Bearing in mind that the original proposal for an ERA was put before Congress in 1923, the difficulty of achieving change is apparent.

---

come about: judicial interpretation. American courts have the power of judicial review which enables them to declare any act or action of Congress, the executive branch or one of the 50 state governments, illegal. They can also interpret the Constitution as they did in the major cases of *Furman v Georgia* in 1972 (concerning the death penalty), *Roe v Wade* in 1973 (concerning abortion), and *Plessy v Ferguson* 1896 and *Brown v the Topeka Board of Education* 1954 (concerning the legality of segregation). These were landmark decisions which significantly changed the law. Not for nothing did Chief Justice Evans Hughes remark back in 1909 that 'the constitution is what the judges say it is'.

In Britain, judges cannot declare laws unconstitutional as Parliament, which passed them, is sovereign, the supreme law-making authority, though since the 1980s they have been much more willing to find ministers guilty of exceeding their powers or otherwise infringing the law. Their contribution to constitutional doctrine has been important in another way. Decisions were taken by judges hundreds of years ago in cases where there was no statute to guide them. On areas such as personal liberty, they made up the rules as common law, and ever since many of these rules have continued to be applicable.

Recent experience of constitutional reform

From the 1970s to the 1990s, several issues and events combined to cast doubt upon British constitutional arrangements. Among others:

- **Adherence to the European Convention on Human Rights** raised the question of conflict between British law and the European code.
- **Membership of the European Community/Union** made community law been binding on the British Parliament and had major implications for the doctrine of the Sovereignty of Parliament.
- **The introduction of Direct Rule in Northern Ireland** in 1972 replaced 50 years of rule in that province via the Stormont Parliament.
- **The growth of nationalism in Scotland and Wales** in the mid-1970s and in subsequent periodic upsurges posed a challenge to the existing arrangements for Scottish and Welsh government.
- **The Referendum on Europe** in 1975, the first held across Great Britain, had implications for the doctrine of Parliamentary Sovereignty. Also, the holding of it led to another breach with tradition. Ministers were allowed to differ in their attitudes to membership of the European Community, temporarily waiving the idea of collective responsibility.
- **The dismantling of the Greater London Council (GLC) and the Metropolitan County Councils** was a significant inroad into the form of local democracy in Britain. Other local authorities found that their powers were circumscribed in the years of Conservative rule.
- **The increasing use of quangos** led many people to feel that too many decisions were being taken by unelected bodies whose members were closely connected – sometimes related – to the government of the day.

All of these developments had a significant impact on the British system of government. The need for constitutional renewal was frequently discussed by academics and commentators. A constant theme among would-be reformers was the need to halt the centralisation of power, which was perceived to be a growing trend in British politics. Arrangements which had once been regarded as near-perfect were becoming the cause of uncertainty and disquiet.

Growing interest in constitutional reform in Britain

The Liberal Democrats and their predecessors have had a long-standing commitment to constitutional reform, but more significantly the cause was embraced by Labour in the 1990s. During the period of the Major administration of 1992–97, the opposition parties began to agree, clarify and popularise their proposals for constitutional change. Conservative ministers were broadly united in wishing to preserve existing arrangements intact, their only wish being to retrieve some powers which had drifted to Brussels.

Other than the Labour and Liberal Democrat parties, various groups and individuals campaigned for constitutional change. Among the campaigning groups were **Charter 88**, **Demos**, the **Institute for Public Policy Research** and the **Institute of Economic Affairs**. The theme of constitutional renewal has never commanded much interest among the voters, but it has appealed to the chattering classes: middle-class intellectuals, journalists, lecturers and teachers in disciplines such as the law and politics.

The Blair government and the constitution

Before the 1997 election, Tony Blair re-affirmed his belief that 'building a proper modern constitution for Britain is a very important part of what we are about'. Since then, action has been taken in many fields, and the programme of constitutional change is well underway. Among the changes made are the following:

- the incorporation of the European Convention into British law;
- the introduction of a new electoral system for European elections;
- the establishment of the Jenkins Commission on the electoral system for Westminster (and a cautious welcome for its recommendations, but no subsequent action);
- the abolition of the hereditary system in the second chamber and the establishment of a commission to work out the basis for a new body to replace the existing House of Lords (with discussion under way on the best means of proceeding to a second phase of reform);
- the introduction of devolution for Scotland and Wales, following the outcome of the referendums of September 1997;
- the creation of a new authority for London, including an elected Mayor – along with provision for the adoption of elected mayors in other parts of the country; and
- talks leading to the Good Friday Agreement in Northern Ireland, with the intention of creating an assembly and power-sharing executive.

Attitudes to the constitution in the United States

Americans tend to regard their Constitution with considerable awe and reverence. Such deference is indicated by poll findings and other statements of popular opinion. They indicate that Americans are both familiar and content with their constitutional arrangements. Indeed, according to US historian Theodore White, the nation is more united by its commonly accepted ideas about government, as embodied in the Constitution, than it is by geography.[11]

On becoming President in 1974, Gerald Ford observed that 'our Constitution works'. He was speaking in the aftermath of the Watergate Crisis, which led to the downfall and ultimate resignation of President Nixon. Nixon was judged to have been involved with a cover-up and various illegal operations, and thereby to have abused his position. As Americans firmly believe in the idea that 'we have a government of laws, not of men', Ford and many other Americans saw his removal as a vindication of their Constitution. It had served to protect freedom, restrain the behaviour of those in high office and define the limits of executive power.

Given such widespread approval of the form of government, it is not surprising that America has not shown the same interest in constitutional reform. Very few people publicly advocate radical changes in the structure of government established in 1787. Those who would tamper with it have to make a strong case for change and tend to talk in terms of restoring it to its original glory rather than making fundamental alternations.

Nevertheless, on occasion, there has been some interest in reform. Both chambers of Congress have voted on proposed innovations since 1995. The Senate has rejected them all and in the House only two changes – flag desecration (approved three times) and the balanced budget (approved once) have passed with the necessary majority. Even these issues tended to be ones of broader national policy, albeit with constitutional implications, rather than straightforward issues directly affecting some aspect of institutional arrangements. Term limits do fall into this category, but despite being a high-profile part of the Republican Contract for America programme in the 1994 election, they have failed to materialise.

Conclusion

Constitutions are important in all countries for they affirm the basic principles according to which they should be governed. In the overwhelming majority of cases, they are written documents, although even where this is not the case the country can still be regarded as having a constitution. They are legally supreme, often difficult to amend and frequently short-lived. In Britain and the United States, they have survived well, even if on this side of the Atlantic there has been interest in and the implementation of a programme of constitutional reform.

Most written constitutions contain a declaration of rights, as does the American one. In Britain, there has traditionally been no such protection of liberties, although the passage of the Human Rights Act (1998) has changed the situation. However, as we see in the next chapter, the mere existence of a constitution and some form of Bill of Rights is no guarantee that essential freedoms will be respected. Liberty ultimately depends more on the political culture of any country than on any particular documentation.

What matters more than whether a constitution is embodied in a single document or not is whether it works effectively. The mere presence of a written constitution is no guarantee that the power of government is appropriately constrained. At any one time, a dozen or so of the world's written constitutions are in full suspension, in many others their provisions are systematically ignored. In both Britain and the United States, there is a basic consensus about how governing should take place. When that consensus is absent, no system of government, whatever the nature of its constitution, is likely to endure.

The constitutions of Britain and the USA: a summary		
	Britain	*US*
General characteristics	Unwritten/uncodified Flexible/easy to amend	Written/codified More rigid/less easy to amend
Constitutional principles	Commitment to democracy, rule of law Monarchical government Unitary system, with devolution Parliamentary system Fusion of powers Parliamentary sovereignty	Commitment to democracy/ rule of law Republican government Federal system Presidential system Separation of powers Popular sovereignty

REFERENCES

1 A. Heywood, *Politics*, Macmillan, 1997.
2 T. Paine, *The Rights of Man*, Everyman, 1998.
3 A. Hanson and M. Walles, *Governing Britain*, Fontana, 1997.
4 K. Wheare, *Federalism*, Oxford University Press, 1947 (reissued as Federal Government, 1963).
5 S. Benn and R. Peters, *Social Principles and the Democratic State*, Allen and Unwin, 1959.
6 J. Dewey, *Democracy and Education*, Macmillan, 1916.
7 E. Wade and G. Philips, *Constitutional Law*, Longman, re-issued 1998.
8 M. Shaw, *Anglo-American Democracy*, Routledge and Kegan, 1968.
9 As note 1 above.
10 Lord Hailsham, *The Elective Dictatorship*, BBC Publications, 1976.
11 T. White, 'The American Idea', in *New York Times Magazine*, June 1986.

USEFUL WEB SITES

www.constitution.org/cons/natlcons.htm The Constitution Society. Constitutions of several countries are provided in an English version, with some commentary.

For the UK

www.ucl.ac.uk/constitution-unit Constitution Unit. Research centre relating to constitutional reform in the UK, with a valuable update section dealing with progress on constitutional reform.

www.lcd.gov.uk Lord Chancellor's departmental site. Coverage of constitutional issues in England and Wales.

www.charter88.org.uk Charter 88 site, with extensive information on constitutional reform, plus useful links.

www.democraticdialogue.org Democratic Dialogue. Northern Ireland-based think tank – includes information on constitutional matters.

For the USA

www.nara.gov/education/cc/main.html. National Archives Classroom web site. Many key historical documents on American government can be found here, notably the Declaration of Independence, the Constitution etc.

www.access.gpo.gov/congress/senate/constitution/toc.html. Congressional Research Service, Library of Congress.

tcnbp.tripod.com/index1.htm US Constitution Resource Center Index. Links to on-line resources about the American Constitution. On-line copy of Constitution, annotated with commentary and relevant Supreme Court cases etc.

www.constitutioncenter.org. National Constitution Center. Useful starting point for study of the US Constitution.

www.americanstrategy.org/foundations.html American Strategy. Introduction to American constitutional history.

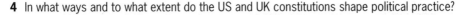

SAMPLE QUESTIONS

1 Does the written constitution of the United States make the country harder to govern than Britain?

2 Discuss the view that the British Constitution is too flexible and the American Constitution is too rigid.

3 Do the similarities between the British and American constitutions outweigh the differences?

4 In what ways and to what extent do the US and UK constitutions shape political practice?

Protecting liberties, advancing rights

3

Liberties and rights are of especial concern in liberal democracies, which claim to provide a broad range of them. The word liberalism is associated with the primacy of the individual. Historically, liberal thinkers have been committed to personal freedom, believing that men and women flourish and progress when they are able to express their creative personalities without undue restrictions. In democracies, governments are empowered by the people. They are given office on trust, and their power should not be abused. There are occasions when there is a need to deploy the powers of the police or security services, and to impose other limitations on freedom. But those restrictions must be capable of justification on grounds of the common good. The more the citizens know of the reasoning behind them, the better. They can then assess whether essential values have been preserved.

For many years the rights which were emphasised tended not to require the government to act (freedom of expression, for example), whereas in recent years more importance has been attached to the passage into law of entitlements which do need positive governmental intervention. In Britain and America, anti-discriminatory legislation has been enacted to allow for the protection of minorities and other disadvantaged groups.

In this chapter, we examine the protection of liberties in both countries, in particular the right of freedom of expression. We move on to compare the positive benefits which have been conferred upon various groups in society.

POINTS TO CONSIDER

➤ Distinguish between civil liberties and civil rights.

➤ How well are the liberties of the citizen protected in Britain?

➤ To what extent is the Human Rights Act an adequate alternative to an entrenched Bill of Rights?

➤ Does Britain need a home-grown Bill of Rights?

➤ Do civil liberties need to be entrenched?

➤ How much tolerance should be extended to extreme minority groups whose opinions are generally out of step with contemporary thinking?

➤ 'Democracy requires the fullest freedom of expression'. To what extent is freedom of expression recognised in Britain and the United States?

➤ How effective is the protection against discrimination towards women and ethnic minorities in the two countries?

➤ Is the idea of affirmative action a good thing?

➤ Should Britain follow the American example of 'open government' and 'freedom of information'?

Most Western democracies have a constitution which sets out the relationship between the state and the individual. Such documents mark out the respective spheres of governmental authority and personal freedom. They do this by defining civil liberties and rights, often in a Bill of Rights. The American Bill has been around for a long time, and is the oldest in the world. The ideas of those who helped to formulate it were an inspiration to the French Revolutionaries in the years at the end of the eighteenth century. The spirit and tone of the early revolutionaries was set in the Declaration of the Rights of Man and Citizens, adopted by the National Assembly at Versailles. The document reflected the thinking of the eighteenth-century Enlightenment. Among its foremost notions was the observation that: 'Men are born free and equal in rights . . . the aim of every political association is the preservation of the natural and undoubted rights of men. These rights are liberty, property, security and resistance to oppression.'

The Declaration became a charter for European liberals over the next half-century. Lord Acton, a Liberal philosopher of the nineteenth century, commented that it was in its impact 'stronger than all the armies of Napoleon'. The principles laid down in 1789 were to enthral and divide the continent, and few European countries remained unaffected by them. Some states incorporated statements of human rights into their own constitutions, as did the Swedes in 1809 and Holland in 1815. In the twentieth century, and especially in the years since 1945, many old-established countries have adopted new constitutions, and new nations have devised their own written statements. Most of these make some provision for the protection of basic rights.

Britain has long been out of step with the rest of the continent, and with the Commonwealth, in not having a Bill of Rights of its own. Indeed, until the passage of the Human Rights Act of 1998, it had not incorporated the European Convention on Human Rights (ECHR) – or any other human rights treaty – into British law. Such isolation is particularly apparent when it is realised that some dependent territories, and most of the African and Caribbean countries, have provision for protecting rights in their constitutions. In the last two decades, the issue of human rights has been one of much

Types of rights

By rights, we mean entitlements. Identifying those to which we are entitled has been a source of controversy over many centuries. Many writers distinguish between **natural or inalienable rights** which derive from people's common humanity and should not be infringed, and **legal rights**, those which are granted to citizens by the governments of different states. Many would further distinguish between those legal rights which are **civil and political**, and those which are **social and economic** in character. Inalienable rights have a moral dimension, as is recognised by Article I of the United Nations Universal Declaration of Human Rights (1948): 'All human beings are born free and equal in dignity and rights. They are endowed with reason and conscience, and should act towards one another in a spirit of brotherhood.'

Legal rights of the civil and political variety include freedom of worship and freedom of expression. They are sometimes referred to as **civil liberties** or **negative rights**, in that they mark out areas of social life where the Constitution restricts or prohibits governmental intrusion on individuals' free choice. They restrain the interference of government, delineating a sphere of governmental inactivity. Social and economic rights are often described as **positive rights**. They extend the role and responsibilities of government into areas such as education, health provision and the right to work. They are more controversial because they expand the activities of government and are also dependent on the availability of resources.

Any listing of positive rights may be disputed. Many would claim the right to education, but what about the right to private education? The same applies to health care and the right to strike (or not to). Particularly controversial is the issue of abortion, on which 'pro-choicers' argue the right of a woman to have total control over her own body whereas the 'pro-lifers' argue for the right to life of the unborn foetus.

interest, and groups around the world have been active in campaigning for more generous provision and better enforcement.

The protection of liberties in Britain and the United States in theory and practice

There was no Bill of Rights in the original American Constitution, not least because the federalists who dominated the gathering felt that it was unnecessary. In their view, liberty would be protected by procedures such as federalism and the checks and balances built into the proposals. They doubted the value of a special document defending personal rights, for federalists claimed that the maintenance of basic freedoms would depend primarily upon the balance of forces set out in the document and on the tolerance or otherwise of the age.

For anti-federalists, the Bill of Rights was a proclamation of their fundamental belief in the natural rights of all Americans. Whether or not another generation sought to deny them, it was crucial to proclaim their existence. Any government resting on the consent of the people must acknowledge them and include them in any constitution. Anti-federalists may have lost much of the battle over the form of government, but they won the debate over the Bill of Rights, which were adopted as the first ten amendments to the Constitution, on 15 December 1791 (see below).

The first ten amendments to the Constitution and their purpose

Protections afforded fundamental rights and freedoms
Amendment 1: Freedom of religion, speech, press, and assembly; the right to petition the government.

Protections against arbitrary military arrest
Amendment 2: Right to bear arms and maintain state militias (National Guard).
Amendment 3: Troops may not be quartered in homes in peace time.

Protection against arbitrary police and court action
Amendment 4: No unreasonable searches or seizures.
Amendment 5: Grand jury indictment required to prosecute a person for a serious crime. No 'double jeopardy' – being tried twice for the same offence. Forcing a person to testify against himself or herself prohibited. No loss of life, liberty or property without due process.
Amendment 6: Right to speedy, public, impartial trial with defence counsel, and right to cross-examine witnesses.
Amendment 7: Jury trials in civil suits where value exceeds 20 dollars.
Amendment 8: No excessive bail or fines, no cruel and unusual punishments.

Protections of states rights and un-named rights of the people
Amendment 9: Unlisted rights are not necessarily denied.
Amendment 10: Powers not delegated to the United States or denied to states are reserved to the states or to the people.

First Amendment freedoms – freedoms of speech, assembly, association, petition and religion – are at the heart of a healthy constitutional democracy. The Amendment explicitly acknowledges freedom of expression. In Britain, by contrast, the traditional protection available in this area has been very different. There was no clear legal presumption in favour of free expression, although judges have in recent years tried to interpret laws and other rules which inhibit free expression as narrowly as possible. People have been free to say what they like, as long as they did not break any existing law such as the law of defamation or the legislation on race relations. In the absence of any law proclaiming the right of free speech, the British relied on what A V Dicey, constitutional theorist of the late nineteenth and early twentieth century, , labelled 'the three pillars of liberty'.[1] He argued that between them Parliament, a culture of liberty and the courts offered adequate protection, operating as they did against a background of respect for the rule of law. The commitment to freedom of expression is now much clearer because Britain has passed the Human Rights Act (1998), incorporating the European Convention into British law. Article 10 of the Convention acknowledges the right of freedom of expression and this can now be cited in British courts. Much now depends on the interpretation of freedom of expression by the judges.

The European Convention on Human Rights and its protocols

Article   2: Right to life
Article   3: Prohibition of torture
Article   4: Prohibition of slavery and forced labour
Article   5: Right to liberty and security
Article   6: Right to a fair trial
Article   7: No punishment without law
Article   8: Right to respect for private and family life
Article   9: Freedom of thought, conscience and religion
Article 10: Freedom of expression
Article 11: Freedom of assembly and association
Article 12: Right to marry
Article 13: Right to an effective remedy
Article 14: Prohibition of discrimination
Article 25: Applications by persons, non-governmental organisations or groups of
                   individuals
Article 28: Report of the Commission in case of friendly settlement
Article 31: Report of the Commission 'if a solution is not reached'

Protocol No. 1
Article 1: Protection of property
Article 2: Right to education
Article 3: Right to free elections

Protocol No. 4
Article 1: Prohibition of imprisonment for debt
Article 2: Freedom of movement
Article 3: Prohibition of expulsion of nationals
Article 4: Prohibition of collective expulsion of aliens

Protocol No. 6
Article 1: Abolition of the death penalty

Protocol No. 7
Article 1: Procedural safeguards relating to expulsion of aliens
Article 2: Right of appeal in criminal matters
Article 3: Compensation for wrongful conviction
Article 4: Right not to be tried or punished twice
Article 5: Equality between spouses

The First Amendment requires judicial interpretation for it is brief and needs to be applied to particular circumstances. This is true of other amendments as well. The Convention contains vague, all-embracing phrases such as the 'right to liberty and security of person' and 'freedom of expression', a deliberate choice on the part of those who drafted it. If the terminology were more precise, it would automatically exclude many issues from consideration. However, unlike the American Bill of Rights, it qualifies the substantial right expressed in the first paragraph of each article. The qualifications list the exceptions to the application of the right. For instance, in Article 10 the right to freedom of expression is modified by the first paragraph:

> This right shall include freedom to hold opinion and receive and impart information and ideas, without interference by public authority and regardless of frontiers. This article shall not prevent States from requiring the licensing of broadcasting, television or cinema enterprises.

Perhaps more controversially, it is modified by a second paragraph which contains other important limitations as

> necessary in a democratic society, in the interests of national security, territorial integrity or public safety, for the prevention of disorder or crime, for the protection of health or morals, for the protection of the reputation or rights of others, for preventing the disclosure of information received in confidence, or for maintaining the authority and impartiality of the judiciary.

Finally, under Article 15, a state can derogate from its obligations in circumstances of national emergency. This let-out has enabled Britain to pass its anti-terrorist legislation (1998 and 2001) without fear that it falls foul of the Convention.

In America, the Supreme Court has been the primary branch of government charged with giving meaning to these freedoms and ensuring that they are observed. It has generally adopted a practical approach, refusing to make them absolute rights beyond any kind of governmental regulation or to say that they must be observed at any price. The Amendment has never been interpreted in such absolute terms, so that the rights to freedom of the speech and of the press are limited (see, for example p. 55 below). But the nine justices on the Court have recognised that a constitutional democracy tampers with such freedoms at its peril and have generally insisted upon compelling justification before allowing the rights to be infringed.

Because essential freedoms are given constitutional status, they are not easy to override and many groups – however unpopular in the country – have been able to cite the clause in their defence. Those who would desecrate the flag or who have adopted extremist right-wing views have often been tolerated in its name. By contrast, in Britain, the Human Rights Act is not entrenched, but part of the ordinary law of the land. If any existing law is incompatible with the Convention, there is a fast-track procedure for its amendment. But it can be expressly overridden. In that sense, American protection is more secure.

The role of judges in interpreting the Bill of Rights and the European Convention

The task of interpreting the broad phrases of the American Constitution and the Human Rights Act in Britain is performed by appointed judges. As we see on pp. 144, 149, justices on the Supreme Court have been much involved in issues concerning civil liberties in the postwar era. The decisions of the Warren Court were notably liberal in their judgements concerning the rights of individuals (especially minorities), equal representation and equality before the law. The Burger Court which followed was more liberal than anticipated, although its decisions on the criminal law were more cautious and it leaned towards more powers for the police.

By incorporating the Convention, Britain has taken a step in the American direction. Previously, especially on the political left, there was much fear of judicial power and an unwillingness to trust the judges to get it right. Some critics of the idea of a home-grown and up-to-date British Bill of Rights worry about the backgrounds, attitudes and method of selection of those in the judiciary. Ewing and Gearty questioned whether it is

> legitimate or justifiable to have the final political decision, on say a woman's right to abortion, to be determined by a group of men appointed by the Prime Minister from a small and unrepresentative pool ... Difficult ethical, social and political questions would be subject to judicial preference, rather than the shared or compromised community morality.[2]

Incorporation of the European Convention has troubled those who argue that it is at Westminster that issues should be decided. It is up to Parliament to defend the people against injustice and to legislate for the type of society the government of the day favours. MPs are elected; judges are not. Moreover, in the Labour Party, there is a long history of doubts about judicial conservatism. Many have argued that judges are more interested in preserving rights of property than in safeguarding the liberties of trade unions, or racial or other minority groups. Some have pointed out that judges tend to be wealthy, conservative in their thinking and out of touch with the lives of people from less comfortable backgrounds. Moreover, their training and the character of their task tends to give them a preference for traditional standards of behaviour, a respect for family and property, an emphasis on the importance of maintaining order and a distaste for minorities – especially if they are strident in their approach as they search for justice.

The tolerance extended to minority opinions

For all of the protection afforded by the Constitution, some groups have not been able to enjoy their full rights. Mark Twain once remarked that God gave the American people 'the three precious gifts of freedom of speech, freedom of religion and the prudence never to exercise either of them'. Justice Oliver Wendell Holmes recognised that there are times when it is not appropriate to exercise First Amendment rights, in his observation that 'the most stringent protection of free speech would not protect a man in falsely shouting "fire" in a crowded theatre'.

Tolerance has been extended in cases where people have engaged in **symbolic speech**. In 1965, Mary Beth Tinker and her brother John were suspended from their school in Iowa for wearing black armbands in protest against the Vietnam War. This was adjudged to have been a violation of the First Amendment, because the right to freedom of speech went beyond the spoken word. Similarly, when Gregory Johnson set a national flag on fire to protest against the build-up of nuclear arms, a state law banning such desecration was overturned because the law fell foul of the same Amendment. It was held that the act was not just a dramatic action, but was in effect an expression of speech.

> **symbolic speech**
> Non-verbal communication or speech-related acts, such as burning a flag or wearing an armband, that are protected by the Constitution because they involved the communication of ideas.

However, there have been occasions when these freedoms have had to yield to societal pressures from the majority. If in theory most Americans believe in freedom of expression, many would have more doubts about extending that freedom to the **Ku Klux Klan** or some other extremist group. Neither would they be keen to allow schools in their neighbourhood to inform schoolchildren about homosexuality or atheism.

At times, anti-communism has been a powerful force in American politics. The Smith Act of 1940 forbade advocacy of the violent overthrow of the government and in 1951 (*Dennis v the United States*) the Supreme Court upheld prison sentences for those leaders of the Communist Party who were said to have supported such action. This might seem more like shouting fire in an empty rather than a crowded theatre, but the Court saw the danger presented by seditious left-wing activity as so great that important rights must be denied. During the early 1950s, in the **McCarthy** era, those alleged to be socialists or communists (even if in reality they were liberal progressives) found themselves in difficulty with the courts who seemed unwilling to defend their constitutional rights. Both in the 1920s and the 1950s, free speech was under threat in America in a way that was not the case in Britain, even though the American protection of freedom of expression was much more explicit.

> **Ku Klux Klan**
> A secret organisation of white protestant southerners formed after the American Civil War to fight black emancipation. The group has terrorised blacks, Jews and immigrants, among others, resorting to lynchings and shootings. At times, its influence in American life has been considerable – in the 1920s, for example.

> **McCarthyism**
> The fear, prevalent in the early 1950s, that America was under great threat from international communism, adherents of which were said to be infiltrating government, institutions and society at many levels. It was named after Senator Joseph McCarthy, the prominent witch-hunter of communists, who led unscrupulous investigations into the lives of those accused of subversion.

In Britain, there is no such thing as the First Amendment. No British court would overturn an act of Parliament for violating someone's freedom of speech, although incorporation of the European Convention might pave the way for change via the fast-track procedure. There is nothing like the same certainty of protection. Freedom of expression in Britain is well established, but there are restrictions which are stronger than those in the United States. These have been evident in the handling of security cases.

In the 1980s, there were many anxieties about the protection of liberties in the Thatcher years. Critics felt that there was an increase in governmental power at the expense of personal freedom. The pressure group Liberty felt inspired to launch an advertising campaign enumerating countless ways in which its members believed that the Conservatives in office were trampling on people's rights, alleging that ministers had

> overseen a major increase in central government and police power. It has curtailed our right to peaceful assembly, to join a trade union, to elect our own local government, to receive information, to be free from discrimination. When these rights are taken from some, the freedom of all is threatened.

In particular, in the 1980s state security became something of an obsession. In the *Spycatcher* case, Peter Wright's book on the security services caused a furore, for his memoirs provided a frank account of his earlier work as a security officer. Ministers took out an injunction to restrain broadsheet newspapers from commenting on aspects of the affair, although they eventually lost a case at the European Court in Strasbourg where it was found that the government was breaching Article 10 of the Convention.

The relationship between security and the media's overage of events in Ireland was a particular theme of that decade. There was an obvious security implication in discussion of events in the province, and coverage often caused problems for broadcasters whose instinct was to probe controversial and dramatic occurrences and find out what really happened. In 1988 the British government imposed a ban on the broadcasting of free speech by representatives of certain organisations, notably Sinn Fein, the Ulster Defence Association and the paramilitaries. Programmes could in future included the 'reported speech' of such supporters or an actor's voice could read a quotation, but they could not speak for themselves. The ban was challenged in the British courts and at the European Court in Strasbourg, but was maintained.

Pentagon Papers
Classified documents which detailed the history of American involvement in Vietnam.

In comparison to the Thatcher gags, which were generally upheld in the British courts, the American administration of President Nixon had no such success when it went to court in an attempt to stop the publication of the illegally obtained **Pentagon Papers** in the *New York Times v United*

States case, 1971. The Supreme Court refused to stop publication of these classified documents by the *New York Times* and the *Washington Post*, noting the heavy presumption against 'prior restraint' (any limitation on publication requiring that permission be secured or approval granted prior to publication).

In another way, freedom to express controversial views is more clearly protected in the United States. It is unusual for someone to win a libel case in America. The courts tend to err on the side of freedom of expression, taking the view that if public debate is not free there can be no democracy. The Supreme Court has allowed considerable latitude to those who make derogatory comments which damage or bruise public reputations. (Libel is not protected under the First Amendment.) In Britain, **libel** laws are stricter than in America or most European countries, and some judges have been severe on those found guilty of defamation. Klug *et al* stress the 'rigidity' of the present law and note that 'it runs contrary to the trend in international law which has placed greater emphasis on the right to free expression'.[3] Under the British law of defamation, it is an offence to make any statement calculated to bring a person into hatred, ridicule or contempt, or which may cause a person to be ostracised. Libel is more serious than **slander**, for it is recorded in a more permanent form. If the observation can be proved true or comes into the category of fair comment, there is no legal liability. The Human Rights Act may make a difference, for in interpreting the Convention the European Court has normally taken the view that defamation has not occurred provided that the facts are reasonably accurate, that the opinion was expressed in good faith and that there was no intent to defame.

> **libel**
> Defamation by printed word or in broadcast form and therefore a permanent attack; defamation refers to comment which is malicious and damaging to a person's reputation.
>
> **slander**
> Defamation by word or gesture and therefore a temporary attack.

Yet if Britain has lacked the formal protection of freedom of expression possessed by the United States, nonetheless it has generally been less harsh on the expression of minority views of a left-wing variety. The hysteria against communists which characterised the McCarthyite era has no British equivalent.

The degree of protection given to basic freedom depends to some extent on the political climate of the times. In the 1960s, the constitutional meaning of free speech was expanded in America, and courts were generally more supportive of a variety of forms of protest. However, in the United States – and in Britain as well – the terrorist threat posed by the events of September 11th challenged the tolerance of many citizens. In both countries, draconian legislation was introduced, much to the alarm of supporters of civil liberties.

Anti-terrorist legislation

Almost every American could agree on the need to ensure greater security of the person, by rooting out terrorists and preventing the danger of further attacks. But critics of the Bush administration claimed that its package of anti-terrorist measures ('Uniting and Strengthening America by Providing Appropriate Tools Required to Intercept and Obstruct Terrorism' – more usually known as 'the USA PATRIOT Act') went far beyond what was necessary to achieve these objectives. They detected signs of a serious erosion of accepted freedoms.

Criticism centred mainly on three broad aspects of the Act:

1 The dedication to secrecy which made it difficult to find out information relating to the 600 or so detainees held in federal prisons.

2 The way in which new powers tilted the balance towards the executive branch and removed from the judicial system some of its power to review the actions of the administration. (For instance, immigration judges now have less opportunity to prevent unlawful detention or deportation of non-citizens.)

3 The traditional distinction between foreign intelligence gathering and criminal investigation at home has been undermined. For instance, information gathered by domestic law enforcement agencies can now be handed to bodies such as the CIA.

In addition, reports concerning a number of individual cases indicated a new spirit of intolerance of dissent. In November 2001, a member of the Green Party USA's committee was surrounded by military personnel as she tried to board a plane in Bangor, Maine, to attend a Chicago meeting on the use of pesticides in war. She was told that because her name had been 'flagged in the computer', the airport was closed to her. Her flight fare was not refunded and she found that her hotel reservation in Chicago had already mysteriously been cancelled. There were also complaints from some academics opposed to the war in Afghanistan of harassment by university and other authorities.

In Britain too, there were allegations from civil libertarians that the restraints on freedom were excessive, not least because the Labour government had already introduced a measure tackling terrorist threats a year or so before. Of course, many people on either side of the Atlantic might point out that, by their actions, the terrorists involved had destroyed the most basic right of all – the right to life – of nearly 4000 people, mainly Americans, but also including British and other people as well. They had threatened the 'life, liberty and pursuit of happiness' of many more people who either lost members of their families or for some time feared such a loss.

The proclamation of positive rights in recent years in Britain and the United States

On p. 48, we made the distinction between negative and positive rights, the former limiting governmental intrusion on the free choice of individuals and the latter extending the role and responsibilities of government into areas such as education, health provision and the right to work, in order to expand the opportunities available to all citizens. The negative rights are often referred to as civil liberties, which are essential if individuals are to be allowed to communicate freely with each other and with the government. Positive rights are sometimes known as civil rights. In postwar Britain and America, governments have acted to ensure the equal treatment of individuals and to give them a better, more satisfying life.

Civil rights are a set of protections from something which could otherwise greatly affect people's lives, such as freedom from arbitrary arrest and imprisonment, and from discrimination on such grounds as disability, gender, race, religion or sexual orientation.

The rights of criminal suspects and those detained in prison

America has always taken a tougher stand on matters of law and order than prevails in Britain. In their attitude to law-breakers, those charged with enforcing the law have been keen to make it clear that 'crime does not pay'. Whether in the matter of the sentences passed, the conditions under which prisoners are detained or the use of the death penalty, the emphasis has generally been on firm punishment rather than on the rights of those charged committing offences. At times, a more liberal attitude has been apparent, as under the Warren Court (see pp. 144, 149) which in the Miranda ruling required police officers to inform suspects of their constitutional rights and created specific guidelines for police interrogations. But exceptions to the so-called **Miranda rules** have been allowed. For instance, in 1991 the Rehnquist Court (see pp. 149–50) in *Arizona v Fuliminante* decided that the admission at a trial of an illegally coerced confession does not mean that a conviction must be overturned, as long as the impact of the confession was in itself harmless.

> **Miranda rules**
>
> In the *Miranda v Arizona* judgement (1966), the Supreme Court decided that no conviction in a federal or state court could stand if evidence introduced at the trial had been obtained as a result of suspects being denied their constitutional rights. The justices laid down the *Miranda rules* which among other things stipulated that suspects must be notified that they are free to remain silent, warned that what they say may be used against them in court and told that they have a right to have attorneys present during questioning.

The Eighth Amendment in the Bill of Rights forbids cruel and unusual punishments, although it leaves the phrase undefined. In recent years, there has been much discussion about the increasing use of the death penalty in states such as Florida and Texas. The Supreme Court tackled the issue of whether the death penalty is inherently cruel and unusual as a form of punishment, in the case of *Furman v Georgia*, 1972. It overturned the law enforced in Georgia, finding that its imposition was 'freakish' and 'random', but in subsequent decisions it has been more sympathetic in its judgements to the use of the capital punishment. In 1976 in the case of *Gregg v Georgia* the nine justices argued that it 'is an expression of society's outrage at particular offensive conduct ... an extreme sanction, suitable to the most extreme of crimes'. There has been much criticism by opponents of the death penalty of the methods employed to implement it in different states, some of which have been condemned as particularly cruel and unusual. There has also been concern at the execution of teenagers over 16 and of mentally retarded individuals, and of the way in which black Americans seem much more likely to attract the ultimate punishment than do white people.

As for the detention of criminals, there has been widespread experimentation with boot-camps and other tough regimes inside American prisons. But what has attracted particular attention is the issue of the treatment of non-American terrorist suspects after the attack on the twin towers in 2001. Instead of establishing prisoner-of-war camps in the Afghan territory it had freed from Taliban control, the US arranged for their transport, in small groups, to a naval base at Guantanamo Bay, in Cuba, instead of to the American mainland. Here, they were not subject to the jurisdiction of the American courts, and critics have complained that basic rights have been denied. As yet, they have not been brought to trial and their detention in crowded conditions has provoked controversy.

At times, Britain has also adopted stronger measures against criminals, most notably in recent years. There is a growing concern among ministers that the rights of suspects and defendants have been unduly emphasised, and that it has proved hard for the police to obtain convictions. But the toughness on crime has been balanced by some interest in the causes of crime and an attempt to ensure that those detained in custody are granted their rights. Moreover, the death penalty was abolished in 1965 and in recent decades there has been no substantial move to reintroduce it.

The extension of rights to disadvantaged groups

The full rights of women and ethnic minority groups were only slowly recognised on both sides of the Atlantic. As in many parts of Europe, in the nineteenth century women in America experienced unequal treatment for centuries. They were seen as goods and chattels, dependants of their fathers and husbands, and denied a range of legal rights, including the right to vote.

In the twentieth century, the 19th Amendment extended the right to vote across the country and once women had a voice in political life they were able to use it to campaign for other rights.

Yet women were slow to benefit from the 'equal protection under the law', as promised by the 14th Amendment. Even the Warren Court, which did much to advance the cause of racial minorities, was less willing to show the same concern for women, Chief Justice Warren noting that 'woman is still regarded as the centre of home and family life'. In other words, they were viewed as having a limited role in society and their anxieties did not receive the same scrutiny as matters of race and national origin. However, in the 1960s a national commitment to civil rights came meaningfully to the fore. The passage of the Equal Pay Act (1963), requiring equal pay for equal work, and the Civil Rights Act (1964), which prohibited discrimination on the grounds of sex (among other things), were important steps forward, and showed a willingness to use the law to advance women's rights a few years before similar steps followed in Britain (1970 and 1975 respectively).

In both countries, the legal position of women has improved substantially and their rights in the work-place have been expanded. However, in politics they have found it difficult to achieve a major breakthrough in the national legislature, until the last few years (see pp. 126–9). This is in spite of the fact that the women's movement for female liberation developed in the United States.

Civil rights for ethnic minorities

The early twentieth century was a bleak time for civil rights in America and it was not until the 1950s and 1960s that the rights of black Americans began to be secured. The decision in the 1954 case of *Brown v Board of Education* (Topeka, Kansas) was a landmark judgement in bringing about the ending of segregation, but it was another decade before they achieved 'equal protection under the law'. The Civil Rights Act laid it clearly down that 'no person in the United States shall, on the ground of race, color, or national origin, be excluded from participation in, be denied the benefit of, or be subjected to discrimination under any program or activity receiving Federal financial assistance'. This was but one of several measures which advanced the cause of black Americans, most notably including the Voting Rights Act of 1965 which prohibited literacy tests and other practices which had a discriminatory impact.

Civil rights activists demanded non-discrimination and equality of opportunity. To achieve the necessary breakthrough for women and members of ethnic minorities, Democratic Presidents were keen to introduce a policy of **affirmative action**, to compensate for the effects of past discrimination.

affirmative action
A policy designed to give special attention or compensatory treatment to members of some previously disadvantaged group.

This provided special benefits to those in the community such as blacks, women and other disadvantaged groups, often involving a special effort to recruit and promote members of these groups.

In its anti-discriminatory measures, America gave a lead which was followed in other countries such as Britain. Segregation had never been a British problem, but the issues surrounding immigration and race relations were becoming a matter of controversy by the 1960s. Several reports pointed to the unfair treatment of the growing number of people from the New Commonwealth, so that in a succession of measures Labour passed legislation to outlaw racial discrimination (1964, 1968, 1976 and 2000). In particular, the 1968 Act was much influenced by American experience. In both countries, the laws might be in place, but there are many examples of discriminatory practices, police harassment and of controversy concerning the position of ethnic minorities in society.

In both countries, there has been strong suspicion of any legislation which confers a seemingly privileged position on some disadvantaged group, whatever the scale of injustice that group may have suffered in the past. Affirmative action ran into political difficulties and has been much challenged in the courts since the early 1990s. Positive discrimination, the preferred British term for such remedial action, has always been controversial in Britain, with critics suggesting that 'reverse discrimination' involving quotas or preference to minority groups is unacceptable.

Open government and freedom of information

In a liberal democracy, the public need to be able to evaluate the performance of a government, in order to decide whether it merits their support. To do this, they need to be 'in the know' about how government works and to have access to information about the basis on which policies are made. **Open government** and **freedom of information** are for many people basic requirements of any democracy. Limits are sometimes placed on this 'right to know', usually because of fears for national security and in order to protect unwarranted intrusion into individual privacy.

open government
The relatively free flow of information about government to the general public, the media and other representative bodies.

freedom of information
Free public access to government information and records. Freedom of information is regarded by many people as a prerequisite for more open government.

America has always had a culture of openness, as befits a country in which there is a suspicion of government and a wish to ensure that those who exercise power do so in an appropriate manner. Its freedom of information (FoI) legislation of 1966 and 1974 provided citizens and interest groups with the right to inspect most federal records. In general, the assumption is that records are subject to disclosure, unless they involve personnel records, court records, national security issues, or business and trade secrets. Access to some information may be initially denied, but appeal to the courts may secure the production of the documents previously unavailable. Such access is a considerable aid to the activities of investigative journalists.

In addition, the so-called 'sunshine laws' adopted by many states are designed to let the sun shine on all governmental deliberations. These laws apply to both legislative and executive officials, and are designed to ensure that policy discussions and decisions occur in full public view and not in closed-door sessions.

In contrast to American experience, Britain has a reputation for secretive government. It is frequently alleged that information kept secret in Britain goes far beyond what is necessary to preserve public safety and often includes material which, if published, would cause political embarrassment. The major legislation which underpinned the British obsession with secrecy was the Official Secrets Act (OSA) of 1911. The measure was draconian in its clampdown. The notorious Section 2 was a catch-all clause which forbade any unauthorised disclosure of information by anyone who had in his possession data obtained whilst that person was holding a position under the Crown. There was no distinction between sensitive information relating to national security, and more harmless trivia. This meant that even the leaking of a Ministry of Defence luncheon menu was against the rules! Clause 2 gave Ministers an arbitrary weapon with which to silence those who would blow the whistle on what happened in government, and could be used to silence anyone who might embarrass those in office.

In 1989, a new Official Secrets Act was passed by the Thatcher government. Ministers claimed that it was more liberal than the previous one and that it abandoned the catch-all clause – which was true. But although the 'reform' narrowed the definition of official secrecy, it tightened it within these narrower confines. Even a disclosure of information about fraud, neglect or unlawful activity cannot now be defended as being in the public interest. Convictions are therefore easier. Some liberalisation has occurred since then, but critics continue to call for greater transparency in the British system of government. They believe that more openness is desirable and necessary, and that democracy works best when citizens are well-informed.

Unlike most countries, Britain had no Freedom of Information Act until the year 2000. Many states had freedom of information enshrined in law. guaranteeing citizens the right to see a wide variety of documents, both state and personal. But in Britain, the right of access to information remained patchy. New Labour, in opposition, talked of reform of the OSA and the introduction of a FoI bill. The former has yet to come, and many observers feel that in office ministers are at one with their predecessors in using security and secrecy in their own interests. The legislation on freedom of information was slow to materialise, but it passed into law in 2000 and will become effective after the next election.

The passage of the Freedom of Information Act is an historic step. But to many observers – including those sympathetic to ministers – it is a watered-down version of what is required. Canada, Ireland, Sweden and the United States all provide considerably greater openness.

The instinct of governments in Britain is to keep secret much that in the United States would be revealed by a vigilant press protected by First Amendment guarantees. There is no tradition of openness and in all of the debate in recent years it has been clear that ministers of either party are concerned to set clear limits to the information that can be made available.

Conclusion

America provides greater formal protection for individual liberty than does Great Britain. The Constitution, via the Bill of Rights, sets out guarantees of essential freedoms, and Americans frequently argue their rights under the First Amendment to express their feelings on any issues of public importance. But such protection has not always been extended to all groups, particularly those belonging to unpopular minorities. In contrast, until the passage of the Human Rights Act, Britain lacked such clearly proclaimed protection, but this did not mean that rights were not recognised.

A bill of rights is not the panacea for all problems arising in the relationship between the individual and the state. History is littered with examples of countries in which formal statements of rights have not proved to be worth the paper upon they were written on. The American document did not stop President Franklin Roosevelt from depriving thousands of native-born Japanese Americans of their liberty in World War Two, and for generations its provisions were not applied to black Americans.

Views have differed across the Atlantic. Thomas Jefferson could not understand why anyone should resist the idea of a bill of rights, seeing it as 'what the people are entitled to against every government on earth, general or particular, and what no just government should refuse or rest on inference'. A British Conservative and former minister, John Patten, sees it differently. He takes the traditional view on this side of the Atlantic that:

> Such documents are meaningless unless they exist within a country which has a political culture that renders them viable ... The greatest protector of citizens' rights in the UK are citizens themselves ... The protector of freedom in the end is the political culture, not some document, however weighty.[4]

Women and ethnic minorities on either side of the Atlantic have campaigned strongly for their rights in recent decades. In the United States, the 14th Amendment gives formal recognition of the rights of all Americans to 'equal protection', but the attempt to pass an Equal Rights Amendment to benefit women by providing that 'equality of rights under the law' could not be denied 'on account of sex' proved unsuccessful and eventually founded in 1982. In both countries, legislation has conferred a range of benefits upon groups seeking greater opportunities and fuller recognition of their rights.

The civil rights umbrella is a large one, with increasing numbers of groups seeking protection for their rights, be they old, young, disabled, gay or victims

The liberties and rights of people in Britain and the United States of America: a summary		
Issue	*Britain*	*United States*
Existence of Bill of Rights?	No, but Human Rights Act (HRA): protection of the law, but no entrenchment.	Yes, many rights guaranteed by Constitution.
Language and interpretation	Articles of HRA require interpretation: several qualifications to articles of European Convention. Much depends on judicial interpretation.	Broad phraseology of Constitution, but terms not qualified. Much depends on judicial interpretation.
Freedom of expression	Now protected by HRA, Article 10, but traditionally more restricted than in US, e.g. libel.	Guaranteed by 1st Amendment: much toleration of symbolic speech, but not always towards minority rights – e.g. communists.
Punishment: rights of suspects, defendants and detainees	Power of police strengthened in recent years, concern over criminals 'going free'. But also concern for right of accused and over causes of crime. No death penalty.	Err on side of police powers. Rights of accused often questioned, tougher regime for many detainees, especially terrorists at Guantanamo Bay. Many states employ the death penalty.
Rights of women	Gained vote in 1918 and 1928. Anti-discrimination measures passed from 1970 onwards.	Vote via 19th Amendment, 1920. Anti-discrimination legislation (1964), before Britain. Women's Liberation Movement developed here.
Rights of ethnic minorities	Anti-discriminatory laws on race relations passed from 1960s. Much still to do.	Anti-discriminatory legislation (1964) earlier than in Britain. Much still to do.

of Aids. Those categorised as belonging to disadvantaged minorities, particularly the elderly, now constitute a significant section of the voting population, and in the new century they are sure to be active in demanding greater recognition of their rights.

REFERENCES

1 A. V. Dicey, *Introduction to the Study of the Law of the Constitution*, Macmillan, 1885.
2 K. Ewing and C. Gearty, *Freedom under Thatcher*, Clarendon Press, 1990.
3 F. Klug, K. Starmer and S. Weir, *The Three Pillars of Liberty*, Routledge, 1996.
4 J. Patten, Conservative Political Centre Lecture on 'Political Culture, Conservatism and Rolling Constitutional Changes', July 1991.

USEFUL WEB SITES

For the UK

www.coe.fr Council of Europe. Access to information on European Convention.

www.echr.coe.int European Convention on Human Rights.

www.lcd.gov.uk Lord Chancellor's departmental site. Coverage of human rights legislation.

www.charter88.org.uk Charter 88. Information relating to protection of rights.

For the USA

www.heritage.org The Heritage Foundation, a conservative group which campaigns to preserve liberties and rights. Has useful links to other conservative organisations with a similar agenda.

www.aclu.org The American Civil Liberties Union, a more liberal campaigning group on rights. Links to other more liberal organisations.

www.findlaw.com FindLaw provides an index of US Supreme Court rulings.

www.ifex.org The International Freedom of Expression Exchange represents more than 50 groups committed to human rights and civil liberties. It describes cases of current concern.

http://nsi.org/terrorism.html Web site of the National Security Institute. Provides links regarding terrorism, including details of policy and legislation in that area.

SAMPLE QUESTIONS

1 Is the passage of the Human Rights Act the first step towards the introduction of a written constitution in Britain?

2 Examine the ways in which liberties and rights are protected in Britain and the United States. In which country is there a greater degree of protection?

3 Is it true that to say that constitutions are meaningless without recognition of basic civil liberties and rights?

Executives

4

The executive branch literally refers to those persons who are charged with responsibility for the administration of government and the implementation of laws made by the legislature. Technically, it includes the head of state, members of the government and the officials who serve them, as well as the enforcement agencies such as the military and the police. However, more usually the term is used to denote the smaller body of decision-makers which actually takes responsibility for the direction and form of government policy. Indeed, we use the term Political Executive **when referring to the government of the day, and the** Official Executive **when we are speaking of the bureaucracy whose task it is to administer the policies which ministers have laid down.**

In the first section of the chapter we are concerned with the Political Executive, in other words with the politicians rather than the civil servants. Who gets to the top? What power do they exercise? Why is that power often said to be growing? Who is more powerful, Prime Minister or President?

In the second section, we briefly review the Official Executive, examining who we can include within the ranks of the bureaucracy, how they got there and the power they exercise.

POINTS TO CONSIDER

➤ Distinguish between the Political and the Official Executive.

➤ What factors led to the broad trend to increased prime ministerial and presidential power in the twentieth century?

➤ What factors constrain the Prime Minister and President today?

➤ To what extent are they prevented from achieving their political goals?

➤ What qualities is it desirable for political leaders to possess in the television age?

➤ Is the personality of a leader today more important than his or her ideology?

➤ Compare the importance of the Cabinet in Britain and the United States.

THE POLITICAL EXECUTIVE

In a parliamentary system such as Britain, the key politicians include the ministers headed by a prime or chief minister, all of whom are members of and responsible to Parliament. In presidential systems such as the United States, the President acts as a single executive, though he appoints Cabinet members to work with him. Neither the President nor his Cabinet officers are members of congress.

The functions of executives

As we have seen, the key function of the executive branch is to take decisions and assume overall responsibility for the direction and co-ordination of government policy; in other words, executives provide political leadership. Providing leadership involves several distinctive roles, of which Heywood has distinguished five main ones:[1]

1 Heads of state (be they monarchs or Presidents), Chief Executives and government ministers on occasion undertake **ceremonial duties** such as receiving foreign visitors, staging banquets and signing treaties. In this capacity, they 'stand in' for the state itself, embodying the national will. In Britain, the Queen has a key ceremonial function, although on frequent occasions ministers – and especially the Prime Minister – are also required to meet dignitaries and engage in discussions with other heads of state or their representatives. In America, the President combines the role of Head of State and Chief of the Executive. He or she is the symbolic head of state and as such a focal point for loyalty. Again, the President has ceremonial functions ranging from visiting foreign countries to attending important national occasions.

crisis
A sudden, unpredictable and potentially dangerous event which calls for constant monitoring, good and consistent judgement, and decisive action. Most American Presidents have been only too willing to seize their chance to lead, whether it be Kennedy over missiles in Cuba or George W. Bush over the terrorist attacks on New York and Washington.

2 Key members of the Executive have to respond in times of **crisis**, and provide leadership. A willingness to shoulder responsibility and a facility for making difficult decisions are important assets for any could-be national leader, and it is in the **management of crises** that their mettle is tested to the limits. The potential dangers range from an upsurge of discontent at home from militant groups to terrorism abroad, from conflict in the world's trouble-spots to the need to cope with famines and earthquakes in territories which fall within a nation's responsibilities. Some Prime Ministers spend much of their time on international affairs, out of choice or preference.

Tony Blair was much involved in helping to build the international coalition against terrorism following the events of 11 September 2001, and George W. Bush was forced into more vigorous action as part of the same struggle. The Bush presidency moved into a higher gear, adopting a more assertive role at home and abroad. Given America's size and strength, the role of the President in crisis management is inevitably greater than that of the Prime Minister.

3 Members of the Executive seek to **mobilise support** for the government to which they belong, for without such support the task of implementing policy is much more difficult. This involves appearing on the media or taking other opportunities via which the ministerial case can be put across to the public. As we see on p. 71, political leaders are normally keen to take advantage of the opportunities presented by television for it can be an invaluable medium for telegenic personalities. These range from extended political interviews and 'soft interviews' on chat shows, to televised appearances in the legislature and televised press conferences. Prime Minister Blair has recently followed American style and opted for the 'presidential' press conference.

4 Above all, the most important day-to-day role of the executive branch is to control the policy-making process, a function which has expanded notably in the twentieth century with the increasing involvement of government in running the economy and providing welfare programmes. As a result of the greater degree of state intervention and regulation, **ministers are constantly involved in making decisions** on a whole range of issues which have a major consequence on people's daily lives. As part of their involvement, they introduce new policies, often requiring laws to be guided through the legislature. For this, they need the consent and approval of a majority of elected representatives, and as we have already seen in 3 above the task of winning support for governmental initiatives falls largely to them.

The Prime Minister is part of the legislature and has a phalanx of party supporters behind him or her who will usually support and vote for the measures he or she introduces. The President is not part of the legislative branch and although Presidents can recommend measures to Congress – and increasingly do put forward packages of proposals to Congress – they may have real difficulty in getting them on to the statute book. Their methods range from subtle and more blatant arm-twisting to threatened or actual use of the presidential veto, but despite such an array of means there is no guarantee that they will achieve the end required. Whereas Tony Blair was able to push through a controversial programme of welfare reform, Bill Clinton was not able to do the same in health policy.

5 Finally, **the Political Executive oversees the work of the Official Executive,** and whilst it is bureaucrats who implement the decisions which have been taken it is nonetheless usually the politicians who get the praise or blame for

what is done. Ministers take the blame for mistakes, and are responsible to the Legislature for sins of omission and commission on the part of their civil servants.

In Britain, both individual and collective responsibility have long been viewed as cardinal features of British government, even if in recent years they rarely lead to ministerial resignations or the downfall of the party in power. At times of political controversy when wrong-doing or maladministration is exposed in a department, the Prime Minister may come under considerable pressure to act, as Tony Blair was over the behaviour of his Secretary of State for Transport, Stephen Byers, in 2001–02. In America, the President and/or Cabinet cannot be brought down by an adverse vote in the legislature. The President will ride out problems within a department, even if its head has to take the flak.

The increase in executive power

In the twentieth century the power of government has been extended significantly as politicians have sought to develop new policy initiatives to please the voters. In an age of mass democracy, they cannot afford to leave the aspirations of the people unmet, and they have been forced to respond to pressing economic and social needs or else suffer defeat at election time.

Heads of state have benefited from the increasing attention of the media over the last few decades, but their powers have for a long time been largely symbolic unless – as in the case of the United States – the President fulfils a dual ceremonial role as head of state and also acts as Chief Executive. Chiefs of the Executive have major responsibilities, and their public profile is markedly higher than that of their ministerial colleagues. Much of their increase in power derives from the growth in governmental interventionism, but the globalisation of economic and political concerns has also added to their responsibilities and recognition.

Prime Ministers – sometimes known as chancellors or as first ministers (or by local names as in Ireland, where the term Taoiseach is employed) – are chiefs of the executive branch. Their power is based upon their leadership of the majority party, and they head either a single party or coalition government. Their formal powers are less than those of a US-type executive President, but their ability to hire, promote and fire colleagues offers much scope for a display of strong, personal leadership.

For first ministers, the degree of power they can exercise depends largely upon two areas:
- The relationship with ministerial colleagues in the Cabinet. Strong leaders will be able to use their patronage to reward party colleagues whom they

wish to bring into the administration and dismiss or downgrade dissenters, and will give a decisive lead to Cabinet discussions.

- Leadership of the party via which they can influence the legislature and the voters. Modern political leadership is based largely on the growth of the party system in the twentieth century. As parties have become more centralised and disciplined, leaders have been given an opportunity to assert their influence over their party supporters and rivals, and if they can keep their ministerial team united they can be in a position to stamp their personal imprint on the party. Of course, this does not always happen, and there are always other potential leaders waiting 'in the wings', so that a leader who loses the willing consent of his followers can find himself or herself in difficulty.

Heywood provides another series of reasons for the growth in prime ministerial power over recent decades, noting in particular

> the tendency of the broadcast media in particular to focus on personalities, meaning that Prime Ministers become a kind of 'brand image' of their parties. The growth in international summitry and foreign visits also provides prime ministers with opportunities to cultivate an image of statesmanship, and gives them scope to portray themselves as national leaders. In some cases, this has led to the allegation that prime ministers have effectively emancipated themselves from Cabinet constraints and established a form of prime-ministerial government.

The position of Prime Minister in Britain was already well established by the end of the nineteenth century, when it was described as *'primus inter pares'* (first among equals), but circumstances in the twentieth century allowed premiers to develop the potential of their office to the full and to become much more than the description implies. In particular, war leadership – whether it be in World War One, World War Two or the Falklands War – provided opportunities for a display of assertive, personal leadership. Managing a war effort requires broad shoulders, a willingness to take tough decisions and accept responsibility if things go wrong and an ability to rally and inspire the nation. It did much for the fortunes of Margaret Thatcher as Prime Minister, for she was able to cast herself in Churchillian mould.

Today, as we see on pp. 78–80, there is talk of prime ministerial or even presidential government in Britain and the comparison with the American President has a well-established place in the minds of examiners.

American Presidents have benefited from similar factors, notably:

- The growth of 'big government' in the years after 1933, as the role of President became identified with increased federal intervention.
- The importance of foreign policy, with the development of an American world role following World War Two.
- The mass media: the media can concentrate on one national office, for the President is news – the Kennedys were almost like a royal family for

journalists. Since the 1960s, television has been increasingly important and Presidents regularly make the headlines.

In addition, the inertia of Congress, which surrendered much influence in the early post-war decades, enabled Presidents to assume a larger leadership role. The mid-1960s saw the peak of enthusiasm for presidential power, for by then it seemed as though there was a broad consensus about domestic and foreign policy (by the end of the decade, division over the Vietnam War had threatened that consensus), and Congress was willing to accept presidential leadership. It gave Truman and his successors *carte blanche* in matters of national security. Foreign policy was recognised as the President's sphere of influence and his initiatives received the near-automatic ratification of Capitol Hill.

Television and political leadership: differing styles
(see also p. 75 and pp. 257–60 in the chapter on the mass media)

The publicity and opportunities for leadership afforded via television are considerable, and some politicians have been able to exploit the medium to great effect. This can be achieved by leaders of sharply contrasting personalities. In the early years of the Fifth French Republic, Charles de Gaulle was skilful in using his televised press conferences to create what Ball refers to as 'the impression of aloof royalty, unsullied by the real world of political bargaining and compromise'.[2] He came across as a national leader who could be counted on as the father of the French people. His appeal was not in any way based upon a telegenic image of the type which is now considered so important for political leaders.

Neither did Margaret Thatcher in her early years as Opposition leader seem to possess obvious television appeal, her voice seeming shrill, her manner unduly hectoring. Abrasive and argumentative politicians can seem unattractive to the voters, and these qualities needed to be managed. Within a few years her TV persona had changed, and her weaknesses were either removed or turned to her advantage. She was able to convey her strength and resolution, and with careful coaching from professionals was successful in adopting a 'softer' style of voice and appearance to accompany her message. In choosing Tony Blair as leader, Labour saw the value in opting for someone who is media-friendly, and endowed with personal charisma. Like Bill Clinton – who was also able to deploy the medium to his advantage – he is easy on the eye and ear. Clinton was often most successful in staging a comeback via the adept handling of television.

Today, as the veteran Democratic Party consultant, Raymond Strother has noted, there are many more appealing, attractive people who get to become political leaders.[3] Conventional good looks are an advantage – fatness or baldness quite the opposite. The Americans have in recent decades chosen some leaders who are 'naturals' for the media age. John F. Kennedy had an image of youth and glamour, and was able to use television to impress the voters with his determination to get America moving ahead and conquer 'new frontiers'. Ronald Reagan was a trained actor, who looked good, and was able to deploy his soft-soap style and easy charm to convince Americans of his warmth and sincerity.

How do politicians acquire political leadership in Britain and the United States?

No one is born to be Prime Minister or President, unlike the person who becomes king or queen in Britain.

BRITAIN

Prime Ministers gain power as a result of a general election victory. As the leaders of the largest party, they win the right to form an administration. On occasion, the existing Prime Minister either resigns in office (e.g. Macmillan, Wilson) or is defeated by a rival candidate in a party leadership contest (e.g. Lady Thatcher). This creates a vacancy which is filled as a result of a leadership contest in the relevant party.

The process of getting elected as party leader

The **Conservatives** were the last of the three parties to allow party members a say in the choice of their leader. For many years up to and including the election of William Hague in 1997, the decision was made by MPs, who had the opportunity to talk to their constituents before they cast their vote. Hague introduced a number of organisational reforms, among them a scheme which first operated in 2001. MPs (who of course had had the chance to see the rival candidates at work in the House of Commons and to assess their parliamentary skills) voted on a range of candidates, which was eventually narrowed down to two: Kenneth Clarke and Iain Duncan Smith. Party members then made the final decision, in this case opting for the less-well-known Duncan Smith, the candidate widely perceived as more right-wing and anti-European.

The **Labour** leader and deputy are elected via an Electoral College, in which there are three equally represented components: the unions, the constituency representatives and MPs. Given the disparity in the size of the three components, the votes of MPs count disproportionately, the vote of one MP being equivalent to some 800 constituency votes and approaching 15,000 trade union votes. Those wishing to be candidates need nominations from 12.5 per cent of Labour MPs when there is a vacancy, or 20 per cent when they are mounting a challenge to an incumbent. To be declared elected, a candidate needs an absolute majority of the votes. The revised machinery was put to the test for the first time in 1994. On that occasion, Tony Blair was elected leader with majority support in all the constituent parts of the College. Although only a quarter of the eligible voters exercised their right, the election was widely seen as the biggest democratic exercise in European party politics, a 'million-vote mandate' as some Blairite supporters proclaimed. (952,109 votes were actually cast).

The **Liberals** were the first party to opt for some scheme for choosing their leader which extended to the party membership, as well as to MPs. **Liberal Democrat** machinery allows for a straight 'one person, one vote' ballot of all party members.

The background of those who enter Number Ten

The road to the premiership in Britain is usually a long one, Prime Ministers normally having experienced a good innings as a backbencher and then served in a variety of ministerial posts. They become leader of the nation by first becoming the choice of their party. In the two main British parties, the leader is now chosen by a combination of MPs and party members, so that many thousands of people have been involved (see opposite) – or had the opportunity to become involved – in the decision. Once the party leader is decided, everything depends upon the outcome of the general election. The leader of the largest party becomes Prime Minister and forms his or her administration.

Of recent premiers, most have had some experience of ministerial office before they reach Number Ten. James Callaghan was elected as an MP in 1945 and served for 31 years before he became Prime Minister. Unusually, he had served in all three great office of state (the Treasury, the Home Office and the Foreign Office). John Major entered the House in 1979 at the same time as Margaret Thatcher entered Downing Street, and within eleven years had replaced her, illustrating that much depends on good fortune, right timing and the lack of an acceptable alternative. He had had a rapid rise through the ministerial ranks, serving for only two years in a major department (the Foreign Office and the Treasury). In the case of Tony Blair, he had entered the House of Commons in 1983, eleven years later was the leader of the Labour Party and within three further years became Prime Minister after a landslide victory.

THE UNITED STATES OF AMERICA

American Presidents gain their position by one of two basic routes. They either take the normal road to the White House, running for the presidency via the electoral process briefly described below, or else they are elevated to the presidency from the vice-presidency. About one in five Presidents reached the Oval Office not by the normal road of elections, but because they were the number two when the incumbent died, was assassinated or discredited. Truman replaced Roosevelt after he had suffered a stroke, Johnson replaced Kennedy after the dramatic shooting of the President in Dallas, and Ford replaced Nixon after his resignation as a result of Watergate and associated scandals. In Ford's case, he bears the unwanted distinction of being the only President never to have been elected to office, for at the first opportunity (November 1976, against Jimmy Carter) the Americans voted him out of office.

The people who have become President have been a very diverse group, some distinguished intellectuals of great moral force, others shallow men of dubious morality. As long as they had the basic qualification of being natural-born citizens of the United States, were at least 35 years of age and had resided in the country for at least fourteen years, they were eligible. All have been white, male and, with the exception of Kennedy, Protestant. On observing Harding (often rated the worst president of all time) in office, a critic remarked: When I was a boy, I was told that anybody could become President. Now I'm beginning to believe it'.

The process of getting elected to the presidency

Candidates firstly need to achieve the nomination of their party. The method of selecting candidates has evolved over 200 years, and three possibilities are available: via the caucus, state conventions or primaries. Primaries are state-wide intra-party elections, the purpose being to give voters the opportunity to select directly the party's candidates.

▶

Nowadays, almost all candidates for presidency begin the campaign via the primary route. The first is held in New Hampshire and most are over by late March. There is an increasing tendency for primaries and caucuses to be brought forward, because states realise that they stand a better chance of affecting the outcome if they hold elections early in the process. Usually, a clear-cut winner has already emerged by time of National Nominating Conventions in July–August, so that these bodies now really only ratify a choice which has been made months previously. Their importance has declined, the Democrat convention of 1952 being the last to take more than a single ballot to select its nominee.

Once the candidates are chosen, then the presidential campaign proper gets underway. It includes whistle-stop tours and speech-making, but nowadays the emphasis is on television advertising, appearances and live presidential debates (see p. 252). When the voter makes his or her choice in November, he or she is actually voting to choose members of the Electoral College (see p. 31), rather than directly opting for a particular presidential candidate. **NB** Candidates may run without the support of a political party, as Independents. To do so, they must present a petition, signed by a specified number of voters who support the candidacy. Ross Perot was able to get on the ballot paper in all 50 states in 1992. Some states make this difficult, as the Green nominee, Ralph Nader, found in 2000.

What are the political backgrounds of those who become political leaders in the United States?

Candidates for the White House have tended to come from the Senate or a state governorship rather than the House of Representatives, where the period of two years in office gives them little time to make their mark. Gerald Ford was the last member of the House to become President, although in this case immediately prior to his elevation he was Vice President. (Nixon had experienced some difficulty in finding anyone who wanted the job, following the downfall of his previous choice in a financial scandal.)

Kennedy was the last person to rise from the Senate to the presidency, although several senators since the 1960s have attempted to gain their party's candidacy. The main route of successful candidates has been the vice-presidency or a governorship. Johnson, Ford and Bush Snr were all Vice-Presidents immediately prior to becoming President, and Nixon had served in that office for eight years before having a further eight years in the political wilderness. Carter, Reagan, Clinton and Bush jnr were all previously state governors. Reagan was well known to Americans, his face being familiar on cinema and television screens as a movie actor, whereas Carter (the peanut farmer from Georgia) and Clinton (the Governor of Arkansas) were little known outside their states.

Strength and weakness in political leaders: changing fashions

Opportunities for vigorous leadership present themselves to some leaders more than others. But individuals as well as circumstances make a difference, for some Presidents and Prime Ministers seek opportunities for giving taking decisive action.

What qualities are needed to be a successful leader in Britain, the United States and elsewhere?

Politicians come in all shapes and sizes, although the demands of the media today make it less likely that anyone who becomes their party's nominee for the highest office will be fat, ugly or unconvincing on television (see p. 71). The tendency in any modern democracy is to choose leaders who are thought likely to be 'good on television'. Those who are not 'naturals' for the medium or at least effective in handling it, such as Michael Foot and William Hague, have often failed to be elected. In Ronald Reagan, Americans found the perfect blend of the worlds of television and politics. Ideally, leaders need wide popular appeal.

The qualities needed to obtain the leadership and stay there are varied. What is evident from a study of recent Prime Ministers and Presidents is that politicians of very different personalities can occupy high office and achieve success. Important qualities might include, among other things, affability, ability (not necessarily the highest academic distinction, but rather nimbleness and vigour of mind, and a certain astuteness), industriousness (not necessarily a massive command of detail), an ability to delegate and concentrate on essentials, a capacity for decision-making, high ideals, vision, judgement, good timing, and courage (the willingness to tackle difficult events and where necessary to give a clear steer to events). Determination and perhaps ruthlessness are also in the mental equipment of most successful politicians.

For America, given its prolonged election campaigns, there are additional factors. The process of becoming American President – unless the President dies in office and the Vice-President takes over – is a long, complex and expensive one. It tests the mettle of any candidate, so that those who emerge have to be able to remain relatively unscathed after the scrutiny of a prolonged campaign. They need endurance and stamina, and to have a private life that will withstand the spotlight of media publicity, unless – like Bill Clinton – their charm enables them to convince Americans that, although not a saint, they are the right person for the job. It is a gruelling process, but it does ensure that the person who eventually emerges has, by the time he of she takes over, become a national figure in his own right. If Carter was largely unknown outside of his state in 1975, he was recognisable to almost all Americans a year later. In Britain, the main national party leaders are more obviously recognisable before reaching Downing Street, for coverage of politics centres on personalities and the Westminster scene. It is still important for them to achieve a broad appeal not just to party members and sympathisers, but to the non-committed voters at large.

Fashions in political leadership come and go. Strong leadership can inspire people and provide a real impetus to government. Colleagues, party members and voters feel that the person at the helm has a clear vision of what needs to be done, and for a time this can be very appealing – especially after a period of drift. The danger is that an assertive display of firm leadership can easily drift into authoritarianism, and the qualities once admired can seem no longer admirable. What was once strength based on personal conviction can easily become arrogance.

The premiership of Margaret Thatcher illustrated how a leader endowed with a towering personality and firm views – assets which were initially admired by many members of the public – could become someone seen as overbearing and out-of-touch. After her leadership, many of her colleagues and people outside Westminster were pleased to see affable John Major take over. Yet when his parliamentary position was weakened after the 1992 election and his administration became beset by internal problems, there was much criticism of his dithering, indecisive leadership. Many voters seemed to want a firm hand in control, and warmed to the personal charisma and sense of direction Tony Blair was able to offer.

The Major administration illustrates the importance of the role of party leadership for any Prime Minister. Though not lacking in appealing personal qualities, he was unable to provide a sense of direction and his government seemed to drift from problem to problem – especially after the humiliating circumstances of withdrawal from the Exchange Rate Mechanism (ERM) on Black Wednesday – 16 September 1992. In his case, it was not lack of ability but a combination of unfortunate circumstances that undermined his position. His party was divided, and he could not dominate a House of Commons in which his parliamentary majority was always at risk. In addition, however, he also seemed to be deficient in what the elder George Bush once called 'the vision thing'. He seemed unable to lead people, and inspire them with the prospect of reaching a promised land. He lacked personal magnetism.

What determines the strength of political leaders?

In any country, much depends on the person at the helm. The observation of Lord Oxford on the office of Prime Minister many years ago applies to the situation in any democracy: 'The power of the Prime Minister is what its holder chooses and is able to make of it'. What the leader **chooses** to make of the office is a matter of personal style and approach. What he or she **is able** to make of it depends on personal ability and the circumstances of the day.

1 Style

Individual British and American Prime Ministers and Presidents have had differing concepts of their office, as we can see from two examples from each country. In Britain, John Major adopted a style which was more collegiate than that of Margaret Thatcher. Less of a conviction politician, he was by inclination more consensual, willing to consult and discuss issues. By contrast, Tony Blair has adopted many of the characteristics of the Thatcher era. As party leader, he has been known for his firm discipline, often derided as 'control freakery'. Party colleagues have been expected to acquiesce in policy changes, some of which have been markedly distasteful to supporters of Old Labour – especially on welfare, the role of the private sector and trade union issues.

The Prime Minister's second election victory provided him with the opportunity to act more decisively and autocratically, and his emergence as a war leader in the battle against international terrorism has focused much attention upon his personal leadership. He has adopted a 'presidential' style, taking to the media on regular occasions and showing much concern with matters of presentation. He has tried to project himself as the voice of all reasonable elements in country who can shelter under his 'big umbrella'. He has downplayed the importance of the Cabinet and is said to be dismissive of Parliament, attending and voting irregularly. He is often charged with lack of accountability, as in his 'down-grading' of Question Time in the House of Commons.

In America, presidents Kennedy and Johnson asserted a more positive role for government than their Republican predecessor. They knew what they wanted to achieve, and put forward a bold programme for social progress. By the time Bill Clinton took over, the opportunities for the White House to display powerful leadership had been much reduced. 'Big government' was out of fashion, so that although he was naturally a leader who wanted to make things happen he found himself constrained by prevailing circumstances, most notably a resurgent and Republican-dominated Congress keen to make life difficult for him.

2 Ability

Of postwar British Prime Ministers, most have been able in some way or other. Ability is not always a matter of intellectual distinction, although a strong intellect can help. Harold Macmillan was an astute leader. In his prime, his abilities were widely recognised by those around him, as was pointed out by a colleague who observed: 'Harold Macmillan's chairmanship of the Cabinet was superb by any standards. If he dominated it (he usually did) . . . it was done by sheer superiority of mind and judgement'.[4]

John Major had many likeable qualities but intellectual prowess and public speaking were not ones for which he was greatly famed. He had other gifts, being notably effective in negotiation. James Callaghan had a reassuring manner which enabled him to see the country through difficult times, even if he was unable to give a decisive personal lead.

The men who have occupied the Oval Office have been similarly diverse, some intellectually eminent (Wilson and Clinton), some not very bright (Harding and Ford). Some have been fine speakers able to sell their policies (Franklin Roosevelt, Kennedy and Clinton), others have been poor speakers who lacked a way with words or had difficulty with them (Nixon, Ford and George W.

Bush). Their quality has been variable, but sometimes even if they were initially seen as unimpressive in comparison with their predecessor, they have grown in stature whilst in office. George W. Bush was widely portrayed as lacklustre, uninspiring and indolent in his early months as President, tainted by the fact that his presidency seemed to many people to be 'illegitimate'. Whatever view is taken of his intellectual qualities and capacity for leadership today, it is certainly true that he and his presidency were galvanised into action and moved into a higher gear after the attack on the twin towers. He took a firmer grip on events, began to shape the political agenda and – in the view of one observer – mutated 'into a figurehead who has the people behind him'. This shows the importance of the final factor, circumstance.

3 Circumstance

Some political leaders have been lucky in the circumstances of their takeover and others less fortunate. Margaret Thatcher was in many respects fortunate. The Falklands War, the Miners' Strike and the activities of the Greater London Council and Liverpool City Council provided her with dragons to slay – General Galtieri, Arthur Scargill, Ken Livingstone and Derek Hatton, among them. Moreover, the economy benefited from North Sea oil revenues, and the Labour Party was divided and led in the 1983 election by a leader (Michael Foot) who lacked popular appeal and had little idea on how to exploit the media. Her successor was less lucky. John Major took over at the end of a long spell of Conservative rule so that in many ways he succeeded to an exhausted inheritance. Within a few years it was 'time for a change'. He also suffered from the fact that Europe was beginning to intrude much more into British politics, the issue of European policy causing substantial problems for his party and administration.

The elder George Bush was primarily interested in foreign policy and won himself many plaudits at the time for his handling of the Gulf War. But within a short time, the concerns of many Americans were more to do with domestic policy and the recession than they were with events overseas. In 1992, he no longer seemed to be the man for the hour. His son, whatever the doubts his personality and ability created among many of his fellow countrymen, was called upon to lead his country through the trauma of 11 September and its aftermath. The event was the making of his presidency, even if it is difficult to judge what its effects will be in the long term.

The case of the British Prime Minister

For much of the twentieth century, writers and journalists debated the idea that the Prime Minister had acquired an unprecedented, even dangerous, degree of power. Back in 1914, one observer, Sidney Low, noted that the incumbents of Number Ten were acquiring 'now and again, enlarged attributes, beyond those possessed as chairman of the executive board, and chief of the dominant party'.[5] He went on to observe that it was 'the increasing size of Cabinets' which 'caused the figure of the Prime Minister to stand out more prominently above the ranks of his colleagues'. RHS Crossman, a former Oxford don and then a Labour MP/Cabinet minister, elaborated upon the idea that Britain had acquired a system in which the Prime Minister had supreme power: 'The post-war epoch has seen the final transformation of Cabinet Government into prime ministerial Government', with the effect that 'the Cabinet now joins the dignified elements in the Constitution'.[6]

Such claims have been repeated frequently since the early 1960s, and many of them were made long before Mrs Thatcher ever became Prime Minister. But her performance led to a burst of renewed comment, for she appeared to stretch the power of the office to its limits. One minister who fell foul of her leadership style, Jim Prior, was to write in 1986 of the 'awesome' and 'still not fully appreciated' extent of prime ministerial power.[7] At around the same time, a left-wing critic of the concentration of power, Tony Benn, was more specific in his challenge:

> The wide range of powers . . . exercised by a British prime minister . . . are now so great as to encroach upon the legitimate rights of the electorate, undermine the essential role of Parliament, [and] usurp some of the functions of collective Cabinet decision-making . . . In short, the present centralisation of power into the hands of one person has gone too far and amounts to a system of personal rule in the very heart of our system of . . . parliamentary democracy.[8]

The central elements in prime ministerial power are well known but difficult to measure. They are:
- the power of appointment and dismissal of Cabinet and other ministerial offices;
- power over the structure and membership of Cabinet committees, any of which the Prime Minister may chair;
- the central, overseeing non-departmental nature of the office
- leadership of the party; and
- a high degree of public visibility.

These features operated for much of the twentieth century (certainly since 1945), but the circumstances outlined above have boosted the potential of the office and given it a much higher profile. No Prime Minister since World War Two has been anything less than very powerful, but individuals have made a greater or lesser impact upon the office. All were subject to some constraints, and even the more powerful among them were not always able to sustain the same degree of performance throughout their term.

Any Prime Minister today has a formidable display of powers at his or her disposal, but it is easy to overstate them. These powers need to be placed in context, and when this is done it can be seen that prime ministerial power can be seriously circumscribed and dependent on the circumstances of the time. It is not merely that some Prime Ministers are more powerful than others, but that any single Prime Minister will be more powerful at certain times than at others in the course of the premiership.

The prime ministerial government thesis can be over-stated, and it suffers from the tendency to over-generalisation. The relationships between the Cabinet, individual ministers and the Prime Minister are complex and fluid. Much depends on the personalities of those involved and on the issues and problems with which they are faced. There has certainly been a remarkable growth in the power of the executive branch of government in the last 100 years, but the distribution of power within the Executive is liable to change at any time.

The case of the USA

Presidential power has increased since the days of the Founding Fathers as people have turned to the presidency for initiatives to get things done. At times, the President has filled the vacuum left by the inertia or inaction of Congress, the states or private enterprise. The growth has not been at a consistent pace, for there was a reaction to Lincoln's autocracy and the increase in governmental power during World War One. There has been an ebb and flow of power because the presidency has flourished during emergencies which are, by definition, a temporary condition. When normality has been restored, presidential domination has come to an end. The fear of dictatorship has re-emerged, and Congress reasserted itself.

At times, Americans seem to want vigorous leadership, but they may then become troubled by the consequences of that assertiveness and yearn for a less active presidency. As Wasserman puts it: 'Americans have swung back and forth in how powerful they want their Presidents . . . [they] have walked a thin line between too much and too little power'.[9]

The modern presidency

The modern presidency really began in 1933, for the Great Depression created – or at least accelerated – a fundamental change in political behaviour in the United States. The sheer scale of economic dislocation and hardship required a national lead, and the administration of Franklin D Roosevelt was only too willing to respond. Since then, the American system has become a very presidential one and the political process now requires a continued sequence of presidential initiatives in foreign policy and in the domestic arena to function satisfactorily.

As we have seen, there was real enthusiasm for presidential power in the 1960s. A broad spectrum of commentators welcomed its expansion. It was felt to be prudent to allow the President a relatively free hand to lead his country. There was general agreement that the federal government should have a significant role in the nation's economy and in creating and maintaining a welfare system. This growth of executive power prompted Arthur Schlesinger to argue that the concept of the constitutional presidency had given way by the 1970s to an **imperial presidency**, a revolutionary use of power very different from what had origi-

> **imperial presidency**
> A label for the increased authority and decreased accountability of the presidency, at its peak by the late 1960s.

nally been intended.[10] He was largely basing his argument on the Nixon presidency and concluded that the institution no longer seemed to be controllable via the supposed constitutional checks and balances. It was an unsatisfactory position, pregnant with the possibility of the abuse of power.

The 1970s to the present day

Such abuses of presidential power did occur – Vietnam and Watergate were but the most significant. Many Americans realised for the first time in 1974 the tremendous accretion of power in the hands of the President. The principle of a separation of powers had been incorporated into the Constitution to prevent a concentration of power in one part of the government. Watergate and the revelations of the misuse of power by the executive branch during several past presidencies reminded people of the message spelt out by the Founding Fathers – a system that placed too much responsibility in the hands of one man must offer temptations for wrongdoing.

Since then, observers have often spoke of the weakness rather than the strength of the presidency. Franck wrote in the 1980s of the 'tethered presidency', one too constrained to be effective and capable of providing the leadership America required.[11] The experience of Bill Clinton illustrated the limitations of the office. In his first term, he had two years in which his own Democratic party had a majority on Capitol Hill, yet he still found that it was difficult to manage Congress and achieve his legislative goals. Thereafter, weakened as he was by congressional enquiries into his personal affairs and ultimately by the process of impeachment, his presidency was a disappointment to those who had had such high hopes in 1992.

The President is a national leader seen by many as the leader of the Western world, a key player on the global stage. As such, the office holds enormous power. The extent to which that power is deployed will depend upon individual incumbents. Some Presidents have adopted a deliberately unassertive style. Their style has been custodial, as they confine themselves to carrying out the powers expressly mentioned in the constitution and leaving Congress to take a lead and get things done. Others have been activists who favoured taking a personal lead. Not content with being mere stewards of national affairs, Franklin Roosevelt, John F. Kennedy, Lyndon Johnson and Bill Clinton have seen the role as one enabling them to give a personal lead. Most modern Presidents have by inclination been more activists than stewards, even if – like Clinton – they have found that the post-1970s presidency is less susceptible to a display of real leadership.

Many of Bill Clinton's 'triumphs' were more concerned with fending off attacks upon existing social programmes than taking America in a new direction. But his effective qualities as a campaigner, with a knack for appealing over the heads of congressmen to the nation at large, enabled him to show remarkable resilience and stage impressive comebacks. He used the presidential office as a pulpit from which to preach his values on issues which mattered to him, such as the family, race and even religion. Theodore Roosevelt – long before him – had adopted the 'bully pulpit' approach, in which he used a policy of active leadership to establish national goals.

Broadly speaking, the more admired Presidents have all been activists, those who used their incumbency to impose their moral authority of the nation, and deploy vision, assertiveness and crisis leadership to good effect. The nature of the presidency at a particular moment depends considerably upon the incumbent. Great men tend to make great Presidents, but the active presidential leadership of the 1960s and the habit of congressional compliance is out of fashion. It is commonplace among academics of recent years to think more about the limitations of the office than of its opportunities for leadership, even if those Presidents they admire have been those who imposed their stamp upon the office.

Neustadt and other writers have stressed the limitations on the power of the President.[12] He first argued this thesis in the early 1960s, using an anecdote about President Eisenhower to illustrate his case. Talking of the election of Eisenhower as his successor, Harry Truman observed: 'Poor old Ike. He'll sit here and he'll say, "Do this! Do that!". And nothing will happen. Poor Ike – it won't be like the army. He'll find it very frustrating.' The experience of recent years has made Neustadt's argument seem considerably stronger than it did when it first appeared.

Prime Minister and President compared

For years, it has been a regular part of discussion on the British and American systems of government to compare the two offices and to decide which is the more powerful, the Prime Minister or the President. In Britain, academics have paid consistent attention to the premiership and written of 'government by Prime Minister', 'prime ministerial government' or of 'presidential government'. So what are the similarities and differences of the two offices and which is the more powerful?

An obvious difference is that in Britain the ceremonial and political roles are separated, so that the monarch is the titular head of state while the Prime Minister is the chief executive or political head of the government. In America the roles are combined in one person, a consideration which imposes considerable demands on the incumbent, but means that he or she has many opportunities to appear on social occasions and attract favourable media coverage. The Prime Minister is relieved of certain time-consuming duties, such as receiving ambassadors and dignitaries from abroad, and there may be an advantage in separating the ceremonial and efficient roles, pomp from power. But wearing both hats gives the President a dimension of prestige lacking in the office of Prime Minister, for he or she is only a politician whereas the President is both in and above the political battle, more obviously representing the national interest.

The holders of both offices have a similar responsibility for the overall surveillance and direction of the work of executive departments of government, and there are advantages of the Prime Minister over the President and vice versa. The Prime Minister is part of a plural executive, and he or she and the Cabinet are collectively responsible to the House of Commons. He or she may, of course, have acquired a real ascendancy over colleagues, and the impact of Margaret Thatcher's tenure in office showed the extent of prime ministerial dominance. Yet the British Cabinet is bound to be concerned in most major decisions during the lifetime of a government.

In the USA, the Cabinet is much less significant, and several Presidents – whilst not formally dispensing with the Cabinet – have been casual about holding meetings and and have treated its suggestions in a cavalier manner. Their Cabinet colleagues tend to be people drawn from the world of business, the ranks of academia or other professions, and return there once their term in office has expired; they have no personal following of their own in Congress or in the country. Cabinet members in Britain have a greater political standing in their own right, and are less easily ignored; they may be contenders for the party leadership.

A key factor in the comparison of Prime Minister and President is that the former is a more powerful party leader. He leads a disciplined party, whereas the President does not. This means that whereas the President can find difficulty in getting his proposals enacted into law, perhaps because of states rights, the views of Congress or the Supreme Court, the Prime Minister, given a reasonable majority, is likely to get most of his or her programme through. In as much as the reputation of a government may depend on what it can achieve, the Prime Minister has far more chance of implementing the proposals he or she wants. Margaret Thatcher could reform the health service along the lines she favoured, whereas a few years later Bill Clinton could not. As Walles observes: 'Whereas a prime minister . . . with the support of party, is ideally placed for authoritative action, a president . . . often lacking the full support of his party in the legislature . . . is poorly placed to translate policies into working programmes.'[13]

In the area of foreign policy, both people are generally in charge of the direction of the government's external relations. On their own or through the appropriate departments, they declare the tone of the nation's foreign policy. There are differences in their position, however, for the President must have any treaty approved by two-thirds of the Senate, and if the policy requires legislative back-up, he or she may have difficulty in getting this through the Congress.

On the other hand, whereas the President may decide administration policy alone or in conjunction with the Secretary of State, a British Prime Minister is much more likely to put his or her policy before the Cabinet where views can be expressed. There may be individual opportunities for the Prime Minister to bypass the full Cabinet and take key decisions in a Cabinet Committee, but in most cases the Prime Minister appoints a Foreign Secretary with whom he or she is in agreement or on whom the Prime Minister feels his or her views can be imposed.

The Prime Minister is of course always liable to be defeated in the House, and therefore may not see out the term. Similarly, as with Margaret Thatcher, the incumbent of Number Ten can be removed when in office. In both cases this is rare. The occupant of the White House has a guaranteed fixed term in office, unless he or she does something very wrong, as over Watergate. The advantage in security of tenure is with the President, although when it comes to choosing the date of the next election (and manipulating the economy to create the 'feel good' factor), the advantage is with the Prime Minister.

Within the two political systems, the Prime Minister has the edge in domestic policy, because of his leadership of a disciplined, centralised party in a political culture which is orientated towards party government. He can get things done and he has considerable freedom of action in terms of how he wishes to do it. By comparison, presidential powers are more constrained. In foreign policy, Prime Ministers such as Margaret Thatcher and Tony Blair have usually been able to get their way, whatever opposition they have faced. Labour leaders in particular may face hostile elements in their party and Cabinet but, as long as they are perceived as an electoral asset, they can override them. In contrast, despite the War Powers Act, Presidents have been able to carry out short-term military forays, commanding American forces without much significant opposition. Presidents dominate the conduct of foreign policy.

Of course, there is a difference between comparing the two offices within their respective systems of government and comparing their power in terms of world leadership. In terms of global importance, the President possesses unsurpassed power. He is the leader of the more significant country in inter-national terms, with enough nuclear capacity to wipe out civilisation.

Has the British premiership become presidential in character?

It is important to distinguish between what is meant by prime ministerial government and what is implied by the term presidential government. There is a strong case for saying that the office of Prime Minister has grown in impor-tance under the influence of a number of strong Prime Ministers. This is not the same as saying that those incumbents have necessarily been presidential in character.

There are clear similarities between the two roles. Prime Ministers have developed powers and a larger apparatus which bear some resemblance to those of the American President. The way in which Prime Ministers use the media is a good example. Blairite spin doctors have seen the opportunities for media manipulation, Alistair Campbell and others being keen to lean on television producers and journalists to get favourable coverage. They have recognised that one way of getting their message across is to speak to the nation directly. Presidents have very direct access to the media and can speak to and for the nation as they require.

Recent Prime Ministers have seen the opportunities presented by television in particular, understanding that the medium is infatuated with personalities. They are often keen to appear 'above the fray' of battle, in the way that Margaret Thatcher and Tony Blair have often seemed to talk of what the government must do, as though they were in some way detached from it. This enables them to retain an aura of dignity and authority, and stay 'unsullied' by the daily reports of stories damaging to the administration. 'Teflon Tony' was a label which stuck to Mr Blair for some years, whatever mire or difficulties his ministers became involved in. In this respect, he was following the example of President Reagan who made himself into a kind of 'outsider', detached from the governmental process in Washington and able to dissociate himself from anything which might endanger his popularity.

Reagan's was a very personal leadership which Michael Foley has described in his study of *The Rise of the British Presidency*.[14] He calls it **'spatial leadership'** and illustrates it by paying particular attention to the comparison with Reagan and Thatcher. He notes the way in which both were able to express their country's suspicion of government and politicians. She relished her role as the individual fighting against ineffective colleagues. Tony Blair has also experimented with the televised press conference as a way of talking directly to the press and to the nation, rather than having his message interpreted by journalists when they write their possibly biased accounts. Presidents have made varying use of such conferences, the more telegenic among them – particularly Kennedy and Clinton – being able to enhance their reputation by an impressive and polished performance.

One way Prime Ministers such as Thatcher and Blair may seem presidential is by trying to present themselves as national leaders of all the people. Their use of new or developed means of support is another. Just as Margaret Thatcher used the Cabinet Office and her relationship with the Cabinet Secretary to strengthen her control, so too the Blairite development of the Prime Minister's Office is a further indication of a wish to increase his influence and control over policy-making and to ensure that the government is run from a powerful nerve-centre, in what Hennessy calls 'a command premiership'.[15]

> **spatial leadership**
> A reference to the way in which recent US Presidents have tried to increase their position in Washington by creating distance between themselves and the presidency.

Foley is very aware of the differences between the two offices, in particular the fact that the President is also head of state, has direct authority from the people and cannot be removed by the legislature except for misconduct. But he detects similarities and concludes that the office of Prime Minister has become presidential but in a uniquely British way. The constitutional position of the two offices does not make for any real convergence, so that Britain has a distinctive presidential model in which the position of the Cabinet cannot be ignored – even if on occasions Prime Ministers by-pass it in making decisions on individual policy matters.

Support for the Prime Minister and President

The main support for the British Prime Minister is provided by the Cabinet (see the box on pp. 88–9). The relationship between the leader and the colleagues he or she appoints is a fluctuating and evolving one, but the Prime Minister would always consult Cabinet colleagues even if at times it is after a key decision has been made. In an umbrella sense, if we use the term Cabinet to include the Cabinet meeting, discussions in the inner Cabinet, Cabinet committees and in bilateral meetings with individual ministers, the Cabinet remains a body of enormous importance.

All Prime Ministers like to gather around them a collection of close friends and advisers, people whom they can trust even if the choices lack any formal position of power. Not surprisingly, this kind of loose and informal 'kitchen Cabinet' can cause much resentment among others in the party, both ministers and those outside the government.

The Cabinet Office and the Prime Minister's Office

Philip Gould, a key figure behind the scenes in the Blair administration, believes that the Prime Minister needs 'his own department that is powerful, talented and fast enough to cope with the speed of changing circumstances . . . without it, good government will become increasingly elusive'.[16] On the other hand, many would say that the Prime Minister in effect has his or her own department, in the Prime Minister's Office which has become a de facto, but not formalised Prime Minister's Department. Large numbers of advisers can be brought in at any moment to help keep the Prime Minister informed on policy developments and the potential difficulties ahead. In particular, there is an emphasis on presentation. The increased role of the Press Office indicates the importance attached to this area.

Prime Minister's Office (PMO)

The PMO has grown in importance in recent years and is now staffed by some 35–40 people who work in four different sections:
1 **The Private Office**. This is run by the PM's principal private secretary, a civil servant. It manages the PM's engagements and relations between Parliament and Whitehall, as well as keeping him or her up-to-date with important developments.
2 **The Political Office**. This links the PM with Parliament and the Party, and advises him or her on matters of political tactics, as well as preparing speeches and important documents necessary for the PM to carry out engagements.
3 **The Policy Unit**. Twelve advisers, mainly drawn from outside of government, who work on short-term appointments. They are there to give policy advice, and under Tony Blair the Unit has a key role. In Peter Hennessy's words, this helps to give the 'justified impression of No. 10 becoming more like the White House'. They are joined by two career officials.
4 **The Press Office**. These five or six people handle relations with television and the press. Press Secretaries such as Sir Bernard Ingham under Margaret Thatcher and Alistair Campbell under Tony Blair can be very influential.

The British Prime Minister also has the support of the Cabinet Office. The support given by the Office has helped to strengthen the Prime Minister's hand by providing the kind of oversight and leadership that departmental ministers, immersed in the minutiae of detail, cannot match. In particular, the axis between premier and Cabinet Secretary has been an important one in recent administrations.

The role of the Cabinet in Britain and America

The Cabinet is not mentioned in the American Constitution, although all Presidents have had one. However, the Cabinet has much lower status than in Britain. If anything, its influence is in decline, and has been since the 1930s. It is up to each individual President to employ it as he prefers and some Presidents such as Reagan in the early years of his administration have been keen to use it as a useful sounding-board and source of ideas. He tended to go round the table and invite individual views. He also experimented with Cabinet councils of five or six members which acted as committees to deal with topics such as economic affairs and human resources, a system comparable to the British system of Cabinet committees. Bill Clinton formed committees of Cabinet and sub-Cabinet members, as in the case of the National Economic Council. The purpose was to better integrate departmental heads and White House officials around particular policy areas.

In Britain and America there is much interest in who is appointed to the Cabinet, for the nature of the appointments gives some idea of the likely tone and style of the administration. Prime Ministers rely on their Cabinets to a greater or lesser extent. John Major used his Cabinet more extensively than his predecessor, and made less use of cabinet committees and bilateral discussions with ministers. Tony Blair uses Cabinet to impose his will, not always staying once his views are known. His meetings are brief and the style less collegiate. He expects cooperation and loyalty from ministers, and emphasises team spirit.

In both countries, Cabinet membership is usually around 20, the British Cabinet usually being slightly larger with 23–25 members, the American one slightly smaller. Whereas the present Bush Cabinet has 19 members, the latest Blair one has 23. In both cases the heads of important government departments will be included. In Britain, there are also a number of non-departmental ministers some of whom play more of a coordinating role and assume special responsibilities placed upon them. In America, other than the President, Vice-President and 14 departmental heads, the other members usually included are the ambassador to the UN and the Director of the Office of Management and the Budget.

Prime Ministers and Presidents include whom they wish, for Cabinets are their personal creation. In Britain, the Prime Minister is constitutionally free to make any appointments he wishes to, but they are politically limited. They choose members of their own party, certain of whom effectively choose themselves, for they are men or women of party standing, key figures in their own right. It was inconceivable that Tony Blair would have omitted John Prescott or Gordon Brown in 1997, just as a Major Cabinet without the rivals he defeated for the leadership (Michael Heseltine and Douglas Hurd) would have been unlikely.

In Britain, most members of the Cabinet are elected politicians, answerable to the House of Commons, although a proportion of members sit in the House of Lords. US Cabinet appointees have not been elected, are not figures of prominence within the party and are not members of Congress. Presidents will bear in mind certain considerations:

- They will normally be careful to ensure that nominees for Cabinet positions are acceptable to the Senate.
- They may choose nominees because of their personal loyalty to the President, or to repay political debts. In particular, Presidents may wish to reward prominent politicians who helped in the national campaign. However, they do on occasion choose someone from the other party: George W. Bush has included a Democrat, Norman Mineta (one of the Asians, see below).
- They will usually be keen to achieve some geographical balance, with representation of regions different from their own. (For example, as a northern liberal himself, Kennedy included a southern segregationist.) A broad social balance is desirable, and recent Presidents have been careful to acknowledge the existence of women and different ethnic groups such as the black, Hispanic and Jewish communities. George W Bush selected a surprisingly diverse Cabinet which includes two African- and two Asian-Americans, a Cuban-American, and an Arab-American. He also included four women.
- [If they are Republican] they tend to include appointees from a business background, so that Nixon, Reagan and Bush Jnr have all included people from the worlds of commerce and manufacturing.

The Cabinet in 2003 is a veritable tycoon's club, by far the wealthiest in US history; 12 out of 19 qualify as millionaires in Sterling and others such as Cheney, Powell and Rumsfeld are very affluent. Democrat Presidents rely more on academia than business.

Once they have been appointed to the Cabinet, British politicians often stay in some Cabinet office for the duration of the administration, even if they are reshuffled. Several of them serve in a series of Cabinets, if the party is long in power or returns to it within a period of a few years from the last spell in office. A few go on to become Prime Minister or deputy Prime Minister. In America, once Cabinet members have been taken from relative obscurity and served their President for the lifetime of his or her administration, they return from whence they came, often having made little impact on the public at large. They are not leading political figures in their own right. Only two people have moved directly from the Cabinet to the presidency: Taft (Theodore Roosevelt's Secretary of War) and Hoover (Harding's and Coolidge's Secretary of Commerce).

In Britain, the Cabinet is the main decision-making body. It takes decisions, coordinates policy and acts as a court of appeal when agreement cannot be reached in Cabinet committee. Even if the Prime Minister is very powerful, the role of the Cabinet is still a major one, although commentators debate the balance of power between the premier and his or her colleagues. Ultimately, Prime Ministers need Cabinet backing. The American Cabinet is an advisory body only and in the final analysis the President may choose to ignore it. Legend has it that Lincoln asked his Cabinet to vote on an issue and when the result was unanimity in opposition to his own view he announced his decision: 'seven nays and one aye, the ayes have it'. Major decisions remain in his hands, which may enhance his power in relation to the Prime Minister but also leaves him very exposed. The role can be a lonely one, for he cannot count on the support of party notables. If he wants it, the President looks elsewhere for policy advice, coordination and support. He may choose to consult his Cabinet, but does not feel bound to do so. Often he will view members as spokespersons for their departments who have little or nothing to contribute on other matters.

In Britain, the doctrine of Collective Responsibility applies to Cabinet members. They are expected to show unanimity in public and to defend agreed government policy. In the USA, there is no such doctrine, and disagreement in public is more apparent. Over policy towards Iraq and Saddam Hussein in particular, the present Bush administration is noted for its very public divisions, the Vice-President and Secretary of Defense taking a more unilateralist and often hawkish view, the Secretary of State a multilateralist one. The Secretary of State and the Defense secretary have also taken a different line on European Union defence policy. Presidents see no particular reason why Cabinet members should be interested in or agreed upon all aspects of policy. As Kennedy remarked when speaking about Cabinet discussion: 'Why should the postmaster sit there and listen to a discussion of the problems of Laos?' No Cabinet member feels the need to rush in and defend a colleague, whereas in Britain – however much the leaks may expose deep rifts and tensions – there is a general need to accept that in public members should tell the same story. Party and the realities of power tend to at least mute their disagreements.

The American and British Cabinets are very different bodies. The American Cabinet contributes much less to the system of government. There are, in Walles' phrase, 'no party pressures to induce a sense of collectivity . . . [and] no electoral demands [to] impose an outward unity'.[18] Presidents often become disillusioned with their creation, so that Carter who initially favoured a strong Cabinet and allowed it to meet frequently in the first two years was by 1979 inviting all of his Cabinet secretaries to resign. There was no question of him and his team sinking or swimming together.

The British Executive is to a much greater extent based on the idea of Cabinet government. In a parliamentary system, there is not the same focus on the person who leads the team, although the exact relationship between him or her and Cabinet colleagues is a variable factor. Increasingly, in many such systems, more use is made of Cabinet committees and the operation of the Cabinet as a whole may be bypassed. It is more of a ratifying body, than the place where key decisions are taken. In a presidential system, the emphasis is on the single chief executive, departmental heads follow their own agenda and Cabinet meetings are – as Hague describes them – often 'little more than a presidential photo-opportunity'.[19]

Support for the President

Presidents do not have the degree of backing and support from the Cabinet that Prime Ministers are accustomed to receiving. However, they have other and extensive sources of help, many of which are located in the Executive Office of the President. Its component elements have changed since its creation in 1939, but central to its work are the White House staff, those personal appointees of the President upon whom he relies for general strategy and policy advice. Such is the power of members of this inner coterie (Haldeman and Ehrlichman under Nixon; Meese, Baker and Deaver under Reagan) that they can sometimes deny access to the President even to members of the Cabinet.

From the earliest days, it was obvious that the new Office would be highly significant, but even so the extent of its impact on American government today

The Prime Minister and the President: a summary		
Issue	*Prime Minister*	*President*
A parliamentary versus a presidential system of government	Prime Minister part of legislature and answerable to it. Must defend himself or herself in House of Commons – e.g. QuestionTime.	President detached from legislature and not required to justify his or her performance before Congress – unless impeached. Does deliver State of the Union speech there.
Chief of the executive branch or head of state?	Chief of the Executive only – smaller ceremonial role.	Chief of the Executive and Head of State – dual role makes job more burdensome but also enables the President to appear as embodiment of the people.
A single executive: position of the Cabinet	Prime Minister has to work with the Cabinet, which meets regularly, and share collective responsibility with it, even if he or she may on occasion choose to side-line it when key decisions are made.	President has a Cabinet but it has considerably less status in American politics. He or she might not consult it when making key decisions. It does not include several powerful politicians, personalities in their own right.
Security of tenure – length of time which can be served in office	May serve for as long as the public and party want him or her, but in practice this is rarely more than for 7–8 years, in most cases; service might not be continuous.	Limited by Constitution to two whole terms, though may also finish out the existing presidential term if Vice-President.

could not have been judged. At the time, it comprised barely 1000 staff, whereas today the total exceeds 5000. But the extent of its operations and of its importance is not to be judged by numbers alone, but more by the centrality of its position in the workings of the executive branch. It has become what Maidment and McGrew call 'the principal instrument of presidential government'.[17]

Today, the President relies on the Executive Office to come up with the background information, detailed analysis and informed policy recommendations that he needs to enable him to master the complexities of his task. It has taken its place at the heart of the administration, giving him the advice he depends upon, conducting many of his dealings with Congress, and helping him to publicise, and supervise the implementation of, his decisions. He is freed to deal with top-level matters of the moment and to engage in future planning.

Issue	Prime Minister	President
Party leadership	Strong party leader: can count on support of back benchers in most circumstances. Also, powerful party machine behind him, to rallyparty beyond Westminster.	Cannot count on party loyalty or support – e.g. in voting lobbies of Congress. National party leadership much weaker. Impact of federalism/separation of powers.
Ability to achieve desired policies and implement programme	High success rate for governmental policies, in terms of amount of programme implemented. Even controversial programmes usually pass into law.	Presidential policies might not be carried out: several Presidents have difficulty with Congress (e.g. Clinton and health reform).
Role in foreign policy and management of crises: national strength	Several Prime Ministers have been very powerful in time of war: opportunity for strong leadership. But l globa influence of Britain has declined postwar; lack offormer industrial or military might.	Presidents tend to thrive on crisis management – e.g. Kennedy and Cuba, 1962, George W Bush and crusade against terrorism following 11 September. Country most powerful in world. USA leader of free world and able to act strongly to try and enforce its world view.

The Executive Office is an umbrella under which exist a number of key agencies which cover the whole range of policy areas and which serve him directly. The Office of Management and the Budget already existed in 1939, but otherwise only the White House Office has been there since the original machinery was set up. Elements have changed in different administrations, but central to the work of the Office are the White House staff to whom we have referred.

The vice-presidency

The Vice-President assumes some of the ceremonial tasks of the President, and represents him or her on formal occasions, whether it be the funeral of a foreign leader or the commemoration of some past event. The role can amount to more than this. For some Presidents, their deputies can be useful in an advisory capacity on matters of politics and policy. Jimmy Carter made more use of Walter Mondale than had been usual in the past, because he needed the support of a Washington 'insider' who could give good advice based upon his knowledge and experience. Reagan allowed Bush to attend many meetings and to represent him in many engagements. However, activity and influence are very different, and whereas Mondale was allowed more say in the decision-making process this was much less true of his successor.

Al Gore was probably the most influential Vice-President in American history. Not only did he preside over important projects such as the 'Reinventing Government' initiative. He also took an active interest in issues ranging from the environment to science and technology, and gave Bill Clinton his advice upon them. Often, he would remain in the Oval Office when all other advisers had departed, so that his voice was the last the President heard. He is said to have been allowed considerable influence over the composition of the revamped Cabinet at the beginning of the second term, the idea being that this would give him influential supporters in key positions to help him prepare his bid for the November 2000 contest. The Gore experience indicates that vice-Presidents take on ad hoc assignments, their number and character depending on the use the President wishes to make of them. Bill Clinton gave his deputy the task of conducting a national review of the workings of the federal bureaucracy. Other Presidents have been much less willing to use their running-mate.

There has been discussion in recent years of 'a new vice-presidency'. Yet in spite of the growing trend towards providing Vice-Presidents with a more worthwhile role, for much of the time they are effectively 'waiting in the wings' in case their services are called upon to assume the burden of the presidency. They stand in readiness to assume command, in the event of death (either through natural causes or assassination), or through resignation or removal from office.

THE OFFICIAL EXECUTIVE (the bureaucracy)

The bureaucracy has been described as 'the state's engine room',[20] advising on and carrying out the policies determined by the Political Executive. The structure of bureaucracies has come under increased scrutiny in recent years, in line with the changing view about the role of government which became fashionable at the end of the twentieth century as the ideas of the New Right came into ascendancy. The task is to 'steer' rather than 'row', to concentrate on broad policy and leave the implementation and delivery of services to others. Here, we examine the role of bureaucracies, the way in which they operate and the attempts by their political masters to make them work efficiently and achieve control over them.

POINTS TO CONSIDER

➤ Who are the bureaucrats and what is their role?

➤ How does the recruitment of bureaucrats differ in Britain and America? What problems do the systems of recruitment create?

➤ What have been the main developments in the structure and development of the British and American bureaucracies in recent decades?

➤ Why have British and American governments been increasingly concerned about the operation of bureaucracies in recent years?

➤ How can political control over the bureaucracy be secured?

The bureaucracy

As society became more complex in the twentieth century, government expanded and a huge **bureaucracy** developed. New bodies were created, some with uncertain jurisdiction. Once in place, these organisations competed for mastery over a particular area of concern, and departments and agencies fended off other organisations which tried to poach their territory.

By the term bureaucrats, we refer to the thousands or even millions of people who operate in the Executive Branch, whose career is based in government service and normally work there as a result of appointment rather than election. Often known as civil servants, they serve in organisational units such as government departments, agencies and bureaux. Wherever they work, they operate under common regulations, with matters such as recruitment, pay, promotion, grading and other conditions of service being determined by a central body. In Britain, it is the Civil Service Commission; in the United States, it is the Office of Personnel Management.

The task of bureaucrats is to carry out the ongoing business of interpreting and implementing the policies enacted by the government. There are several aspects to their work:

- they give advice to their political masters concerning the direction and content of policy;
- they implement policy, turning legislative policy goals into actual programmes;
- they administer policy, an often routine role although it involves exercising a degree of discretion; and
- they are regulators who develop rules and regulations.

> **bureaucracy**
> Technically, a hierarchical organisation in which offices have specified tasks and employees are assigned responsibilities, based on their merit, knowledge and experience. Term often used as a synonym for administration or rule by the officials who conduct the detailed business of government, advising on and implementing policy decisions. Bureaucrats behave according to specific rules so that treatment of each case they handle is relatively predictable and fair.

Bureaucrats do more than follow orders. Because they possess crucial information and expertise, senior figures act as partners in making decisions about public policy. Because of the power of their position, the problem of management and control of bureaucracies has become a central issue of modern democratic government. Unelected, their work needs to be regulated by politicians, the elected decision-makers, who are concerned to rein in their power.

The bureaucracy in Britain and the United States

Appointment and ethos

The development of the bureaucracy has varied from country to country. In Britain and the United States, there was a major reform of the system of appointment in the nineteenth century and a constant feature of recent decades has been a new emphasis on managerial efficiency.

Britain

In Britain, following the Northcote–Trevelyan enquiry (1854), reform was introduced to ensure that those key figures in the civil service whose work required intellectual ability should be appointed on the basis of merit rather than nepotism (favouritism shown to relatives of those in power). Competitive examinations were introduced, open to all suitably qualified persons, from 1870 onwards. Since that time, appointment on merit has been the order of the day, although since the 1980s there have been allegations that promotion in the higher civil service has been influenced by political leanings. In the 1980s, there were suggestions of a 'politicisation' of officialdom, with the Thatcher government keen to advance the careers of those who were 'one of us'. Leading officials became closely identified with the policies pursued by ministers, thus threatening the principle of political neutrality. These suggestions have again surfaced under the Blair administration.

After 1870, the civil service developed along distinctive lines. It was generalist in character, with certain qualities of mind (intelligence, education, experience and personal skills such as the art of judgement) being seen as more important than expertise in a specialist subject area. Recruitment was to the service as a whole, rather than to a specific post. Officials could be moved from one department to another, thus developing the idea of a unified service. In addition, the bureaucracy was noted for three qualities which have been much written about ever since:

- **Permanence.** The job was viewed as a career, rather than as a temporary position based on political patronage. Civil servants do not change at election time, as they do in the USA. This permanence is associated with experience and continuity, so that an inexperienced incoming government will be able to count on official expertise. Permanence, coupled with confidentiality, means that civil servants can speak frankly to ministers, without fear of dismissal. It makes a civil service career seem attractive.

- **Neutrality.** As a result of the permanence, it was essential that any official should serve any government impartially, whatever its political complexion. Officials must not let their personal political leanings affect their actions. They must carry out decisions with which they personally may disagree and not involve themselves in any partisan activity. If they were to be partisan, this would make it difficult for them to remain in office and serve as permanent officials.

- **Anonymity.** Civil servants were to stay silent on issues of public policy, their political masters (the ministers) being accountable for their actions and discussing issues in the public domain. If officials became public figures, this would endanger their reputation for neutrality, for they could become identified with a particular policy. They might then be unacceptable to a new administration. Identification might also prevent them from offering frank advice to ministers: if they knew that they could be named they might feel the need to be very discreet.

These traditional characteristics have been called into question from the late 1980s onwards. Partly this was because of the managerial reform undertaken by successive governments (see pp. 99–101), but it was also related to the monopoly of one party in power. Conventions which developed under alternating governments gradually lost their force, particularly when strong Prime Ministers sought to change the culture of Whitehall. Business advisers to the Thatcher government saw anonymity as having its own disadvantages, such as concealing poor advice and reducing the incentive to act efficiently. They also argued that permanence meant officials lacked any appreciation of other modes of working and removed the incentive to change or improve.

The United States

As in Britain, appointment based on favouritism to those of similar political inclinations was the order of the day for most of the nineteenth century. President Andrew Jackson (1829–37) is credited with the development of a '**spoils system**' by which it was seen as legitimate to reward personal and political friends with public office in the federal bureaucracy ('to the victor go the spoils'). Appointments were made on the basis of patronage, 'who you knew, rather than what you knew', and membership of the

> **spoils system**
> A patronage system for filling appointive public offices with friends and supporters of the ruling political party.

successful party was important in gaining government jobs. Pressure for change culminated in the passing of the Pendleton Act (1883), which required candidates for some positions in the public service to pass a competitive examination. Ability, education and job performance became the key criteria for appointment, rather than political background. Today, 95 per cent of federal civilian jobs are covered by 'civil service rules' laid down by the Office of Personnel Management. Appointment is to a specific department or job, so that the civil service is specialist rather than generalist. These posts are permanent, so that – as in Britain – there is continuity and stability in administration.

The American civil service is also expected to be politically neutral, as in Britain. Officials are unable to take part in overt political activity. However, neutrality is undermined by the fact that several thousand posts in the federal civil service remain in the gift of the President. He or she can nominate more than 3000 senior civil servants to serve in the administration and these include the heads of the fourteen major departments (the secretaries), as well as assistant and deputy department secretaries, deputy assistant secretaries and a variety of other appointive positions. Political appointees are not expected to be neutral and they can be blamed for policy failures. Once in office, their tenure of office depends on how the White House judges their performance.

In making political appointments, the President is likely to choose personnel whom he regards as loyal and competent, and who share his political outlook. Abernach notes that whereas in the past many appointees had been people who had established good connections with interest groups or congressional committees, in the Reagan era 'ideology was the key'.[20] Sharing a number of Thatcherite attitudes (see pp. 99–100), he established an appointment system which ensured that appointees would be faithful to him and pursue his objectives of reduced governmental activity.

Yet the importance of political appointments in the United States can be exaggerated. They may seem to provide the President with an opportunity to change the direction and character of government policy, but in reality the number of appointments he and his aides can make amounts to only a small percentage of those who work for the federal bureaucracy. Overall, Bill Clinton chose less than 0.2 per cent of the total civilian, non-postal federal work force. Moreover, the appointments have to be made in the brief period between the day of the presidential election and Inauguration Day. Inevitably, the President must concentrate his or her attention on appointments at Cabinet level and leave many of the rest to other members of the team.

Size and organisation

The size of any bureaucracy is broadly linked to the demands placed upon it. In the twentieth century, the responsibilities of government were significantly widened, as voters began to expect more from those who ruled over them. Accordingly, civil service employment increased dramatically. By the end of the century, there was a new emphasis on streamlining government, as ministers had reduced expectations of what governments might or ought to try to achieve.

Britain

There are now well under 500,000 civil servants, a marked drop on the number in the early 1980s. Many of these are clerical or managerial staff, distributed in government offices up and down the country. The ones who concern us most are those who belong to the top administrative grades, often referred to as the 'mandarins' or, collectively, as 'the higher civil service'. These 750–800 senior officials are based mainly in the large Whitehall departments such as the Treasury, the Home Office and the Foreign Office, although some work in the Next Step agencies which were introduced in the 1990s (see p. 100).

The United States

The American civil service expanded considerably during the days of the New Deal, as 'big government' came into fashion. Today, some 5 million people work in the Executive Branch, 60 per cent of them civilians, the rest being military personnel. America has a decentralised bureaucracy, only 12 per cent of federal officials working in Washington, the rest being based around the country. The federal administration is organised around most of the same vital functions which exist in any other national bureaucracy. The administrative apparatus responsible for fulfilling them is divided into three broad categories.

- **Government or executive departments.** There are fourteen cabinet-level departments, which vary greatly in size. By far the most important department is the State Department, but others include the Treasury, the Defense Department, and the Justice and Interior departments. They are sub-divided into bureaus and smaller units, often on the basis of function. Within the Commerce Department, there is the Bureau of the Census, and others such as the Patent and Trademark Office.

- **Independent agencies.** Many agencies help to keep the government and economy operating smoothly. They include several types of organisation with differing degrees of independence. Some (such as the Veterans Association) are executive agencies which provide special services to the people, whilst others are regulatory commissions which supervise particular sections of the economy (e.g. the Environmental Protection Agency).

- **Government corporations.** These are a cross between business corporations and regular governmental agencies and manage projects of massive public importance, such as the St Lawrence Seaway Development Corporation and the Tennessee Valley Authority.

Influence: civil service power

In recent decades, it has often been suggested that the work of civil servants goes beyond the mere task of giving advice and implementing decisions. They exert significant influence over the policy-making process, helping to create and shape rather than just advise on public policy.

Britain

In theory, civil servants advise and ministers decide. Ministers weigh up the options available to them in the light of the evidence given to them. They take the praise and blame for the decisions made and for the way in which they are implemented, via the doctrine of individual ministerial responsibility. However, the reality is somewhat different.

Ministers are very reliant on the performance of the civil servants who work in their department. They are transient. They come and go, perhaps serving for a full administration or maybe being moved after a couple of years. By contrast, their officials may have been in the department for a long time and have developed considerable expertise. They become familiar with the realistic range of policy choices available and know the advantages or otherwise of various lines of policy. Their views will reflect a 'departmental view', but this may conflict with the government's or minister's priorities. In this situation there is scope for conflict between them.

Much has been written about 'mandarin power', mandarins being the very senior officials who have close and regular contact with ministers. It is suggested that often, because of their ability, experience and expertise, they exert a powerful influence over what happens in a department, especially over the policies that emerge. Radical commentators and MPs (and premiers such as Margaret Thatcher who wanted to 'get things done') are wary of mandarins, seeing them as a conservative force hostile to necessary innovation. At worst, they might frustrate the minister and be obstructive, concealing information.

The United States

In America, there has long been discussion of the difficulties of taming the bureaucracy. Because the President normally appoints people who share his outlook to key positions, it might be expected that he would achieve control over the bureaucratic process. Yet this often does not happen, for once in position, those appointed may 'go native' and become part of the administrative machine, rather than agents of the President's will. As with relations with Congress, Presidents soon find out that it is important to persuade, for they lack the power to command. In the frustrated words of President Truman: 'I thought I was the President, but when it comes to these bureaucracies I can't make 'em do a damn thing'.

The American bureaucracy has a large degree of freedom, each agency having its own clientele, power base and authority. Much of that authority derives from Congress which creates or destroys agencies, authorises and approves reorganisation plans, defines powers, and appropriates agency funds. Yet even Congress is unable to control the operation of bodies once they are established and many of them have a life of their own. There is popular suspicion of bureaucratic power and many commentators suggest that federal bureaucrats misuse or even abuse it.

Organisational and attitudinal reform: controlling the bureaucracy

Britain

Under Margaret Thatcher, change in Whitehall was 'in the air'. As Prime Minister, she was instinctively suspicious of the civil service. She associated a large bureaucracy with the 'big government' of the consensus years (see pp. 192–3) which she so despised. She wanted to roll back the frontiers of the state. This involved curbing a civil service that had become unnecessarily large and was urging or pursuing misguided policies. Moreover, she was suspicious of the power and type of senior civil servants, some of whom might use their permanence and expertise to develop their own view of what was needed, rather than assist in carrying out the wishes of the government of the day. Not only were they excessively powerful, they were also sometimes poor managers, ill-equipped for the task of running a large department. They often lacked training in management skills, many being generalist all-rounders rather than expert administrators.

Among other things, she tried to bring in people at the top who were 'one of us'. Several early retirements enabled her to sweep away several long-serving officials. She also brought in outside advisers such as Sir John Hoskyns and Sir Derek Rayner, businessmen who might help to transform the ethos of the civil service and place a new emphasis upon managerial efficiency. The development of the Next Step agencies was an important part of this process.

Sir Derek Ibbs was appointed during the late Thatcher years to run an Efficiency Unit. Ibbs was dissatisfied with the pace of change in the civil service and in 1988 produced the very influential report, 'Improving Management in Government: The Next Steps'. It wanted the creation of a slimmed-down, better-managed civil service. He argued that the civil service was too vast and complex to be managed well as one organisation. Departments varied and needed their own systems of management. Accordingly, he recommended a division of work. New agencies would be responsible for 'blocks' of executive work (operational matters), and a smaller 'core' civil service would work in the departments to 'sponsor' the agencies and to service ministers with policy advice and help. All government departments have been affected by Ibbs' thinking. Gradually, throughout the 1990s, the functions of departments were handed over to these new bodies. There are now about 150 and most civil servants work in them, rather than in departments. The agencies are headed by appointed chief executives, often very well-paid individuals brought in from the business world.

In 1997, the incoming Blair administration accepted the idea of such agencies. The old days of hierarchical departments staffed by permanent officials had long gone. By the time of Tony Blair's arrival, it looked as though Whitehall was in a state of continuous upheaval. He wishes to deliver effective public services. He was anxious to achieve 'performance targets' and was more interested in reaching them than in worrying about the means by which this might happen. Cutting waiting lists for hospital appointments was a goal, as was cutting class sizes in infant schools. Ministers were less interested in the department or agency which delivered the outcome, than in ensuring that it was attained. He wanted to see the civil service act as an efficient enabling body, in the same way that councils had become enabling authorities in the 1980s. The White Paper *Modernising Government* (1999) discussed the role of central and local government, and the role of the private sector in service delivery.

To improve policy coordination and implementation and get away from the 'short-termism' of traditional governmental thinking, the Prime Minister has established the Performance and Innovation Unit in the Cabinet Office. Specifically, it was to examine cross-governmental policies, sorting out departmental disputes. The Prime Minister is committed to 'joined-up' government, and uses non-departmental ministers to ensure that officials plan for the future and work with those in other departments.

To open up government, the Prime Minister is keen on changing the culture of senior civil servants. He suspects that many are resistant to new thinking and doubts the quality of some of them. Above all, he fears 'departmentalitis', the idea that civil servants have adopted a policy view and keep to it whichever party is in power. To break the stranglehold of traditional attitudes, he is keen to see new people brought in from outside the service. His fondness for political advisers illustrates his enthusiasm for changed thinking. The idea is to enable ministers to get a grip on their officials. Advisers add a political dimension to the opinions gained from civil servants and are there to help ministers who are in danger of being too susceptible to official advice. Most ministers are keen on this more independent source of advice.

The United States

In the United States, efforts have also been made to make the bureaucracy more efficient and more responsive. Presidents may seek to exert control by various means. They establish commissions and enquiries to scrutinise the operation of the bureaucracy, amalgamate or reorganise departments and make use of political appointees in a bid to advance policy initiatives. But they find the task difficult, not least because of the fragmented nature of officialdom, functioning as it does via the network of departments, bureaux, agencies and commissions. Ronald Reagan was deeply suspicious of bureaucrats and introduced a series of changes including privatisation of some operations, contracting out and the handing over of some federal programmes to the states. In addition, cuts were made in personnel in areas such as welfare.

In 1993, Bill Clinton gave his Vice-President the task of reviewing the bureaucracy and making recommendations to improve its efficiency and flexibility. His report *Reinventing Government* (1993) pointed to the wastefulness of many governmental organisations, the traditional preoccupation with familiar working practices and the lack of incentive for experimentation and innovation. Recommendations included cutting red tape, placing more emphasis on customer service, delegating more authority to those operating at lower levels of government and pruning unnecessary expenditure.

The bureaucracy in Britain and the United States: a summary		
	Britain	*United States*
Key personnel	Permanent secretary and higher civil servants who serve for several years and acquire wealth of knowledge and expertise, derived from functioning under different party administrations.	No comparable job to permanent No comparable job to permanent secretary; senior figures are political appointments of incoming administration.
Use of outside personal advisers	Less used in past, though recent governments have employed more in a bid to ensure that the political will of ministers is reinforced as they seek to impose a sense of direction on their departments. Act as minister's eyes and ears.	Secretaries of various departments surrounded by a coterie of appointees, political figures who help departmental heads to impose their will on the career civil servants below them. System most evident in Executive Office, especially White House Office where advisers act as a counter-bureaucracy.
Traditional principles	British civil service noted for its permanence, neutrality and anonymity. Now less neutral and anonymous, with increasing comment about a 'politicisation' of service under Thatcher and Blair administrations. Senior civil servants now liable for interrogation by select committees, making them more accountable.	95 per cent permanent civil service, politically neutral, though appointments made by President undermine the idea. Political appointees not anonymous or neutral, but discussions between departmental heads and their advisers are kept secret to allow officials to 'think the unthinkable'. Never same reluctance to allow officials to appear before congressional committees.
Power and influence of bureaucracy	Increasing comment in recent years about influence of civil service over policy-making. Suggestion that they wield real political power and dominate their political masters. But theory remains that civil servants advise and ministers decide. Minister takes praise or blame for conduct of department and its officials, answering in Parliament for what is done.	Bureaucracy not a single, monolithic institution, and various elements of bureaucracy differ in the degree of independence they exercise – e.g. bureaux in departments have great autonomy. Bureaucracy a powerful institution, large and complex, often seen as burdensome by American public. All senior members are appointed by the President who can remove them, but once in office often act independently.
Recent characteristics	Increased politicisation. Use of political appointees. Use of agencies and other unelected bodies. Appointment of chief executives in agencies in gift of government of the day.	Characteristics of modern British bureaucracy long familiar in United States – e.g., politicisation/ political advisers.

Conclusion

Political executives have a key role in political life for it is members of the government who devise policies in the light of information and advice they receive, and get them on the statute book. The Official Executive has the task of implementing the policies the political executive has devised.

Because of the expansion of governmental activity in the twentieth century, the powers of the Executive have grown, and the Chief Executive is today far more powerful than a hundred years ago. Various other circumstances ranging from television to the new importance of international summitry and overseas visits have provided political leaders with a new pre-eminence, and they are no longer national leaders alone but also world statesmen. Because of these trends, many writers discern a trend towards prime ministerial government in parliamentary systems, and comment on the extent of presidential power in countries such as the USA. Such offices are indeed very powerful today, but the extent of that power and influence can vary according to the incumbent and the circumstances of the time.

Official executives have expanded in size and influence as a result of changes in economic, social and political conditions. The number of civil servants broadly increases in accordance with the tasks imposed on them. The twentieth century was an era of huge growth but in recent years there has been an emphasis on streamlining officialdom and ensuring that it works with greater efficiency and responsiveness.

REFERENCES

1 A. Heywood, *Politics*, Macmillan, 1997.
2 A. Ball, *Modern Government and Politics*, Macmillan, 1993.
3 R. Strother, as quoted in L. Rees, *Selling Politics*, BBC Books, 1992.
4 Lord Hill, *Both Sides of the Hill*, Heinemann, 1964.
5 S. Low, as quoted in Cabinet and Prime Minister, *Heart of the Body Politic?*, Politics Association/SHU Press, 1995.
6 R. Crossman, in an introduction to W. Bagehot, *The English Constitution*, Fontana, 1963.
7 J. Prior, *A Balance of Power*, Hamish Hamilton, 1986.
8 T. Benn, 'The Case for a Constitutional Premiership', in A. King, *The British Prime Minister*, Macmillan, 1985.
9 G. Wasserman, *The Basics of American Politics*, Longman, 1996.
10 A. Schlesinger Jnr, *The Imperial Presidency*, Houghton Mifflin, 1973.
11 T. Franck, *The Tethered Presidency*, New York University Press, 1991.
12 R. Neustadt, *Presidential Power: The Politics of Leadership/Presidential Power and the Modern President*, Wiley & Sons/Free Press, 1960/1990.

13 M. Walles, *British and American Systems of Government*, P. Allan/Barnes & Noble Books, 1988.

14 M. Foley, *The Rise of the British Presidency*, Manchester University Press, 1993.

15 P. Hennessy, *The Prime Minister*, Allen Lane, 2000.

16 P. Gould, as quoted in note 15 above.

17 D. Maidment and D. McGrew, *The American Political Process*, Sage/Open University, 1992.

18 As note 13 above

19 R. Hague and M. Harrop, *Comparative Government and Politics*, Palgrave, 2001.

20 As note 19 above.

21 J. Abernach, 'The President and the Executive Branch' in C. Campbell *et al.* (eds), *The Bush Presidency: First Appraisals*, Chatham House, 1991.

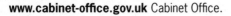

USEFUL WEB SITES

For the UK

www.open.gov.uk The official government web site, covering the whole government structure.

www.number-10.gov.uk 10 Downing Street. As with the above, but more emphasis on the centres of power.

www.cabinet-office.gov.uk Cabinet Office.

www.civil-service.co.uk Statistics and information, as well as details of recent changes.

www.britishcouncil.org British Council. Coverage of recent changes in civil service and governance of UK.

For the USA

www.whitehouse.gov/ Official presidential site for the White House. Useful for following the day-to-day activities of the President, including daily briefings and press releases, as well as materials from the Executive Office of the President, the Council of Economic Advisers and other such bodies.

www.whitehousehistory.org White House Historical Association. General overview of the presidency and the White House; offers a virtual tour of the White House, showing its objets d'art.

SAMPLE QUESTIONS

1 To what extent is it true that executives have gained at the expense of legislatures?

2 Compare the methods by which British Prime Ministers and American Presidents attain their office and the backgrounds of those who reach the top in Britain and the United States.

3 'The idea that the British Prime Minister has become a presidential figure like the American incumbent ignores the substantial differences in the two roles.' Discuss.

4 How accountable are British Prime Ministers and American Presidents to the legislature and to public opinion?

5 To what extent does party act as a restraint upon the British Prime Minister and the American President?

6 Discuss the view that not all heads of government are effective political leaders.

7 Consider the ways in which the Executive in Britain is different from the Executive in the United States.

8 Compare and contrast the role of the Cabinet in British and American government.

9 What is the political significance of the different ways by which senior civil servants are recruited in Britain and the United States?

10 How do politicians seek to control the bureaucracy in Britain and the United States, and with what measure of success?

Legislatures

5

The constitutions of most countries describe the legislature, parliament or congress as the key decision-making body in the realm, or else accord it equal status with the Executive. Yet in practice the reality is different. Few legislatures make important decisions and in many cases neither do they initiate laws. Over recent decades, writers have often drawn attention to the alleged 'decline of legislatures'. In Britain, chapters have been written on the 'passing of parliament', 'parliament in decline' or 'the loss of parliamentary control'. Yet in spite of their relative decline, in many cases they remain very significant in any democracy for they usually comprise the elected representatives who are there because they reflect the sentiments and feelings of the electorate.

In this chapter, we are primarily concerned with the nature and work of Parliament and Congress and of the members who serve in them. We also comment on the characteristics of second chambers and their role, before finally assessing the theory of legislative decline and its application to Britain and America.

POINTS TO CONSIDER

➤ Are bicameral legislatures a good thing?

➤ Are legislatures policy-making bodies? If so, in what sense?

➤ Consider the changing role of legislatures.

➤ 'Today, the functions of legislatures are more to legitimate than to legislate'. Why is this so?

➤ 'A key function of legislatures is to scrutinise and control the work of the executive branch'. How do Parliament and Congress attempt to do this and with what success?

➤ Compare the contribution of committees in Parliament and Congress.

➤ Compare the pay and conditions of MPs and members of Congress.

➤ To what extent does the membership of Parliament and Congress respectively reflect the social composition of Britain and the United States?

➤ Does it matter that most legislatures are socially unrepresentative of the populations they serve?

➤ Does the experience of Britain and the United States support the idea of 'postwar legislative decline'?

The exact number of **legislatures** across the world varies from year to year, but broadly it has been on the increase, as a number of countries have returned to democratic rule and new states have been established in parts of formerly communist-controlled Eastern Europe.

The names accorded to legislatures vary. The term Congress is used in some countries, as in America. Parliament is employed in Britain and the Commonwealth. On the continent, it is more common to speak of the National Assembly (as in France) or the Chamber of Deputies (as in Italy). Scotland has its own parliament, but Wales – with its weaker measure of devolution – has a National Assembly.

> **legislature**
> The branch of government which is empowered to make law. The term also refers to the often-elected bodies which consider public issues and give assent to measures of public policy. Sometimes they are known as assemblies or parliaments. In either case, they are forums of debate and deliberation.

Structure and purpose

Some legislatures are **bicameral** (two chamber) and some are **unicameral** (single chamber). Where two chambers exist (see box on pp. 108–9), it is often argued that the possible 'excesses' of the popularly elected assembly need to be balanced by the experience and wisdom of a more reflective upper house, as has been the case in Britain. However, if the second chamber is not elected, there is the danger that it will be considered undemocratic, a denial of the popular will – the more so if its membership has been chosen on the basis of heredity, as the House of Lords was for many centuries until 1999.

Many second chambers have lost much of their power, so that in Britain and France they retain only the right to revise or delay legislation. In federal countries, the second chamber is often more powerful (for instance in Canada and Germany). In such examples, the size of the country, the need for regional representation and the sometimes-sharp geographical cleavages make a second chamber seem desirable.

There are more unicameral legislatures than bicameral political systems. Unicameralism has been on the increase in recent years and Hague and Harrop note that in 2000 112 out of 178 legislatures had only one chamber.[2] Countries such as Denmark, New Zealand and Sweden abolished their upper house without any obvious serious effects, and as a general trend across the world the number of two-chamber assemblies is slightly in decline. They are more common in federal countries and those which are geographically extensive. It is significant that the countries which have opted for abolition are small, Sweden having about 8.9m, Denmark 4.5m and New Zealand 2.5m. In such countries, the pressure of legislation is much less than in a country the size of Britain.

SECOND CHAMBERS: THEIR VARYING MEMBERSHIP AND SIZE

Britain and America both have bicameral systems, having a lower chamber (in both cases called the House: 'of Representatives' in the USA and 'of Commons' in the UK) and an upper one, the Senate and House of Lords respectively. In Britain, as in many other large democracies, a second chamber is widely considered necessary as a check upon the lower house, the government-dominated House of Commons, but it is also useful because it shares the parliamentary workload (and so reduces pressure on the House of Commons), has a significant role in legislation (especially the task of scrutiny and revision, but also of delay) and provides opportunities for careful deliberation of matters of public policy by people many of whom are expert in their chosen fields. In America, apart from its law-making and other roles, the second chamber provides territorial representation, with each state – however large or small – being represented by two members.

At present, in both cases, members of the upper house serve a longer period in office than do members of the lower house. Composition is determined differently in the Lords from in the Senate, and there are more members. Membership of the Lords was based substantially on heredity, until the phasing out of selection through inheritance in 1999 (Phase One). The present membership (June 2003) comprises:

544	Life peers, appointed under the terms of the 1958 Life Peerages Act
92	Hereditary peers: under a compromise deal in 1999, elected from amongst their number on a party basis (they were allowed to remain until Phase Two gets underway)
24	Archbishops/bishops
27	Law lords
687	**Total**

Phase One is a transitional period for the House of Lords. Ministers intend that it should be followed by Phase Two, which is meant to resolve the long-standing issues surrounding its future. As yet, no agreement has been reached in the House of Commons about the form of a revised chamber. In a series of free votes, MPs rejected all the options available (Feb. 2003). If reform occurs, then the tenure of office of members will have to be decided. At present, members of the House of Lords serve for life, although serving bishops cease to be members when they lose their position. Members of the Senate serve for six years. This longer period of service provides for greater stability and continuity, as befits reflective bodies. A further degree of stability in the Senate is achieved by the use of phased election, with one-third of members retiring every two years. It was Madison's original intention that senators, serving a longer innings and taking a broader view than members of the lower house, would exhibit 'superior coolness . . . and wisdom'. The same qualities are often attributed to life peers in Britain.

Size and membership of lower houses

Legislatures range in size from the larger at one extreme (Britain has 659 members, India 545, and America 435) to the very small at the other (Iceland 73, Luxembourg 60, and Costa Rica 57. Unsurprisingly, size is related to

In Britain, the House of Commons is the more dominant chamber. The Lords has a role in the legislative process, mainly as a revising body, although new – usually non-controversial – legislation can be initiated there. It is unable to reject bills passed by the House of Commons, although it has a power of delay under the 1949 Parliament Act. This is not the case in America, where the two houses have a very different relationship and are in theory co-equal. The Senate has some distinctive responsibilities (such as in the field of foreign affairs) and also has higher status. It plays a large role in the legislative and budgetary processes. It also has an important role in checking the Executive, via its powers of checking presidential appointments, and ultimately being the body which conducts any trial for impeachment.

Various factors make the Senate a more significant second chamber than the Lords. The Constitution, with its separation of powers, requires the legislature to act as a curb upon the Executive. Also, in a presidential system, the President is not answerable to one chamber only, so that there is not the same focus of attention on one house more than the other. Strong second chambers are more often found in federal countries and those which provide for effective regional representation. In the case of America, such considerations make it the strongest upper house in the democratic world.

Membership of second chambers

Other than by inheritance or Britain's Phase One arrangements, there are four main ways of choosing members of an upper house, although of course a combination of any of these approaches is possible:
- **Direct election**, which is the most common and is used in 27 out of 66 chambers.[1]
- **Indirect election** (21 chambers). Sometimes, indirectly elected houses are selected by members of local authorities, sometimes by members of the lower house. The now non-existent Swedish body was composed entirely of members elected by local councillors, whereas the French Senate is elected by a series of electoral colleges, comprising members of local authorities and deputies in each department.
- **Appointment for life** (16 chambers), as in Canada where members are nominated for life by the Governor-General in theory, but by the government of the day (Prime Minister) in practice. Nominations tend to be made on the basis of a candidate's support for the party in power.
- **Vocational representation** (1 chamber). The Irish Republic is unique among democratic countries in employing a form of vocational representation. The Senate has members elected by graduates of Irish universities, others nominated by the Prime Minister and 43 more elected from five vocational panels (Cultural and Educational, Agricultural, Labour, Industrial and Commercial, and Administrative).

population, though the proportions vary considerably in various states. Broadly, India has on average one representative for just under every two million people; the USA one per 420,000 for the House of Representatives; Germany one for 120,000; France one for 100,000; Britain one for 90,000; Switzerland one for 35,000; Sweden one for 25,000; Norway one for 27,000;

and Ireland one for 20,000. From such figures, it can be seen that smaller countries are at an advantage. The legislatures are intimate, giving members more chance to participate in the proceedings. Moreover, since these members represent fewer constituents, the bonds between people and representatives are close. For these reasons, legislatures in smaller countries are more likely to function effectively than those in much larger ones.

The work and importance of the British Parliament and the American Congress

A distinction is sometimes made between legislatures (assemblies which do not force the executive to resign, and therefore are less likely to be dissolved)[3] and parliaments (which can censure the government and therefore do risk the possibility of being dissolved). The distinction has some validity, so that in presidential systems such as the United States and many Latin American countries the legislature is powerful and secure but cannot vote the President out of office (except for an impeachable offence), whereas in parliamentary systems such as those of Britain, most of Western Europe, the Commonwealth, Japan and Israel, assemblies do have the power to censure the government. Here, we use the words interchangeably.

By their very existence, legislatures perform an important representative function. They reflect the people's wishes, for they comprise the elected representatives of the voters. For this reason, they are said to be sovereign bodies, embodying the principle of popular sovereignty or 'people power'. However, constitutions usually accord legislatures a substantial array of other powers.

Legislatures have six main purposes, the last two of which we will consider in more detail.

1   Representation

This is a term with several meanings. Here, we are using the term to mean the authority to act on behalf of another, as gained through the process of election. In this sense, the elected representative acts to safeguard and promote the interests of the area represented. In Britain as in most Western democracies, representation operates via political parties. The successful candidate gets elected because of his or her party label, but he or she must seek to balance the sometimes conflicting pressures of representing the country, party and constituency, as well as being true to his or her own conscience and feelings. In America, the House of Representatives was originally seen as the body which represented the mass of the people although since the introduction of the direct election of the Senate it has lost that distinctive position. The importance attached to the representative function is very great in America, in comparison with other legislatures. Congressmen attach the highest priority to the attitudes and concerns of those who elect them and other considerations, such as party, matter less.

2 Deliberation

Members apply their knowledge, understanding and judgement to consider the nation's affairs, especially in the process of debate. When contemplating the issues of the day, they are expected to balance their responsibilities to party and constituency with those to the nation. Writing to his constituents in Bristol in 1774, **Burke** outlined in classic style the case for a representative of the people exercising this balancing function:

> Parliament is not a congress of ambassadors from different and hostile interests . . . which . . . each must maintain, as an agent and advocate . . . Parliament is a deliberative assembly of one nation, with one interest, that of the whole . . . You choose a member indeed; but when you have chosen him, he is not a member for Bristol, but he is a member of Parliament.

In a talking assembly such as Parliament, discussion occurs on the floor of the chamber in formal debate. In Congress, it centres on the committee rooms and is more detailed and less stylised.

Edmund Burke (1729–1797) British statesman and orator. Burke was a Whig MP until his death in 1797, but was an acknowledged and persuasive advocate of the conservative cause. He had clear views on the duties of an MP, arguing that should his deliberations ever force him to the conclusion that there is a divergence of interest between the nation and his constituency, he must always remember that he is a member of the UK Parliament first and foremost. Parliament was 'a deliberative assembly . . . where not local purposes or prejudices ought to guide, but the general good resulting from the general reason of the whole'.

3 Financial control

Raising taxation is a traditional function of parliaments, associated with the redress of grievances. In bygone days, the representatives of the people demanded concessions of their king prior to conceding the demand for extra taxes.

Lack of power to control spending effectively has been a weakness of many parliaments, for the amounts are vast, the issues complex and elected members lack the time and expertise to monitor the situation in any detailed manner. Such controls as there are operate after the event, by which it is too late to have an effect.

In most countries, financial control is an area in which the legislature is at its weakest. Governments set out their budget before the assembly and with few modifications they are passed. This is untrue in America, for the Constitution specifically placed the duty of raising of money on the House of Representatives and money spent by government departments has to be allocated under headings approved by Congress. Flammang *et al.* observe that 'without the agreement of members of Congress, no money can be doled out for foreign aid, salaries for army generals or paper clips for bureaucrats'.[3] Similarly, the President's federal budget is subject to congressional agreement which may not be forthcoming. Since the early 1970s, the expertise of members of Congress in handling budgetary issues has been increased, following the establishment of the Budget Office.

4 Political recruitment

Assemblies often act as a recruiting ground for ministerial office. In parliamentary systems where the government is chosen from parliament, the performance of elected representatives can be assessed. Service in the House, showing up well in debates and voting loyally with the party, are admired virtues for those who wish to tread the career path to high office. This applies less in America, for the President and his Cabinet do not derive from the chamber. It may be that presidential candidates have cut their teeth by service in Congress (Kennedy and Nixon), but as we see on pp. 73–5 this is much less true today when the route to the White House often seems to be service as a state governor.

5 Legislation

Law-making is a key function of legislatures, as the very word suggests (by derivation, *legis* means law, and *lator* means proposer or carrier, hence the idea of someone who proposes or carries law). In most cases, it is not the function where they exert most influence, for representative assemblies are by their nature often ill-equipped to generate and develop laws. In the days when Locke and Montesquieu argued that laws should be made by legislatures, the scope of law-making was much more narrow than it is today. Often it was concerned with matters affecting the family, law and ownership of property.

What changed in the twentieth century was the massive growth in state intervention in a whole range of areas of policy-making. Laws are no longer just about regulating private relationships between citizens, but they are concerned to introduce or amend arrangements for providing many services in the fields of education, consumerism, health, housing and social security, amongst many others. Often the details involved in such laws are highly complex, and there are a great variety and amount of them. They involve vast expenditure, and need the input of those who possess the relevant knowledge and technical expertise.

Such interventionism also extends to the running of the economy, where the trend to detailed economic management has grown in the post-war era. Governments are expected to produce policies for inflation and unemployment, and to regulate state and private industries. We live in an age of managed economies and a welfare state. Against this background, it is inevitable that executives will assume a growing role, the more so as so many matters require continuous action and on occasion urgent decisions.

Hence the task of deciding what laws are needed and of preparing legislation has been largely surrendered to governments, and parliaments are more concerned with scrutinising what is proposed, making amendments and voicing objections, rather than playing a key role in the actual making of law. Members of legislatures who wish to play an effective role increasingly need to be specialists rather than generalists, and for this reason they need to be equipped with assistants and facilities which enable them to find out information quickly and to develop a genuine expertise in their subject. Only then can they hope to challenge ministers who have the resources of a government department from which they can draw support.

Law-making in Britain and the United States

Law-making is the main feature of Congress. It uses up most of the available time, a greater proportion than applies at Westminster. There is much more legislation to be handled than there is in Britain. In a typical session in Britain there may be approaching 100 public bills from the government or private members. This compares with some 1000 in America, many of which will have a short existence before their life is terminated. However, in Britain there is a real expectation that legislation introduced will pass through the House, especially if it derives from government. (The fate of private members bills is variable. A few will pass each session, less controversial ones usually having the most chance, because they do not arouse intense opposition and obstruction. The fate of controversial bills is more dependent on the attitude of the government. Ministerial acquiescence or support will increase their chances of success, not least because some parliamentary time may be made available for them.)

Most British bills become law, because ministers impart a sense of direction to the legislative programme and steer their creation through the chamber in all its stages. The party managers control the timetable of the bill and the whips will ensure that important votes are taken on party lines. Party loyalties dominate the voting and although there are examples of dissent this rarely leads to governmental defeats. From this brief review, it becomes apparent that Parliament is not the place where bills originate. It is the place where constitutional authority is conferred on bills that have come from the government departments. The initiative in introducing legislation comes from the Executive and party organisation within the House is used to see that ministerial policies pass through the chamber. This is why Walles could describe the House of Commons as being more a 'a legitimiser than a legislature'.[5] As Shaw remarks, 'Parliament . . . is where the merits of legislation are discussed, but not where the laws are made. In Congress . . . there is both discussion and law-making. Parliament is a *deliberative* assembly. Congress – to the extent that any legislature can be so described these days – is a *law-making* assembly'.[6] Indeed, Truman has written that Congress today is more nearly a legislature in the strict sense than is the national assembly in any other major country in the world.[7]

Congress is a legislative body in the full sense of the term. It passes more legislation than the House of Commons, even if more laws today derive from the Executive than used to be the case. There is no certainty that they will pass through the chamber. Executive influence in Congress is weakened by the separation of powers, an even more powerful factor when reinforced by a divided government in which different parties control the White House and Capitol Hill. If laws from the Executive are passed it may not be in the form that the President or the Cabinet team would wish. Bills can be transformed (or lapse), so that the legislature has a significant impact on the content of legislation. In Britain, the impact of the parliamentary process is often minimal. For all of the time spent in the House examining bills, the overall effect is often modest.

The differences between the role of Parliament and Congress with regards to law-making are not just in terms of the amount of bills or the overall impact of the procedure. They concern the actual process itself, the method of examining bills being very different in the two countries. In Parliament there are eleven stages, five similar ones in each chamber, culminating in the Royal Assent. The role of the second chamber can be important in modifying the content of legislation or rather slowing it down, but the key work is done in the House of Commons

In America, legislation is sometimes introduced into the two chambers at the same time. In whichever house it begins its existence, it must ultimately pass both of them in the same wording. Most of the work is done in standing committees which, unlike the British equivalents, are specialist bodies, comprising members who may have served for some years on the committee dealing with agriculture, education and labour or public works and transportation.

In Britain, much of the discussion of a bill is done on the floor of the House, in the second and third readings, although the detail is examined by a standing committee. In America, committees are central to the legislative work of Congress as it tries to cope with the vast legislative burden placed upon it. After introduction, a bill is assigned by the Speaker to an appropriate standing committee. In the majority of cases it will get no further The role of chairman is crucial in deciding whether or not the bill merits further consideration and if it does whether this should be in full committee or be carried out by one of the many subcommittees. At these hearings, interested parties will be present.

They may provide a written submission or perhaps be called upon to give oral evidence.

If they survive the committee hurdle, bills go to the Rules Committee which stands 'as a strategic gateway between the legislative committees and the floor of the House'.[8] The Committee is empowered to issue a rule which will allow the bill to proceed further and be discussed by the chamber. The rule will specify the length of time available for debate and the types of amendment which can be moved. If the bill is acceptable to the House after proponents and opponents have had their say, then it is sent to the Senate which as we have said may already have been dealing with its own version of the bill. Procedure there is similar, but the process is more relaxed; there is no time fixed limit for debate and there is no Rules Committee. There are opportunities for senators to obstruct or **filibuster** the bill's progress, and senators have been known to speak for hours in their attempts to talk a bill to death. A closure can be applied only if 60 per cent of members vote in favour of it.

> **filibuster**
>
> A delaying strategy whereby opponents of a piece of legislation try to talk it to death, based on the tradition of unlimited debate. Today, 60 members present and voting can halt a filibuster in the senate.

Once agreement between the versions of the bill passed by the two houses has been achieved in the conference committee, the final version is sent before the two chambers for their approval before going to the White House for the President to sign. He or she may leave the bill unsigned or veto it, and Congress may override the presidential veto, although this is uncommon.

If Congress is more influential as a law-making body, it would be fair to say that it is better at obstruction than creation. This is why Shaw could write that 'Congress may be said . . . to be status quo oriented, while the Administration is action-oriented'.[9] President Kennedy once observed that 'it is very easy to defeat a bill in Congress. It is much more difficult to pass one'. As Hague and Harrop remark: 'Because legislation is still difficult to pass even when the need for change is widely recognised, the America experience suggests that an assembly which really does control the legislative process is more of a mixed blessing than might be imagined'.[10]

6   Control of the Executive

Scrutiny of the work of the Executive is perhaps the key function of legislatures today, as most have lost much their law-making as opposed to law-passing role. Via this watchdog role, those in government are held to account for their actions. Their right to govern is acknowledged, but so too is parliament's right to take them to task. In Britain, opportunities for criticism and control of executive action arise in the passage of legislation, in question time, debates, votes and via the select committee system (see pp. 117–18 for more detail of committee activities).

THE WORK AND VALUE OF COMMITTEES IN THE BRITISH PARLIAMENT AND THE AMERICAN CONGRESS

Modern assemblies require a comprehensive array of committees to assist them in their work. Such is the volume and complexity of business, they are indispensable. They are used in the areas of examination of bills and of financial proposals, acting as a check upon government administration and investigating issues of current importance and concern.

In America, much of the main work of Congress is done in the committee rooms, which is why it can be described as a working assembly, whereas in Britain it is on the floor of the House that reputations are made, key issues discussed and government held to account. The British system is floor-orientated rather than committee-orientated, which is why Hague and Harrop describe the House of Commons as a talking rather than a working assembly.[10]

Congress developed a comprehensive network of highly specialised standing committees well in advance of the House of Commons. The Senate has 17 and the House 19, each specialising in one area of legislation and being responsible for scrutiny in that area. There are far more subcommittees. Each house can adjust the number and size of its committees from session to session, but in 2000 the House Agriculture Committee had 4 subcommittees, the International Relations Committee had 5, the Senate Agriculture, Nutrition and Forestry Committee also had 4, the Foreign Relations Committee 7 and the Indian Affairs Committee 0. Membership of committees varied between 10 and 61.

Legislative committees in Britain are non-specialist, as is apparent from their labels: Standing Committees A–H. Bills are assigned to them at random. Fewer members partic-ipate in the committee system of the House of Commons than in Congress, where every Senator serves on two committees, every Representative at least one. Because they may serve for several years on the same committee, they develop a specialist knowledge of the issues involved in their subject area and, given their more important role in the legis-lature, it means that members on committees exercise real influence and power. The committees are better staffed and resourced, each having a budget to employ in its service.

Chairmen of committees have often served for some years. Until the 1970s, they were appointed on the basis of seniority, whereas now seniority is an important criterion when the steering and policy committee of the parties put forward nominees on whom members can vote. In fact, the party leaderships have taken more control of the process in recent years, ensuring that loyal members gain key positions.

Unlike the position in the House of Commons, chairs of committees and subcommittees always belong to the majority party. In their period of dominance since 1995, the Repub-licans have limited their committee chairs to six consecutive years of service. The chairs control the order of business, and their ability to make and unmake subcommittees and hire staff combine to make theirs a very influential position. At Westminster, standing committee chairmen have no comparable specialist knowledge, powers or status.

Scrutiny of legislation in American standing committees is much more meticulous because it is carried out by specialists. Partly because of the operation of separation of powers, the party allegiance and degree of party cohesion of Congress members matter less that they do in Britain. This means that in their consideration of bills they are willing to think beyond the convenience of those who lead the party.

Committees of scrutiny

Select committees have been around for a long time at Westminster but the system was a haphazard one, in which experiments were tried and then dropped. Those who served on them did not have the opportunity to acquire and develop any expertise, and scrutiny was often piecemeal. Of course the big breakthrough at Westminster in the committee system was the establishment in 1980 of a system of select committees, each of which focused on the work of one government department. Their task was and remains to examine 'the expenditure, administration and policy' of the department whose activities they monitored. Via their investigations, members acquire detailed information about the work and problems of departments which is essential if they are to engage in intelligent debate. They also tend to behave in a less partisan manner than is common in the charged atmosphere of the House. As a result, those in the Executive are called to account for their policies and administration by effective watchdogs who throw the spotlight of publicity on their actions. They have other advantages, among them being those identified by Philip Norton:

- the House is better informed about government work, because a number of members have developed a degree of specialist knowledge;
- the committees have a deterrent effect on the behaviour of government, for ministers know that their handling of affairs is being publicly scrutinised;
- there is more openness in government as information is placed in the public domain and ministers and their officials are cross-examined in public;
- the reports may have more influence on policy than is immediately apparent, for recommendations are often taken on board when ministers refine their proposals.[12]

There are still complaints about these committees, which lack adequate resources and are under-staffed with specialist help. They cannot match their American counterparts in terms of personnel, nor are their reports always taken as seriously. Often, there is a lack of time for debates on their reports and findings. Governments have been reluctant to countenance any strengthening of their resources and powers, being wary of their influence. The whips have a significant role in their appointment, via the Committee of Selection but their attempts to replace awkward members backfired in 2001 when Gwynneth Dunwoody and Donald Anderson were reappointed after an attempt to drop them. At the present time there are moves afoot to make the system of select committees more powerful.

As we have seen, American standing committees deal with legislation and scrutiny of a specified policy area. In addition, temporary select committees can be established to investigate particular issues, such as that which in 1986 investigated the Reagan administration's sale of arms to Iran and the diversion of the proceeds to forces trying to bring about the overthrow of the Nicaraguan government. The committee system has long been in existence and these powerful investigative bodies were for years held up by parliamentary reformers as a model of how influential British select committees could be. For several years, ministers were resistant to anything akin to the American experience, a view summed up by a leading British Conservative, R. A. Butler, in a debate on procedure.

▶

Dismissing them as 'committees à l'Americain', he was worried that 'the activities of such a committee would ultimately be aimed at controlling rather than criticising the policy and actions of the department concerned. In so doing, it would be usurping a function which the House itself has never attempted to exercise . . . [committees] would undermine the authority of the executive.'

Committees in America are powerful and have a life of their own. Back in 1880, Woodrow Wilson remarked that the American political system did not have party government but instead 'government by the chairman of the standing committees of Congress'. The remark might now be extended to include subcommittees and their chairmen, for they have acquired an autonomy and freedom of action once reserved for the parent committees. Given their responsibility for policy and scrutiny, and their permanency, members can develop their expertise and become well versed in the issues surrounding their particular area. In effect, American committees are mini-legislatures in their own right.

Question Time is a much-vaunted British way of holding ministers responsible. Its merits – particularly those of Prime Minister's Questions on Wednesday afternoon – have been much questioned, but the fact that he and other ministers must appear before the House and face often hostile questioning helps to keep their feet on the ground and brings them into contact with the comments and criticisms which people are making about government policy. As well as advancing an alternative approach, the Opposition party has the specific role of holding the government to account, throwing the spotlight of publicity on its acts, demanding a full exposition of the ministerial case and censuring ministers when it finds their policies and activities condemnable.

America has no such institution as Question Time, nor does it have a body equivalent to Her Majesty's Opposition. The system of government is very different. Whereas in Britain ministers are members of the legislature and via the doctrine of individual ministerial responsibility are accountable for the work of their departments and their own performance, in America the President is appointed directly and the Cabinet is hand-picked according to the President's requirements and preferences. Cabinet members are not members of Congress and do not have to justify their policies before the elected representatives in Congress, though they may be summoned to appear in committee hearings. The prospect of being subjected to such investigation is bound to influence the behaviour of those who make decisions.

As we have seen, American investigative committees are powerful organs of scrutiny which are the more effective because the 'freedom of information' legislation makes it easier to gain access to key documents. They have the right of subpoena, which means they can force witnesses to appear and answer questions on the issue under investigation. In 1997 the Senate Finance Committee (a permanent standing committee) conducted hearings into the operations of the Internal Revenue Service. Temporary select committees have in the past conducted full-scale investigations of such issues as the conduct of the Vietnam War, the problems surrounding the Watergate break-in, and American involvement in the Iran–Contra affair. The McCarthy hearings of the early 1950s are but the most notorious example of the power of such committees, which have no real counterpart in Britain. Select committees probing the Westland issue in 1986 or the behaviour of ministers in the sleaze cases of the 1990s found it difficult to ever obtain a full picture of what was happening. Even after a lengthy investigation, it can be difficult to discern what actually took place.

Congress also has the key judicial power of **impeachment**. The House decides on whether the accused official has a case to answer and if it believes that he or she has, then the trial takes place in the Senate. A verdict of guilty results in dismissal from public office. Bill Clinton survived the process in 1999, but the ability of Congress to appoint special prosecutors to probe every aspect of a President's affairs and then bring impeachment charges (and the relentless media interest this creates), make it difficult for the incumbent to concentrate on achieving his or her policy goals.

impeachment
The process by which Congress can remove officers of the national government, including the President. The House votes on a charge or series of charges, and a trial on these charges is then conducted in the Senate.

Congress has two main advantages over the British parliament whether in scrutinising legislation or in holding members to account. The first is the doctrine of Separation of Powers, which was designed to prevent undue concentration of power in one location, and which denies members of the Executive the chance to sit in Congress. The second is the absence of strong party bonds, which mean that congress members can act more as free agents, acting and voting as they think it appropriate to do; they do not feel beholden to their party leaders for their advancement.

The decline of legislatures: British and American experience

Most legislatures are relatively weak. They are often thought to be much weaker than they were in some 'golden age' of the nineteenth century. In reality, the 'golden age' theory can be exaggerated. Some nineteenth-century assemblies were easily manipulated by dominant leaders who could often get their way. Several governments always have exercised firm control over legislative arrangements. This was true of Britain, though it is certainly fair to argue that the House of Commons was less predictable in its voting patterns then than it is today. Cross-voting was more common, and governments were liable to be brought down by an adverse vote in the chamber.

In his classic work written in 1921, Lord Bryce wrote of the decline of legislatures, identifying parties as the most serious threat to them.[13] He pointed also to the increased complexity of policy-making and to the incompetence or corruption of many legislators, which also served to strengthen the executive branch. His views have been echoed by many subsequent commentators. In 1989 Petersson felt able to conclude that 'every description of the form of government of the modern state seems to end up with a discouraging conclusion about the actual role of parliament'.[14] For many years, parliaments have been criticised as 'rubber-stamps' for those in power.

Legislatures do tend to be weak, not least because governments need to make urgent decisions on what are often complex items of business – perhaps a crisis in foreign policy (such as the events of 11 September 2001), a difficult discussion in the United Nations, a sudden problem on the financial markets or a leaky oil tanker polluting the coastal regions. Elected representatives inevitably find themselves responding to what has already been done. The influence of legislators at the broad policy level is therefore necessarily limited, and in matters of law-making or on financial provisions their main role tends to be one of ratification rather than of initiative or real influence. In Blondel's words: 'Legislatures do not initiate: they follow'.[15] They cannot initiate because in many cases, as we have seen, the legislation often introduced by modern governments is too complex and technical, and requires preparatory work to be done by civil servants before it is ready to emerge for consideration.

Today, attention is often more focused on the executive branch of government than on the legislature. Often the latter appears to be reacting to the work of the former. In Britain and many other countries, government may be dependent on parliamentary support, but party discipline ensures that this is normally forthcoming, and as a result it is governments which dominate parliament rather than parliaments which dominate government. As Budge, Newton *et al.* point out:

> It is government which can impose procedures and timetables, limit questioning of its activities, pass legislation, and, if necessary win votes of confidence. Even opposition parties tolerate governmental domination of this kind, hoping to benefit from it when their turn in government comes. The power of the government is even greater if the prime minister is free to call an election. The threat of losing seats often has the effect of reinforcing party loyalty and intimidating internal party opponents.[16]

The same writers go on to point out that in Britain the fact that about a third of the majority party and a sixth of all MPs are in the government further strengthens the position of government at the expense of Parliament. There is only one main opposition party, so that 'Parliament simply becomes one of the forums where opposition leaders criticise government policy without being able to defeat it'.

Where minority or coalition governments are more common, in countries ranging from Ireland to Sweden, from Denmark to the Netherlands, there is greater likelihood that parliament will exercise more influence. Governments tend to seek more cross-party agreement to get their bills through, and often seek to gain a broad consensus of opinion behind them. This search for agreement is particularly true of Scandinavian countries, and in Denmark especially parliament can be very effective. The Danish body is always liable to defeat a minority administration, and the average life of governments is around two years, half the figure for Britain or Sweden. In order to survive, Danish governments are very reliant on parliamentary acquiescence, and often tend to seek agreement over a whole range of policy areas. They build coalitions according to the issue under discussion.

In the light of the above considerations, Budge, *et al.* conclude that in Denmark, rather untypically, governments depend on parliament rather than the other way round.[17] This is unusual. But it is generally true that wherever coalitions are weak and quarrel internally, much more importance is attached to negotiations within parliament than where governments are confident of winning legislative votes. Generally, coalitions are weaker the more parties they include.

Broadly, the more powerful the government the weaker the parliament, but a weak government does not necessarily mean a strong legislature. The situation varies considerably, and on a broad spectrum we may include the following European examples:

Strong parliaments						*Weak parliaments*	
Denmark	Norway	Netherlands	Germany	Switzerland	UK	France	
	Sweden	Ireland	Portugal	Poland	Spain	Russia	EU

Source: Adapted from Budge, Newton *et al.*, *The Politics of the New Europe*, Longman, 1997.

In America, Congress – with the different constitutional status accorded to the legislature – clearly has greater power than other assemblies or parliaments. On the spectrum above, it would be placed to the left of Denmark, as the 'strongest of the strong'.

As a result of the growing trend towards executive power, some parliaments are rather compliant. Even so, Hague and Harrop warn against generalisation, and conclude that:

> To speak of the decline of assemblies in an era of big government is too simple. In several ways, assemblies are growing in importance; as arenas of activity, as intermediaries in the transition from one political order to another, as raisers of grievances and as agencies of oversight. The televising of proceedings in many countries is making assemblies more, not less central to political life . . . [Moreover] in the assemblies of Western Europe, backbench members are now more assertive; party leaders can no longer expect well-educated and well-researched backbenchers to be loyally deferential.[18]

The same writers point out in a later edition that other legislatures have benefited from American experience. In particular, 'Congress led the way in equipping assembly members with the resources to do their jobs professionally . . . throughout the democratic world, backbench members have become more assertive: party leaders can no longer expect career politicians to be totally deferential. Specialised committees, and members with a driving interest in policy, are increasingly successful in contributing to political debate'. They divide assemblies into various categories: Active, Reactive, Marginal (e.g. legislatures in many communist states where the assembly is but a minor partner in policy-making) and Minimal (e.g. one-party African states where the assembly is a rubber stamp under executive domination). The US Congress is described as Active, an assembly which 'makes policy autonomously', whereas Britain is in the second category, a Reactive Assembly, which 'reacts to but can influence government policy'.

The performance of the American Congress is much criticised by American commentators who often lament its lack of effectiveness and in particular its slowness to act. As Walles has explained, 'in the absence of firm control and leadership, Congress is ill-equipped to establish priorities which can then be readily translated into action'.[19] It does not perform its legislative and investigative functions as impressively as many would like, and at times it has seemed to surrender too much initiative to the White House.

Relations with the presidency are an important aspect of congressional power and influence. Writing in the 1880s, Woodrow Wilson (later himself to be a 'strong' President) observed that 'in the practical conduct of the federal government . . . unquestionably, the predominant and controlling force, the centre and source of all motive and of all regulative power, is Congress'. With only a very few other exceptions, greater power resided on Capitol Hill than in the White House right down to 1933. Then for many years Americans became used to a more assertive presidency. It seemed that Congress could not act effectively in an age when federal activity had expanded so rapidly, and most Presidents were only too willing to step in to the vacuum and seize their chance to lead. But since the early 1970s, when Congress finally decided to assert itself, Presidents from Jimmy Carter to Bill Clinton have found relations with Capitol Hill difficult to manage, and there has been talk of a 'tethered' or 'restrained' presidency and an emphasis on presidential weakness rather than strength.

In other words, congressional influence has varied over time. It is now a more powerful body vis-à-vis the White House than it was at the beginning of the 1970s. When the Founding Fathers devised the Constitution, it was always intended that Congress would act as a check upon the influence of the other two elements of government: the executive and the judiciary. Some recent Presidents have been only too aware of its ability to obstruct their efforts to implement their programme.

The tendency towards the 'decline of legislatures' is certainly less true of presidential systems. Congress has more opportunity to modify proposals than most assemblies. But its main strength has usually depended more on blocking or frustrating presidential ambitions, or scrutinising the performance and membership of the Administration, than in actually in determining policy. The power is one of delay rather than of initiative.

Elected representatives in Britain and America: their role

Elected representatives have a variety of different responsibilities. They have loyalties which often conflict and different members will reach differing conclusions about where their main duties lie. They have an obligation to the nation, to their constituents, to the party whose label they employ, to the pressure groups which they may represent and to themselves, their own consciences.

In most democracies, elected members are creatures of their party; parties are the vehicles through which they entered the legislature. Without the label, they would almost certainly not have been elected. They were nominated by a party organisation, elected on a party ticket, pledged to a party line. They are expected to give support to the party in the chamber and most do so without much complaint. They accept the constraints of party discipline, knowing that there are opportunities in which they can vent their concerns other than in the voting lobbies.

Like other elected representatives, MPs also have responsibilities to the country and especially to their constituents and any constituency interests. As MPs they are expected to play a full part in the proceedings of the House, attend regularly, speak and vote in debates and serve on committees. They should also try to view issues from a national as well as from a party and constituency point of view. Today, they receive a mass of correspondence from aggrieved constituents and especially deal with welfare matters such as social security benefits, housing allocation and educational provision. Some MPs specialise in handling such problems and have made a name for themselves as good constituency MPs.

Congress members have similar responsibilities, although the priorities they attach to them are often different. In virtually every case, they were elected on a party label, but once in the House or Senate loyalty to party does not have the same hold over their activities as it does in Britain. Committee and constituency pressures are much greater. The representative function is all-important, for Senators and Representatives have always attached high priority to the attitudes and concerns of those who elected them.

Congress members – especially members of the House who only serve for two years – place much emphasis on getting re-elected. Mayhew distinguished three types of behaviour in which they might indulge to enhance their prospects: self-promotion, credit-claiming and position-taking.[20] In each case, the aim is to ensure that constituents view them as the right person for their congressional district. 'Pork barrel' politics have always been a feature of American politics, for the success of politicians in bringing home the pork or bacon (gaining advantages or concessions for the district) will substantially affect their chances. They know that their prospects of survival will depend to a large extent on their ability and effort, and so they spend much of their time in assessing and acting upon the wishes of those who sent them to Washington.

Taking care of constituents amounts to more than gaining pork or advantages. It also involves acting as a kind of ombudsman, taking up grievances and sorting out problems. Bailey concludes that 'the increased emphasis on constituency service has transformed members from national legislators to narrowly focused ombudsmen' and sees dangers in a situation in which Congress is 'filled with ombudsmen rather than legislators'.[21] It encourages short-term thinking rather than a concern for what is in the best interests of the nation over the longer term. Because of this, the emphasis on representation can be said to be at the expense of good policy-making, and Congress is often criticised for its failings in terms of efficiency and in representing the national interest.

There is no easy answer to the question of which is the most important responsibility of congress members any more than there is for MPs. In a country where so many live at great distance from Washington, people expect that the representatives they sent to the federal capital will voice the feelings of the folks 'back home' and deliver them tangible benefits. Congress members are alive to this and a survey conducted in 1977 showed that 52 per cent of the 140 representatives interviewed saw their tasks as being to represent their 'district only' or 'nation and district'. 45 per cent thought that their duty was 'to the nation' and 3 per cent were unsure; party was not a response any of them were invited to stress.[22] Just how they react will depend on the issue. On some topics there is no clearly expressed constituency view and members can argue the national or party case, or feel free to follow the dictates of conscience. But on many more topics there is a local interest to consider and this may influence their prospects for re-election. Congress members are constantly looking over their shoulder to the people who put them there. They also have to bear in mind the wishes of the lobbyists and Political Action Committees who gave support to their campaign.

Note: Figures for the US in the following subsection relate to the 108th Congress (elected in November 2002) unless otherwise stated.

The social backgrounds of members of legislatures

In general, legislatures tend to be overwhelmingly male, middle aged, middle class, and, in North America and Europe, white. Berrington points out that 'almost every study of legislators in Western democracies shows that they come from more well-to-do backgrounds, are drawn from more prestigious and intellectually satisfying backgrounds and are much better educated than their electors.'[23]

Working-class representation is low in many countries, so that representatives of the middle and upper classes predominate. As a broad trend, parties of the right tend to draw more heavily on business and commerce, whereas parties of the left have many professionals within their ranks, especially from the world of education. For both right- and left-wing parties, law has always been a useful background for political service, particularly in the United States. It has lost some of its former impact today, and professions involving communications, such as newspaper and television journalism and public relations, have increased in their representation.

In many democracies certain political families always seem to have one of their members in the legislature. In India, the Gandhis and Nehrus have always been well represented, just as among the British the Soames, Hoggs and Benns, and among the Americas the Kennedys, Gores and Bushes have provided representatives in two or more generations. In some families there is a tradition of public service, and at some level – local or national – many members get involved in political activity.

In America, work on Capitol Hill was always regarded as a full-time activity. Members are not allowed to earn from outside an income more than 15 per cent of their congressional salary. Pay and conditions are good: more of an incentive to full-time membership than they are in Britain. There was never the same idea of members of the privileged classes going to Westminster as a social activity in the afternoon and evening, after a day's work elsewhere. The part-time British politician is now in retreat, a process accelerated by the Labour landslides in 1997 and 2001. More common today is the career politician who may have begun life working as a research assistant and then worked in the party organisation ('political staffers') or served on a local council before entering Parliament. Such people are committed, well versed in political issues and

> **career politicians**
> People committed to politics which they regard as their vocation. They know little else beyond the worlds of politics, policy-making and elections.

understand their party and those who work within it. However, some would argue that **career politicians** lack the sense of broad perspective that comes from having done another job. They have not inhabited the 'real' world of ordinary people and may not always possess the judgement that comes from knowing about the preoccupations of people from all walks of life – in other words, what 'makes people tick'.

In America, it has long been the case that congress members have served in some other political activity. They may have been state administrators or legislators, or served as county, city or town officials. Some will have been judges or governors, others Representatives, before they bid for a Senate seat. Shaw found that in the early 1960s 98 per cent of Senators and 88 per cent of Representatives had such a political apprenticeship in public offices, a far higher figure than at Westminster.[24] Far fewer British MPs have served in local government, proportionately more on the Labour side.

Female representation in legislatures

For several years, the United Nations has taken the view that for a legislature to be considered gender-representative, there should be at least 30 per cent of women in the elected chamber. By 2000, seven Western European countries had reached the target, although the number of women has increased in most assemblies over the last decade. The position is patchy, as the table indicates:

Female representation in the 'top ten' countries and in America

Country	Year of last election	% of women MPs	Electoral system
Sweden	1998	43	List PR
Denmark	1998	37	List PR
Finland	1999	36	List PR
Netherlands	1998	36	List PR
Norway	1997	36	List PR
Germany	1998	31	AMS – Hybrid
New Zealand	1999	29	AMS
Australia	1998	22	AV
Canada	1997	20	FPTP
Britain	1997	18	FPTP
World average*	**2000**	**14**	
America	1998	13	FPTP

Source: Table adapted from R. Hague and M. Harrop, *Comparative Government and Politics*, Palgrave, 2001, using information provided by Inter-Parliamentary Union 2000.

Notes: Figures are for lower houses in two chamber countries. * figures calculated from countries for which data available.

Both Britain and America have lagged far behind the rest of the world in the representation of women in the national legislature. In 1995, UNICEF found that Britain came 18th in a list of 22 industrialised countries,[25] and the Inter-Parliamentary Union put Britain in joint 65th place in its list of women MPs world-wide. First was Sweden, with 40.4 per cent, followed by the other Scandinavian countries and Holland. However, many developing countries had a better record than Britain. Prior to the 1997 election, Britain and the USA had a lower percentage of female MPs than African states such as Mozambique and

South Africa (both on 25 per cent), and Namibia, Uganda and Chad, and South American countries such as Cuba (23 per cent), Argentina (22 per cent) and Nicaragua (16 per cent). Women also fared better in some Asian nations such as China (21 per cent), North Korea (18 per cent) and Vietnam (18 per cent). While some of the countries included in the list were hardly known for their democratic credentials, it is surprising that Iraq (on 11 per cent) could claim to have a better record on the representation of women than Britain. More women were also elected in many of the new Eastern European democracies. In Slovakia 15 per cent of MPs were women, in the Russian Federation and Poland it was 13 per cent, and in Hungary 11 per cent.

Clearly, the representation of women in national parliaments varies considerably. They have fared badly in the USA, and in some European countries such as France, Greece, Ireland and Italy (all Catholic or Orthodox in religion) representation has traditionally been low. Scandinavia has the best record, and there are several possible explanations for this:

- it could be a reflection of a cultural and legal framework which is generally more sympathetic to female advancement;
- it could be a result of their use of party list proportional systems, by which the parties present lists of candidates to voters rather than individual candidates;
- it could reflect the strong commitment of Scandinavian parties to promoting women as candidates, which encourages women to come forward.

The situation is confusing, for in the USA the Women's Movement has been stronger than in Scandinavia, yet women are less well represented. Again, all European states use some form of proportional representation, but this has not always produced an outcome favourable to women, as the experience of Italy indicates.

Female representation in Britain and the United States

In both countries, women made only incremental gains in the 1970s and 1980s. The situation steadily improved through the 1990s. In both countries, the number of women sharply increased in 1992. In 1997, there was the highest ever intake of women at Westminster (120, of whom 101 were Labour and 13 Conservatives). In the 2002 mid-term elections, more American women were elected to the House (59) and to the Senate (13) than ever before. In June 2001, 118 women were elected to the House of Commons and the number of women in the reformed Lords at the same time was 111. In the case of the three elected chambers, women have more often been elected for the more progressive of the two main parties: Labour and the Democrats. The same is true for members of ethnic minority groups (see p. 129).

What explains the under-representation of women in both countries?

There are some common factors and some which apply more to one country than the other:

- Women are under-represented in the 'top jobs' of many areas of national life, from the management of 'big business' to finance, the civil service to the church, the armed forces to the law. In the circumstances, it is hardly surprising if they are under-represented in politics.
- Those who hold political office are office elected by First Past The Post which is less conducive to the election of women and minority groups. In choosing only one candidate, it is sometimes considered better to play safe and choose a candidate unlikely to lose any support.
- Interest in and more particularly opportunity for becoming an elected representative is limited by domestic home-making and child-rearing responsibilities.
- Politics is often perceived as an aggressive and often macho preoccupation and many women might be put off by the hurly-burly, shouting and abuse which characterise some legislatures.
- Discrimination – some people do not wish to see women elected, seeing politics 'as a man's world', with men being more suited to political activity (terms such as 'less emotional' are often bandied about!).
- The fear that women may lose votes, by comparison with male candidates.

What is significant is that in the British Conservative Party, it has often been older middle- and upper-class women on selection committees who have been most reluctant to choose women, a common early question to would-be candidates often related to whether they have any children and who is looking after them. Some local Conservatives have often expressed the view that in choosing a male candidate, they are really getting 'two for the price of one', for the wife of a married man may be able and willing to help on the social side of political activity (staging garden parties and fund-raising events, speaking to local gatherings of women's organisations, etc.), whereas the husband of a political wife may have a job of his own which prevents him from being such a source of support.

In both countries there is a tendency for elected representatives to serve for a long period because of the existence of safe seats. Members serve an average of 20 years in the House of Commons, 12 in the House and 11 in the Senate, according to one study.[26] (In America the incumbency factor works in favour of male re-election to the Senate). It is difficult for women to achieve a breakthrough, because the low turnover means that few vacancies are created.

Finally, what can make a difference to the level of representation of women is the use of positive discrimination in some form. Following the 1992 election, Labour used quotas to ensure that there were women-only shortlists in some constituencies, as a short-term means of redressing the balance. Inevitably, the effect was to raise the proportion of women among new recruits to the following election. As New Labour won a landslide in 1997, it meant that many women were elected. Labour's method eventually fell foul of the courts in the **Jepson case**, but ministers intend to legislate to ensure that in choosing candidates the provisions of the Sex Discrimination Act do not apply. In other words, the use of quotas or other methods of advancing the female cause would be acceptable again, should any party wish to employ it. All main British parties express concern about the level of female representation. There has been increased debate within the Conservative Party as to whether it is appropriate in some way to give it a boost, perhaps even by forcing some associations in 'safe' seats to choose women as their candidates.

> **Jepson case 1996**
> In 1995, Peter Jepson took the Labour Party to court, claiming that the process for selecting candidates was discriminatory. He argued that he had been excluded from seeking selection in certain constituencies, purely on the basis of his gender. This was, in their view, contrary to the Sex Discrimination Act, 1975. The court found against the party in January 1996, ruling that the exclusion of men from certain selection contests was unlawful. The decision was, in effect, later confirmed by a judgement of an Employment Appeal Tribunal.

Ethnic minority representation

Ethnic minority representation in Britain is low. Following the 2001 election, 12 out of 659 members come from the black and Asian communities, including 2 Muslims and 3 Sikhs; 21 Jews were elected. African-Americans and Hispanics are similarly under-represented in the 108th Congress, there being no representation of either group (some 72m in the USA) in the Senate and 39 and 25 respectively in the House out of 435 members. Jews (5 per cent of Congress) and Catholics (25 per cent) are better represented than in the past, but not on the scale in which they are represented in the population at large.

Age

Elected representatives still tend to be middle aged, so that those elected usually attain their position only after doing some other job and making a mark in their chosen career. This can be said to provide them with experience of life, but it also means that the voice of young people is neglected, causing some to feel alienated from the political system. In Britain, after 2001, the average age of Conservative members is 48, the figure being slightly higher for Labour (50) and lower for the Liberal Democrats (47). Four years earlier Labour had ten members who were under 30 at the time of the election and a lower average than the Conservatives: 48 against 50. Low Labour turnover in 2001 meant that the overall age was boosted as existing members were now older. In the new Scottish Parliament, the average age is lower than at Westminster; 45 in comparison with 49.1 (the latter figure is that for the three main parties).

MPs tend to be younger than American Representatives and Senators. To enter the House a Representative has to be 25, a Senator has to be at least 30. The average age of members of Congress is usually in the early 50s, with senators averaging about five years older than Representatives (currently 59.5 per cent as against 53.9 per cent).

Social class: occupational backgrounds

As for the middle-class nature of representatives, in some states this is now more apparent than was once the case. For instance, the British Labour Party evolved as a party to represent working people in Parliament, and in its early years it always contained among its ranks a large trade-union element. From the 1960s onwards, the trend towards middle-class representation grew, with an influx of academics from the universities and polytechnics. In the Blairite party of today there are many members drawn from the worlds of public-sector professionals, teachers and political staffers. The percentage of Labour MPs drawn from a manual working-class background has taken a sharply downward turn, now being at its lowest ever. In its early days, the Parliamentary Labour Party had 83 per cent working-class membership (1918); since 2001 the figure is 12 per cent. Manual workers are but a small minority in the Labour Party, as they are in most countries, even those where socialist parties are strong.

American workers have never been keen to go to Capitol Hill themselves. They never felt the same for working-class representation in the legislature that motivated trade unionists and other working people in Britain at the beginning of the twentieth century, perhaps because feelings of class consciousness were never so acute. More affluent than British workers, they seemed more content to elect representatives of one of the main parties, particularly the Democrats.

Labour's changed composition over recent decades reflects what has been happening in many other countries. Those who dominate legislatures tend to be lawyers, managers and professional workers such as teachers. In North America, lawyers predominate in both Canada and the United States; in Western Europe they are often around a quarter of the total. Teachers are numerous in Western Europe, and businessmen and managers are well represented. Similar patterns apply in Asia, the Middle East and in South America. In communist states, teachers and white-collar employees have tended to replace working men and trade unionists.

The legal background is now less important than it was in America, but still a greater proportion of congress members have a legal background than do MPs.

Law attracts people interested in politics; after all, lawyers work in the law and parliaments make law. Their strong representation is in many ways unsurprising. In particular, law provides a flexible work situation for candidates as they wage their campaign. They can also leave their job with relative ease and return to it as they wish, their experience of having served as an elected representative almost certainly increasing their public visibility and possibly the earnings they can then command. About 40 per cent of members of the 108th Congress are lawyers, compared with around 10 per cent of MPs.

Business and banking are also common backgrounds for legislators. Business people are often members of private or family-owned companies, in which another member of the family can keep the enterprise going whilst their relative takes a place in the chamber. It is more difficult to get on and off the corporate ladder without losing ground to rivals within a large firm. Business people make up about 35 per cent of Congress, and half that figure in the House of Commons.

Overall, congressional membership is more heavily skewed to the middle and professional classes than the House of Commons, which itself is very unrepresentative of the British people. The Senate has sometimes been called a 'millionaire's club', which may be an exaggeration, but the proportion of millionaires and nearly millionaires is high. In the House of Representatives, too, members have generally served in occupations with substantial incomes (well above the national average) and of high esteem.

Education

On average, congress members have a higher educational attainment than MPs, although to make the comparison raises difficult issues about the standards of education in either country. Most congress members have a college degree and many have graduate degrees (70 per cent in the 108th Congress) or some qualification such as a degree in law (JD) or business (MBA). At Westminster, an ever-rising number of MPs have attended a university or – as they were then called – polytechnic. A very high proportion (440 members) of the three main parties have a degree and in particular the percentage of Conservative graduates has never been higher (81 per cent). The Conservatives continue to have a large number of members who have been to public school (109 out of 165), although the Old Etonians are in retreat within the party (15 at present).

Should parliaments be a microcosm (mirror image) of the nation? In particular does the under-representation of women and members of ethnic minorities in Britain and the United States really matter?

In every democracy, the legislative chambers – upper or lower – are socially **unrepresentative** of the nation at large. Indeed, in a democracy it would be virtually impossible to get an elected house which is a microcosm of society. Election results are at the mercy of the electorate. Moreover, the over-representation of people who are middle aged, highly educated, white and male is hardly surprising, given that the people who come forward for election usually have those characteristics.

> **unrepresentative**
> In this sense, untypical of a class. Parliaments do not provide a fair representation of the community at large. In other words, membership does not mirror or is untypical of the characteristics of the persons represented.

In certain respects, many people would be relieved to know that level of educational attainment is higher among elected representatives than the population at large. Members deal with complex issues of public policy and it is essential that they are literate, as it is that they are able to express themselves fluently in speech and on paper. Even if illiterates wanted to stand – which is unlikely – they would probably be unable to cope with the type of work involved. Neither would it usually be considered a good thing if there was en exact representation of people who are in some way inadequate, bewildered or suffering from serious emotional disorders.

More serious, is the under-representation of women and ethnic minorities in Parliament, Congress and other legislatures.

'Yes! Under-representation matters for several reasons'

It is dangerous in a democracy if groups with less wealth and power are under-represented, not just women and members of ethnic minorities, but also young people and members of the poorest section of the community. If they feel excluded and see their elected representatives as being something of an out-of-touch elite, there is a real danger that they will regard the legislature with some contempt and turn to other forms of political action to get their message across. The election of a more socially representative assembly would strengthen its legitimacy in the eyes of the public, reducing the risk of law-breaking, violent protest and of alienation from the democratic process.

Again, as long as certain groups are under-represented, there are likely to be fewer debates on issues affecting them, and the quality of debate may be poor as many members do not take the matters under discussion seriously. As a result, full scrutiny by the media of the impact of government policy on such groups may be largely absent from the political process.

The election of more women is particularly important, for as a majority group in the country they have long been seriously under-represented at Westminster and on Capitol Hill. Many highly competent people of large minority groups have also been denied the chance to fulfil their potential. Legislatures need the services of the most able people available, but at present much talent goes unrecognised. This is unfortunate, because the more that get elected, the more role models there are to encourage others of their own type to come forward and see politics as a realistic, attractive career option.

All the mainstream parties talk of their aspiration to achieve a society in which people are able to progress on merit. They claim to dislike discrimination and to wish to encourage equal opportunities. It is therefore hypocritical for the legislature not to reflect these worthy principles in their composition. Achieving more balanced representation in Congress and Parliament would be an inspiring signal to those striving for equal opportunities in other workplaces and institutions.

'No! Under-representation does not matter'

In a representative democracy, we select MPs broadly to reflect the interests of their constituents. To achieve this, it is not necessary for Parliament to be a mirror-image of British or American society. The system is supposed to produce representation of people's political views. It is not essential or realistic to expect that membership will exactly be in proportion to the size of all the various groups within society, from 'teenage Rastafarians to eighty year old organic gardeners'.[27]

MPs should be able to represent the views of all their constituents, and it is not necessary to belong to a particular group or interest to put a case on their behalf. It was, after all, a male Parliament and Congress which eventually voted to extend the franchise to women. MPs and congress members exercise their best judgement on what is right for the whole community, and to do this they do not need to be socially representative – only to possess an ability to empathise with the needs of all sections of the population. You don't have to inhabit a slum dwelling to appreciate that slums need to be cleared, even if your recognition of the full horrors might be more acute if you do so. Many MPs have taken up the problems of the poor in inner cities, in the same way that Senator Edward Kennedy (born into one of America's wealthiest families) has for years championed the underprivileged. Neither do you need to be a woman to understand that discrimination against women is hurtful, wrong and damaging to society.

Furthermore, women and other social groups are not homogeneous. They do not all possess the same needs and views. Some women are pro-choice on abortion, others are pro-life. They may have widely different views on divorce as well, and on a range of issues their political outlook can be as diverse as that of men. Class, employment, age, locality and lifestyle may be more important in determining political views than gender or race. For this reason, it is impossible to represent all women or minority peoples as a group, even if one wanted to do this.

Above all, what we need are competent and caring people to represent us. The personal ability and party allegiance of any candidate should be the main determinants of who gets elected. To draw attention to irrelevant factors such as gender in deciding on the selection of candidates may be unfair and result in reverse discrimination against the most suitable candidates for the job.

The pay and conditions of legislators

For many years it was customary for British MPs to lament their inadequate facilities. Many of them found that the vast size and splendour of their surroundings were poor compensation for the conditions in which they had to operate. It was common for both members themselves and academic and journalistic commentators to make adverse comparisons with the situation in other countries. On matters of pay too there was general dissatisfaction until comparatively recently, although in recent decades the level of remuneration has considerably improved. In 2002, an MPs had a salary of £51,822, as well as a range of allowances for office help, staffing and accommodation. Some members still often voice criticism of the lack of constituency help they receive, whilst others feel that they could do with more research assistance at Westminster. Most MPs employ a couple of people to help them, and also make use of the services of unpaid research assistants. The lack of office equipment and particularly of information technology services are frequently condemned, for the House makes no central provision for such facilities. Poor facilities are often mentioned by MPs who have had previous experience of the business world where they came to take good provision for granted.

Legislatures in Britain and the United States: a summary		
	Britain	*United States*
Unicameral or bicameral?	Bicameral.	Bicameral.
Size	House of Commons 659. House of Lords 687.	Representatives 435. Senate 100
Method of selection	Commons: direct election. Lords: mainly appointment.	Representatives and Senate: direct election.
Nature of membership	Both unrepresentative: too few women and minorities.	Both unrepresentative: too few women and minorities.
Status of chambers	Commons: significant. Lords: secondary role.	Theoretically equal, but Senate has higher prestige.
Type and role of committees	Standing (non-specialist) for legislation: select for scrutiny.	Standing (specialist) for legislation and scrutiny: select for special enquiries.

Such inadequate rewards and conditions of work were perhaps justifiable when the task of being an MP was widely regarded as being a part-time occupation. Today, however, many members take the view that it is impossible to do two jobs well, and that in trying to reconcile employment in commerce and industry with membership of the House, there may be a conflict of interest. In other words, pay and allowances need to be appropriate for those who wish to work full-time at Westminster, as most MPs do.

It remains the case that, in comparison with other legislatures, elected representatives in Britain are relatively deprived, for pay and facilities elsewhere are often considerably better than those in the Mother of Parliaments. In terms of accommodation, equipment, staffing, library assistance and other amenities, American congress members are notably better placed. Senators have up to 30 staff serving them and Representatives around 25. (Of course, in both cases they service a much larger geographical area than do MPs.) Pay is markedly higher at $150,000, and perquisites are more lavish in terms of offices, equipment, staffing and other amenities. In particular, library assistance for congress members is far superior to such assistance at the House of Commons. The Library of Congress is the largest in the United States and attached to it is the Legislative Reference Service. Senators and Representatives can benefit from these research facilities, which are far more advanced and much better staffed than the research division of the library at Westminster.

	Britain	United States
Law-making	Commons has main role, Lords does work of revision: most bills pass and impact of process limited.	Key legislative role for both houses, though relatively few bills pass into law: lack of party support.
Watchdog role, investigation	Questions, Opposition and select committees.	Powerful investigatory committees: no Question Time or official Opposition.
Relative power	Loss of power: talk of 'Parliament in decline' and need for reform.	Most powerful legislature in world, though often talk of 'congressional paralysis'.
Pay and facilities	Pay low by European standards: conditions poor.	Generous pay and excellent facilities, especially staff support.

Conclusion

In liberal democracies, governments have often succeeded in muzzling parliamentary powers, and Britain is no exception, for the reasons described. Yet legislatures are not without influence, and can still play an important role. They may not have the power to initiate, lacking as they do the necessary technical competence. But they can play a part in starting up a great debate on policy issues which can be taken up elsewhere, particularly in the media.

Philip Norton has stressed that there needs to be a wider focus than mere concentration on parliament's role in the making of public policy.[28] He regards the British Parliament as 'not just significant', but also as 'indispensable'. He points out that legislatures today are multi-functional, their task of 'manifest legitimation' (giving the formal seal of approval) being a core defining purpose. But also in articulating interests, redressing grievances, recruiting ministers, mobilising and educating citizens and acting as a safety-valve when tensions in society arise, they perform an invaluable role.

The experience of America is rather different. It is the most influential legislature in the world, even if at times there has been an ebb and flow in the power relationship it has with the presidency. If the White House and Congress are under the control of different parties, then elected representatives may be particularly keen to curb presidential aspirations.

REFERENCES

1 Figures based on those provided in R. Hague and M. Harrop, *Comparative Government and Politics*, Palgrave, 2001.
2 As note 1 above.
3 I. Budge, K. Newton *et al.*, *The Politics of the New Europe*, Longman, 1997.
4 J. Flammang, *American Politics in a Changing World*, Brooks/Cole, 1990.
5 M. Walles, *British and American Systems of Government*, Philip Allan/Barnes Noble Books, 1988.
6 M. Shaw, *Anglo-American Democracy*, Routledge and Kegan, 1968.
7 D. Truman, *The Governmental Process*, Knopf, 1951.
8 G. Edwards *et al.*, *Government in America*, Harper Collins, 1996.
9 As note 5 above.
10 As note 1 above.
11 As note 1 above.
12 P. Norton, *Does Parliament Matter?*, Harvester Wheatsheaf, 1993.
13 J. Bryce, *Modern Democracies*, Macmillan, 1921.
14 O. Petersson, *Maktens Natverk*, Carlssons, 1989.
15 J. Blondel, *Comparative Government: An Introduction*, Prentice Hall, 1995.

16 As note 2 above.

17 As note 2 above.

18 As note 1 above.

19 As note 4 above.

20 D. Mayhew, Congress: *The Electoral Connection*, Yale University Press, 1974.

21 C. Bailey, 'Ethics as Politics: Congress in the 1990s', in P. Davies and F. Waldstein (eds), *Political Issues in America*, Manchester University Press, 1991.

22 *Report of The Commission on Administrative Review*, House of Representatives, 1977.

23 H. Berrington, 'Political Ethics: The Nolan Report', *Government and Opposition* (30), 1995.

24 As note 5 above.

25 UNICEF findings, referred to in *The Times*, 9 June 1995.

26 A. Somit, '. . . And Where We Came Out', in *The Victorious Incumbent: A Threat to Democracy?*, Dartmouth, 1994.

27 J. Longmate, *Women and Politics*, Politics Association/SHU Press, 1997.

28 As note 11 above.

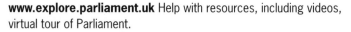

USEFUL WEB SITES

For the UK

www.parliament.uk House of Commons Information Office. A useful source of information on many aspects, including lists of women MPs etc. Produces valuable factsheets.

www.explore.parliament.uk Help with resources, including videos, virtual tour of Parliament.

www.scottish.parliament.uk Scottish Parliament. Help with queries and resources.

www.wales.gov.uk National Assembly for Wales. Help with queries and resources.

www.democratic.org.uk Democracy UK. Information on Parliamentary Reform.

For the USA

www.thomas.loc.gov Thomas (named after Thomas Jefferson, the Library of Congress). The congressional site which offers a comprehensive look at Congress in the past and today; useful information about current activities.

www.house.gov House of Representatives.

www.senate.gov Senate.

Both give valuable details about the work of both chambers, reports about current legislation, the activities of congressmen, their conditions etc.

www.vote-smart.org Vote Smart. An easy-to-understand guide to current legislation going through either US chamber.

www.rollcall.com The newspaper read by those working on Capitol Hill: information re. congressional politics, including news and analysis.

SAMPLE QUESTIONS

1 Why is the upper house in Britain less powerful than the Senate in the United States?

2 Does bicameralism operate more effectively in the United States than in Britain?

3 Compare the effectiveness of the law-making process in Britain and the United States.

4 Compare and assess the effectiveness of the ways in which Parliament and Congress seek to control the work of the Executive.

5 Has the American government more to fear from the scrutiny of Congress than the British government from that of the House of Commons?

6 Is it true that the real work of Congress is done in the committee rooms? How does the American committee system compare with that in the British Parliament?

7 Why are congressional committees more powerful than those of Parliament?

8 Why is Congress a more powerful legislature than the British Parliament?

9 Explain and discuss the view that MPs and congress members are subject to very different pressures.

10 Compare the background and roles of MPs and congress members. What might an MP like and dislike about the American legislature?

11 Discuss the view that senators and representatives are better paid and better equipped to fulfil the tasks demanded of them.

12 Consider the importance of socio-economic background when assessing the performance and effectiveness of members of Parliament and of Congress. What barriers prevent the development of a more representative cross-section of the populations of Britain and the United States from getting elected?

13 Could British parliamentary reformers benefit from an acquaintance with the experience of the US Congress?

6

Judiciaries

Courts of law are part of the political process, for governmental decisions and acts passed by the legislative body may require judicial decisions to be implemented. Courts need to be independent to be respected, but this is difficult to achieve in practice. There is never full independence as far as appointment is concerned, and Blondel warns that in their verdicts judges cannot be expected 'to go outside the norms of the society'.[1] In Britain and America, the courts have traditionally diverged in their behaviour, but today there are more similarities than there were a few decades ago. Judges have become more active players on the political scene. Even so, many British people would probably not consider the courts to be part of the political system, whereas in the United States their political role sometimes becomes very apparent.

We are primarily concerned with the courts in their political capacity rather than with their criminal and civil caseload. We shall explore the role of judiciaries, how judicial independence is protected in both countries, the types of person who become judges, and the differing conceptions of their role and we shall assess the extent to which they are involved in political matters.

POINTS TO CONSIDER

➤ What mechanisms exist to ensure judicial impartiality? To what extent is the idea of an independent judiciary put into practice in Britain and the United States?

➤ In making appointments to the Bench, should the personalities and opinions of individual judges be taken into account?

➤ As judges perform an increasingly political role, should they be elected?

➤ Does it matter that the social background of leading judges on both sides of the Atlantic is unrepresentative of society as a whole?

➤ Should the courts lead public opinion or should they follow it?

➤ To what extent are the courts of law political?

Liberal democracies such as the United Kingdom and the United States, along with Australia, Canada, France, Italy and many other countries, have an independent judiciary which is charged with responsibility for upholding the rule of law. Even those in power, be they Presidents or British ministers, have the same duty to act within the law. Any transgression of it should not go unchallenged. The rule of law is a cardinal principle in any democracy, and where it does not prevail then this is a clear indication of a regime which is in some degree despotic.

In democratic countries, it is expected that the judicial system will be enabled to function freely, without any interference from the government of the day. Judicial independence implies that there should be a strict separation between the judiciary and other branches of government. In most cases, the independence of judges and law officers is ensured by their security of tenure, although their independence could be compromised by the close involvement of politicians in the manner of their recruitment and promotion. Moreover, once recruited, bias can creep in, as a result of the type of person who gains advancement. Judges in many countries do tend to exhibit a remarkable homogeneity. This might pre-dispose them to defend the existing social and political order, and make them unsympathetic to groups who seek to challenge it, such as representatives of racial or other minorities, and militant women.

The operation of the courts in Britain and America

In both countries there is an elaborate network of courts which have responsibility for upholding the law. The guilt or innocence of those involved in criminal offences is determined, after defendants have been given the opportunity to defend themselves. Those involved in civil disputes can get them resolved.

In Britain, there is one basic judicial system for criminal law and a second handles civil law. The United States has a more complex judicial structure. As a federal country, it has two court systems: a series of federal courts and a series of state/local ones. It is the state system which is used in the overwhelming majority of cases.

In Britain and America, courts operate along adversarial lines, with the prosecution and defence each seeking to discredit the arguments advanced by the other side and persuade the judge and/or jury of the merits of their case.

Whereas in America, those who handle cases are all lawyers, in Britain there is a distinction between barristers who in most cases put forward the arguments before judge and jury and the solicitors who are the initial point of contact for those in need of legal assistance. Solicitors do much of the preliminary, out-of-court work.

The functions of judiciaries

There are three main functions of the judicial branch of government. Judiciaries:
  • resolve disputes between individuals, adjudicating in controversies within the limits of the law;
  • interpret the law, determining what it means and how it applies in particular situations, thereby assessing guilt or innocence of those on trial;
  • act as guardians of the law, taking responsibility for applying its rules without fear or favour, as well as securing the liberties of the person and ensuring that governments and peoples comply with the 'spirit' of the constitution.

A key function of the judiciary is that concerning **judicial review**, to which we now turn.

Judicial review

Under the doctrine of judicial review, the courts are granted the power to interpret the constitution and to declare void actions of other branches of government if they are found to breach the document. As explained by Stone, in reference to the situation in the United States, it is 'the power of any judge of any court, in any case at any time, at the behest of any litigant party, to declare a law unconstitutional'.[2] Constitutional issues can therefore be raised at any point in the ordinary judicial system, although it is the Supreme Court which arbitrates in any matter which has broad significance.

> **judicial review**
> The power of any court to refuse to enforce a law or official act based on law, because in the view of the judges it conflicts with the Constitution.

Judicial review is particularly important in federal systems to ensure that each layer of government keeps to its respective sphere. The function was not written into the American Constitution, but the ruling of the Supreme Court in the case of *Marbury v Madison* in 1803 pointed to the key role of the Court in determining the meaning of the Constitution. In the United States some of the measures of Roosevelt's New Deal thus fell foul of the Supreme Court, as did Truman's seizure of the steel mills in 1952 to prevent a strike. In exercising its power of review, the Court normally decides on the basis of precedent (*stare decisis* – stand by decisions made), but on occasion it has spectacularly reversed a previous decision and thus enabled the Court to adapt to changing situations and give a lead. The judgement in *Plessy v Ferguson* (1896), which allowed for segregation on the basis that separate facilities were not necessarily unequal was reversed in the *Brown v Board of Education (Topeka, Kansas)* ruling (1954), when it was decided that such facilities were 'inherently unequal'. The case referred to public education, but campaigners rightly saw its wider implications.

The doctrine applies in many countries ranging from Austria and Ireland to Germany and India, as well as in a number of South American states. Normally, it is a duty placed upon special constitutional courts created for this purpose, whereas in the United States review is conducted by regular courts. The German Federal Constitutional Court is the nearest equivalent to the US Supreme Court. It has extensive powers of judicial review which were introduced with the specific intention of ensuring that never again would an extremist party such as the Nazis be allowed to gain office by means which were seemingly constitutional and legitimate.

Judicial review in Britain

In America, the Supreme Court interprets not only the law, but also the Constitution. Britain has no provision for judicial review. No court can declare unconstitutional any law that has been lawfully passed by the British Parliament, which is the sovereign law-making body, a principle that has never been challenged. In the absence of a written constitution, there is – as Heywood points out – 'no legal standard against which to measure the constitutionality of political acts and government decisions'.[3] What it does have is what the same writer refers to as 'a more modest form of judicial review, found in uncodified systems', which allows for the review of executive actions, deciding whether the executive has acted *ultra vires* (beyond its powers).

In the last two or three decades, the influence of Europe upon British politics has increased and this has made inroads into parliamentary sovereignty, requiring judges to view European as superior to British law. The habit of challenging legislation has developed, so that there is now something of a tradition of **judicial activism**, in which ministers as well as civil servants and local authorities are found to have acted unconstitutionally and exceeded their powers.

> **judicial activism**
> The view that the courts should be a co-equal branch of government, and act as active partners in shaping government policy – especially in sensitive cases, such as those dealing with abortion and desegregation. Supporters tend to be more interested in justice, 'doing the right thing', than in the exact letter of the text. They see the courts as having a role to look after the groups with little political influence, such as the poor and minorities.

British judges began to assume a growing political significance in the 1980s, and were more than willing to issue judgements which were highly critical of government ministers and declared their actions unlawful. This trend was in part a response to increasing anxiety about the misuse of executive power, but it also reflected a developing interest in the area of human rights. For instance, as Home Secretary, Kenneth Baker was found to be in contempt of court following the deportation of an immigrant which was carried out without the correct procedure being followed. Between 1992 and 1996, his successor,

Michael Howard, was defeated on ten occasions in the courts, and as we shall see his policies aroused strong hostility from some members of the Bench.

In both Britain and America, there is provision for decisions of the courts to be overridden. In Britain, this requires only the passage of an Act of Parliament, although in cases involving law emanating from the European Union this takes precedence over British law and cannot be so changed. In America, on many issues Congress can pass a law to deal with court decisions it dislikes and ensure that future rulings are different. If the matter is a constitutional one, as we have seen in chapter two (pp. 39–40), the arrangements for amending the Constitution are more complicated.

The independence of the judiciary

Courts should be independent, but from whom? It is generally acknowledged at least in theory that they should be subject to no political pressure from the political leaders of the day, but independence may mean more than this. It may imply freedom from what Blondel refers to as the 'norms of the political and social system itself'.[4] In other words, judges operate within the context of the principles on which the society is based, so that they are separate rather than fully independent of the government. In reality, they tend to act in defence of the existing social order rather than as 'independent bodies striving for justice or equity'.

The degree of independence of judges from political interference varies from country to country, and even within a single country's history. When judicial officers displease the ruling group, they can be ignored, removed or even eliminated. In some cases, under particular regimes, the pressure has been overt. Judges might be wary of handing out judgements which are seen as damaging to the interests of those who rule. In the 1970s, the Argentinian dictatorship took a strong line against 'difficult' judges. More than 150 were said to have disappeared, the allegation being that ministers ordered their execution. More commonly, pressure is of a more subtle and indirect character.

The independence of the judiciary is dependent on the existence of certain conditions.

The selection of judges

Their appointment should not ideally be influenced by political considerations or personal views. In practice, there are two methods of selection: appointment, as is practised in most countries (especially for senior judges – the American Supreme Court, for example), or election, as is the means by which most American state judges are chosen. Appointments may also be made on the basis of co-option by existing judges.

As a means of choosing judges, appointment has built-in dangers, namely:

- that it becomes a means of rewarding relatives and friends (nepotism); and
- that people might be chosen not according to their judicial merit but rather on account of their political persuasions and known views on public affairs such as the appropriate scope of state intervention in economic and social life (partisanship).

Election may have the advantage of producing a judiciary which is more representative of the voters and therefore responsive to prevailing feelings, but it carries no guarantee of technical competence. Moreover, those elected may feel unduly beholden to those who nominated them as candidates or to the majority of voters who favoured them.

It does not follow that because judges are appointed for political reasons they will necessary act in the way that those who choose them predict. Several appointees to the US Supreme Court have exhibited a remarkable degree of independence when on the Bench, most notably **Chief Justice Earl Warren**. Appointed by the conservative Dwight Eisenhower, he presided over a remarkable series of liberal decisions, and the Court in his era became a pace-setter in the area of advancing civil rights, much to the surprise and dismay of the President. In the same way, the Nixon appointee Chief Justice Warren Burger was a disappointment to the President. It was Burger's Court which insisted in 1974 that the Nixon White House handed over the damaging tapes in the Watergate controversy.

The appointment of British judges is less overtly partisan than in America. Appointments are made by the Lord Chancellor, who will consult the Prime Minister when dealing with the most senior posts. This provides an opportunity to favour those who broadly share his views, but in practice the pool of barristers from whom the choice is made tend to be of a similar background and type. Many of those selected have, at some time, had to pass examinations in order to demonstrate their abilities, before they are even allowed to be considered for service as judges.

> **Earl Warren**
>
> A Republican from California who served as Governor, 1943–53 and stood as the unsuccessful vice-presidential candidate in 1948. He served as the Chief Justice of the US Supreme Court between 1953 and 1968, presiding at a time when controversial decisions were made on desegregation, the rights of criminal defendants and support for press freedom.

The security of tenure of judges

Once installed in office, judges should hold their office for a reasonable period, subject to their good conduct. Their promotion or otherwise may be determined by members of the government of the day, but they should be allowed to continue to serve even if they are unable to advance. They should not be liable to removal on the whim of particular governments or individuals. Judges may in some countries serve a fixed term of office.

US Supreme Court judges normally serve for a very long period, their appointment being initially made for their life even if they decide to retire after several years of service. Although theoretically they may be removed by impeachment before Congress if they commit serious offences, this provision has never successfully been employed. In Britain, judges are hard to remove, and those who function in superior courts are only liable to dismissal on grounds of misbehaviour, and this only after a vote of both Houses of Parliament.

Judges are politically neutral

Judges are expected to be impartial, and not vulnerable to political influence and pressure. They need to be beyond party politics, and committed to the pursuit of justice. As we see below, individual judges interpret their role differently.

The independence of judges in practice

In many countries, judges are able to work independently and without fear of undue and improper interference. This is true of some communist or other authoritarian regimes, as well as of liberal democracies. Once appointed, judges have a habit of donning the clothing of judicial fairness, and even when there are insidious pressures they can be singularly resistant and willing to offend the ruling administration. In India, in the 1970s, the increasingly autocratic Mrs Gandhi ran into trouble with the courts. They were willing to cause offence by deciding against the government on key issues. She was actually found guilty of electoral malpractice and disqualified from holding office for five years, though the disqualification was later suspended on appeal. Within days there was a declaration of a state of emergency in which the Prime Minister was able to order mass arrests and impose strict censorship. Thereafter, even when emergency rule was lifted, the challenge to the government from the judiciary was never again so overt.

In several Latin American states, especially those functioning under civilian rule, judges are noted for taking a strongly liberal and independent line which is displeasing to those who exercise political power. In Zimbabwe, the courts have often showed a willingness to offend the ruling Mugabe regime by producing judgements which conflict with the aims of the regime.

The background of judges

A more subtle threat to the notion of judicial independence derives from the social background of judges. In many liberal democracies the type of person appointed to the Bench tends to be middle class and better-off, and as such they are not fully representative of the society in which they operate.

Judges are often seen as conservative in their approach, and as possessing an innate caution and a preference for order in society. This may make them unsympathetic to minorities, especially strident ones, and hostile to ideas of social progress. Militant demonstrators have often received harsh words and stiff punishments from judges who dislike the causes and methods with which strikers and others are associated. Similarly, legislation which seeks to broaden the scope of governmental action may fall foul of the judiciary. This happened in the United States during the Roosevelt presidency, when key parts of the New Deal were struck down.

The backgrounds of British and American judges

In Britain, judges have been drawn from a narrow social base and are often criticised for being out-of-touch with the lives of the majority of the population. They tend to derive from the professional middle classes, often having been educated privately and then at Oxbridge. They tend to be white, wealthy, conservative in their outlook and are therefore often portrayed by critics as elitist. Of particular concern to some people is the lack of female, and ethnic-minority judges on the Appeal or High Court, and their serious under-representation on the Circuit Bench where in 1995 there were 28 and 4 respectively.

A judge's generally privileged background does not necessarily make him or her biased or unsympathetic in outlook. However, critics would claim that the nature of their training and the character of the job they undertake tends to give them a preference for traditional standards of behaviour, a respect for family and property, an emphasis on the importance of maintaining order and a distaste for minorities (especially if they are militant in their approach to seeking justice for their cause).

Much of the Labour concern in the past about the idea of a British Bill of Rights or incorporation of the European Convention into British law has been based on anxieties about passing power from elected politicians to unelected, unaccountable and often right-wing judges. Labour suspicion did not rest purely on the grounds of their background. It was much influenced by a series of unfavourable verdicts from which the labour movement has suffered in the nineteenth and twentieth centuries in the courts. Throughout much of its history, many in the party and in the unions have felt that their cause has suffered from the decisions made by those on the Bench, particularly in the area of industrial relations.

Labour now appears to have overcome its suspicions about the judiciary, for in office it has incorporated the Convention as a step in the direction of providing people with a Bill of Rights. However, there are still those who question the wisdom of passing policy decisions and the resolution of any conflicts of social and political values over to the judges. JA Griffiths has spoken for such critics, suggesting that judges have a particular view of the national interest, and that in issues where there is a dispute between the state and citizen they are more than likely to side with the Executive than with striking miners, militant unions, leak-prone civil servants or minority activists. He has claimed that they have a poor record in upholding specifically civil libertarian legislation, and that in particular they have tended to minimise the effects of the Race Relations Acts by adopting a narrow and unhelpful interpretation of statutes. He suggests that

> they define the public interest, inevitably from the viewpoint of their own class . . . Those values are the maintenance of law and order, the protection of private property, the containment of the trade union movement and the continuance of governments which conduct their business largely in private and on the advice of what I have called the governing group.[5]

In the United States, all federal judges and Supreme Court justices are appointed by the President. The typical Supreme Court justice has generally been white, Protestant, well-off and of high social status, although there were two female and one African-American members of the Supreme Court at the turn of the twenty-first century. In the lower federal courts, middle class appointees are common, but there has been an attempt by recent Presidents to appoint more women and members of ethnic minority groups. Bill Clinton appointed more than 200 judges in his first term and their composition was notably diverse: 31 per cent were women, 19 per cent were African-American and 7 per cent Hispanic. In general, he leaned towards the appointment of moderate, centrist judges whose nomination would not create difficulties in the Senate.

Much media interest centres on the nominations for judicial office made by modern Presidents. In the 2000 election campaign, commentators speculated on the differing approaches to nomination which George Bush jnr and Al Gore might adopt. It was realised that the impact of a Bush or Gore presidency on abortion rights and other controversial issues could be considerable, if a vacancy arose on the Supreme Court. Since January 2001, the new President has shown signs of seeking to adjust the composition of the judiciary in a more conservative way. In so doing, he has taken advice from the Federalist Society for Law and Public Policy which was formed in the early 1980s. Its members draw inspiration from James Madison, one of the Founding Fathers, who on occasion railed against the power of central government. Members played an influential role in the impeachment proceedings against President Clinton and in the Florida legal offensive which brought Bush to power in 2001. They are trying to steer the judiciary away from the liberalism of the past and as a means of fulfilling this agenda they seek out ideologically acceptable candidates who might become suitable judges. Most members of George W. Bush's vetting panel for nominees belong to the organisation.

The political involvement of judges in Britain and America

Alexis de Tocqueville noted that 'hardly any question arises in the United States that is not resolved sooner or later into a judicial question'. He was certainly correct, although he could not have anticipated the extent to which the Supreme Court (the highest judicial body) in particular would become involved in controversial decisions. Much of the work of the Court is related to social and political matters that have a direct impact on everyday life – for instance, whether an abortion should be performed, convicted murderers executed or minimum working standards be imposed.

In America, the Supreme Court is clearly a political as well as a judicial institution. In applying the Constitution and laws to the cases which come before it, the justices are involved in making political choices on controversial aspects of national policy. The procedures are legal, and the decisions are phrased in language appropriate for legal experts. But to view the Court solely as a legal institution would be to ignore its key political role. A Chief Justice Hughes once put it: 'We are under the Constitution, but the Constitution is what the judges say it is'.

In interpreting the Constitution, the nine justices must operate within the prevailing political climate. They are aware of popular feelings as expressed in elements of the media and in election results. They know that their judgements need to command consent, and that their influence ultimately rests on acceptance by

> **judicial restraint**
> The idea that the courts should not seek to impose their views on other branches of government, except in extreme cases. Supporters of this view are 'constructionists', those who want the courts to limit themselves to implementing legislative and executive intentions. They want a passive role for the courts.

people and politicians. This means that the opinions expressed on the bench tend to be in line with the thinking of key players in the executive and legislative branches, over a period of time.

Judicial activism or judicial restraint?

The question of how to use its judicial power has long exercised the American Court, and different opinions have been held by those who preside over it. Some have urged an activist Court, whilst others err on the side of **judicial restraint**. The latter is the notion that the Court should not seek to impose its views on other branches of government or on the states unless there is a clear violation of the Constitution. This implies a passive role, so some justices have urged that they should avoid conflict, and that one way of doing so is to leave issues of social improvement to the appropriate parts of the federal and state government. Advocates of this position have felt that it would be unwise and wrong to dive into the midst of political battles, even to support policies they might personally favour. Anthony Kennedy is a member of the Rehnquist Court (1986–) who has taken this view, asking: '. . . Was I appointed for life to go around answering . . . great questions and suggesting answers to Congress?' He has provided his own answer: 'That's not our function . . . it's very dangerous for people who are not elected, who have lifetime positions, to begin taking public stances on issues that political branches of government must wrestle with'.

By contrast, judicial activists argue that the Court should be a key player in shaping policy, an active partner working alongside the other branches. Such a conception means that the justices move beyond acting as umpires in the political game, and become creative participants. An exponent of judicial activism was Chief Justice Earl Warren. As we have seen, his court was known for a series of liberal judgements on matters ranging from school desegregation to the rights of criminals. In his era, decisions were made which boldly and broadly changed national policy. So active was his court that members of rightwing groups posted billboards around the country carrying the message 'Impeach Earl Warren'. In some respects the Burger Court which followed (1969–86) was less liberal in its approach, although it confirmed many decisions of the Warren Court and was responsible for a series of bold judgements, including *Roe v Wade* on abortion and support for affirmative action programmes. In such cases, critics argued that the judges were making policy decisions which were the responsibility of elected officials.

The present Rehnquist Court was always expected to be more conservative and it soon began to chip away at liberal decisions on abortion and affirmative action. The majority of its members do not see it as their task to act as the guardian of individual liberties and civil rights for minority groups. It has handled fewer cases than previous courts each term and struck down fewer federal and state laws. Biskupic has commented on these trends: 'Gone is the self-consciously loud voice the Court once spoke with, boldly stating its position and calling upon the people and other institutions of government to follow'.[6]

Yet this view of the Rehnquist Court and its alleged judicial restraint has been questioned. Its greater ideological conservatism is generally accepted, although its record on civil liberties is more mixed than the term might imply. Some commentators have suggested that it has been highly activist in its willingness to challenge the elected branches of government. Rosen is an exponent of such thinking. Comparing the Warren and Rehnquist eras, he argues that both courts were committed to an increase in judicial power: 'Both combine haughty declarations of judicial supremacy with contempt for the competing views of the political branches'.[7] Others too have observed that for all of the lip service paid to judicial self-restraint, 'most of the current justices appear entirely comfortable intervening in all manner of issues, challenging state as well as national power, and underscoring the Court's role as final arbiter of constitutional issues'.[8]

Growing judicial activism in Britain

In recent years a new breed of judges has begun to emerge. The number of applications for judicial review in Britain has increased sharply, and judges have been markedly more willing to enter the political arena by declaring government policy invalid. Few governments have been subjected to more scrutiny in the courts than those of the Conservatives between 1979 and 1997. In addition, several eminent judges argued publicly for the incorporation of the European Convention on Human Rights into British law, a goal achieved by the passage of the Human Rights Act 1998 which gives judges the opportunity to make judgements based on cases brought under the European document.

Leading judicial figures were also willing to challenge Home Secretary Michael Howard over his policy on sentencing. Many of them disliked the way in which he was laying down rigid guidelines which limited their freedom to pass the sentences which they felt to be appropriate. His successors, Jack Straw and David Blunkett, have also fallen foul of eminent members of the judiciary who, among other things, have criticised ministers for the inroads proposed into jury trial, the limitations of the Freedom of Information Act (2000), the increased use of and conditions in prisons, and stringent rules for asylum seekers who make welfare claims. It seems to be a strange turn-around that appointed liberal judges are willing to take on elected politicians, commanding much sympathy in the media in so doing.

The scope for judicial creativity in policy-making is limited by the way in which British legislation is drafted in considerable detail. Judges are supposed to content themselves with interpreting the law rather than with helping to develop it. In many parts of Europe, there is more opportunity for judges to take a hand in making the law, as laws passed do not cater for all contingencies; judges need to think about the intention behind legislation. Where there exists a written constitution and where legislation is framed in broad phraseology, there is considerable scope for judicial activism. Judges are required to fill in the gaps in laws so that their policy-making role is well established. French judges are frequently required to make laws, the effect of their decisions being not only to clarify but also to reinforce and reshape the law.

Judicial activism is a feature often commented upon by British critics of the European Court of Justice. Euro-sceptics dislike the way in which the decisions of the court have taken the Union ever further down the federal route. The justices have indeed at times been instruments of integration, and this policy-developing role is one unfamiliar to British observers until recent years. There has traditionally been a differing approach between continental judges and their British counterparts in the execution of their task. Continental judges adopt a more policy-orientated attitude. They tend to interpret the law in the light of what they see as its intentions and thus shape the law in a particular direction. In Britain, judges have in the past taken a more conservative stance and confined themselves to strict interpretation of what the law says, although this attitude is changing.

With the passage of the Human Rights Act, there is the prospect of a politicisation of the judiciary in Britain which could become embroiled in the political arena as judges seek to decide on the interpretation and/or validity of a particular piece of legislation. In the words of an opponent of the move, Lord Lloyd, 'To try to bring the judiciary into this sort of contest can only have one effect and that is to destroy the standing of the judiciary in the eyes of the people as a whole.'[9]

Judicial activism has a longer history in America than in Britain. Its written constitution, federal system, traditional of judicial independence, preference for limited government and ease of access to the courts all point in this direction. As Hague and Harrop explain: 'The United States is founded on a constitutional contract and an army of lawyers will forever quibble over the terms'.[10]

Conclusion

As a broad trend, the role of judges in the political system has increased in liberal democracies but also even in authoritarian societies. Fifty years ago, politicians paid relatively little attention to decisions of the courts. Since then, judges have been more willing to enter into areas that would once have been left to national governments and parliaments, striking down laws and regulations passed by those elected to public office. The process has been aided by the increased use of international conventions in the postwar world. There has also been a proliferation of international or transnational courts to enforce them, ranging from the European Court of Human Rights to the European Court of Justice, from the World Trade Organization panels to the North American Free Trade Agreement panels. They test national law against some other body of law, usually treated as being superior. In some cases, these agreements or conventions have involved members of the Bench in any member country ruling against the decisions of the party in power.

The judiciaries of Britain and the United States: a summary		
	Britain	*The United States*
Liberal democracies, based on rule of law?	Liberal democracy, based on rule of law.	Liberal democracy, based on rule of law.
Approach to judicial review	Modest form of judicial review of executive actions.	Strong version of judicial review, courts able to strike down laws or other official acts as 'unconstitutional'.
Selection of judges	Judicial appointments made by Lord Chancellor's office.	President appoints Supreme Court justices and federal judges (election of judges in state judicial systems).
Security of judges	Judges very hard to remove.	Appointments normally made for life, though in theory possibility of impeachment.
Background of judges	Chosen from narrow social base, often seen as white, male and middle class, and deeply conservative. Few women and ethnic minority members on Bench.	Presidential appointees vary, Democrat Presidents more likely to appoint women and members of ethnic minorities – e.g. Clinton's willingness to diversify composition.
Judicial activism v judicial restraint?	Judges traditionally confined themselves to interpretation of law, shunned political involvement or controversy. Influenced by European experience, many now more willing to take on ministers, criticising their policies and reviewing their actions.	Republican Presidents tend to prefer judges who adopt a more passive approach to their role and seek only to interpret the Constitution. Many Democrats favour judges who take a more activist approach and who see courts as having a key role in shaping policy.

Other factors are involved in the 'judicialisation' of politics. Among them, Richard Hodder-Williams has mentioned:

1 'the failure of the political process to meet the aspirations of those who are governed under it and with the rise of the administrative state and a bevy of bureaucracies the decisions of which affect so much of so many people's lives';

2 the rise of 'a more educated, more challenging electorate that is less deferential to government in all its forms and is more aware of deficiencies through a lively, and often vulgar, press';

3 the development of 'an ideological shift throughout Europe, which has enhanced the status of rights-based demands and has redefined a substantial part of what politics is about, away from struggles between classes and religious groups towards conflict between the coercive powers of the state and the individual';

4 the influence of particular and influential individuals 'like Lord Denning in Britain and Earl Warren in the United States, who had the strength of character and self-belief to challenge the old orthodoxies and help usher in new values and expectations'.[11]

Some fear that this political involvement has gone too far, and that judges are too often noticed by politicians. The Florida Supreme Court and the Supreme Court in Washington are even involved in deciding who shall be the President of the United States. They feel that there are dangers for the standing of judges if this process is unchecked. Others worry less about the damage which may be done to the judges' reputations, but instead place their emphasis upon fear of judicial power. They are concerned that judges are unrepresentative and argue for a reformed judiciary. Lord Lloyd, speaking from a very different perspective, is less concerned about the backgrounds from which judges are chosen, their competence or their capriciousness in adjudication. For him, Parliament – comprising the elected MPs – should decide on whether abortion or capital punishment is permissible, and what the age of consent should be: 'The fact of the matter…is that the law cannot be a substitute for politics. The political decisions must be taken by politicians. In a society like ours, that means by people who are removable.'[12]

REFERENCES

1 J. Blondel, *Comparative Government: An Introduction*, Prentice Hall, 1995.
2 A. Stone, 'Governing with judges: the new constitutionalism' in J. Hayward and A. Page (eds) *Governing the New Europe*, 1995.
3 A. Heywood, *Politics*, Macmillan, 1997.
4 As note 1 above.
5 J. Griffiths, *The Politics of the Judiciary*, Fontana, 1991.
6 J. Biskupic, 'The Rehnquist Court: Justices want to be known as Jurists, not Activists', *Washington Post*, 9 January 2000.
7 J. Rosen, 'Pride and prejudice', *New Republic*, 10/17 July 2000.
8 T. Yarborrough, 'The Supreme Court and the Constitution' in G. Peele *et al.*, *Developments in American Politics (4)*, Palgrave, 2002.

9   Lord Lloyd, as quoted in P Norton, ' A Bill of Rights: The Case Against', *Talking Politics*, summer 1993.
10 R. Hague and M. Harrop, *Comparative Government and Politics: An Introduction*, Palgrave, 2001.
11 R. Hodder-Williams, *Judges and Politics in the Contemporary Age*, Bowerdean, 1996.
12 As note 6 above.

USEFUL WEB SITES

For the UK

www.lcd.gov.uk Lord Chancellor's departmental site. Information relating to judicial appointments.

For the USA

www.supremecourtus.gov The official web site of the Supreme Court, providing background information about the Court's history, mode of operation and calendar.

www.uscourts.gov Federal judiciary home page. Comprehensive guide to federal court system, with court statistics, answers to frequently asked questions etc.

www.law.cornell.edu/supct Cornell Law School. Provides a diverse array of legal sources and full text of Supreme Court judgements.

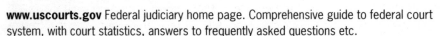

SAMPLE QUESTIONS

1   Discuss the view that an independent judiciary is essential in order to protect the rights of the people.

2   How are senior judges recruited in Britain and the United States? Do and should they reflect certain interests?

3   Compare the political significance of judges in the United States and the United Kingdom.

4   'Legislatures may make laws by passing statutes, but judges have to apply them in particular situations'. To what extent do judges in Britain and the United States make the law?

5   In what ways do judges act as law-makers? Should they?

6   Is judicial activism necessary because some issues are too difficult and contentious for the political branches of government to be able to resolve?

7   To what extent is the judiciary a powerful factor in politics on either side of the Atlantic?

Governance beyond the centre

7

Even the most authoritarian government would find it difficult to take all decisions at the centre. Leaving aside any considerations of the desirability of decentralising decision-making, it would be impractical for any set of ministers to understand the needs of every area and to involve themselves in the minutiae of detail concerning its public administration. Governments recognise the need to allow some scope for regional or local initiative.

Britain has a unitary system in which legal sovereignty lies entirely at the centre, whereas the United States has a federal structure in which there are what Hague and Harrop refer to as 'multiple layers of governance'.[1]

In this chapter, we examine sub-national government (those bodies which cover only a part of the country) and its relationship to the centre. Sub-national governments take many forms. We are concentrating on devolution in Britain and on the Washington–state relationship in America, noting the differences between the two forms of government and the trends within them. Broadly, Britain has made some moves to decentralisation, and America – always a markedly more decentralised country – has a stronger centre than was ever intended by the Founding Fathers, although the emphasis in recent years has been on greater partnership between Washington and the state capitals.

POINTS TO CONSIDER

➤ What are the differences between federalism and devolution?

➤ 'Britain is moving towards federalism and the United States is more centralised than the Founding Fathers ever intended'. How true is this?

➤ Why has power generally shifted towards the centre in liberal democracies?

➤ Is the national government in Britain and the United States too weak or too dominant?

➤ For Britain, which is the most suitable: devolution or federalism? Could federalism work in Britain?

➤ Does local government perform an important role in Britain and the United States today?

➤ Assess the strengths and weaknesses of unitary and federal forms of government.

In those countries where the bulk of decisions taken by public bodies are made at the centre, the country is said to be centralised. Where the proportion is small to very small, the country is said to be decentralised. However, in practice, it is less easy to measure the degree of **decentralisation** than this summary suggests, and opinions tend to be impressionistic. To complicate the situation even more, some countries have deliberately opted for a form of state organisation which is federal. Federalism is often regarded as being the answer in those countries where it is desirable to balance unity against diversity, in that it caters for national and local requirements.

> **decentralisation**
>
> The process of transferring responsibilities and powers from national bodies to more local ones.

It may seem to provide the very essence of decentralisation, yet in reality the experience of federal countries shows that there almost as many federalisms as there are federal states. As Blondel points out:

> Since it has many 'faces', federalism is but one of the formulas which can bring about decentralisation. There are other formulas, such as confederacies or supra-national arrangements, in the context of unions of states, and regionalism or semi-autonomous local authorities, in the context of single states.[2]

The degree of centralisation or decentralisation in any state is often related to its history, so that the French and the Japanese have been long familiar with centralised control, as have many South and Central American peoples. By contrast, the North Americans and the Germans (with the exception of the interwar era) are more used to decentralisation. In Britain too, no ruler was ever able to ensure that key decisions were always taken in the capital. There has been a long tradition of local government, and in the localities many imaginative municipal enterprises were once initiated. Yet Britain, along with some other countries, has in the postwar era often been said to have excessively centralised administration. Labour in opposition tended to repeat the allegation, and since 1997 has embarked on some policies designed to lessen central control. Indeed, in most Western countries there has been pressure for decentralisation in recent years, and the changes in Spanish administration are but one example of this trend.

At this point, some definitions are necessary, in order that we may more easily categorise the various countries under consideration.

Types of governmental systems

Bullman has provided a typology of European states, in which he distinguishes four main categories.[3]

1 **classic unitary:** local government exists, but no regional structure other than for centrally-controlled administrative purposes (e.g. Greece, Ireland and Luxembourg);

2 **devolving unitary**: local government exists and there is some elected regional machinery with a degree of – but not necessarily uniform – **autonomy** (e.g. Finland, France and the United Kingdom);

3 **Regionalised**: a directly elected tier of regional government with significant legislative powers (e.g. Italy and Spain);

4 **Federal states**: powers are shared according to the Constitution and the regional/state tier cannot be abolished by central government (e.g.Austria, Belgium, Germany and the United States).

Such distinctions reflect the differing structures which have emerged in recent years, given the pressures for regionalisation. However, the basic distinction is that between unitary and federal countries, with confederalism being a weaker, looser variety of federalism.

In **unitary states**, all legal power flows from one source: for example Parliament in the United Kingdom, the Chamber of Deputies in France, the Knesset in Israel and the House of Representatives in Japan. Most European governments are of the unitary type. Power is concentrated in national government, and the operation of lower tiers of government derives not from a written constitution but from the centre. In Britain, local authorities exist but they do so at the behest of Westminster, and they are entirely subordinate to it. Some devolution of power is possible, but this does nothing to breach the idea that control derives from Parliament; local and devolved power can be revoked. Unitary systems normally exist in relatively homogeneous countries which lack significant ethnic, geographical, linguistic or religious distinctions.

> **autonomy**
> The right or state of self-government: literally self-rule, a situation allowing peoples to be governed according to their own preferences and laws.

Devolution involves the idea that there should be some redistribution of power away from the centre to subordinate assemblies which can, if necessary, still be overridden by the parent authority. It usually springs from dissatisfaction with centralised government when ministers appear to be unwilling to recognise local needs. Devolution does not mean that a country ceases to be a unitary state, for as Enoch Powell, a late constitutional traditionalist and rightwing MP, explained: 'Power devolved is power retained'.

> **devolution**
> The transfer of power in a unitary state from central government to subordinate elected bodies, without there being any sharing of legal sovereignty.

In **confederacies**, the regional authorities exercise much of the power, and central control is relatively weak. Historically, the best example of a confederacy was probably that found in the United States under the Articles of Confederation, but many years later the eleven southern states seceded from the Union in the American Civil War and they declared themselves to be a Confederacy. Switzerland today is often described as having confederal administration, its 26 cantons exercising much of the power in the country. At the international level, the Commonwealth of Independent States (CIS) formed out of the old Soviet Union in 1991, the United Nations, and the European Union as it has operated until recently can be seen as examples of states joining together for their mutual interest without ever relinquishing much control to a powerful central body. Elazar quotes the Azerbaijan President as dismissing the CIS in disdainful terms – 'a mere soap bubble . . . pretty on the surface but empty inside'.[4]

In **federal states**, legal sovereignty is shared between different tiers of government: a federal (central) government and regional governments (known as states in the USA and Länder in Germany). Under federalism, the states have guaranteed, protected spheres of responsibility, and the central government conducts those functions of major importance which require policy to be made for the whole country. Both tiers may act directly on the people, and each has some exclusive powers. Federalism thus diffuses political authority to prevent any undue concentration at one point, but lacks the very high degree of decentralisation which characterises a confederation. Under federalism, it is still likely that there will also be a system of local government, although it can vary significantly in form. In the USA, the federal government has little role in regulating the functioning of this tier, which falls under the direction of the states.

Broadly speaking, countries vast in size tend to have federal systems which decentralise the running of government and the administration of services. Some of the world's largest countries by population or area are federal, notably Australia, Brazil, Canada, Germany, India and the United States. Yet China and Indonesia are large unitary countries, and tiny Malaysia and Switzerland are federal in differing degrees. Today, there are 22 federations, covering some 40 per cent of the world's population.

Developments in the British unitary state: the move towards devolution

As we have seen, devolution involves the ceding of power by parliament to some new elected body. Bogdanor defines it as 'the transfer to a subordinate elected body, on a geographical basis, of functions at present exercised by ministers and Parliament'. As such, it differs from federalism which

> would divide, not devolve, supreme power from Westminster and various regional or provincial parliaments. In a federal state, the authority of the central or federal government and the provincial governments is co-ordinate and shared, the respective scope of the federal and provincial governments being defined by an enacted constitution . . . Devolution, by contrast, does not require the introduction of an enacted constitution.[5]

Until the 1970s, Labour had not seriously contemplated devolution. It was unmentioned in its 1974 (February) manifesto, but the shock-waves produced by the election of six Scottish National Party MPs (two in Labour seats) meant that the party could no longer afford to ignore the issue. The Wilson leadership was convinced that unless it conceded the need for devolution, the minority government would suffer further losses when the inevitable second election took place. The shift of opinion was originally therefore one of tactics rather than of principle, and it was not until party spokespersons began to prepare their manifesto for the October election that the case for change was couched in more democratic language.

The attempt to introduce devolved assemblies in the late 1970s was unsuccessful, but what had been a sometimes hesitant and uncertain commitment to the principle of devolution became a more developed and convincing one over the coming years. In the 1990s, Labour argued the case strongly that devolution was the only way to keep Scotland in the United Kingdom. It accepted that the Scots wanted far greater control over their own lives, and felt that ministers in London too often did not understand or care sufficiently about conditions north of the border. The Blair leadership took up the devolution theme, resting its case on firm democratic foundations. The truth of a remark by the nineteenth-century Liberal Prime Minister, Gladstone, was appreciated: 'Making power local, makes it more congenial'. Ministers certainly hoped that devolution would stave off the threat from the Scottish National Party (SNP), and ensure that the unity of the kingdom was preserved.

A Devolution Act for Scotland was on the statute book by 1998. First elections took place in 1999 and the Scottish Parliament began to function later that year. A watered-down version of devolution was made available to the people of Wales, who obtained an assembly rather than a Parliament with tax-varying powers. Finally, as a result of the Good Friday Agreement, a Northern Ireland Assembly is up-and-running in Northern Ireland. The three countries have therefore been singled out for special treatment, in comparison with England. Moves to go ahead with the regionalisation of England have been initiated, through the creation of indirectly elected Regional Chambers and government-appointed Regional Development Agencies, which might in time evolve into elected regional assemblies. The pattern of centralisation in British government is being slowly eroded.

The merits and difficulties of devolution

Devolution is widely seen as democratic, in that it allows people to express their distinctive identity and have a say in the development of the life of their own particular regions. It has the merit of countering the dangers of an overpowerful, excessively centralised state. Indeed, in celebrating the referendum

Devolution in practice: power in Edinburgh, Cardiff and Belfast

In May 1999, **Scotland** elected its first Parliament for 292 years. It has extensive legislative powers over areas such as criminal law, education, environment, health, judicial appointments, local government, police and transport, and has a tax-varying power of up to three pence in the pound on the level of national income tax. Several areas of policy are reserved to Westminster, among them defence, foreign policy, macro-economics and some existing Home Office responsibilities. Labour now governs Scotland as the leading partner in a coalition with the Liberal Democrats, the logical outcome of a devolution strategy evolved by both parties in the 1990s. Ministers espouse the language of cooperation rather than conflict, in recognition of the fact that politics north of the border have moved in an entirely new direction.

In **Wales**, the National Assembly has less responsibility and influence. It has secondary law-making powers, enabling it to fill in the details and expand upon legislation passed in London. (Under this delegated legislation, the Assembly could for instance define the content of the National Curriculum in Wales.) It can also make appointments to Welsh quangos, and has discretion over the 'Welsh block' of funding (enabling it to allocate some £7m between its various responsibilities). It cannot pass its own Acts (primary legislation) and has no tax-varying powers.

In **Northern Ireland**, the Assembly has powers in between those of Scotland and Wales. It can make primary legislation in a number of important areas – including education, economic development, environment, finance, health and social services – but has no tax-varying powers. It has been suspended on five occasions, because of the acute difficulties involved in power-sharing between the Unionists and Sinn Fein, especially over the controversial issue of decommissioning terrorist weapons.

victory which preceded the passage of the Bill, Tony Blair observed that 'the era of big centralised government is over'.

Opponents see devolution as fraught with danger, often claiming that although in the United Kingdom the sources of unity are much greater than the sources of diversity, once parts of the whole are allowed to enjoy a measure of self-government then there is a danger of the whole edifice splintering apart. Moreover, the Conservatives who resisted the Blairite proposals in the 1997 referendums in Scotland and Wales suggested that there was no real necessity for change, because unlike the situation in some other countries, the UK has not developed as a result of previously autonomous states coming together recently. They feared a 'Balkanisation' of the British Isles if parts were able to go their separate ways, because the Scottish Nationalists would not be satisfied with devolution which is a half-way house between unity and independence. The SNP is a separatist party, its long-term goal being national independence for Scotland. It would do its best to expose the flaws in devolution and this would fuel pressure for separation.

One of the difficulties of devolution which is often mentioned by its critics is the West Lothian (now more usually referred to as the English) Question: 'Why should Scottish MPs at Westminster be allowed to have a say on purely English matters while English MPs will no longer have a say on Scottish matters?' Such a dilemma would not arise under a federal system, for under federalism the division of functions is clear-cut. If ministers had opted for a system of elected regional councils for England, then each region (and Scotland and Wales) could have similar devolved powers, leaving the United Kingdom Parliament to deal with the residue of issues, those key ones affecting the four countries collectively. But as yet there is no widespread public demand for legislative devolution across the UK, and even if this were ever introduced it is doubtful whether the powers granted to regional bodies would ever be equal to those of the Scottish Parliament, so that statutory responsibility for English devolution would probably remain at Westminster.

The Question was never a source of contention when, prior to Direct Rule, Northern Ireland had its own parliament at Stormont while the province sent members to the House of Commons. (The situation arises again under the Good Friday Agreement which provides for an Assembly and an executive body.) However, logic does not always apply in these matters, and there is a possibility that English people might increasingly feel disadvantaged. They may come to resent the fact that an issue primarily relevant to England is being decided on the basis of Scottish votes in the House of Commons.

Bogdanor points out that the difficulties inherent in the West Lothian Question have been resolved – or at least accommodated – elsewhere without much difficulty. Devolution has proved perfectly feasible in countries such as Italy, Portugal and Spain. For instance, in Italy 15 out of 20 regions have no exclusive legislative powers, but the other 5 have wide responsibilities in economic and social affairs. In Spain, 7 out of 17 have greater autonomy than the others. But 'there is no West Sardinian Question nor any West Catalonian Question'.[6]

Be that as it may, the West Lothian Question does raise the issue of whether in a unitary state it is possible to devolve substantial powers which are denied to other regions. Many commentators might argue that in Britain there was little choice. It would have been politically unrealistic to deny recognition to the Scots whose wish for a change in their constitutional status had been so clearly stated in the elections between 1987 and 1997. If the price of meeting their aspirations was the creation of an anomaly, then this was a price which had to be paid. However, Bogdanor does go on to observe that

> devolution will alter the role of Westminster very radically, by introducing the spirit of federalism into its deliberations. Before devolution, every Member of Parliament was responsible for scrutinising both the domestic and the non-domestic affairs of

every part of the United Kingdom. After devolution, by contrast, MPs will normally play no role at all in legislating for the domestic affairs of Northern Ireland or Scotland, nor in scrutinising secondary legislation for Wales ... Westminster, from being a parliament for both the domestic and the non-domestic affairs of the whole of the United Kingdom, is transformed into a domestic parliament for England, part of a domestic parliament for Wales, and a federal parliament for Northern Ireland and Scotland. The West Lothian Question, then, draws attention to the fact that devolution will transform Westminster into the quasi-federal parliament of a quasi-federal state.[7]

Is Britain becoming a federal state?

Britain is a unitary state, but some of the changes in recent years to the pattern of government seem to indicate a move in a more federal direction. Devolution has been the British route to decentralisation, so that power remains theoretically in Westminster's hands although it is politically hard to imagine any administration in London seeking to recover control over areas which have been delegated to Edinburgh or Cardiff.

Northern Ireland had a devolved assembly in the days before Direct Rule, so that the relationship between London and Belfast was essentially federal in character, with certain functions allocated to the national level of government and the rest to the provincial one. The new assembly formed as a result of the Good Friday Agreement (1998) has similar powers, so that Northern Ireland, Scotland and Wales all have devolved administrations. At some point in the future, Regional Development Assemblies in some areas may well be accountable to elected regional assemblies rather than as at present to an indirectly elected forum of local councillors. This leaves open the possible emergence of a Spanish-type structure, in which the peoples of some parts of England have more control over their future than their counterparts in some areas of Spain.

The creation of the devolved assemblies, the possible development of democratic regional machinery and the arrival on the local scene of elected mayors who could in time become a kind of 'Mr London' or 'Ms Birmingham', are all indications of a less centralised structure of government than we have previously witnessed. This has led some writers to speculate on whether Britain is becoming more federal in character. In Britain, we might perhaps experience what Coxall and Robins envisage as: '[the development from] a unitary state to a mosaic of federal, devolved and joint authority relationships between core and periphery, with the English core becoming more decentralised as regional and urban identities find political expression.'[8]

When commentators speculate on moves towards a federal structure in Britain ('creeping federalism'), they do not usually imply a uniform division of power between Westminster and provincial units formally set out in a written document. Rather, they envisage a situation in which the policy of devolution is gradually applied to all parts of the United Kingdom, just as it is now applied to Scotland and Wales. Such a pattern is more akin to the model proposed by some Liberals in the late nineteenth century, a pattern then labelled as 'Home Rule All Round'. Bogdanor seeks to distinguish this from a strictly federal system, and refers to it instead as 'federal devolution'.[9]

The European dimension

Of course, another line of possible development is to imagine a more federal Britain as part of a federal Europe. The pioneers of post-war Europe who created the European Economic Community (now the European Union) always envisaged that their attempts at cooperation would take Europe towards some kind of 'United States of Europe'. British Conservatives have long feared the idea of a federal Europe, seeing this as a form of centralisation, involving the creation of some giant Euro super-state. The formal creation of such a 'monster' may be as yet a long way off, but they see moves to integration (such as 'Euro-land', with its single currency) as steps in that direction.

The British take a different view of federalism from most Europeans, who see federalism as decentralisation in practice. Whereas John Major was keen to insist on the notion of subsidiarity being written into the Maastricht agreement and sought to sell the Maastricht treaty as a decentralising measure to halt the drift of power to Brussels, several other European leaders were bemused, for they could also endorse subsidiarity. They view it as the very essence of federalism because it involves the idea that decisions should be taken at the lowest level of government possible. As the Treaty puts it in article 3b:

> In areas which do not fall within its exclusive competence, the Community shall take action, in accordance with the principle of subsidiarity, only if and in so far as the objectives for the proposed action cannot be sufficiently achieved by the Member states and can therefore, by reason of the scale or effects of the proposed action, be better achieved by the Community. Any action by the Community shall not go beyond what is necessary to achieve the objectives of this Treaty.

The creation of devolved assemblies in Britain is therefore the logical outcome of accepting subsidiarity in Europe. It is hard to see how one can argue the case for government at the lowest possible level in the EU, whilst not being willing to concede that the Scots, Welsh and Northern Irish should be able to benefit from the same degree of local control.

What has been happening in Europe since the 1980s is that the pressure for decentralisation or the strengthening of existing regional machinery within countries is coinciding with a developing move to closer integration of national states within the EU in the last two decades. On the one hand, there is more recognition of local or regional diversity, on the other a desire to bring about a more effective Union in which more policies are carried out on a common basis.

A note on quangos

Quasi Autonomous Non-Governmental Organisations (quangos) are so named because they are established by ministers and funded from the public purse, but yet have an independence of action usually denied to officials in the bureaucracy. Examples include the BBC, one of the oldest quangos, and a variety of other authorities such as the Charity Commission, the Tourist Boards and the Welsh Development Agency.

Quangos have been a growth area since the 1980s. Although the Conservatives had committed themselves to curbing the growth of such non-elected bodies in 1979, their numbers grew rapidly, according to several analyses. The definition of quangos varies, but if the term includes the recently created Executive Agencies (part of the *Next Steps* programme), Health Service Trusts, opted out-schools and hospitals and Training and Enterprise Councils (TECs), then the opposition attacks based on 'the number's game' were justified. In any case, the reasons for criticism were wider than their alleged growth. Critics disliked the way in which those appointed to quangos were usually men connected with or sympathetic to the Conservative Party, or – in some cases – wives of Conservative MPs. They were seen as being unaccountable to the general public.

The first Nolan Report (1995) was concerned about appointments to quangos, and wanted to ensure that in future they were based solely on merit. Sensing an easy target, Labour went further and condemned them as a symptom of an excessively centralised and undemocratic – even corrupt – state. It promised that it would democratise rather than dismantle the quangocracy at an early stage in any new administration it formed. As yet progress has been modest. Some quangos have disappeared as a result of the introduction of devolved assemblies, but in the main Labour ministers appear to have accepted that these non-elected bodies can actually serve rather than threaten the communities in which they operate. What is necessary, in their eyes, is to ensure that appointments to such powerful organisations are made only after a thorough investigation. Yet again, there have been suggestions that appointments to some Health Service Trusts have been made on an overtly political basis.

Developments in American federalism

In its early days, the USA operated a system of **dual federalism** as laid down in the Constitution. Sometimes known as layer-cake federalism, the model presupposed a clear division of responsibilities between the central and state governments. James Bryce summed it up as: 'two governments covering the same ground yet distinct and separate in their action'.[10] The system prevailed until the 1930s, although from the early days it was apparent that various factors were leading towards an accretion of central influence and control. These were:

- **Constitutional amendments:** e.g. the 14th Amendment gave 'equal protection 'of the law to all citizens, and the 16th allowed the federal government to raise money via income tax. The 16th considerably broadened the financial base of the federal government, providing the funds for the third factor, below.

- **Decisions of the Supreme Court:** e.g. the Inter-state Commerce Clause allowed Congress to regulate trade 'among the several states'.
- **The financial relationship:** e.g. the demands for more education, health and welfare proved onerous for the states, and the federal government stepped in with more financial aid. The dependence of the states on federal financial resources to support their services has inevitably coloured the relationship.

When Franklin Roosevelt introduced his New Deal for Americans at a time of deep economic depression, the programme of interventionist economic and social changes led to an increase in governmental action. The new model was known as **cooperative or concurrent federalism**, a system in which both parts, federal and state, worked together to resolve the nation's difficulties.

Some strings were attached to the **grants-in-aid**, although states retained considerable discretion on how money was to be spent. The federal government was more concerned to supplement, stimulate and assist states than to pre-empt them, as they sought to handle pressing economic and social problems.

> **grants-in-aid**
> Transfers of money from federal government to states and localities, in order to finance state policies and programmes.

This was not true of the experience of the 1960s, for in the years of President Johnson's Great Society programme a new, more active version of **creative federalism** emerged, in which the motivation was political rather than economic or social. Washington set out to insist on certain uniform standards, so that there were measures to ensure an end to discrimination in education, employment and housing. By the end of that decade, this variety was sometimes called **coercive federalism**, for as Kincaid puts it there was 'unprecedented federal reliance on conditions of aid, pre-emptions of state and local authority, mandates, court orders, and other devices intended to ensure state and local compliance with federal policies'.[11] Another label was **redistributive centralism**, again a recognition of the way in which Washington was insisting on bringing about changes in the nature of state policies. This creative or coercive form survived the attempt by President Nixon after 1969 to return power to the states. It survived in part because Congress and many state governments remained under Democratic control throughout the period.

Nixon may not have had much success in implementing his desire to see states assume more responsibilities and powers, but he firmly believed in what he called the **New Federalism**. In the Nixon years there was a new emphasis on **block** instead of **categorical grants**, so that states were more free to decide how to spend their money. His primary concern was not essentially to curtail the amount of money which reached the localities, but to determine how it got to them.

The next Republican President, Ronald Reagan, had more success. His wish to see a change of direction in the functioning of American government was clear from the beginning. In 1981, he proclaimed that 'all of us need to be reminded that it was not the federal government that created the states, it was the states that created the federal government'. He cast himself firmly in the dualist mould, emphasising his determination to 'demand recognition of the distinction between the powers granted to the federal government and those reserved to the states or to the people'. He wished to re-structure the federal system as it had developed, so that Washington would withdraw from several areas, and the states would gain the right to take initiatives and operate more programmes if they so wished. By the end of his 'devolution revolution', the states were funding more of their own programmes, and the number run by the federal government had been substantially curtailed.

categorical grants
Grants of the type commonly made in the Johnson presidency. Money was given from the central government to the states and localities for specific, often narrow, purposes and to be used in specified ways.

block grants
Discretionary grants handed over by the federal government to states or communities; recipients are able to choose how the money is spent within the broad area covered by the transfer.

Bill Clinton stressed the importance of cooperation between the federal and state/local governments, and was keen on the idea of local experimentation. Twin forces determined his thinking. His background as a Governor in the South – an area where there was a history of resistance to federal demands – made him sympathetic to states' rights, whereas his belief in more active national government inclined him to be a centraliser in his approach. Under Clinton, as under Bush Snr before him, there was a modest increase in federal aid to the states and localities.

Above all, Clinton emphasised the importance of improved cooperation between the federal and state governments, and spoke of increased opportunities for local initiative and experimentation. He established a framework in which federal officials were able to loosen programme requirements to allow states and localities more flexibility. Washington was no longer seen as 'knowing best' and there was much more recognition of the role and importance of the states in producing effective government. The Clinton years saw a renewal of state governments and a shift of balance in the federal relationship. The new-found vitality of state capitals has sometimes been referred to as what Dye has called 'competitive federalism'.[12] Nowadays, good practice in one state may be copied elsewhere and just as state initiatives have often in the past reflected national thinking, so today national thinking may be influenced by what is happening across America.

Over the last two decades there has been a greater emphasis once again on the role of the states, a trend pleasing to conservatives who always doubted the wisdom of surrendering state rights over key economic and social functions. American states found themselves more dependent on their own sources of income, for at a time of growing budget deficits there was less scope for revenue sharing. In the circumstances, states were forced to become more creative and since the Reagan presidency they have been keen to develop a spirit of innovation and enterprise. Walker felt able to describe them as 'laboratories of democracy'.[13] There has been some highly creative thinking in individual states, which have looked for new means of solving public problems and meeting challenges. Examples of novel and influential programmes include:

- Hawaii and Oregon have experimented with new schemes for the delivery of health provision, the Hawaiian example being modelled on British lines. Via its Death with Dignity, Oregon has legalised euthanasia for those who feel beyond the help of medical assistance.
- Wisconsin has been in the forefront in developing new arrangements for its educational programme, its legislators showing interest in parental choice and developing a voucher system, which has aroused much interest in Washington under the Bush Jnr presidency.
- California led the way in developing building construction standards to help reduce energy costs and in setting out new emission regulations for cars to assist in combating air pollution
- Vermont allows same-sex 'civil unions'.

It is early days to comment on developments in the George W Bush presidency. He labelled himself a 'faithful friend of federalism' on entering the White House, as might be expected from an ex-Republican state governor. In the early days, he leaned on the advice and services of leading state officials and established a study group to see how the role of states might be advanced. Yet there are factors which have worked against such a pro-devolution policy: the business community is sometimes unenthusiastic about regulatory state laws; the religious right dislikes some features of state autonomy, not least Oregon's suicide law; and sympathetic state governors fear the electoral consequences of trying to impose measures on standards and accountability in schools. More seriously, perhaps, two issues have come to the fore on which federal leadership has been needed. Firstly, the attacks on the twin towers of 11 September and their aftermath have shifted the focus of attention away from the states and more to Washington. Secondly, after the 'good years' in which the economy has been performing well, recession may make it more difficult for states to fund programmes for which they have now assumed responsibility.

Relations between the states and the centre are at the very heart of federalism, for federalism seems to provide for an in-built tension between the two levels of government. Hague and Harrop point out that in the United States

> The original federal principle ... was that the national and state governments would operate independently, each tier acting autonomously in its own constitutional sphere. In particular, the federal government was required to confine its activities to functions explicitly allocated to it, such as the power 'to lay and collect taxes, to pay the debts and provide form the common defence and welfare of the United States'. In the circumstances of eighteenth century America, extensive coordination between federal and state administration was considered neither necessary nor feasible. This model of separated governments ... has long since disappeared, overwhelmed by the demands of an integrated economy and society.[14]

The experience of American history reveals that the nature of federalism has changed over time. There was a broad tendency towards central control from the beginning and it accelerated with the greater state regulation following the establishment of the New Deal. The trend reached its peak in the 1960s. Sometimes this greater central power came about as a result of constitutional amendment; more often it was a response to prevailing economic and social conditions. Sometimes too the tendency towards central control was given a push by judicial decisions, so that clauses in the Constitution were interpreted widely to provide the federal government with a broad scope for legislation. The result was that in America the centre gained power at the expense of the 50 states, especially in the area of major economic policy.

The centralising tendency has been arrested in the closing decades of the twentieth century. In practice, American federalism has experienced growing interdependence. There is a developing trend to improve relations between federal, state and local governments and find common ground between them. In several areas of policy such as education and transport, policies are made, funded and applied at all tiers. States have regained much of their lost autonomy and are very important in their own right, but on occasion the national government steps in. When California experienced a serious electrical power shortage in 2000, Washington became inevitably involved as the state began to make demands on the supplies of surrounding states.

The relationship between states and the centre is not static. America has, as Gillian Peele points out,

> a vibrant but complex system which displays enormous variety and contradiction ... Bush may expect, or indeed, want to continue the rebuilding of a genuine partnership with the states. The evolution of the American system has, however, produced a complex labyrinth of relationships which are less than easily navigated. It is thus likely that although the American federal and intergovernmental system will continue to tilt away from Washington, change will be relatively slow and incremental'.[15]

The British unitary and American federal systems compared

It is important not to emphasise unduly the formal differences between unitary and federal systems, for in practice the distinctions are less clear-cut than at first appears. In a country such as Britain or Spain which have devolved bodies and/or regional structures, no likely government would in practice seriously contemplate reducing their autonomy. To do so would invite political difficulties. Power is actually more widely diffused than the term 'unitary' implies. Similarly, in any federal structure, the federal government is bound to exercise enormous power, the exact extent of that power varying from country to country. This is because any country needs strong, effective leadership, especially – but not only – in times of crisis. It is in recognition of this requirement in twentieth century America that examiners have sometimes asked whether the United States is becoming a kind of unitary state. So too have they asked whether Britain is moving in a more federal direction.

In the 200 or more years since the writing of the American Constitution, there has been a broad move towards central control to such an extent that critics have lamented the trend towards creation of what seems to be a unitary system in disguise. Yet if much of the autonomy of the states – as laid down in the constitution – might have been eroded, the states remain significant, and there are in America plenty of examples of state experimentation and initiative. A spirit of partnership has developed between Washington and the states, which as Blondel observes 'goes against the ideas of separation at the root of the federal model'.[19] In his discussion of trends in federalism in recent decades, Grodzins has argued that rather than a layer-cake model of separate and independent spheres of influence, the appropriate model to describe the United States is really a marble cake.[20] There is now a mix of overlapping relations, which has again done much to break down the old distinction between federal and unitary states, which often have a strong tradition of local government.

The old distinctions between the British and American systems are less clear-cut than used to be the case. However, by British standards, America remains a very decentralised country in which political power is diffused across the country, whereas even allowing for recent experiments in devolution Britain is still much more centralised than even many other unitary states. The way in which national governments removed the powers and in some cases termi-nated the existence of local government is an indication of that process. This could happen in Britain by the passage of national legislation, whereas in America whenever Washington has attempted to increase its power at the expense of the states there has usually been considerable state resistance. Local feelings and the tradition of self-government count for more in America

Local government in Britain

The position of local government in Britain has undergone dramatic change in the post-war era. In the years after World War Two, it had expanded to take on new roles as a direct provider of welfare services such as education and housing. Both parties seemed happy to increase expenditure on such services and allow local authorities to exercise considerable discretion as to how it was used, within the broad parameters of public policy. Councils had the freedom and the resources to meet local demands and needs, and regular local elections ensured that this was 'a golden age of local government'. There was a widespread feeling that local authorities were doing a reasonable job, and many people seemed content to leave them.

This picture is perhaps unduly rosy, and in that golden age there were chapters in textbooks which urged the case for local government reform to make it more effective and efficient. In particular, the tendency towards centralisation of power in Whitehall and to reduce the freedom of local authorities was something which needed to be addressed. Much of the dispute was about structure and finance, but from the 1970s onwards there were also attacks criticising councils for their excessive bureaucracy, for their remoteness from local people, for policy disasters such as high-rise housing and occasionally even for corruption. New Right thinkers were unimpressed with local government. They wanted to see Britain escape from what they saw as a prolonged age of municipal socialism.

The period since 1979 – largely coinciding with the years of Conservative rule – has been one of decline, characterised by

> cost reduction, resource restriction and tight central government control over local government expenditure. In addition, there has been a questioning of the role of local government. Functions have been removed from local authorities and given to unelected single-purpose agencies. At the same time, local government services have been subjected to competition and a large part of the work previously performed by local authorities is now carried out by private companies. Moreover, those services for which local authorities do remain responsible have been subjected to much greater central control over their content, for example through the National Curriculum in education, thus diminishing local government discretion.[16]

Today, local government is viewed more as an enabler rather than as a provider of services, although it would be wrong to underestimate the extent to which councils do provide services and spend public money. Wilson and Game point out that even in the area of education where much power has been lost to central government, councils still exercise much control.[17] Moreover, they remain responsible for some 25 per cent of all spending.

With a new government after 1997, it was likely that the importance of local authorities would increase. The Prime Minister soon let it be known that he was keen to revive this ailing area of British democracy. It would be 'modernised . . . re-invigorated . . . reborn and energised' under Labour rule. There was much interest among commentators as to how the wider policy of massive constitutional change would impact on the world of local government, for policies such as devolution, electoral reform and the use of elected mayors all had clear implications for the existing form of local government.

In office, Labour has been keen to make local councils more efficient, increase popular involvement in their activities and rid them of sleaze. Whereas the Conservatives had got rid of the Greater London Council, Labour wanted to restore democracy and end a situation in which London was the only national capital in the West without a single voice. It has created a mayor and assembly for Greater London, in the hope that a dynamic mayoralty might provide a new leadership to the city. Other cities have been given the chance to follow

London's example and opt for executive mayors, as some have done. In this respect, they are following American experience, as well as that of other well-known cities from Barcelona to Paris. New York's Rudi Giuliani provided a good illustration of what could be achieved in his period of office, which ended in 2002. His job is arguably the second toughest in the United States after the presidency and he exploited its potential to full effect. He was widely credited with turning around the situation in a city well-known for its theft and violence. However, he became considerably more famous world-wide for his response to the terrorist attacks of 11 September, as he galvanised attempts to organise recovery and tried to lift the morale of anxious New Yorkers.

Labour's attempts to restore interest in local democracy have yet to yield fruit, especially in the area of election turnout. Experiments have been tried to make it easier for residents to vote, by such means as postal and internet voting, extended polling hours and placing polling stations in places of easier access. But although experiments with postal voting did increase the numbers voting in 2002, the other forms made little beneficial impact and in the last few years the overall number of voters has on occasion fallen well below 30 per cent.

Local government in America

In addition to its 50 state governments, America has a vast and complex maze of local governments numbering nearly 88,000 types of authority. Generalisation is difficult, because they range from the extremes of small, rural, sparsely populated townships to huge, densely populated metropolitan areas, with cities, towns, counties and districts in between. Every American lives within the jurisdiction of the national government, a state government and perhaps ten to twenty local bodies. For instance, the six-county Chicago–Illinois metropolitan area has more than 1200 different governments, some serving the people in broad ways, others providing more specialised services.

Since the Reagan era, states have been willing to decentralise their governing arrangements to the local level ('second-order devolution') and the smaller units encourage individual participation and promote the value of individualism. There is a strong tradition of grass-roots democracy in America, which fits in well with the widely shared belief that government should be kept as close to the people as possible. The very existence of so many governments to deal with so many different and necessary services seems to indicate that democracy flourishes in the localities, a situation far removed from British experience.

Yet the health of local democracy in America can be over-exaggerated. As in Britain, local politics are often poorly covered by the media and as a result the public often are ill-informed about what goes on. This in turn makes it difficult to hold those who represent them accountable. Moreover, levels of turnout in some elections are often very low. Some cities such as Birmingham (Alabama) have done much to encourage neighbourhood democracy by creating neighbourhood boards which have meaningful control over important policy decisions. In this way, voters can see that participation is worthwhile and they feel that it is worthwhile to take their involvement beyond voting alone.

Writing of Britain and the United States, McNaughton gets the balance about right:

> In the USA, if anything, citizens are more interested in the politics of their state and their community than in the goings-on in Washington. Their daily lives are clearly affected more by the nature and performance of local government than those of British citizens. American local democracy is, therefore, more lively, more meaningful and more cherished than it is in the UK.[18]

than they do in Britain. The Constitution guarantees to the states a degree of independence and self-government never recognised by sub-national units in United Kingdom, where the Scots and the Welsh faced along wait in the struggle for devolution. Federalism in America is very much alive today.

As for local government, it is not mentioned in the American Constitution and the diverse array of units has no constitutional standing recognised by the Supreme Court. Such sub-state governments were created by legal charters granted to them under state law, and their pattern varies enormously as does the amount of power they exercise. In Britain, local government has no constitutional status. It has been created by legislation and the functions of the different councils are only those which are specifically granted to them. This tends to limit the autonomy of British local authorities. In Britain, there is far more talk of the death of local democracy, whereas in America the various local units are often held in higher esteem.

Which is the better system?

Federalism has been beneficial to the United States in many ways, its advantages to Americans including:

- The states act as a safeguard against excessive centralisation and the overbearing control of Washington.
- It recognises the distinctive history, traditions and size of each state, allowing for national unity but not uniformity. If the peoples of one state such as Texas want the death penalty, they can have it; people in other states such as Wisconsin which voted to abolish it are not forced to follow suit.
- It provides opportunities for political involvement to many citizens at state and local level; state governments provide thousands of elective offices for which citizens can vote or run.
- Citizens can identify strongly with their state as well as with their country. In Elazar's phrase, states 'remain viable because they exist as civil societies with political systems of their own'.[21]
- States provide opportunities for innovation, and act as a testing-ground for experiments which others can follow.

On the other hand, at times reliance upon the states has served to hinder national progress. At the time of the Great Depression, states were unable to cope with the scale of the catastrophe which they faced and turned to Washington for a lead. On issues such as civil rights too, the granting of full recognition to African-Americans was slowed down because southern state governments were committed to segregationist policies and unwilling or slow to accept the decisions of the machinery of the federal tier. Moreover, the inability of the states to cope with major problems has meant that they were forced to rely more heavily on funding from the national government which inevitably carried strings attached to it and erodes state independence. This has at times made for tensions in the relationship, but as it has evolved in recent years federalism seems to have operated in a way that allows for constructive cooperation between the layers of government, making it more the 'marble cake' of which Grodzins has written.

The unification of the United Kingdom came about largely as a result of the extension of royal authority and conquest, as happened in many other unitary states. The unitary system has worked relatively well because there is a widely held preference for strong, effective government. In a relatively small country lacking substantial regional differences, federalism would be hard to implement, not least because of the population dominance of England over other parts of the United Kingdom.

For years many people accepted royal authority in London, or in the days of a constitutional monarchy the sovereignty of Parliament. If Parliament was sovereign, then it was understood that this supremacy applied across the Kingdom. In the postwar years, there was no serious outbreak of national feeling, perhaps because the economy was performing well and living standards were rising. When in the 1970s those factors no longer applied, there were increased feelings of neglect in the areas further from the capital.

Advantages and disadvantages of unitary and federal states		
	Advantages	Disadvantages
Unitary states	Clear hierarchy of authority, with centre supreme and centre–periphery tensions few.	Excessive concentration of power at the centre.
	Provide clear focus of loyalty for all citizens, who identify with country as a whole.	Inadequate representation of regional and minority diversity.
Federal states	Act as check on central power, preventing undue concentration.	Some overlap of powers, possible competition and conflict between centre and states.
	Provide unity in large state, but cater for diversity and responsibility.	Broad tendency for power to be increasingly exercised at centre, especially on key economic issues.
	Offer an acceptable compromise between the need for effective government and for a strong periphery.	Sluggishness – difficulty in getting things done quickly.

This was particularly true of Ireland, Scotland and Wales, the parts of the Kingdom which were brought in last and which have always retained a sense of their own distinctiveness. Nationalist feelings were strong in these countries. In Ireland, 26 counties gained independence in 1921, but in the north and the other two countries devolution was the eventual answer. As other countries in Western Europe have found also, the combination of unitary government plus devolution seems to many observers to be a pragmatic and appropriate solution for government in the UK.

Conclusion

Britain is a unitary state. As such, sovereignty resides at the centre, in Parliament, even if power may be delegated to other bodies. By contrast, America is a federal country in which sovereignty is divided between Washington and the regions, the division of responsibilities being set out in the Constitution. The constitutional position of the two countries is therefore very different. In practice, there are some similarities, now that Britain has gone down the route of creating devolved bodies in Scotland, Wales and Northern Ireland.

The trends in federal states such as America indicate that there has been in the modern world a tendency towards more centralisation, as national governments have been forced to deal with national problems such as regulating the economy or protecting the environment. Yet at the same time in countries such as Britain which have long exhibited a high degree of central control, there has been a move in recent years towards some decentralisation. Usually, the motivation for decentralisation has not derived from an ideological belief that there was excessive centralisation which needed to be reversed. Rather, it has sprung from a recognition that it was necessary to concede some ground to the people in those areas of the country which have felt aggrieved, for otherwise electoral damage or social disharmony might come about. Blondel concludes: 'one could argue that the regionalism which has been introduced in [Britain and Spain] constitutes an imitation of federalism – indeed, is federalism in all but name ... the difference between federal and unitary states is becoming smaller, not only in practice but formally as well'.[22]

America is less centralised than Britain. Its constitutional arrangements, history and geography mean that it is almost certain to retain a federal system into the long distant future, the more so now that central and state government are acting in greater partnership with each other. Its arrangements provide for a more straightforward allocation of power between Washington and the states than exists between London and the national capitals, with their differing degree of autonomy. However, in a relatively small country such as Britain, there would be difficulties in making federalism work effectively.

Governance beyond the centre in Britain and the United States: a summary		
	Britain	The United States
Unitary or federal?	Unitary.	Federal.
Degree of centralisation	Traditionally centralised, but now a 'developing unitary' system.	Decentralised, but as broad trend more power at the centre now than 200 years ago. Move from 'dual federalism' to other forms such as 'creative federalism'.
Developments in devolution and federalism	Devolution introduced in Scotland, Wales and Northern Ireland differing degrees: 'creeping federalism'. Scotland developing distinctive policies.	Despite broad trend above, more initiative at state level since the 1980s – new emphasis on partnership and local experimentation, since days of 'new federalism'.
Quangos	Development of quango state: quangos replaced many traditional local government functions. Attract much criticism.	Term unknown in US politics.
Local government	Flourished after World War Two, but increased central control especially after 1979: and attempts to rationalise structure and reduce number of authorities. Much talk of death of local democracy – low turnouts. Labour's attempt to re-invigorate, by use of elected mayors.	Responsibility of each individual state. Vast range of local units. Great theoretical interest in public participation, but local democracy not as flourishing as some would like. As in Britain, suffers from low level of media coverage and interest.

REFERENCES

1 R. Hague and M. Harrop, *Comparative Government and Politics: An Introduction*, Palgrave, 2001.
2 J. Blondel, *Comparative Government: An Introduction*, Prentice Hall, 1995.
3 U. Bullman, 'The Politics of the Third Level' in C. Jeffery (ed.) *The Regional Dimension of the European Union: Towards a Third Level in Europe*, Cass, 1997.

4 D. Elazar, 'From Statism to Federalism: A Paradigm Shift', *International Political Science Review* (17), 1996.

5 V. Bogdanor, *Devolution in the United Kingdom*, Oxford University Press, 1999.

6 As note 5 above.

7 As note 5 above.

8 B. Coxall and L. Robins, *Contemporary British Politics*, Macmillan, 1998.

9 As note 5 above.

10 J. Bryce, *Modern Democracies*, Macmillan, 1921

11 J. Kincaid, 'American Federalism: The Third Century', in *Annals of the American Academy of Political and Social Science*, May 1990.

12 T. Dye, *Understanding Public Policy*, Prentice Hall, 1997.

13 D. Walker, *The Rebirth of Federalism*, Chatham House, 2000.

14 As note 1 above.

15 G. Peele, 'Federalism and Intergovernmental Relations' in G. Peele (ed.) *Developments in American Politics*, Palgrave, 2002.

16 H. Atkinson and S. Wilks-Heeg, *British Local Government Since 1979: The End of an Era?*, Politics Association/SHU Press, 1997.

17 D. Wilson and C. Game, *Local Government in the UK*, Macmillan, 1994.

18 N. McNaughton, *Success in Politics*, Murray, 2001.

19 As note 2 above.

20 M. Grodzins, *The American System: A New View of Governments in the United States*, Rand McNally (Chicago), 1966.

21 D. Elazar, *American Federalism: A View from the States*, Harper and Row, 1984.

22 As note 2 above.

USEFUL WEB SITES

For the UK

www.scottish.parliament.uk Scottish Parliament. Help with queries and resources.

www.wales.gov.uk National Assembly for Wales. Help with queries and resources.

www.charter88.org.uk Charter 88. Information relating to constitutional changes.

www.lcd.gov.uk Lord Chancellor's departmental site. Coverage of constitutional issues.

www.record-mail.co.uk The *Daily Record* Devolution Site

www.local.gov.uk, **www.local.detr.gov.uk** Two general local government sites.

For the USA

http://newfederalism.urban.org The Urban Institute (a Washington think-tank). Monitors changes in federal social policies that affect the states and local governments.

www.governing.com/govlinks.htm *Governing* magazine (published by Congressional Quarterly, Inc.). Site has links concerning state and local government matters.

www.csg.org Council of State Governments. Links with the home pages of individual states, providing information about the states and the way their systems of government are organised.

In addition, the web sites of particular state and local governments can be consulted.

SAMPLE QUESTIONS

1 'America has a federal and Britain a unitary form of government, but in reality the influence of the national government over the states and local and devolved authorities respectively is broadly similar'. Discuss.

2 Discuss the similarities and differences between British devolution and American federalism.

Political parties

8

Political parties are organisations of broadly like-minded men and women which seek to win power in elections in order that they can then assume responsibility for controlling the apparatus of government. Unlike interest groups, which seek merely to influence the government, serious parties aims to secure the levers of power.

In this chapter, we examine their relevance in Britain and America. The emphasis is on the competition between the two main parties in either country for the control of public offices, although the nature, role and difficulties experienced by third parties are also considered. In addition, we note other aspects of party activity, including membership, finance and organisation.

POINTS TO CONSIDER

➤ Compare the functions of parties in Britain and the United States.

➤ Should British parties adopt the system of primary elections for choosing its parliamentary candidates?

➤ What are the main types of party system?

➤ What role do third parties have in Britain and the United States?

➤ What barriers do they face?

➤ Why have socialist parties made headway in Britain and Europe, but not in the United States?

➤ What are the similarities between (a.) the Conservative Party and the Republicans and (b.) the Labour Party and the Democrats?

➤ What is meant by the 'third way'? Compare the approaches of Tony Blair and Bill Clinton as exponents of the idea.

➤ 'Parties are in decline'. Does the evidence from Britain and the United States bear this out?

The varying significance of parties in modern democracies

Political parties are now accepted as an essential feature of any liberal democracy. They are ubiquitous, existing in different forms under different political systems. They bring together a variety of different interests in any society, and by so doing 'overcome geographical distances, and provide coherence to sometimes divisive government structures'. Via the electoral process, they determine the shape of governments.[1]

The competition of parties was not always regarded as inevitable or desirable. In the American Constitution there is no provision for party government. The Constitution – federal in character and characterised by competitive institutions – actually makes the operation of parties more difficult. The Founding Fathers did not want party government and within a few years of the completion of their task President Washington was still speaking of the 'baneful effects of the spirit of party'.

Parties have contrasting significance in different democracies. In Britain and the rest of Western Europe they are much stronger than in the USA, where they are noticeably weak. In much of Western Europe, they have a large but declining dues-paying membership, a reasonably coherent ideology and a high degree of discipline among members of parliament. In the USA, none of these factors apply. In parts of the country, they hardly seem to exist between elections.

Britain has party government. At election time, a party seeks to capture the reins of power and win a mandate to govern. To do this, it requires a majority of seats in the House of Commons. If it obtains a working majority, it can then expect to control the machinery of government until the next election is called. Having control of the executive branch and being in a position to dominate the legislature, it will be able to carry out its manifesto. Its leaders know that they can normally count on the backing of their MPs to ensure that their legislative programme passes through Parliament. As Shaw puts it: 'The government will have its way, and the opposition will have its say'.[2]

The situation is very different in the United States. Party politics are more parochial than national and as Walles explains: 'the promises made are not about supporting a national programme so much as about doing something for the district or the state'.[3] America lacks the concentration of power possessed by the British Executive and has a more dispersed system of government. Presidents may have grand ideas for action, but as the experience of President Clinton and his first-term programme for health reform indicates, they cannot anticipate such a relatively easy ride for their plans. Because Congress has the role of acting as a counter-balance to the executive branch, it takes the task of scrutinising White House proposals seriously. Even if the

President has a majority in one or both chambers, he or she may be unable to achieve his or her goals, as Kennedy, Carter and Clinton all came to realise. Parties are much less disciplined than in Britain and congress members are likely to think in terms of constituency and other pressures as much or more than party allegiance. This is why Shaw could refer to the American system as 'government by individuals rather than by party'.

The functions of parties

As we have seen, the primary purpose of political parties is to win elections. This is what distinguishes them from pressure groups, which may try to influence elections but do not usually put up candidates for office. They articulate the needs of those sections of society which have created them and look to them to advance their interests. But they must go further, for to win an election they need wider support. If they wish to be in government – either in a single-party administration or some form of coalition – then they cannot afford to follow a narrow doctrinal programme, for this would alienate important groups in the community and make it difficult for other parties to contemplate cooperation with them. In the words of an old examination quotation: 'Pressure groups articulate and political parties aggregate the various interests in society'.

European and other democracies are party democracies. Parties perform important functions in forging links between the individual and those in office. Without them, individual voters would have less control over those in power than they do today, and governments would function in a less cohesive and effective manner. When that cohesiveness breaks down and is replaced by factionalism, government is likely to be ineffective and more remote from the needs and wishes of the people.

Much party activity is concerned with the election period, but parties offer other opportunities for participation and involvement over a continuous period. Among their specific functions, they:
- contest elections in order to compete with other parties for elective office;
- select candidates who would have little chance of success but for their party label;
- coordinate political campaigns;
- put together coalitions of different interests, for a variety of groups and individuals can come together under one broad umbrella, so that any government which emerges is likely to have widespread support in the community;
- organise opinion, providing voters with cues for voting, because most of them can identify in some way with the image of the main parties; they can therefore be a basis for making their political choices;

- articulate policies, educating the voters and providing them with a choice of alternatives;
- activate voters by mobilising their support via campaigning, rallies and emblems of identification varying from banners to lapel badges, giving them an opportunity for political involvement;
- incorporate policy ideas from individuals and groups which are outside the political mainstream, responding to changes suggested by third parties and protest movements.

American elections are much more candidate-centred than European ones, so that some of the above functions do not apply or apply with less force in Britain and other Western democracies. The choice of candidates is made in primary elections (see box on pp. 182–3) and the financing and organising of campaigns is carried out by Political Action Committees (PACs) and the candidate's array of advisers. Parties have a more 'supportive' role in recent years, with the downgrading of party machines in the twentieth century.

Party systems

There is an obvious distinction between party systems which allow for the existence of only a single party and those which allow competition between a range of parties. Single-party systems are now on the retreat, particularly since the fall of the former Soviet satellite governments in Eastern Europe. They are to be found on the African continent in countries south of the Sahara such as Mozambique and Zimbabwe, and in parts of what used to be termed the Third World; they also exist in communist countries such as China, Cuba and North Korea. The majority of countries have a variety of parties from which voters can make their choice. There are a few authoritarian military regimes which do not allow parties of any kind. These are to be found in parts of Africa, Latin America and the Middle East.

Systems with more than one party

Party systems which allow a choice of parties fall into three main categories:

1 **Two-party systems.** In two-party systems, only the two main parties have a meaningful chance of achieving political power. Heywood identifies three main criteria of two-party systems:
   1 although a number of 'minor' parties exist, only two parties enjoy sufficient electoral and legislative strength to have a realistic prospect of winning government power;
   2 the largest party is able to rule alone (usually on the basis of a legislative majority), the other providing the opposition;

The selection of candidates in Britain and America

Parties can employ many different procedures for choosing candidates. In most democracies, the choice is made by local party activists, possibly subject to central approval. In Britain, the choice is made by a selection committee of the constituency organisations. Candidates chosen are those thought likely to appeal to the voters and be loyal to the party. In the Conservative Party, an individual may submit his or her name for consideration, but in the Labour Party an individual must be nominated by an affiliated body. Particularly in the Labour Party, the approval of party headquarters is required for all selected candidates.

Candidates can be chosen by party headquarters, the decision perhaps taking the views of local organisations into consideration. In some countries where closed-list electoral systems are employed, parties have a major role in deciding who is on the ballot paper and in what order the names are placed.

In America, the choice of candidates is made locally, with no central review of the selections made. There are no approved lists at party headquarters in Washington, neither is there any power of veto. Decisions are made by the rank-and-file of the supporters in primary elections. Those who seek office circulate petitions and if sufficient they can gain a sufficient number of signatures, then their name appears on the party's ballot.

Primaries were adopted to democratise procedures, by placing the nomination in the hands of the party membership rather than the party bosses who had dominated the procedure of election in the past. Most states have closed primaries, with participation limited to actual party members (those who have registered as supporters of the party some months before the date of the primary), whereas in open primaries voters may participate in either party's choice of candidate (they decide on the day which primary ballot paper they will take). Either way, the voters choose directly the candidates they will be called upon to vote for in the subsequent general election.

The method of candidate selection is very important, for in many 'safe' seats there is a strong likelihood that nomination will result in membership of the legislature. The merits and disadvantages of the British and American systems for choosing candidates are therefore of much significance. In Britain, the choice is made by a relatively small committee, often dubbed a 'selectorate'. The mass of loyal supporters of a local party are denied what could be a perk of membership, the right to participate in the political process and have a say in who

3 power alternatives between these parties: both are 'electable', the opposition serving as a 'government in the wings'.[4]

Britain is often cited as a good example of a two-party system. Southern Ireland and the United States also fall into this category, although Ball points out that in both cases the parties lack the centralised hierarchical structures and mass membership characteristic of British politics. Neither are ideological differences in either case clear-cut. The political divisions between Fianna Fáil and Fine Gail are largely historical and the Democrats and Republicans in America often have more internal than inter-party differences. In his view, it is

represents them. They may find that the person chosen does not reflect their views, on a divisive matter such as membership of Euro-land, or immigration and race relations. This is the more likely because the activists who dominate selection committees may be unrepresentative of local party members.

In America, most states allow the ordinary voter to take part in the choice. Instead of trying to persuade a small number of party workers of his or her merits, the candidate must convince a significantly larger proportion of the electorate. The process involves creating a personal machine to canvass for support in a full-blooded, professional campaign which in a safe seat will be more important than the later contest between the parties. There are disadvantages with both open and closed primaries (see opposite) and it is easy to over-stress the 'democratic' case for their use. In reality, turnout in primary elections is often low, and they enhance the prospects of better-funded candidates and thereby increase the significance of money in American election. But there might be advantages if they were used in Britain. They would:
- provide a means by which individuals can be politically involved;
- attract attention to the process of choosing a candidate;
- offer a choice of person and perhaps of policy as well;
- take power away from cliques who may dominate the local party scene;
- (for anyone who believes that the system of party discipline in the House of Commons is too rigid) act as a counter-balance, for the person elected would be there more because of his or her own personal qualities than as a creature of the party organisation.

There are possible objections to the adoption of primaries in Britain, notably that they would:
- increase the cost of elections, for candidates would end up fighting two elections instead of one; this would increase the importance of money in elections and make the amount of funding a candidate can attract all the more important;
- tend to place greater emphasis on the personality and appeal of the candidate at the expense of the policies he or she represents;
- be unnecessary, for there is no obvious public interest or demand. After all, the pressure for primaries in America arose because party caucuses were often dominated by narrow oligarchies which were often in some way corrupt – not a problem which has been evident in Britain.

difficult to place any of these four parties clearly on a Left–Right spectrum, so that he describes them as having **indistinct two-party systems** as opposed to the **distinct** ones of Britain and parts of the Commonwealth.

2 **Dominant-party systems**. In these, there are two or more parties, but only one party ever wins an election in normal circumstances. The Congress Party in India monopolised Indian government in the 30 years after independence, but in recent years it has lost its pre-eminence. Nearer to home, Fianna Fáil held office in Ireland for 37 out of 43 years between 1932 and 1973. Some commentators felt that Britain was moving in this direction in the years after 1979, when the Conservative Party won four successive elections. However,

Labour's victory in 1997 illustrated the danger of constructing such theories which wait to be disproved.

3 **Multi-party systems**. Multi-party systems of four, five or six parties are common on the continent, in part a reflection of the widespread use of list systems of proportional representation, which help all parties to get reasonably fair representation. In such systems, it is highly unlikely that one party could ever gain an outright victory and form a single-party government. Governments are coalitions, which vary from the stable to the unstable.

The two-party systems of Britain and America

The American experience is not straightforward. The system allows one party to capture the White House (the presidency) and the other to dominate on Capitol Hill (the legislature), so that a British-style divide between government and opposition is absent. Also, some writers have quibbled about applying the term 'two-party system' to one in which there are really 51 party systems: one national and one for each of the fifty states. The national parties are a loose aggregation of the state parties, which are themselves 'a fluid association of individuals, groups and local organisations'.[6] As Vile puts it, 'politics operate in a framework of 50 systems, for much decentralisation has occurred'.[7]

There is a variety of forms of party competition throughout the country, with no two states being exactly alike. In some, parties are weak, in others rather stronger. Kay Lawson writes that California 'has political parties so weak as to be almost non-existent . . . it has been run by special interests for so long that Californians have forgotten what is special about that'.[7] By contrast, Pennsylvania has well-organised parties, with sizeable staffs and plenty of money to spend. In some states, there is a genuine competition for power, with both parties having a chance of capturing the governorship or control of the legislature. In others, only one party ever wins and there is no little or no prospect of a change of political control. Yet in spite of such difficulties, most observers think of America as having a two-party system. When they think about American parties, they think in terms of the Democrat and Republicans, which between them possess almost every congressional seat and almost every state governorship.

Britain has in the past often been portrayed as having a model two-party system. In reality, there have been periods when this was not the case, most notably in the interwar years and from the mid-1970s onwards. The years 1945–1970 saw a classic two-party confrontation. Each of the main parties won four elections and between them Labour and the Conservatives monopolised the votes cast and seats won in any election. In 1951, this domination reached its zenith when, in combination, they attracted 96.8 per cent of the votes and 98.6 per cent of the seats. Then and in other elections, the third-party

Liberals played an insignificant role. But from 1974 onwards, the third force (as represented either by the Liberals, the Alliance or the Liberal Democrats) has been a sizeable one, regularly commanding about 15–20 per cent of the votes and in 1997 and 2001 winning 46 and 52 seats respectively. The nationalists in Scotland and Wales have also often performed well, so that the British political arrangements can be described as a two-party system but three- or four-party politics.

Both Britain and America have two major parties, and have – with rare exceptions – done so since national party competition began. In neither case does such a system preclude the existence of other parties and, as we shall see, in both countries many minor parties have run candidates. If anything, the dominance of two parties has been more apparent in America than Britain. The Democrat–Republican stranglehold has endured in America since the 1850s and is much more entrenched than the duopoly of British politics. Whereas American third parties have tended to be absorbed by one of the main organisations, this has not happened in Britain. When the Social Democrats left the Labour Party in the early 1980s, they did not – as a body – return to the fold.

In both party systems, division (to the extent of breakaways) in one of the major parties has usually occurred on the Left rather than on the Right. The Liberals of the late nineteenth century divided over Home Rule, as did Labour in the 1950s over disarmament and public ownership and in the early 1980s over a range of issues. The Democrats split seriously in 1948, with the Truman mainstream under attack from the Dixiecrats of Strom Thurmond on the Right and the Progressives of Henry Wallace on the Left. In both cases, they were embraced back into the party within a few years.

Why Britain and the United States have two-party systems

Some writers stress the natural tendency for opinion on issues to divide into a 'for' and 'against' position which often follows the basic distinction between people who generally favour retaining the status quo (the conservatives) and those who wish to see innovation and a quicker pace of change (the progressives). In his famous analysis of political parties, Duverger long ago argued that a two-party system conformed to the basic division in society between those who wish to keep society broadly unchanged, and those who wish to see improvement and reform.[8] The liberal–conservative, progressive–stand-pat distinction has not always been clear-cut, for the main parties in either country have at times had their more forward-looking members as well as those who oppose social advance.

Institutional factors also make a difference. The nature of the presidency is one. It is the focal point of all political aspiration, but it is a single executive whose leadership cannot be shared. To capture the office, it is best to take a broad middle-of-the-road stance and create a coalition behind one person. For any minor party, 'presidential contests are a mountain to climb which can only be conquered by a major party capable of assembling a broad national coalition'.[9] In Britain, the requirements of the parliamentary system promote two-partyism. The nature of the House of Commons makes it necessary for elected members to decide whether they are on the government side or that of the Opposition. There is no in-between. The confrontational Westminster system has always attached a high priority to firm government and strong opposition. The electorate seems to prefer a strong executive and is unconvinced about the merits of coalitions which are often seen as weak and unstable.

There are more important and fundamental reasons for two-party dominance. Both countries use the same First Past the Post electoral system, under which whoever gets the most votes wins the election. There are no prizes for coming a good second. Even if the largest party gets less than an overall majority, it is declared the winner and other parties are out in the cold. In this way, third-party activity is discouraged, for unless a party wins there is no reward for the votes it receives: the 'winner takes all'. Duverger argued that 'the simple majority, single ballot system favours the two party system; the simple majority with second ballot and proportional representation favour multi-partyism'.[10]

Also, most Britons and Americans have a broad consensus about basic matters in society, so that large and generally moderate parties can provide adequate avenues for political expression. There has often been substantial agreement on the desirability of present constitutional arrangements and the broad objectives of party policy, in addition to a spirit of compromise which makes it possible for one party to accept the innovations initiated by the other. Both Labour and the Conservatives, and Democrats and the Republicans, are broad coalitions in which people of a variety of political persuasions can co-exist. They are flexible enough to cater for most sections of the electorate, each having more die-hard and less partisan members.

Finally, there are the difficulties which affect any third party which tries to break through the system. In America, there may be real barriers in getting on the ballot paper in a number of states, but in both countries, lack of money, staffing and organisation are a problem. Moreover, there is also the argument used by their opponents, that under the voting system used a vote for a third party is a wasted vote. Most voters prefer to opt for a party which has a meaningful chance of victory.

Third and minor parties

Most countries have very many parties, although in several cases we never hear of them. Britain has a large **third party**, the Liberal Democrats, and in Scotland and Wales nationalist parties are second only to Labour in size and impact. Since the 1970s, third parties have been of growing significance. Whereas in 1945, third and **minor parties** combined managed to win only 12.4 per cent of the votes, in February 1974 the figure had reached 25 per cent, a performance bettered in 1997 and 2001.

> **third party**
> A party capable of gaining a sizeable percentage of popular support and which regularly gains seats in the legislature. On occasion, it may win or threaten to win enough support to influence the outcome of an election.
>
> **minor party**
> A party which polls only a tiny percentage of the national vote and almost never gains representation.

Butler and Kavanagh quote twelve parties as having put up more than fifty candidates in the 1997 election: 'There were also interventions from the Scottish Socialist Alliance (16) and other left-wing dissidents, as well as from over 200 other more or less independent "Independents"'.[11] In 2001, the number was down, with the disappearance of the Referendum Party and the Natural Law Party of four years earlier. Many of the groupings in either contest were minor parties which only stood in a very few places and do not regularly stand in every set of elections. In 1997, Socialist Labour and the Pro-Life Alliance put up 64 and 53 candidates respectively. In 2001, the numbers were 114 and 37. The Scottish Socialist Party contested all 72 Scottish seats.

In American presidential contests, there are usually approaching 20 candidates. Some have had an impact on the outcome. Ross Perot's intervention in 1992 was very impressive. He gained 19 per cent of the popular vote and came a good second in Maine and Utah. However, his was more a personal movement (United We Stand, America) than a formal political grouping. Four years later, it had been transformed into the Reform Party, again with Perot standing as the candidate. In 2000, it did much less well, gaining only 0.4 per cent support.

Some parties contest presidential elections regularly, such as the Libertarians and the Greens. In 2000, Ralph Nader won 3 per cent of the vote for the Greens, winning enough support in Florida to deny Al Gore victory in the state and – because the outcome was so pivotal in the country – in the presidential contest as a whole. For the congressional and state elections in the same year, there were very many more parties, just over fifty getting on the ballot papers.

The useful role of third and minor parties

1 They articulate the thoughts of a section of society and represent a segment of public sentiment, however incoherent or even weird those thoughts may be.

In a democracy they have the right to be heard and expressed. In particular, they enable certain causes such as that of the Prohibitionists in America or the 'Pro-lifers' in Britain to be ventilated.

2 They air certain grievances which are not being sufficiently recognised by existing parties, as with the Perot platform on the need to balance the budget in 1992, and the Plaid Cymru and SNP campaigns of recent decades, which have both served as an outlet for nationalist discontent.

3 They can be a source of new thinking and act as spurs to prod majority parties into action, saving them from apathy and indifference. For instance, the constitutional amendment providing for direct election of Senators were first produced by the Populist Party, in the same way that the British Liberals were early pioneers of closer British involvement in moves towards postwar European integration.

4 On occasion, a third party may be in a position to hold the balance of power or at least affect the outcome. On the basis of seats won, the Liberal Democrats might have expected to wield greater influence after the last two elections, but were denied because of the overwhelming number of seats won by the preponderant Labour Party. Ross Perot's intervention in 1992 was probably decisive enough to cost George Bush re-election.

The fate of socialist parties in Britain and America

There are many shades of socialism and many varieties of socialists, but they share in common a belief that unrestrained capitalism is responsible for a variety of social evils, including the exploitation of working people, the widespread existence of poverty and unemployment, gross inequality of wealth and the pursuit of greed and selfishness. Socialists would prefer to see a social system based on cooperative values and emphasise the values of community rather than of individualism. They also believe strongly in the need for a more equal and just society, based on brotherhood and a sense of social solidarity. In the words of Arthur Greenwood, an old-style socialist: 'Socialism is a philosophy of life which, when translated into policies and programmes, offers this country and the world the means of establishing human society as a real community based upon cooperation'.[12]

For generations, socialists argued over the means by which a socialist society can be achieved. Some have advocated revolution, assuming that owners of wealth and property would never surrender their power voluntarily; others have preferred the democratic route to socialism. Parties calling themselves Socialist, Social Democratic, Labour or Communist have been major forces in every democratic country in the world, except for the United States. Many on the political Left have tried to make sense of the failure of socialism in

America, sometimes expressing surprise at 'the conundrum that working class consciousness was stronger in Europe than in the most developed capitalist industrial society of the world'.[13]

Socialism in Britain

In Britain, this gradualist route has been preferred. In its 1918 Constitution, Labour officially committed itself to socialism, which was often then defined in terms of a commitment to the public ownership of key industries or services. Clause Four of that constitution set out the goal: 'To secure for the workers by hand or by brain the full fruits of their industry and the most equitable distribution thereof that may be possible upon the basis of the common ownership of the means of production, distribution and exchange'.

Clause Four was for years a 'sacred cow' of the Labour Movement. Traditionalists on the Left resisted any attempt to downplay its importance, and some members of the party today continue to define their socialism in terms of their commitment to public ownership. By the 1950s, many Labour thinkers ('revisionists') were reconsidering the commitment to nationalisation. Aware that it seemed to be an electoral albatross they instead stressed the need for greater equality and a fairer distribution of resources. For Tony Crosland, socialism was 'a set of values, of aspirations, of principles, which socialists wish to see embodied in the organisation of society'.[14]

The process of revisionism has gone much further in recent years, particularly under the Blair leadership. Tony Blair has only very rarely used the word 'socialist' in his public utterances and when he has done so it has usually been to elaborate on his interest in 'ethical socialism'. He believes that ideas of socialism based on class conflict and public ownership are no longer relevant to today's post-Thatcherite society. Recognising the need to make New Labour electorally attractive, he quickly set out to rewrite Clause Four, which is now more lengthy in the revised version. It purports to be an expression of Labour's aims and values today. It describes a cause no longer based on a particular idea of economic ownership, but one based on a commitment to community values. It speaks the language of 'common endeavour', 'equality of power, wealth and opportunity', 'rights and duties' and 'solidarity, tolerance and respect'. It wants power to rest in the hands of 'the many, not the few'.

This is a much modernised statement of socialist thinking and many commentators would say that it is not socialist at all. They would see New Labour as having more in common with the New Liberals of the early twentieth century, and note that the party now embraces the ideas of a modern market economy. It wants an active role for government and supports the search for a 'third way' somewhere between the state control which Labour used to support and the individualism associated with capitalism. New Labour has been much influenced by a process of Clintonisation. There are many similarities with Bill Clinton's approach in the America of the 1990s.

Frustrated by the way in which New Labour has strayed from the socialism of its roots, some people on the British Left have turned to other organisations in recent years. They despair of Blairism and want to see more commitment to socialism and to the causes which Old Labour used to espouse. Such thinking finds expression in some of the smaller socialist parties which remain true to the earlier vision. Three avowedly socialist parties contested the 2001 election: the Scottish Socialist Party, the Socialist Alliance and Socialist Labour. In combination, they obtained 0.7 per cent of the popular vote.

Socialism in America

Socialism has gained a small but influential following among a section of middle-class adherents, but the working classes have never taken up the cause with much enthusiasm or in any significant numbers. Groups have developed to represent the various shades of socialism, most notably the American Socialist Party (and others such as Socialist Labour and the Socialist Workers parties); as in Europe, left-wing organisations have been prey to internal schism, factional strife and secession. Socialists have never been part of the political mainstream and few have ever achieved national prominence.

America has not proved to be fertile ground for socialist thinkers and their ideas. As V. O. Key explained: 'American socialism is largely a transplanted growth that has failed to take political root in new soil'.[15] The main writers and philosophers of socialism have been Europeans, and their ideas and approach derive from European experience. Perhaps because of the influence of German and Jewish believers, socialism has often been regarded as an alien import unsuited to the conditions of American life. Explanations of socialist weakness in America are numerous, some dwelling more on the failures of socialist leaders and organisation, others suggesting the incompatibility of socialism with core American values (see pp. 7–10) and yet more emphasising the nature of the American Constitution and the difficulties posed by the electoral system. Four major explanations emerge:

1 **The American Dream**, which is a very individualist one. According to that vision, everyone can climb from 'rags to riches', if only they work hard and are given the right encouragement and incentives. Fundamental to this is a belief in free enterprise. Americans generally want the freedom to go ahead and make their own money, rather than benefit from a redistribution of someone else's riches.

2 **The relative absence of class antagonism** in a young country which never had the traditions and institutions of previously feudal systems. There were no

lords and ladies at the top, and serfs or peasants at the bottom. The principle of egalitarianism is little disputed for, as de Tocqueville put it, Americans were 'born equal'.

3 **Over-riding social factors such as racial and religious attachments** are stronger than class solidarity. America has a very diverse population, the ethnic divisions cutting across economic considerations.

4 **The absence of a tradition of strong, left-wing trade unionism**. Trade unionism has never been the force in America that it is in much of Europe (see pp. 224–5) and the unions which do exist often tend towards individualist rather than collectivist solutions. Groups which have attempted to foment industrial strife have often been actively discouraged.

The passing of socialism

With the fall of the Berlin Wall in 1989 and the collapse of socialism in Eastern Europe, socialist ideas have gone out of fashion in many countries. Freed from Soviet domination, these countries have cast aside their former way of life and established new democracies and free markets. They saw the Western lifestyle as preferable to their own, and were aware of the marked discrepancy in the prosperity of capitalist and communist nations. In Britain, faced with the challenge of Thatcherism and new Right policies, the Left moved some way to the Right. In this movement away from pro-state policies, Labour was echoing similar trends in Australia and New Zealand, two other countries where the working class often seemed to be more unionist than socialist.

Labour has drifted further to the Right than many other 'left-wing' parties, and many would say it is no longer socialist. Blairite comments such as 'the era of big government is over' and 'we shall govern from the centre' have inspired commentators such as the American Samuel Beer to speak of 'the final purge of socialism from the Labour party'.[16] But the move away from traditional socialism has been a characteristic of parties of the Left in most European countries so that the absence of a socialist party now distinguishes the United States less sharply from other developed nations.

The Labour and Conservative, Democrat and Republican Parties: ideas, attitudes and approaches

Budge *et al.* describe ideology as 'a theory about the world and about society, and of the place of you and your group within it'.[17] These ideologies are important 'not only in telling leaders what to do but in telling their supporters who they are and thus making them receptive to leaders' diagnoses of the political situation'. Ideology is particularly important for political parties which have to operate across different levels of society. It helps them to link up often complex governmental decisions with the broadly defined interests of their supporters and voters.

In Britain, Labour has traditionally been an ideological party, its members often engaging in internal dispute over some aspect of party thinking. It used to believe that a large percentage of public ownership, and control of industry and government planning were necessary to achieve its socialist ends. The Conservatives were always the party which carried little ideological baggage and some of their electoral success was often attributed to their capacity for adapting to changed circumstances. In the 1980s, under Margaret Thatcher the party adopted a distinctive, right-wing ideological stance on economic and social policy, and ever since her departure in 1990 it has had internal arguments between those who maintain and uphold the Thatcherite legacy and those who wish to see the party moving closer to the political centre ground and putting forward parties of broad appeal to all sections of the community. At the same time as the Conservatives were becoming more ideological, Labour was shedding large sections of its past ideas and policies in an attempt to make the party more electorally attractive.

Unlike British or European parties, American ones have never been ideological or class-based. There has never been a conflict of capitalism versus socialism. The emphasis of politics under successive Presidents has overwhelmingly been on pragmatism and consensus, sometimes the centre of gravity moving to the left as in the 1930s and sometimes to the right as in the Reagan years. Only very rarely has that broad consensus on foreign or domestic policy been seriously under pressure.

The two main parties in both the USA and the UK are sometimes considered to be broker parties, especially the American ones. Broker parties are not founded on strong ideological or social foundations; their doctrines are heterogeneous. The two parties in each country are coalitions of sometimes conflicting groups, which are able to co-exist under the same umbrella. Sometimes, British parties are seen as more governed by ideas and principles than American ones, but in all four main parties there is a wide range of views, gradations between left and right.

Britain

Especially in the years of the postwar consensus in Britain until the 1970s, the differences between the two main parties was often more a matter of degree and timing, rather than of fundamental principle. Shaw could write in 1968 that 'British and American parties agree on far more things than they disagree on'.[18] As an American observer of the British scene, he noticed the gulf between the rhetoric of weekend speeches of government and opposition spokespersons, and what actually happened when either party was in government. Another American scholar and observer of British politics, Samuel Beer, noted that 'the ideological gap between the parties [has] narrowed as Labour's retreat and the Conservatives' advance left the two parties occupying the common ground of the Welfare State and the Managed Economy'.[19] At around the same time, Robert McKenzie wrote: 'I would argue that in practice the gulf between the [British] parties in our own day, is not really vastly greater than the gulf between American parties . . . the two main parties conduct furious arguments about the comparatively minor issues that separate them'.[20]

It may be that the consensual nature of British politics was slightly exaggerated. Ben Pimlott issued a timely antidote to the view that the differences between the British parties had narrowed as much as the above writers suggested.[21] He pointed out that the word consensus was little used before the 1980s, and that it was then coined to distinguish Thatcherism from the era which preceded it. He felt that it was easier to detect consensus in retrospect than it had been at the time when it was supposed to have occurred.

What happened in the 1980s was that the approach adopted by Margaret Thatcher in Downing Street shattered the old ideas of consensus and introduced a new era of party strife. Her free-market economic policies, her approach to taxation, the role of the state, trade unions and privatisation were highly distinctive and many would say divisive. For a while there was a real conflict between the parties, the more so as Labour veered to the Left in the early 1980s. But, rejected by the electorate on four successive occasions, Labour had to respond to the Thatcherite agenda and throughout the 1980s and 1990s policy moved its position to accept free-market policies, a process continued under Tony Blair who has adopted some Thatcherite policies and hijacked some Conservative terminology. The centre ground in British politics is significantly further to the right than it used to be and the differences between New Labour and Conservative less clear-cut than they were in the Thatcher years.

America

The election of Franklin Roosevelt in 1932 highlighted the differences between the two American parties, the Democrats becoming the more radical party, the Republicans more committed to laissez-faire and conservative in attitude. The Rooseveltian Democratic New Deal Coalition of the 1930s welded together intellectuals, labour unions, ethnic minorities, big city machines, blacks and the farmers. Except for the more fitful farmers, that coalition was to survive for more than thirty years. The coalition was held together by the Roosevelt's liberal 'New Deal' formula – a moderate welfare programme involving increased federal intervention in the economy. With entry into World War Two, America suddenly became the force in global politics for which its resources seemed to destine it. By 1945, when war was over, America had emerged as leader of the Western world. Truman turned a new commitment to internationalism into a general commitment to world-wide anti-communism.

In Congress, the Republicans opposed what they denounced as measures of 'creeping socialism' – big government in general, high taxes, welfare handouts, communism at home and abroad, and foreign aid. But the presidential branch of the same party reacted differently, so that Eisenhower as Republican President (1953–61) adopted a moderate conservative stance, essentially 'me-tooist', leaving the New Deal intact but proceeding with reform at a much more cautious pace. As Rossiter put it several years ago: 'The Republicans have been travelling the same road as the Democrats, but they are ten to fifteen years behind and have not enjoyed the trip so much'.[22]

There was broad agreement between the parties that the federal government should have a significant role in the nation's economy and in creating and maintaining a welfare system. The Johnson era (1963–69) was the high point of the postwar domestic consensus which was about to crumble. Till then there was a belief that social ailments were amenable to the application of money. In foreign policy, too, there was a consensus which aroused even less dissent than did its domestic counterpart. Few raised a voice against the direction of American policy after Truman had laid down the 'Truman Doctrine', which outlined America's place in the world and was to become the foundation of policy for many years. America was the world's policeman and had abandoned its prewar isolationism, stationed troops abroad and played an increasingly interventionist role.

From the late 1960s, the Democratic coalition of the Roosevelt era began to disintegrate. The South, once so safe and solid for the Democrats, became by the 1980s the best region for their opponents. Further disarray in that old coalition was caused by the erosion of support among blue- and white-collar workers for the party. Such people had lost much of their faith in Democratic policies. They felt that the party had been taken over by minority groups such as blacks, Hispanics, feminists or gays. It had become a coalition of the disad-vantaged; it had grown out of touch with their ideas and hopes.

In particular, many northern whites had become uneasy about the level of crime and disorder in the inner cities, which they often associated with black activism and poor policing; they were also uneasy over some policies adopted to assist the cause of civil rights, such as bussing and affirmative action. Race and crime were key issues over which the Democrats suffered problems, but there were others. Whilst in the northern states the trade unions were still influential within the party, the southern Democrats were often less sympathetic to organised labour. The new industries which had developed in the South were often ones in which union membership and activity were strongly discouraged.

By contrast, the Republican policies pursued by Reagan in particular were more in tune with popular expectations. Voters were attracted to the Reagan approach by the prospect of lower taxes, less union power, less government and more emphasis on the rights of states and the duty of individuals to fend for themselves. In foreign policy, they liked his wish to emphasise American strength and influence in the world. All this, added to the skills of the Great Communicator as a media performer, was a strong pull.

By 1992, the Democrats had learnt their lesson and their programme was carefully devised. Bill Clinton's policies appealed more broadly than those of his recent predecessors, and he was able to put together a winning combination which gave him eight years in the White House. (see pp. 202–3 for Clintonisation of the Democrat and Labour parties).

In the last few years, more thoughtful members of the Republican Party have been aware of the danger of allowing themselves to become too narrow in their appeal. Mainstream supporters see potential problems in the rise of the Christian Right, for whilst the religious fundamentalists provide a powerful amount of support and are extremely successful at registering and mobilising voters, there is a danger that they might take over the party. This might limit the breadth of their appeal to Americans who do not share those convictions, and who worry about the alleged intolerance of the Christian Coalition. The choice of George W. Bush as the presidential candidate in November 2000 was a victory for pragmatism.

Today, both parties still seek to appeal as widely as possible, but neither can count on the support of key groups. As in Britain, party identification has been in decline. Fewer Americans now see themselves as supporters of either party ('partisan **dealignment**'), and the trend is more evident among the better-off and better-educated, and also among the young. The number of Americans who now view themselves as 'strong' or 'weak' Democrats or 'strong' or 'weak' Republicans is less

> **era of dealignment**
> A period in which the public increasingly dissociates itself from both parties; party identification is weakened.

than it was, and more electors are now interested in issues than was once the case. They tend to be the better-educated and upper-income voters.

Policy attitudes: similarities and differences between the Democrats and the Republicans today

To non-Americans, the policy differences between the two main parties may seem modest, if at times almost non-existent. Lord Bryce once suggested that they were 'two bottles, each having a label denoting the kind of liquor it contains, but each being empty'.[23] The parties certainly do seem to have much in common. If one looks beyond the speeches and the party literature and examines the record of the parties when they have won the presidency in recent years, then often there has been a broad acceptance of much that has been accomplished by their opponents.

Both parties agree about far more things than they disagree about. Both attach great importance to the Constitution and are committed to maintaining America's present form of government. Both accept the pioneering American values of free enterprise and individualism, on which there is little discord in society. Neither favours root-and-branch change in the economic system. There is certainly no deep ideological divide, and in particular no contest between socialism in its various Western European forms and those who oppose it. Even when differences are more discernible, it is important to realise that the differences within parties can be more significant than those between them. A Democrat from New York may be a very different political animal from a colleague from Arkansas or the Deep South, as is often an east-coast Republican from one out in the Midwest.

However there are differences of emphasis and style, degree and method between American parties, and distinct bases of support. Moreover, in their attitudes on issues ranging from abortion to affirmative action and taxation to the role of government, it is not usually difficult to spot a Democrat and a Republican. Americans still recognise the Democrats as the more reform-minded of the two parties, the one whose party platforms in the twentieth century often involved the ideas of moving forward and creating greater social justice for the disadvantaged – Wilson's New Freedom, Roosevelt's New Deal, Truman's Fair Deal, Kennedy's New Frontiers and Clinton's New Covenant. To see American politics as an entirely straightforward divide between the parties of the 'have nots' and the 'haves' would be misleading, but nonetheless the campaigning cry of Adlai Stevenson (the Democrat opponent of Republican President, Dwight Eisenhower in the 1950s) still carries some resonance: 'Vote Democrat so you can live like a Republican'.

The Right–Left divide in both countries: Conservatives and Republicans v Labour and Democrats

If we employ a Right–Left continuum to British and American politics, the Conservatives and

Republicans are parties of the Right, whilst Labour and the Democrats belong on the Left. But as a broad generalisation for the postwar era, the centre of gravity in American politics is further to the Right than in it is in Britain. Therefore, their relative positions in linear terms would be as set out below (but note the attitudes of New Labour as described on pp. 202–3):

Left			*Right*
Labour	Democrats	Conservatives	Republicans

Shaw, writing in the age of consensus when the two parties had come closer in their attitudes and policies, suggested that in both countries the ideological distance between the two parties was not a wide one and that in America it is even narrower than in Britain: 'In the case of the Conservative and Republican parties, the tendency is to look long before leaping, while the Labour and Democratic parties tend towards innovation. Labour party members and Democrats are more receptive to programmes of social welfare and governmental intervention in the economy than their conservative opponents. There is more nationalism in the Conservative and Republican parties than in the other two'.[24]

Advice to students on studying party ideas and policies

As you study party ideas, similarities and differences, bear in mind that there are three useful ways of comparing parties:

1 Look back and examine the policies pursued during particular periods of office in the past (as we have briefly done on pp. 192–5), to see what each has achieved and how ideas have developed.

2 Study the literature and publicity they put out, to extract an understanding of what they stand for; this tells us the way in which the parties like to portray themselves.

3 See what the voters think about the parties, to check if they detect any particularly close associations and preferences; see also which groups support each party.

Shaw's judgements still have much truth in them today, even though in both cases the centre of gravity in the party spectrum has moved to the Right in the light of the experiences of the Thatcher–Reagan years. If we take a series of issues which have been of importance in American politics in recent years, we find a similar Left–Right divide would apply between the British parties:

1 abortion;
2 civil rights for blacks and other disadvantaged groups;
3 affirmative action;
4 the role of the federal government in education;
5 anti-poverty policies and welfare reform;
6 the provision of medical care;
7 the problems of urban renewal;
8 defence spending and the role of America in the post-Cold-War era.

The Republicans oppose or have been reluctant travellers as far as the first seven are concerned, and on the eighth have generally supported a high level of spending and a more isolationist position. The terms used might be different and some issues such as abortion have particular importance in

American politics, but many Conservatives in Britain would echo several of those attitudes. In the past the party did not originally support legislation on racial discrimination or some of the measures associated with the Welfare State, and has shown less interest in inner-city conditions and renewal. Their broad approach is to favour less governmental intervention in aspects of economic and social policy, and to emphasise the importance of low direct taxes. Smaller government, 'getting government off the backs of individuals', more private provision and lower taxes are attitudes that Republican and Conservatives have in common. (See p. 204 for a comparison of Conservative and Republican policies.)

KEY POLICY AREAS IDENTIFIED FROM PARTY LITERATURE

Main priorities of the American parties for the 2000 elections, as listed by them in two states

The Democrats of Massachusetts
- creation of opportunity, recognition of responsibility and building of community;
- commitment to the tenets of Life, Liberty and the Pursuit of Happiness;
- domestic tranquillity requires good jobs, a good education and quality health care;
- 'blessings of liberty' require the maintenance of public safety, the securing of a sustainable environment and the exercise of fiscal responsibility;
- Promotion of general welfare, involving honouring families, investing in communities and safeguarding the political rights of all citizens;
- Democratic government and the power of good governance.

The Republicans of Washington State
- support for Constitution and importance of respect for religion;
- the family and the role of the individual within it;
- free enterprise;
- right to own property;
- encouragement of individual initiative;
- fulfilling America's sense of mission, as a nation of freedom living under God;
- enabling Americans to live the American dream.

Main priorities of the British parties from their 2001 manifestos

Labour
- *Economy/taxation:* no increase in income tax, economic stability, minimum wage increase, referendum on Euro if economic tests for membership met.
- *Home affairs:* extra funding for police, harsher sentences for persistent offenders, set up register of drug dealers, confiscate earnings from crime.
- *Education/health:* recruit more teachers, increase educational spending, introduce more specialist secondary schools, increase spending on health by 6 per cent a year, recruit more doctors and nurses.

'Clintonisation' of the Democrats and Labour: New Democrats and New Labour

Labour and the Democrats have traditionally been seen as the two left-wing parties in Britain and the United States. To Verba and Orren, writing in the mid 1980s, the differing attitudes of the Democrats and Republicans to economic equality was the issue which 'divided [them] most unequivocally'.[25] The same was true of Labour and the Conservatives. The preference for greater social equality was reflected in attitudes to taxation (Labour and the Democrats more in favour of taxing-and-spending, their opponents favouring lower taxes) and welfare (Labour and the Democrats wanting to see more help for

---

- *Transport*: increases spending by 20 per cent a year
- *Other issues:* give MPs a free vote on fox-hunting: remove remaining hereditary peers from House of Lords

Conservatives
- *Economy/taxation:* cut fuel tax, no stealth taxes, lower taxes and less regulation for businessmen, hold local referendums before any increase in Council Tax, keep the pound (no membership of 'Euroland', the single currency).
- *Home affairs:* increase police numbers, take persistent young offenders off the streets, criminals to serve full sentences, a 'safe haven, not a soft touch' for asylum seekers.
- *Education/health:* more freedom for head teachers to run schools, remove tax penalty on private medical insurance to make it more attractive, increase NHS funding.
- *Other issues:* less tax for families, more help for farmers and businesses hit by foot-and-mouth, protect rural shops and general way of life in countryside, a more flexible European Union and no more transfer of powers to Brussels.

Who supports the two American parties? Consider how appropriate such a categorisation is for the British parties?

(See p. 287.) A 'typical Democrat' might be a member of an ethnic minority, non-Protestant, an urban dweller, and belong to a trade union and the working class. He or she would support measures of social welfare to assist the poor and needy, favour regulation of big business and a fairer distribution of wealth and support the global role of America as leader of the free world. A 'typical Republican' might be white, male, middle class, suburban/small town, college-educated and Protestant. He or she would support law and order, believe in limited government and individualism, support big business and free enterprise, be wary of American involvement overseas and see himself or herself as a conservative.

Of course, this is too simplistic, as generalisations invariably are. The Democrats have supporters who are white and black, working and middle class, urban and rural dwellers, combining as they do workers in the northern industrial cities and more wealthy farmers in the west. The Republicans have within their ranks business, professional and working people, many whom are small-town religious fundamentalists and some who are city agnostics, many who support curbs on abortion, others who believe in free choice.

---

those in poverty and hardship, their opponents being more concerned to limit the extent of such help and stress personal responsibility).

There are clear parallels between the position and fortunes of the Democratic Party of the early 1990s and those of the British Labour Party after 1979. Both had experienced prolonged electoral disappointment, had lost the support of many of their traditional voters and had become embroiled in fratricidal warfare as radical groups sought to foist their own agenda on the bulk of the party. They both needed to find a new identity which would appeal to the electorate, and found that their traditional policies were no longer seen as necessary or relevant to today's generation.

Bill Clinton and Tony Blair led their party in similar directions. Both turned their backs on the old attitudes of tax-and-spend and wanted to carve out a new role for government. Both were strong supporters of the 'third way' (see pp. 202–20).

Clintonisation of the Democrats

In opting for Bill Clinton as their presidential candidate in 1992, the Democrats chose a man who was acceptable to almost every section within the party. He was not too identified with any wing or shade of opinion, and he seemed to have more ability and electoral appeal than any of the others in a generally unimpressive field. With a policy platform designed to appeal as widely as possible within the party and outside, the Clinton–Gore ticket was a strong one. It was more liberal than many southern Democrats would have wished, but not too liberal for the party's neo-conservatives and regulars. The message conveyed by the Clinton team reflected this careful balancing act.

The Clinton message

Research carried out for the Democrats showed that many voters regarded their party as too preoccupied with 'eccentric' and minority causes. It was an unattractive home for the average factory worker whose stake in society had improved and who now wanted more of the trappings of material success. The Democrats seemed to be out of touch with the popular aspirations of a growing number of Americans. They needed to consider the interests of the blue- and white-collar workers – the working middle class, in American terminology – many of whom felt squeezed between the needs of the undeserving rich and the undeserving poor. To younger voters, New Deal liberalism meant very little, and a preoccupation with the socially deprived and disadvantaged seemed to offer little prospect of winning their allegiance.

Party strategists decided that the approach required must target their anxieties and preoccupations. The slogan adopted was *People First*. The Democrats identified themselves with the 'work ethic', in the sense that everyone should be allowed to benefit from their work. They aimed their proposals for tax increases at the top 2 per cent, for it had become apparent to Democrats in the Reagan days that no party which advocated higher general taxation would capture the presidency. They were therefore seeking to gear their proposals and policies to the broad working–middle-class coalition; whose interests were different from those relatively few people who were very rich and never likely to be sympathetic to the party anyway. That small percentage had done so well out of the Reagan–Bush years that they were seen as a lost cause, as far as electoral support was concerned.

The Democrats consciously re-examined their stance, and having listened to what people were saying they ensured that their message was in tune with people's needs as well as the core values of the party. They spelt out the need for active government, that the state must counterbalance the markets, for free markets do not give 'the common man a fair shake' – but the vocabulary used reflected how much they had learnt: 'tough love', 'creative government' and 'invest and grow' were key Clinton phrases. They rejected 'something-for-nothing' welfarism, and were prepared to be 'tough' on welfare mothers, giving them training and childcare for two years, but then expecting them to take a job. Welfare should be a second chance, not a way of life, so that the central values were work, reward for effort and responsibility.

Above all, Clinton and his strategists understood the need to address the concerns of the majority and not the minorities, although he was concerned to meet representatives of all groups. His message was spiced with a dash of under-30s idealism and an element of modern-day feminism. He met members of unexpected groups, and was keen to talk to African-American churchmen about crime, and to young people in white suburbs about drugs. The emphasis always was on finding out what bothered people, and ensuring that party policies fitted the situation.

Of course, there are dangers in asking what people want and then offering to give it to them, although defenders of the President would argue that though the party repositioned itself it was ready to stand by its basic commitment and attitudes, and ready to go out and sell the case for positive government action to balance the limitations of the market. Critics have subsequently pointed out that there was an absence of a firm ideological basis to his approach. Some would argue that one of the reasons for uncertainty and drift when he became President was the lack of an underlying coherence in his thinking and programme.

Democrat renewal and the lessons for Labour

Both Labour and the Democrats were suffering from electoral difficulties in the early 1990s. By mid 1992 Labour had lost four successive elections, and apart from the Carter interlude the Democrats had been out of the White House since 1968. Like the Democrats, Labour in the 1980s had also been involved in internal battle, committed to 'eccentric' and 'minority' causes and unappealing to the average factory worker who said: 'This is not my party'. They had seemed arrogant, elitist and out of touch with aspirations. However, in 1992 the Clinton team had reinvented the party as the New Democrats. They had discovered a new identity which was more in tune with contemporary feeling, and in 1992 they had put together a winning combination – a credible candidate, a strategy for economic growth, and a social identity which could appeal to all working people. Labour was bound to wonder why it had lost and the Democrats won in the two elections of that year.

According to the modernising tendency in the Labour Party – represented especially by Tony Blair and Gordon Brown – the lesson from America was that the party has to rid itself of the trappings of the past, and show that it was not a minority-based party but one for all wage and salary earners, a broad working–middle-class coalition which might appeal more widely. In particular, Labour enthusiasts for the Clinton approach felt that Labour must appeal to the majority rather than to the minorities, and that by so doing it could again identify with the working middle-classes of Britain, just as the Democrats

Blair, Clinton and the third way

The third way is a strategy for reshaping politics and society. It is also a strategy about creating a new left-of-centre progressive consensus, in Britain and elsewhere. In April 1999, Bill Clinton (President of the USA), Gerhard Schroder (Chancellor of Germany), Wim Kok (Netherlands Prime Minister) and Massano D'Alence (Italian Prime Minister) attended a conference in Washington specifically about third way politics. In July 2003, leaders from Europe, Latin America and, for the first time, Africa, met to discuss a programme for 'progressive governance'.

Tony Blair and Bill Clinton have been widely recognised as the two main supporters of the third way. The British Prime Minister has embraced the concept to describe New Labour's ideology. In Britain this concept is most closely associated in academic circles with Anthony Giddens, Director of the London School of Economics and Political Science.[26] Essentially the third way is an attempt to find a middle way between left and right, between state socialist planning and free market capitalism. It appeals to centre-left progressives and moderate social democrats. Giddens uses the term to refer to social democratic renewal. For renewal was necessary in the late 1990s to adapt to the probably irreversible transformation of Britain by Thatcherism, the revival of free-market capitalism and the realities of globalisation.

Under the 'third way':

1 The role of the state will be far more flexible, working in new ways. It will be pro-active, devising new policy instruments to produce essential outcomes. It will be a facilitator and a regulator, more than a provider of services. For example, a new hospital may be

showed that they were not the people who gave way to special interests but governed in the national interest. This assessment inspired Labour to re-invent itself as New Labour, abandon the old Clause Four and show a new concern for the needs of Middle England.

Party membership

Party membership declined in most of Europe and in the United States in the last few decades of the twentieth century. There are exceptions to the trend, such as Greece, Portugal and Spain, but as their peoples were living under or recovering from authoritarian regimes early in this period the comparison is made more complicated. Now living in more open societies, citizens of these countries have taken the opportunity to benefit from their newly won freedom. Of course, even where there is a mass membership, this is no guarantee that members will have a say on matters of policy.

Not all countries have parties with a mass membership. In America, supporters do not 'join' a party in the way that they have the opportunity to do in Britain. Arrangements are less formal and no fees are paid; members make a simple declaration of their allegiance at the time of registration.

---

desperately needed in a town; the state may work here as both facilitator and part-provider in a public–private partnership.

2 The need for a competitive and dynamic market is recognised, and Labour has accepted that nationalisation is dead. It argues that it is possible to combine social justice with economic efficiency in a market economy. Both markets and state should be disciplined by a public interest test. Legislation should provide redress for consumers and monitor the quality of state services – for example, the Blair government's introduction of a minimum wage and measures against failing schools.

3 There will be 'inclusion'. The 'New Politics' of the third way defines equality as 'inclusion' and inequality as 'exclusion'. Social inclusion refers in its broadest sense to citizenship with its civil and political rights, its obligations and its opportunities for self-fulfilment and to make a contribution to society. It involves everyone having access to the requirements for a decent life, including education, healthcare, work and income. Measures need to be put in place to reduce the involuntary exclusion of the disadvantaged.

4 The rights of citizens are accompanied by reciprocal duties and it is vital that there is mutual responsibility between individuals and institutions. For example, parents have the right to send their children to school but parents also are responsible for encouraging their children and supporting their school.

5 Expenditure on welfare should come from the state, but from other agencies too. The choice of language here is important. In the past, the money for the welfare state was called public spending; now, as we hear so much from Tony Blair, it is called 'investment'.

6 The slogan 'what matters is what works' sums up the approach to policy-making.

The Conservatives and the Republicans: some broad similarities

1 The centre of gravity in American politics is more to the right than in Britain. Both parties fell into the hands of the New Right in the 1980s, emphasising policies such as pursuit of the market economy, hostility to organised trade unionism and low taxation. Since then, party 'moderates' have had a difficult time. More liberal, pro-European Conservatives such as Kenneth Clarke have found it difficult to get their ideas accepted under Hague and Duncan Smith, just as more liberal elements among the Republicans such as Senator Jeffords (and especially pro-choice Republicans) have been squeezed out or left isolated in the Bush years.

2 Republicans have been traditionally more anti-socialist and unwilling to accept any public ownership. Conservatives are also very much in favour of free enterprise, and opted for privatisation in Thatcher–Major years. In the years of postwar consensus policies, they were pragmatic on nationalisation, though it is out of favour today.

3 Both parties dislike 'big government' and favour low taxation

4 Neither party is very sympathetic to the position of trade unions in recent years. The Thatcher–Reagan administrations were keen to weaken union power. Trade unions have never been as powerful in America as they have in Britain.

5 Both parties are very patriotic, and see themselves as upholding national interests. Both are firm believers in strong national defence; both are traditionally very anti-communist in foreign policy, though no longer a key issue.

6 Both are keen to align their countries with the 'New Europe' and share a common suspicion of the 'Old Europe'. US Defense Secretary Rumsfeld and Duncan Smith are wary of the Franco-German axis in the EU and urge the applicant nations such as Poland and the Czech Republic to be willing to stand up against Paris and Berlin. Duncan Smith is keen to see a 'Europe of democracies' and upholds the rights of nation states, as opposed to any idea of a European superstate.

7 Both parties are committed to firm policies on law and order, and wish to see more emphasis on tough treatment for criminals and support for victims. Americans of all parties more committed to capital punishment.

8 Both parties see a major role for the private sector and charitable bodies in welfare policy. America has never had anything like the NHS and the nature and scale of the universal benefits of the British Welfare State. Many Conservatives are keen to re-model both, and encourage individuals to make provision for their own security.

9 Both parties stress the value of the traditional family as the best means of bringing up children.

10 Many supporters of both parties also emphasise the value of religion in speeches and policy documents, but religion is more of an issue in American politics, especially for the Republicans. The Religious Right (Christian Coalition) plays a key role in the Republican Party, influencing its attitudes on school prayer, abortion, censorship, etc. It sees religious values as the cement which holds the fabric of society together. (Note that there has been a small but increasing role played by fundamentalist religious groups in Britain in recent years, as in the Brentwood and Ongar constituency, where there is said to have been a takeover of the local Conservatives.)

Party members as approximate percentage of electorate in 2000

Austria	18
Finland	10
Norway	7
Italy	4
Germany	3
United Kingdom	2

Source: Adapted from P. Mair and I. Van Biezen, 'Party Membership in Europe, 1980-2000',
Party Politics (7), 2001.

Party membership in Britain, 2002

Labour	270,000
Conservatives	320,000
Lib Dems	74,000
SNP	30,000
Plaid Cymru	8,000

Source: Figures provided in The Guardian, September 2002.

Some writers see declining membership as an indication of a lessening of enthusiasm for and interest in political parties. They point to the loss of members by established parties and adversely compare it to the growth in pressure-group activity. This is certainly true of the British Green Party, which has fared disappointingly after its high peak in the 1989 European Election, whereas some green groups have grown rapidly in support. However, to some extent the figures quoted may equally reflect the fact that parties today spend less time on recruiting than in the past, for they once needed activists to engage in voluntary work and rally the local voters to turn out in support of their candidate. Nowadays, the local campaign in most constituencies is less important than the one on television, by which the leaders and their senior colleagues can address the whole electorate in one brief appearance.

Of course, although changing electoral methods may provide an explanation, parties would be foolish to allow this to deter them from seeking to revive their membership. In the 1990s, New Labour enthusiasts saw it as essential to create a mass membership, the more so at a time when its trade union links were being downplayed with consequent implications for party finance. However, the drive has lost momentum, for many of the 405,000 members at the turn of the millennium have disappeared.

Party organisation

The last few decades have also seen developments in party organisation. Originally spurred on by the creation of a mass electorate in the days when universal franchise was granted, parties saw the need to create national and local organisations to ensure that they were in a position to maximise their support. They needed to raise funds, organise canvassing and provide opportunities for the new voters to become involved, among other things. Usually the organisation operated on a top-down basis, under which national organisations were created and they were given the task of supervising the activities of local branches established throughout the country. Decisions were taken at the centre, and policy statements and lists of likely candidates were handed down to the local associations where much of the day-to-day voluntary work of mobilising the voters was carried out.

This pattern has not been as true in recent years. Older parties have had to adapt to changing conditions, and the arrival of television has, as we have seen, made local organisation less essential; indeed, some party clubs have lapsed to such an extent that they have effectively disappeared, only to be briefly resurrected at election time. In Britain, Labour has been concerned to modernise its image and organisation, and since its defeat in 1997 the Conservative Party has engaged in an overhaul of its traditional approach, streamlining the party and making it more open in its operations. In both cases there has been a new emphasis on making the party more democratic in the sense that members should have a greater say in how the party functions, whilst also seeking to ensure that the leadership retains key powers to act to keep out dissidents who might bring discredit to the organisation.

Whereas British and European parties tend to be highly integrated and centralised, with control resting in the hands of the party leaders and various 'paid' agents, this has not been so in America. Power is more decentralised, and the party's national organisations have only been important during presidential election years. Although the man in the White House might be seen as the leader of his party (in truth he is more of a national than a party leader), there is no equivalent in the defeated party. The presidential challenger acts as leader between the Convention in August and the November election, but once the election is lost his or her authority disappears and there is no one who can really be said to issue policy on behalf of the party. For a long while, national organisation in the British sense barely existed. There were national committees, staffed largely by volunteers, and national chairpersons, who hire staff, raise money, pay bills and attend to the daily duties of the party.

In recent decades, American parties have seen the importance of employing new techniques to galvanise the electorate via mass mailings and other devices. The Republican Party has been effective in using the modern technology of campaigning and in mastering the complicated laws that affect how money is raised and spent. Since the 1980s, they have employed a substantial professional staff to conduct such activities. The Democrats, with a smaller staffing, have nonetheless followed suit, although they contract out much of their work, such as direct mail fund-raising, to campaign consultants. In both cases, the national party has been significantly strengthened and is now more active and effective than ever before. Although the parties expand and contract their activities according to the election cycle, they are continuously involved in the tasks of party development, including recruiting and training candidates and their staff, conducting polling and issues research, and handling relations with the media, among other things.

Party finance

State funding is almost universal in modern democracies. In many cases, state aid is the main source of party revenue, so that only in the Netherlands, Britain and the USA do membership contributions clearly exceed funding from the public purse.

Parties obtain their funding from other sources which include:
- individual subscriptions from party members;
- individual donations, sometimes in the form of one-off gifts from generous benefactors;
- contributions from associated organisations: Labour has traditionally benefited from trade union funding – especially in election years – although in recent years the proportion of income received from unions has dropped sharply.

The issue of funding has become particularly controversial in recent years. The common assumption made by many commentators and critics is that 'he who pays the piper calls the tune'. People – individuals or business corporations – only give if something can be expected back in return. The pay-off might include influence with the party leadership – especially when it is in power – over decisions which might affect the benefactor's particular interests.

Resolving the dilemma: state aid for political parties?

Most countries have attempted to resolve the problems surrounding party financing by opting for a scheme of state funding. In the United States it has been available since 1976 to candidates contesting the presidency, as long as they accept the overall cap on their total spending. In almost all cases, aid has proved generally acceptable not only to the parties themselves, but also to the voters.

Aid has been given for various reasons, among them:
- to assist candidates and parties with financial difficulties;
- to lessen corruption;
- to avoid excessive reliance upon 'special interests' and institutional sources of finance;
- to equalise opportunities between candidates and parties;
- to stimulate political education and research.

Types of state aid

Aid to political parties can be of two types: conditional and unconditional. A majority of countries which have state funding opt for the unconditional approach, whereby the receipt of aid is related to the votes which parties receive in Parliamentary and other elections. In most countries where such aid is given, it appears to be acceptable not only to the parties but also to the electorate. Critics of this idea argue that it is not the role of the state to assist parties solely because they are in financial difficulties. If they have problems, they should seek to raise more money by voluntary means and to reduce or rationalise expenditure. It cannot be in the interest of the taxpayers to be compelled unconditionally to subsidise a party which cannot finance itself. Moreover, given much public disquiet about politicians and parties, unconditional state aid might increase alienation from politics and public cynicism about those who serve as elected representatives. Finally, such a direct subsidy does nothing to encourage political participation. It may even discourage it, if parties become over-reliant on public funds.

Those who favour conditional aid wish to preserve rather than to undermine the voluntary nature of political parties. They recognise the importance of financing parties via means which lessen the dominance of particular interests and encourage individual involvement. Such a change could help to invigorate political parties. They turn to American experience as a guide to what might be achieved. The 1971 Federal Elections Campaign Act (FECA), subsequently amended in 1974, 1976 and 1979, provided – among other things – for the public financing of presidential elections and presidential primaries. Funds are provided for candidates by means of a tax check-off box on individual income-tax returns. This allows an individual to allocate so many dollars of their tax liability to a Presidential Election Campaign Fund. The money collected is then distributed to those candidates who have chosen to opt for public funding. Candidates in receipt of such money accept strict limits upon raising and spending corporate money.

There are difficulties with such a scheme from a British point of view, not least that fewer taxpayers receive a tax return in Britain than in America. Again, critics would say that it is unfair, even discriminatory, if the scheme only applies to those who pay income tax, for this would exclude such groups as the vast majority of students, pensioners, the unemployed and the disabled. But the basic principle, that aid should be triggered by the private and personal decisions of individuals, finds some support. Parties should gain state backing according to the number of people who are willing to contribute funds to them. This could be done by saying that for every £5 or some similar amount duly contributed to a political party, a matching payment would be made by the state.

Arguments in favour of state aid for political parties

Parties need money from sources which do not undermine the integrity of the political process, and many academics and commentators have pointed to the example of state aid overseas where state funding is the norm in Europe and other developed areas. The concept is supported by Labour and the Liberal Democrats who have most to gain from such an experiment.

The principle of some state assistance to British political parties has already been conceded. Help is given to opposition parties (the so-called 'short' money) to assist them in the performance of their parliamentary work, and at election time facilities are made available to them at no cost. The amount of money involved in terms of government spending on such assistance is small, and by ensuring that payment is dependent on a certain level of success in the last election, the difficulty of the state financing small and extreme parties such as the Communists or the British National Party is removed.

The positive case for state funding in Britain rests on a number of propositions, namely:

1 It would reduce the excessive dependence of the two main parties on their large backers, companies in the case of the Conservative Party and trade unions in the case of Labour. If parties turn to private donations from wealthy individuals or corporate backers – as New Labour has done – this creates problems as many people assume that any such money is donated in the expectation of some kind of political benefit (perhaps a favourable business decision or a title). State funding avoids the perception that wealthy backers are able to buy influence over the operations of a political party.

2 Parties of the Centre-Left tend to be at a disadvantage, for they do not have the means to compete. Labour has traditionally drawn heavily on its bedrock working-class support, and it still derives much strength from the inner cities, where voters tend to be relatively poor. By contrast, many Conservative voters are better-placed. More affluent people can afford to be more generous in their political giving. They are also more likely to join a political party, for working people do not tend to be 'joiners' of organisations to the same extent.

3 Political parties which do not have such backing are placed at an unfair disadvantage. The Conservatives outspend other parties in general elections, having more extensive poster campaigns and usually spending more in each constituency. Labour is less well-placed than the Conservatives, but for smaller parties the situation may seem particularly unfair.

4 These difficulties are accentuated when several elections arise together, as in 1979 and 1997. For most councils, there is today a political contest, and since 1979 we also have Euro-elections. The impact of all of this

electioneering on funds is considerable: serious for a major party, dire for a smaller one.

5 Perhaps the core of the case for political funding by the state is, however, less concerned with the disadvantages suffered by one party or the other, and more with the importance of party activity to the democratic process. Representative government depends on political parties competing for power and engaging in the process of public education on political issues. Parties organise opinion and represent the people in the corridors of power. With state aid, they would be in a better position to carry out their functions. They would be less preoccupied with ensuring their survival, and more with genuine political activity. At present, the trend is for parties to reduce their expenditure in an attempt to balance the books, and this means fewer agents than before, and less staff at headquarters to deal in research or answer queries from the public. This can be said to be detrimental to the political process. By investing in political parties, therefore, we would be investing in democracy.

Arguments against state aid for political parties

Some people are much less concerned about reliance on institutional backing, and see nothing sinister in parties gaining financial support from interests with whom there is some similarity of outlook and aspiration. Payment does not equal 'undue influence', and the history of the past generation suggests that governments have often felt free to act in a way that their backers may not like. Labour in the late 1960s and 1970s felt free to pursue policies with which the unions were unhappy, and the CBI, the employers' organisation, often felt that Thatcherite Conservative policies in the 1980s were not as favourable as they might have liked. Several companies lamented the 'hands off' approach to industry which the Conservatives followed after 1979, and would have preferred more intervention to help them through the more difficult times.

Others might argue that state aid could be beneficial to 'third parties', and therefore lessen the chances of either of the two main ones of winning an election outright. Another fear is that aid could be channelled into the funds of parties of doubtful democratic credentials.

More fundamentally, however, critics of state funding tend to make these broad points:

1 Politics is essentially a voluntary activity, and that if the parties are currently short of funds then they must either curtail their costs or seek funds in other ways. This means more local fund-raising; the answer to a shortfall is for volunteer workers to engage more wholeheartedly in their profit-making endeavours. With state funding available, there is little incentive for parties to go out and recruit a mass membership.

2 The decline in membership and waning popularity of the two main parties suggests that they are not as popular as they once were. The answer is that they need to pursue policies which are more in tune with the needs and wishes of the voters, and that when they make themselves more attractive to them, they can expect to increase their support and gain new recruits.

3 Many taxpayers, especially those not interested in politics, might resent being asked to finance party activity. The amount per person of any state scheme might be small, but many voters would probably prefer not to pay it. Cynicism and disillusion with politicians (already widely prevalent in 2002) might be increased if the public was expected to spend money on their activities. Moreover, voters might have a suspicion that if more money were available, it would be spent on needless extravagances, such as glossy brochures and advertising material.

4 Popular support for state funding has often increased when corruption seems to be all-pervasive, but there is little evidence that state funding ends corruption, and some people even argue that it can increase rather than diminish it. In Italy, assistance was initially introduced in 1974 to reduce the bribery and scandals so endemic in political life; by 1993, as details of illegal payments and the abuse of power were exposed, it was dropped because of its misuse. Other countries which have state aid have also experienced financial improprieties – France, Germany and Spain among them. Much depends on the traditions of public life in the country concerned.

5 For many, even if in principle they can see something in the case for state assistance, then 'the time is not ripe'. If the country was doing well, then maybe a little money might be sent to the parties. In times of recession, or when the country is emerging from 'hard times', subsidising parties seems a low priority.

The decline of political parties – do they still matter?

Criticism of political parties is not new, their initial emergence being originally greeted with grave suspicion and mistrust. As we have seen, Jefferson and others founders of the American Constitution were highly critical, seeing parties and factions as promoting conflict and destroying the underlying unity of society.

In 1972, in America, the political columnist David Broder wondered whether the party was really over, and detected signs of 'a growing danger to the prospects for responsible party government' in 'the technological revolution that has affected campaigning in the past decade'.[27] He noted that the development of new forms of campaigning – associated with television, polls, computers, political consultants, media specialists and such things – meant that candidates did not need parties to provide what they could hire for themselves. He suggested that parties were no longer the main source of political information and affection, and argued that any voter who wished to find out more about a candidate's qualities and political stance could now do so via television rather than via the agency of the party, and that pressure groups were in the forefront of much political education and campaigning.

Subsequently, many political commentators began to ask whether parties were obsolescent if not actually obsolete, a theme much discussed after Broder first wrote on the subject. Some writers are encouraged by the trend. Mulgan has argued that – as with dinosaurs – parties are incapable of adaptation to a changing political environment.[28] He sees this as a healthy development if it means that people are drawn into the politics of new social movements, such as the environmental or peace cause. Others see a cause for anxiety, and express concern that as politics become increasingly candidate-centred in an age of television, then the importance of political ideas may be diminished and that of more superficial values such as personality or more harmful influences such as money may be increased.

Evidence of party decline

Most political parties have not been stable over a long period. Stability is associated more with the Atlantic and Commonwealth countries than the rest of the world. However, even in such countries as these, there has been a noticeable decline in the fortunes of once-strong parties in the last two or three decades of the twentieth century. Several have lost members and voters in large numbers. They function in an era of partisan and class de-alignment which has led to a far greater volatility in voting behaviour than ever before. Voting is no longer 'habitual and ingrained', as Punnet described it back in the 1970s,[29] and parties can no longer count on the degree of support which they once could almost take for granted.

The European scene provides plenty of examples of party decline. The erosion of party strength has been particularly marked among some of the larger, established parties which have suffered in an age of greater volatility in voting behaviour. This has affected countries with traditionally stable party systems such as Austria, Denmark and Germany. For instance, there has been a long-term decline in the aggregate vote of both main German parties at federal level. Extreme right wing parties have been beneficiaries of the decline in support for established political parties. Such parties as the Front National in France, the Progress Party in Norway, the Danish People's Party, the Swiss People's Party, the Italian Northern League, and Vllaams Blok in Belgium have gained considerable support in recent years. Austria's far-right Freedom Party secured more than 33 per cent of the vote in 1999 and as a result formed a coalition government with the conservative People's Party.

Blondel distinguishes between the situation in continental Europe and that in the USA, and divides the Western scene into three distinct scenarios:

1 In Europe he finds that the traditional parties have lost ground to newer parties which seem to be more attuned to the people's interests. This has resulted in the development of a growing number of significant parties, this fragmentation making it more difficult for any one party to emerge with 'a true grip on political life'.

2 Britain and the older Commonwealth countries have largely avoided the above trend, because of their attachment to the First Past the Post electoral system, which has enabled them to think still in terms of the old adversarial conflict of government and opposition.

3 In America, he detects a different scenario. Parties have a more symbolic role: 'They do not propose programmes; they do not even select candidates, since these are in effect chosen by primaries which are outside the control of party leaders. On this basis, they survive . . . [but] remain in existence because people apparently feel that there have to be parties in a democracy.'[30]

Britain and the United States

In Britain, in 1955 the two main parties received 97 per cent of the popular vote. By 1964 this had declined to 88 per cent, by 1992 76 per cent and in 2001 72.4 per cent. In addition, they have suffered from falling membership and there is increased cynicism about those who lead them. Yet in spite of the erosion of their electoral support and membership, the two main parties have still managed to dominate the political scene. Every election since 1945 has produced a single-party government, with either Labour or the Conservatives in office. No other party has ever looked as though it could form a single party or coalition administration. In Parliament, in spite of the growth of support for third and minor parties, it remains the case that between them the same two parties won 578 of the 659 seats in 2001.

In twentieth-century America, there was plenty of evidence that political parties had fallen on hard times. They have never had the solid class-based electoral support common in other developed countries, and given the weakness of party discipline have never been sure that they could turn any detailed policy commitments into legislative effect. Maidment and McGrew regard them as 'vast and disparate coalitions with no coherent sets of beliefs'.[31] Other commentators have written about public disillusion with the two parties and the politicians who belong to them, suggesting that they are all as bad as each other.

Historically weak, American parties had by the 1970s become weaker than they were at the turn of the twentieth century for various reasons, including:

- The growth of the system of primary elections which took power away from the party bosses.
- The erosion of the North–South divide, so that the traditional attachment of the South to the Democratic cause was seriously undermined.
- The development of the mass media, which placed more emphasis on the merits of individual candidates; electioneering has become more candidate-centred.
- The arrival of new issues on the agenda in the 1960s and 1970s, such as feminism, environmentalism, civil rights and Vietnam; on occasion, these issues cut across the party divide, and divided some members of the party from others.
- The increasing importance of pressure groups and Political Action Committees which meant that there were more causes in which Americans could participate and alternative bodies for fund-raising for candidates.
- Changes in voting behaviour associated with changing attitudes among key groups of voters. Party loyalty has declined in an age of increasing de-alignment. Most surveys pointed to the loosening attachment of many Democrats and Republicans to their party over the last three decades of the twentieth century, and a growing sense of party neutrality (see also pp. 288–9).

America does not possess disciplined and cohesive parties of the type associated with Britain and Western Europe in the twentieth century. But fears for their continued relevance have been greatly exaggerated, and Epstein's conclusion that they will continue to be important players is not difficult to accept. Noting that they have become 'frayed', he concludes that parties 'will survive and even moderately prosper in a society evidently unreceptive to strong parties and yet unready, and probably unable, to abandon parties altogether'.[32]

Party loyalty may have waned, but of late there have been some indications of renewal. Organisation has become more effective, as first the Republicans and shortly afterwards the Democrats saw the potential of high-tech fund-raising. Hence Herrnson's observation that: The parties' national, congressional and senatorial campaign committees are now wealthier, more stable, better organised and better staffed than ever before.[33]

For all of their weaknesses, American parties have not been displaced. They:
- still serve as a reference point for the electorate which – as many surveys confirm – still think in terms of Republicans and Democrats;
- remain a reference point for congressmen, almost every one of whom belongs to one of the major parties;
- have regained some importance in the last generation as the 'new issues' have lost much of their earlier impact;
- have become more organised at the federal level;
- have shown a greater ability in recent years to raise money by new techniques of fund-raising.

Conclusion

Both Britain and America have long had two-party systems. Britain has developed a 'two and a bit' party system or a 'two-party system and three- (or in Scotland and Wales, four-) party politics'. At national level the American two-party system is more deeply entrenched and the United States has not had a consistently powerful third force in recent decades. In both cases, support for the two main parties is buttressed by the First Past the Post voting system.

In the 1980s, in both countries there was a highly influential period of right-wing rule, in which Margaret Thatcher in Britain and Ronald Reagan in America introduced policies much influenced by New Right doctrines. The influence and popular support for these policies has had a lasting effect not only on their own parties but on the main opposition ones as well.

However, there are key differences between parties in the two countries, of which two are most important:

1 In Britain, parties are centralised and highly disciplined, enabling the governing party to bend Parliament to its will. Not so in the United States, where although American parties can exert some influence they are weaker, have less party discipline and a markedly less-developed national headquarters.

2 In the United States, the two parties are closer together on the ideological spectrum than in Britain. America is the only industrialised liberal democracy which has never developed a significant socialist party, and although the Democrats are the more left-wing or 'progressive' party, in ideological terms they are nearer to the Liberal Democrats and New Labour than to the Labour Party which existed in Britain for most of the last century.

For all of the signs of weakness and fragmentation in party systems, parties are unlikely to become extinct. Even if the bonds are somewhat tenuous, they remain as the main mechanism which links the voters and those who rule them, and they continue to perform useful tasks which today can be summarised as:

- recruiting representatives for national legislatures, and thereby at least influencing – in the British case determining – the choice of those who serve in government;
- educating the electorate by developing, elaborating and 'selling' policies;
- offering an opportunity for popular participation in the political process, even if in many cases this chance is shunned by the majority of voters.

Two-party systems in Britain and the United States: a summary		
	Britain	*United States*
Similarities	One more progressive (Labour) and one more conservative (Conservative) party.	One more progressive (Democratic) and one more conservative (Republican) party.
	Both parties have different wings and wide appeal: Conservatives have recently had more problems with ideological differences, moderates have lost much of their former influence.	Both parties have different wings and wide appeal: Republican moderates have been squeezed out in recent years, partly because of the influence of the Christian coalition on moral issues.
	Dominance of two parties in votes in postwar elections to 1970s, but not so apparent now. Still dominate House of Commons.	Two parties usually dominate presidential elections. In some states, there is regular one party domination in elections for Congress. Hardly any independents sit in Congress.
Differences	Two-party system, but very significant third-party representation: four parties in Scotland and Wales.	Two-party system, or 51-party system? No significant third-party success.
	Big role for parties in elections, including choosing candidates.	More supportive role for candidates. Americans choosing a President more than a party.
	Traditionally more importance attached to ideology, with fairly clear Left–Right differences.	Less ideological parties, more catch-all in character: greater role of religion, especially in Republican Party.
	Strong party unity: sense of party loyalty in voting lobbies and important role of Whips.	Loose party discipline, never same emphasis on party voting in Congress.
	Key role of headquarters in party organisation, especially in Labour Party: centralised parties.	Decentralised parties, with traditionally weak role of national party organisation: growing importance of head-quarters in campaigning.

REFERENCES

1 A. Ball, *Modern Government & Politics*, Macmillan, 1993.
2 M. Shaw, *Anglo-American Democracy*, Routledge and Kegan, 1968.
3 M. Walles, *British and American Systems of Government*, Philip Allan/Barnes & Noble, 1988.
4 A. Heywood, *Politics*, Macmillan, 1997.
5 As note 1 above.
6 G. Edwards *et al.*, *Government in America*, Harper Collins, 1996.
7 M. Vile, *Politics in the USA*, Hutchinson, 1978.
8 M. Duverger, *Political Parties*, Methuen, 1962.
9 A. Gitelson *et al.*, *American Government*, Houghton Mifflin, 2001.
10 As note 8 above.
11 D. Butler and D. Kavanagh, *The British General Election of 1997*, Macmillan, 1997.
12 A. Greenwood, as quoted in S. Lipset and G. Marks, *Why Socialism Failed in the United States: It Didn't Happen Here*, Norton and Company, 2000.
13 As note 12 above.
14 A. Crosland, *The Future of Socialism*, Cape, 1956.
15 V. O. Key, *Politics, Parties and Pressure Groups*, Crowell, 1964.
16 S. Beer, *Britain Against Itself*, Faber & Faber, 1982.
17 I. Budge, K. Newton *et al.*, *The Politics of the New Europe*, Longman, 1997.
18 As note 2 above.
19 S. Beer, *Modern British Politics*, Faber, 1965.
20 R. McKenzie, *British Political Parties*, Heinemann, 1955.
21 B. Pimlott, *Contemporary Record*, Summer, 1989.
22 C. Rossiter, *Parties and Politics in America*, Signet, 1960.
23 Lord Bryce, *Modern Democracies*, Macmillan, 1921.
24 As note 2 above.
25 S. Verba and G. Orren, *Equality in America*, Harvard University Press, 1985.
26 A. Giddens, *The Third Way*, Polity Press, 1998.
27 D. Broder, *The Party's Over*, Harper and Row, 1972.
28 R. Mulgan, *Politics in New Zealand*, Auckland University Press, 1997.
29 R. Punnett, *British Government and Politics*, Gower, 1971.
30 J. Blondel, *Comparative Government: An Introduction*, Prentice Hall, 1995.
31 D. Maidment and D. McGrew, *The American Political Process*, Sage/OU, 1992.
32 L. Epstein, *Political Parties in the American Mould*, University of Wisconsin Press, 1986.
33 P. Herrnson, *Party Campaigning in the 1980s*, Harvard University Press, 1988.

USEFUL WEB SITES

For the UK

www.labour.org.uk The Labour Party.

www.libdems.org.uk The Liberal Democrat Party.

www.tory.org.uk The Conservative Party.

www.greenparty.org.uk The Green Party.

www.keele.ac.uk/depts/por/ptbase.htm Keele Guide to Political Thought and Ideology. Guide to political thinking and ideas.

www.ukpol.co.uk Coverage of various political topics and links to various web sites.

For the USA

www.democrats.org Democratic National Committee. Details of many aspects of recent election campaign and party platform; issues of interest to the party.

www.rnc.org Republican National Committee. Details of many aspects of recent election campaign and party platform; issues of interest to the party.

Several third parties have interesting sites, explaining their histories and different policy positions:

www.lp.org Libertarian Party.

http://reformparty.org Reform Party.

www.greens.org Green Parties of North America.

www.dsausa.org Democratic Socialists of America.

SAMPLE QUESTIONS

1 Compare the main British and American parties in respect of their ideas, sources of support and organisations.

2 'The decline of political parties'. To what extent does experience in Britain and America suggest that political parties are in long-term decline?

3 Are politics today in Britain and the United States more about personalities than political parties?

Pressure groups

9

Unlike political parties, pressure groups do not aspire to govern the country and are concerned with a relatively narrow range of issues. Much of their work is non-political, but in as much as their concerns and aspirations are affected by government they seek to acquire an influence over the conduct of public policy.

In this chapter, we are concerned with examining the range of groups in Britain and the United States, the ways in which they operate and their effectiveness. In addition, we consider the changes in pressure-group activity on both sides of the Atlantic over the last two or three decades.

POINTS TO CONSIDER

➤ What are the differences between movements and pressure groups, and what are the distinctive characteristics of New Social Movements?

➤ Why have single-issue groups become so much more significant in recent years?

➤ In what respects does lobbying of the Executive branch differ in Britain and the United States?

➤ Which access points are most important in British and American politics, and why?

➤ Distinguish between iron triangles and policy networks.

➤ Why have some groups resorted to direct action in recent decades?

➤ Do pressure groups make a positive contribution to British and American democracy?

Free societies are **pluralist**, in that a variety of organisations are allowed to exist and compete for influence over government. No single group can exert a monopoly of power and manipulate the system for its own advantage. In a number of pluralist societies, there are strongly antagonistic ethnic, linguistic or religious organisations; others may be more class-based. Political parties are the most significant of these bodies, and their composition may reflect some of the differences to which we have referred. But in Western liberal democracies there are thousands of other bodies which seek to influence the conduct of power and make their views known. Those people who represent business interests tend to be among the most powerful players in pluralist societies such as Britain, France, Italy and the United States. In all societies there are groups which seek to influence the way the political process operates.

> **pluralism**
> Describes a political system in which numerous groups compete to exert influence over the government. New groups can easily be created, so that further competition can emerge in the market place.
>
> **pluralist societies**
> Those in which the power of the state is limited and there is a political market place in which group activity can flourish. Governments are responsive to group interest. Not everything is politicised, and fundamental freedoms such as free speech and the rights of groups such as professional bodies and trade unions are guaranteed. The USA and UK are examples, as are countries ranging from Australia to France, from Canada to Japan.

These groups differ considerably in their internal operation, some being democratically structured, others led by a powerful elite which dominates proceedings on a regular basis. Some are large, others are small; some operate at a national level, others do so regionally or locally; some are particularly effective and have popular appeal, others cater for minority interests and needs. Some are durable and make a great impact; others are short-lived and make little impression.

The growth of group activity

Pressure groups actually have a long history. In the nineteenth century, the Anti-Corn Law League was a classic case of an organisation which was formed to influence government. At around the same time, de Tocqueville observed that in America too what he called 'associations' were becoming 'a powerful instrument of action'.[1] Yet most groups are of much more recent origin. Their number has markedly increased since the war. Governmental intervention in economic and social life has expanded enormously. As voters expect those who rule them to produce policies on a range of issues from health to consumer protection, there are groups established to press their own claims, interests and ideas.

In countries where proportional representation is used, groups representing some interests have formed political parties. In Scandinavia, farmers' parties have long existed and the presence or absence of their support can be critical in determining the fate of governments. In two-party systems such as Britain and America, the farmers are more likely to seek influence through the organisations set up specifically to defend their interests – the National Farmers' Union in Britain and various organisations in the United States including the American Farm Bureau Federation, the National Farmers' Union and the Grange, the latter being as much social as political in character. In addition to these large and general agrarian organisations, there has in recent years been a vast expansion in the number of agricultural groups representing the interests not only of producers but also of refiners and distributors, of different cereals, fruits and vegetables, and other farm produce.

Especially since the 1960s there has been what Heywood has referred to as an 'explosion in pressure and protest politics'.[2] In his view, this burst of activity 'may be part of a broader process that has seen the decline of parties and a growing emphasis on organised groups and social movements emerging as agents of mobilisation and representation'. Since the 1970s, another type of organisation has emerged: the New Social Movements, whose structure is looser than political parties and whose aims are broader than those of pressure groups. Among the most conspicuous are those which deal with environmental matters, and issues such as nuclear power and weapons, the advancement of women's rights and the protection of minority interests.

Classification of groups

Pressure groups are voluntary organisations formed to advance or defend a common cause or interest. They are unlike political parties in that they do not wish to assume responsibility for governing the country, rather they seek to influence those who do so. They also have a narrower range of concerns than parties, which seek to aggregate a variety of interests in order to broaden their appeal; pressure groups have a more limited focus, many of their aspirations being non-political. However, because their concerns are liable to be affected by government decisions, they need to be organised in order to influence ministers and respond to what they propose.

There is no agreed terminology to cater for pressure-group activity across the world. The Americans talk mainly of interest groups, lobbying and single-issue groups, whereas in Britain the tendency is to use the term 'pressure groups' and then to sub-divide them into different categories. The word 'pressure' has an unfortunate connotation, and many groups operate without resorting to any degree of coercion. They may employ a variety of approaches to press their case, ranging from passing information to writing letters of protest, from having informal consultations to staging popular demonstrations. There are similar difficulties with many of the labels which are sometimes used by political scientists. For instance, the use of the term 'interest groups' fails adequately to cater for the myriad of groups which are more concerned to promote a particular idea than to look after any specific interest. Given such difficulties, there is little point in further discussing terminology. In reality, most groups represent some interests and most interests are concerned to promote themselves to those who make policy. Whatever the label, Wilson-points out, they all, as 'have some autonomy from government or political parties and try to influence policy'.[3]

Movements and pressure groups

Movements are different from pressure groups, although closely related to them. Broadly, a movement may be described as a large body of people united – but loosely organised – around a central idea, issue or concern whose goal is to change attitudes or institutions, as well as policies. Their activities often arise at grass-roots level and later evolve into national crusades. Within our definition, we may speak of the women's movement or the anti-abortion movement. From time to time, new movements arise as people discover new needs and old ones have been tackled. At the present time, a vocal and newsworthy example is the animal rights movement, which falls more easily into a specific category, the New Social Movements.

New Social Movements emerged in the 1960s. The student protesters of the 1960s were an early example, but since then the women's movements, the black movement for civil rights in the USA and the various environmental movements have provided useful illustrations. Often these New Social Movements have a core group which provide strength and direction to the movement, and then a broader amount of less-organised support. Sometimes, the whole movement lacks tight organisation, is less cohesive and lacks the structure normally associated with a pressure group.

This type of social movement has made a great impact in recent years. They are different from what might be termed the old social movements of the nineteenth century, which were primarily concerned to confront the harsh working conditions of the times and to press for change. As Doyle and McEachern explain:

> Like the preceding social movements they have a radical edge and visions of a world transformed by their demands . . . [They] are characterised by their informal modes of organisation; their attachment to changing values as a central part of their political challenge; their commitment to open and ultra-democratic, participating modes of organisation (at least in the initial stages) and their willingness to engage in direct action to stop outcomes which they see as harmful.[4]

In the United States, the movement for civil rights included many bodies within its membership. They ranged from those often associated with Dr Martin Luther King (the National Association for the Advancement of Colored People and the Southern Christian Leadership Conference) to the more militant and separatist Black Power and Black Panther organisations. Movements are wider and more all-embracing than pressure groups and as this example shows often contain groups which have their own distinctive agendas and approaches.

Accepting that the term 'pressure group' is a convenient and general one to embrace the whole range of organisations with which we are dealing, it is possible to be more specific about the types of body which come under that umbrella. A common distinction is between those groups which seek to defend the interests of people or categories of people in society, and those which seek to advance particular ideas and opinions. The former are interest groups – associations designed to protect the interests of their members. The latter are promotional or cause groups.

Environmental movements saw the birth of environmentalism. In the eyes of many observers there may seem to be one broad environmental movement in each region, country or continent, but those in the know would make a distinction between several different ones. Thus Doyle and McEachern point out that there are those which are traditional nature conservation movements, and those which are more radical – concerned as they are with political ecology and anti-nuclear issues, and sometimes referred to as 'New Left movements'.[5] Some would quibble about the term New Left which is often associated with the anti-imperialist protest politics of the 1960s. 'New Social movements' more clearly describes movements which have arisen since the New Left, such as the anti-globalisation protests which seek to show that intensified global competition is not a natural and inevitable development of modern life.

The main thrust of nature conservation movements is to protect species threatened with extinction, and as a consequence of this aim they are often in the forefront of the fight against pollution. They are willing to work within the existing economic structure in society and push for reforms to improve the prospects for animal and plant life. They work to 'green' the political parties so that their ideas might be implemented within the foreseeable future. American environmental movements tend to be of this type, concerned as some of them are with the fate of wolves and grizzly bears, and the management of national parks and the protection of species of fauna.

By contrast, the New Left or post-New Left movements seek more dramatic change in which ecological and social needs are seen as having greater importance than the existing pattern of society, based as it is on the obsession with economic growth. Increasingly, anti-globalisation and other movements within the radical environmentalist category now conduct much of their planning and advertising via the new medium of the Internet. The anti-nuclear movement is an offshoot of the ecology movement, often sharing a similar membership and a common outlook. Its main preoccupation is with the danger posed by nuclear power stations and the search for alternative energy sources. Within its orbit, the emphasis has been on decentralisation and individual or small-group activity, sometimes of a more radical and unconventional kind.

Many well-known environmental movements are based in Western Europe, but they exist elsewhere too. In poorer parts of the world, they tend to be more concerned with issues of survival and security in conditions worsened by environmental misuse and damage – for example, the struggles of the Ogoni peoples of Nigeria against environmental degradation brought about by oil-drilling.

There are thousands of economic interests in modern societies, ranging from the vast to the very small and covering the activities of powerful groups such as big business, investment houses and agriculture and those of small employers who run a plumbing or electrical concern. **Interest groups** are concerned with one section of the population. They are primarily self-interested bodies which often offer services to their members, as well as looking after their sectional interests. Many are found in the economic sphere of society among the interests just listed, although they are also important in the public sector. Professional associations and trade unions fall into this category, as do the peak or umbrella associations of major firms. Most notable among

---

TRADE UNIONS AND THEIR DECLINING INFLUENCE AS INTEREST GROUPS

Trade unions have in most countries suffered from a shrinking membership, partly as a result of the decline of manufacturing in countries ranging from Britain and the United States in both of which new, less-unionised service industries have become ever more significant. As a general trend, unions have failed to cater for the growing number of office workers and those in services (often small-scale and harder to motivate), but membership has suffered from other factors such as:

- unemployment, which has hit workers in traditional industries;
- public attitudes to unions, which were influenced by the hostile approach adopted by conservative governments across the continent and in the USA in the 1980s and 1990s;
- the increase in the amount of part-time working, especially by women, which made union activity difficult to organise;
- the increased diversity of work-forces in terms of qualifications and working conditions.

The decline has not been universal or at the same rate, because of differing economic and social conditions prevailing in different countries. Some unions have been skilful in making adjustments in their attitudes and appeal.

Union strength in Britain, Europe and America

Union membership varies considerably across the continent. It is high in Eastern Europe where once union systems were controlled by communist parties, and where frequently membership was associated with additional attractions such as cheap holidays and welfare benefits. The introduction of market economies, which have produced harsh economic circumstances for workers at least in the short term, has meant that unions continue to enjoy popular backing. Budge et al. point out that Eastern European unions have a defensive function and are strongest where there is most opposition to market economics.[6] As in the West, older employees tend to be well represented among trade union members. Younger workers are more employable and more mobile, and are often less concerned with the defence of their collective rights and see less need for solidarity.

In Western Europe, union bargaining power has been reduced, for the high unemployment of the 1980s and the trends to globalisation of national economies have generally taken a

the peak organisation are the confederations which bring together within one organisation a whole range of other organisations, the Confederation of British Industry and the Institute of Directors in Britain being such bodies. They seek to coordinate activity and speak on behalf of all of their constituent organisations. They may not confine themselves to work in one country, and instead operate on the international scene – in the way that Eurogroups such as UNICE represents business interests beyond the European Union.

In America, there is again a vast array of interest groups, ranging from trade associations such as the American Pharmaceutical Association and the American Electronics Association, to professional bodies such as the American

---

toll of union influence. Unions tend to be consulted less, though in countries which maintain the corporatist tradition they are stronger. Where that tradition has lapsed (Belgium, Netherlands and Sweden) they have diminished. British unions were never so involved in the national economies as is common on the continent, and after the era of strong union power in the 1960s and 1970s they have lost much of their influence; they were never strong in terms of European comparisons.

In America, the unions reached their peak in the 1950s when around a third of the non-agricultural workforce was unionised. Since then the drop has been substantial, with current membership around 15 per cent, even lower in the South. The job market in key manufacturing industries has been hit by imported supplies, from Korea in the case of steel and Japan in the case of cars. As a consequence, unions have found that they have lost much of their former muscle in bargaining. Another reason for decline is the difficulty which unions have had in making membership seem necessary and relevant to today's society. Paul Johnson argues that the task has been made all the more difficult because employers of non-unionised workers have made greater efforts to satisfy their workforce.[7] Whatever the explanation, labour – never strong in the United States – has lost much of its clout in recent decades, and millions of workers – particularly in the growth areas of the economy – are unorganised. Even so, the AFL/CIO still has more affiliated members than any other interest group apart from the 35-million-strong American Association of Retired Persons (AARP), and can still mobilise millions of people. Nearly 14 million workers are members of unions affiliated to the AFL-CIO. Millions of others belong to unions not in the AFL/CIO, among them the teachers.

Union membership in selected countries, 2000
(per cent of workforce)

- **80 and above** Denmark Sweden
- **70–80** Norway
- **40–70** South Africa
- **30–40** Australia Germany Italy UK
- **under 20** France USA

(Adapted from figures provided by International Labour Office.)

Medical Association and the American Bar Association. In the world of industry, the major umbrella organisations are less representative of big business than in Britain. The Chamber of Commerce, the National Association of Manufacturers and the Business Roundtable cater for fewer than a quarter of American businesses. Many large corporations – Chase Manhattan, Chrysler, and American Airlines among them – are formidable in defending their own sectional interests. Among labour organisations, the American Federation of Labor and Congress of Industrial Organisations (AFL/CIO) is the umbrella group of nearly 70 trade unions, such as the Teamsters (lorry drivers) and the united Auto Workers.

Promotional groups cover a vast array of activities. They seek to advance (promote) the beliefs, ideas and values in which their supporters believe, but these are not ideas which are of benefit to their membership, other than in a most general sense. They are therefore 'selfless' in their concerns, and may be concerned to promote long-term goals. They tend to stick to their own agenda, and are liable to lose support if they stray from their original path. Such groups are sometimes short-lived, their membership fluctuates considerably and they are prone to secession as dissatisfied members feel that the organisation has lost its way.

'Promotional groups' include within their realms a wide variety of organisations. Among them are various civic, educational and leisure bodies, as well as charities, social clubs and many others. Examples in Britain are the British Association for the Advancement of Science, the Electoral Reform Society, the Howard League for Penal Reform, and Shelter. American groups include Common Cause and the Americans for Democratic Action. Some promotional groups deal with a range of concerns within their area of interest, others are single-issue groups.

Among the promotional groups, there has in recent years, been a considerable increase in the number and appeal of those concerned with **single issues**. As Davies writes: 'First identified as such in the United States, many were perceived to be on the left of the political spectrum and in the past the people they attracted may have joined the Democratic Party'.[8] Today, there are single-issue groups operating on both sides of the Atlantic which deal with a specific issue of popular interest, such as gay rights, the export of live animals and the siting of some social amenity. They particularly tend to operate in areas such as civil liberties, birth control, abortion, environmental protection, nuclear power, nuclear arms, and the sale of firearms. Snowdrop in Britain had a brief existence in which it lobbied hard and ultimately successfully for a ban on hand-guns. In America, the pro- and anti-abortion groups are of a similar type.

Protective associations are traditionally stronger, and better organised. They are also better resourced, because they benefit from subscription fees from their members. They take up contentious issues of the moment which affect their membership, so that organisations of businessmen and trade bodies in Britain will currently have great interest in the single currency, just as farmers have recently been concerned about BSE and other animal diseases in the news, and about the desirability or otherwise of genetically modified foodstuffs.

NIMBY ('Not In My Back Yard') groups are a sub-category within the general orbit of protective associations, whose importance has grown considerably in recent years. They are protective groups based on geographical rather than functional interests. Their formation has been inspired by various causes, often relating to land use (the threat of development) in the countryside. They arise when inhabitants of the same areas feel threatened. People opposed to proposals for such things as a new road, prison, hostage for women or chemical-waste dumping site are worried that their lifestyle may be affected adversely. The greater availability of media attention today has meant that local action campaigns built around such issues can achieve the desired results.

Examples of protective and promotional (interest) groups in Britain and America

	Britain	United States
Protective		
Big business	CBI	Business Roundtable
Labour	Trades Union Congress	AFL/CIO
Professional	The Law Society	American Bar Association
Agriculture	National Farmers' Union	The Grange
Promotional		
Civil liberties	Liberty	American Civil Liberties Union
Environment	Friends of the Earth	Sierra Club
Public interest/Civic	Electoral Reform Society	Common Cause
Welfare	NSPCC	American Cancer Society

A different type of categorisation of groups is that between insider and outsider ones. Developed by Wyn Grant, this distinction is between those groups that have most influence with government because of the expertise they can provide and the help they can offer in making and implementing policy (for example in Britain, the British Medical Association and the National Farmers' Union (NFU), in the United States the American Farm Bureau). Others are less influential, being able to give little assistance or trade-off in return for policy influence. Some groups are outsiders because they cannot achieve insider status. Other – often ideological – groups do not want such status. For ideological reasons, the Campaign for Nuclear Disarmament would not seek influence with a Conservative government whose approach to matters of defence and nuclear policy would be very different from its own. Neither would it much care for Labour policies, particularly when the party is in office.

The insider/outsider categorisation works less well in the United States than in Britain, because of the different structure of government. The separation of powers gives a greater role to the legislature than in Britain. An American administration lacks the capacity of a British government to push its programme through the legislative chambers, so that there is much more concentration by large pressure groups on Congress.

How groups operate

In free societies, groups seek to exert influence via many avenues or **access points**, mostly peaceful, although on occasion they may resort to more violent forms of protest. Pressure groups have traditionally operated at four main levels, seeking to influence the Executive, the Legislature, the Judiciary and the public at large. In Britain and Europe, they tend to be more closely associated with government than is the case in America.

> **access points**
> Those formal parts of the governmental structure which are accessible to pressure-group influence. There are many such outlets via which groups can present their case, the more so in America given its constitutional structure.

Influencing the Executive

Governments need information, much of which is highly technical and specialised. Interest groups in particular are in a position to offer such information, for they contain experts in their field and have access to the views of their members who understand the problems they confront in their daily operation, know what the impact of government policy is and what needs to be done. Governments also need consent for their policies, and leading interest groups – particularly those which are representative of most people who work in their field – are in a position to assist ministers in carrying out their policies. For instance, the British Medical Association can not only inform the Department of Health about any epidemic of a virulent form of influenza or meningitis, they can also help by carrying out a programme of mass immunisation. Similarly, the NFU, representing as it does the vast majority of farmers, can help the Department of Farming and Rural Affairs (DEFRA) not only by tendering advice, but also by ensuring that its members take careful precautions to ensure that an outbreak of foot-and-mouth disease is contained. In America the American Farm Bureau has traditionally been close to government and enjoyed a successful relationship with the Department of Agriculture, whereas the US National Farmers' Union has never had the same proximity to those charged with making key decisions.

Interest groups wish to influence government in order to see the implementation of policies favourable to their membership. After all, it is ministers and the officials who advise them who have the power of decision, and they are inevitably therefore the target of lobbying activity. This will mean that there is close consultation between the executive branch and group leaders, many of whom will be in daily contact with officials in a government department, having a mix of formal and informal links. The relationship is normally a cordial and cooperative one, for each side has something to offer the other.

Business groups have an advantage at this level. They play a crucial role in the economy as producers and employers, and leading business figures often enjoy a particularly close relationship with senior officials. Sometimes there are social links as well, for many of the people who have a key role in industry may come from a similar social background to those with whom they deal in the bureaucracy. Indeed, so close are the links that there can be what the Americans term a 'revolving door', through which leading figures in government leave to find themselves a lucrative job in private industry when the administration in the White House changes.

In Britain, some insider groups such as the NFU are very close to government. In the 1960s and 1970s – the age of tripartism or **corporatism** – it became fashionable for leading economic bodies such as business/trade organisations and trade unions to work with representatives of government in the management of the economy. Each side contributed its views, and ministers sought to get agreement about what the economy could afford by way of price rises and wage increases. Such corporatism has gone out of fashion since the 1980s, although it is still practised in some European countries.

One study of American groups found that no American interest groups focused exclusively on the executive branch.[10] The majority concentrated their attention on both the Executive and the Legislature, but a sizeable minority lobbied Congress only or Congress and some other target. The Washington representatives of large companies attach more importance to Capitol Hill than the government departments, as do labour unions. According to research by the same writer, many lobbyists in the national capital spend more time on gathering information from government that is relevant to their groups' interests (perhaps about changes in laws and regulations) than they do in providing information to government with the intention of influencing its policies.[11]

> **corporatism**
> The term used to describe the various forms of tripartite bargaining between governments and interest groups (representing business and labour) which have been common in Europe and were employed in Britain in the 1960s and 1970s. The aim is to make the process of government inclusive, by institutionalising group consultation, to avoid open conflict, and to foster harmony among the competitive interests in a market economy. Since the 1980s, there has been a marked reduction in corporatist activity across Europe, as governments have increasingly moved to free-market competition, with greater use of competition and de-regulation.

POLICY NETWORKS IN MODERN DEMOCRACIES

The concept of policy networks has attracted much attention in recent years. They describe the different kinds of relationships between groups and government. The term is a generic one denoting a continuum from close and stable policy communities to looser, more open and discontinuous policy or issue networks.

Iron triangles and policy communities

For many years, there were particularly close links in America between interest groups, committee chairmen and government departments, an arrangement often referred to as 'iron triangles'. The three elements were often in close contact with each other and enjoyed cosy relationships based on interdependent self-interest. Such iron triangles often dominated areas of domestic policy-making, possessing a virtual monopoly of information in their sector. Examples were the smoking and tobacco triangle (the Department of Agriculture, the House and Senate agricultural committees, and the tobacco lobby of farmers and manufacturers) in which there was a focus on crop subsidies to tobacco farmers.

The term triangles was particularly applied to the USA, whereas elsewhere there was more talk of 'policy communities'. Such communities involved a high degree of interdependence between insider groups and government, without the involvement of committee chairmen in the legislature. They were characterised by close, mutually supportive ties, based on a stable relationship between the participants and a high degree of contact. The idea of policy communities fitted in well with Grant's classification of insider and outsider groups, the former having close involvement in decision-taking. In Britain, policy communities were formed around subjects such as food and drink policy, technical education and water privatisation.

Since the 1980s, the autonomy of such triangles or sub-governments in America has been challenged by alternative centres of power, often known as 'issue networks'. Issue networks are wider and looser, and – in addition to the three elements above – describe other players involved in discussion of a policy area, including the research institutes and the media. Media scrutiny and the attentions of consumer protest groups have led to a more critical analysis of policy-making processes, so that secret deals and mutual backscratching are now less frequent or effective. As Hague and Harrop have explained, 'the iron has gone out of the triangle; now influence over decisions depends on what you know, as well as who you know'.[12] In America, the policies supported by the tobacco triangle came under challenge from health authorities, who had been excluded from the area of tobacco policy-making.

Policy communities have begun to decay in most democracies and the trend is towards the more open style of policy-making which characterises issue networks. The impact of any particular group may vary from time to time or issue to issue, partly depending on the expertise it possesses. There are more participants in issue networks, relationships are not continuous or particularly close and there is less interdependence.

Influencing the Legislature

Today, many professional lobbyists and pressure group activists seek to influence elected representatives. As we have seen, Congress is noted as a focus of such interest, but all parliaments are a natural target. In America, the fact that the two houses are powerful assemblies with a major legislative role makes them particularly useful to those who seek influence. Capitol Hill is very accessible to American groups, not least because many legislators are financed by sizeable PAC contributions, but also because they may come from an area where a substantial proportion of the population is engaged in a key interest, for instance farming in the Midwest. As Richardson remarks, 'they often see themselves as having a duty, as well as an interest in re-election, in helping interests important to their constituents'.[13]

Activity at the legislative level is usually more overt than that aimed at the executive branch, much of which tends to take place behind closed doors. Much of the contact is transparent, and may receive widespread popularity – though this does not necessarily make it more effective. It is more effective in France and the USA, which have less strict party discipline, so that there is a real chance that pressure-group activists may sway votes by their campaigning. In Britain and Canada, tight party discipline makes such parliamentary action less effective. Even in the United States, the emphasis on individual contact with congress members and committee chairmen has increasingly been supplemented by greater commitment to supporting sympathetic candidates at election time and 'going public'.

Influence at this level can be with individual representatives, committees or with a political party In Britain, trade unions have traditionally had a strong and close relationship with the Labour Party ever since they helped to create it at the beginning of the century. In recent years, the constitutional and financial ties have loosened, and the emotional and historical bonds count for less than they did in the past. Nonetheless, the relationship is still much closer than that which exists between left-wing parties and the industrial labour movement in most other countries. In America, there have never been similar institutional links between the Democrats and organised labour.

Influencing the judiciary

On occasion, British groups may turn to the law and use test cases to highlight an issue and bring about pressure for change. In 1994, Greenpeace and Lancashire County Council challenged the opening and commissioning of the Thorp nuclear processing plant. They gained valuable publicity even though they lost the battle. Bodies such as the Equal Opportunities Commission and the Commission for Racial Equality have also used the law to gain redress for individuals who have suffered discrimination, having been alerted by campaigning groups.

In the past, there has been little concentration on the courts as a target for action. However, the general trend towards judicial activism and the number of cases concerning civil liberties following the passing of the Human Rights Act (1998), may prompt groups to see this as an avenue which can be exploited. In Britain and in several other democracies, the courts are likely to become more important as an access point in the future. Judicial challenge to national legislation is ruled out by the doctrine of Parliamentary Sovereignty, but groups can mount test cases and challenge the way a law has been implemented.

In countries in which the Constitution provides the courts with a formal role of judicial review, activists will use the courts more readily. In the USA, the method is much more well-established, not least because Americans are traditionally a litigious (ready to go to law) people. Notable progress has been made by civil rights groups and anti-abortion campaigners via lobbying of the Supreme Court. Consumer and environmental groups have also found the legal outlet a useful means of advancing their concerns. American judges have wide constitutional powers to overrule decisions of the Executive and considerable latitude in interpreting the meaning of legislation, so that bringing test cases may prove invaluable in winning a friendly judgement. Of course, much depends who is on the Bench, and US groups often seek to influence the selection of judges, pressing the claims of those whose political and social leanings they find acceptable.

It is not just civil rights groups who have used this route. 'Going to law' requires substantial resources, so that it is often the large and powerful business corporations which have been successful in adopting this approach. They regularly challenge government statutes and regulations, and have their own lawyers to advise them and handle the passage of cases through the courts. In other cases where they met not be a party to the litigation, groups may submit an **amicus curiae** ('friend of the court') brief, in order they can have their views represented and taken into account.

> **amicus curiae**
> A brief filed by an individual or group with the permission of the court. Such briefs provide information and argument additional to that presented by those immediately involved in a case. In effect, a group is acting in the privileged position of being an adviser to the court, a role popular with campaigners in the debates on abortion, consumerism, law and order, and the environment.

Influencing public opinion

In Britain, it used to be said that 'more noise equals least success', and that those groups which operated at the public level did so only because of their impotence at the parliamentary and executive levels. The most effective groups seemed to be those which operated behind closed doors, lobbying discreetly those with the power of decision. Only those groups denied access to the corridors of power needed to resort to lively protest and take more militant forms of action; militancy was a sign of weakness rather than of strength. Indeed, going public was often a sign that that they were operating in the face of considerable hostility from many elected representatives and officials.

direct action
Any action beyond the usual constitutional and legal framework, such as obstructing access to a building, preventing the building of a motorway or – at worst – terrorism. Usually a last resort after other approaches have failed, it is an attempt to coerce those in authority into doing something they would not otherwise do.

Today, the picture of group activity described above is less true than it once was, because of the rise of the media. Activity on a national or local scale in the public arena can – if it is conspicuous – attract the television crews. A piece of **direct action** – such as obstruction of a highway, occupying a tunnel under an airport or climbing a tree – will engage much popular interest, especially if several people are involved. The protests against the transportation of live animals to the continent organised by Compassion in World Farming in 1995 were a good example of the use of this means of securing public support (see pp. 238–40 for more information on the use of direct action).

American groups recognise that one way of impressing Congress is to gain public sympathy. They adopt a dual strategy of going public and lobbying on Capitol Hill. They may seek to exert influence over the public not just by all-the-year-round background campaigns or by shorter blitz, fire-brigade activity. They may also intervene in the electoral process, perhaps by organising the petition for an initiative and then involving themselves in the arguments surrounding the issues at stake. Sometimes, they try directly to influence the outcome of election contests. This may be done because they wish to see certain candidates elected and certain ideas advanced, or because they wish to stop the candidatures of other candidates and oppose the outlook they represent. Often this may involve publishing and grading the voting records of sitting congress members, in an attempt to show the extent to which they fulfil the group's requirements. Environmental groups have in the past singled out the 'Dirty Dozen' legislators with the worst voting records on issues within their orbit; in 2000, eleven were Republican.

Groups can also have an enormous impact on the funding of American elections. Political Action Committees (PACs) assist the candidates in several ways, by providing research material and publicity, by raising election funds and by providing organisational back-up to a candidate who lacks a strong personal political organisation or the support of a party machine. The number of PACs has mushroomed since the 1980s, following the controls on party funding under the FECA legislation of the 1970s. (For further discussion of PACs and the role and control of spending in American elections, see pp. 293–4.)

Other targets for pressure groups

In Britain and America, there are other targets for the lobbyist besides the Executive, Legislature, judiciary and popular opinion. Such 'pressure points' include:

- **Government beyond the centre.** In Britain, local councils may have lost many of their former powers, but they still make important decisions affecting the lives of people within their boundaries. The new devolved bodies in Scotland and Wales provide obvious opportunities for influence. As a vast federal country, the USA offers enormous scope for group activists to lobby at a variety of different access points. The shifting balance of influence in the era of New Federalism has led to a surge of activity in the states and at the local level. Key areas of policy such as welfare are increasingly handled at state level, so that campaigners find it worthwhile to establish offices in state capitals, and lobby governors and state legislatures. There has also been an increase in intergovernmental lobbying, with states and local governments taking offices in Washington to press their claims at the federal level.

- **The media.** Many groups have realised the importance of the media as a means of bringing their cause to a significantly wider audience. In his 1992 survey, Baggott found that 80 per cent of British groups claimed to be in contact with the media at least once a week.[14] American pressure groups exploit the communications media to influence voters at election time, and to motivate constituents to contact their representatives between elections.

- **Companies.** Large firms (some of them multinationals) with great economic power are of increasing interest to campaigners. Environmentalists from several countries have often concentrated their fire on Shell International, as in 1995 over the plans to dismantle the disused Brent Spar oil rig at sea. Some Greenpeace activists see business rather than politics as the best arena within which to seek to further group aims.

- **Pressure groups.** Some lobbyists are concerned to influence other groups whose views may be susceptible to change. In Britain, the pro- and anti-hunting lobbies have long concentrated on seeking to persuade the National Trust (NT) to come out in their favour. 'Anti' campaigners are particularly active within the NT itself. American groups have been successful in forging alliances with other bodies. For instance, the thirty-year-old Food Group comprises some sixty or so business and trade organisations, who work together to lobby Congress and government departments.

- **The European Union.** For Britain, the European Union (EU) has become an important target for pressure groups since the 1980s, as more and more decisions have been taken in Brussels.

Trends in recent years: the changing pressure-group scene

Business interests continue to exercise political muscle in most countries, for their role is essential to the success of the national economy and governments are likely to listen to them. Businessmen have the power to make or withhold key investment decisions which can influence the levels of employment and prosperity in their countries. Hence there is a widespread feeling that what is good for business is good for everyone. However, the former dominance of traditional peak associations has been undermined by the growth in number of other lobbying organisations such as those representing small businesses, trade associations and individual companies.

There have been significant changes in the number, campaigning methods and effectiveness of various other types of groups.

think tanks
Policy institutes which carry out detailed research and provide analysis of and information on a range of policy options. They are often ideologically based, their ideas sometimes being influential with the parties which share a broad affinity of perspective – e.g. the Institute for Public Policy Research and the Labour Party. In America, think tanks such as the Progressive Policy Institute have taken on much of the work of developing new policy options. The role of parties in this area has diminished.

There are far more groups than ever before

Over the last two or three decades of the twentieth century, the number of single issue, local action and other campaigning organisations soared. The ecological concerns of the greens have been well publicised on both sides of the Atlantic. Pre occupations have ranged from pollution to the ozone layer, from conservation to the need to limit economic growth as part of the search for a better means of organising society. Consumerism has become a growth industry, so also has the development of research institutions and **think tanks** such as the Adam Smith Institute and Demos in Britain and the Brookings institutions and the Heritage Foundation in America.

Some groups have lost and others gained in influence

The lobbying scene in Washington was once dominated by three interests, but the influence of these traditional agricultural, business and labour organisations has declined. As we have seen, corporations do more of their own lobbying and rival business organisations have emerged. Unions have lost members and there are now more specialist agricultural associations. The same is true in the field of medicine, which is no longer dominated by the American Medical Association. Its activities are now just part of the campaigning on health matters by groups ranging from that of the insurance companies to the work done by specialist groups such as nurses and paramedics, and organisations representing health delivery (clinics and hospitals, among others). In Britain, too, certain interests carry less weight today than was once the case. Labour has lost much of its previous influence and the impact of the CBI on policy has declined from the corporatist days of the 1960s and 1970s when it exerted real influence. Many campaigning social groups such as the Child Poverty Action Group and Shelter have faced a harsher climate in which to operate in recent decades, as governments have been more stringent with the nation's finances.

There are additional outlets at which groups can target their propaganda

Many British groups have taken opportunities to lobby in Europe, as increasingly, key decisions affecting aspects of British life are being taken in Brussels.

The merits of pressure-group activity

Writers have taken differing views of pressure-group activity, many of them regarding groups as inevitable if not actually beneficial to good government, others being more alarmed at the methods by which they operate and the influence they can attain. The two views are well expressed in the observations of two famous Presidents. John F. Kennedy saw groups as an essential part of democratic activity, performing an invaluable role in American life: 'the lobbyists who speak for the various economic, commercial and other functional interests of this country serve a very useful purpose and have assumed an important role in the legislative process'. By contrast, one of his distinguished predecessors, Woodrow Wilson, was alarmed because he saw the government of the United States as being 'the foster child of special interests . . . not allowed to have a will of its own'.

Groups aid democracy in several ways. They:
* provide detailed and valuable information on areas of economic and social activity, thereby helping to promote better decision-making;
* perform an educative role by raising and explaining issues for public attention, often alerting journalists in the media to matters which need a public airing;
* help to maintain dialogue between government and the governed between elections;
* defend the interests of minorities in the community, particularly those which do not gain a powerful outlet via political parties;
* allow for increased participation in politics by people who might otherwise be inactive on the political scene;
* counter the monopoly of political life by parties, allowing for the taking-up of issues which often fall outside the agenda of party politicians – for instance, cause groups took up environmental concerns before politicians did so;
* ensure that political power is dispersed, thereby acting as a brake on the power of more centralised institutions and players.

Group activity has inbuilt disadvantages:
* The leadership of pressure groups may be unrepresentative, as was the case with British union leaders until the reforms of the 1980s. Officers may wield considerable influence, without being accountable for their actions, and often voluntary organisa-

American groups have made increased use of opportunities for lobbying in the states and localities.

Groups have changed their approach

Pressure groups have developed a more sophisticated approach to the ways by which they seek to influence 'pressure points' in the political process. Some have turned to the use of the new commercial 'lobbying industry', which developed in America and has been imported into Britain since the 1980s. Professional lobbyists were defined in a House of Commons report as those who are 'professionally employed to lobby on behalf of clients or who advise clients on how to lobby on their own behalf'. These agencies trade their

---

tions are liable to be led by elites which are self-perpetuating and out-of-touch with the feeling of less active members.

- Insider groups are too active behind the scenes, engaging in discussions with civil servants which are beyond the public gaze. They may in this way exercise enormous influence, as in the days of corporatism in Britain and of iron triangles in America. Professor Finer – in an early study of group activity – wanted more information and more public scrutiny, ending his book with the plea for 'Light, more light'.[15]
- Groups do not represent all sections of the community equally. The voices of industry and unions, as well as of many professional organisations, are heard loud and clear. Consumer organisations have traditionally exercised less clout, and some groups in the community – the poor, the old, racial minorities and others – are less well-organised and lack muscle, having no strong bargaining stance. The influence groups can exercise is excessively influenced by the resources at their disposal and the relationships they can construct with governments. Moreover, they are a sectional interest. Governments must listen and take all views into account, but govern in the national interest rather than being dominated by any single one.
- The methods employed by campaigners may be unhealthy. Some use money and other means to influence elected representatives. Increasingly, activists turn to militant, direct action to achieve their ends, much of which is illegal.
- The sheer volume of group activity has a detrimental effect on government, undermining the capacity of those in power to get things done. The view was expressed by Douglas Hurd, a British Home Secretary in the 1980s. He attacked groups as 'strangling serpents' which created unnecessary work for ministers and made it difficult for them to reach decisions in the public interest.

Pressure groups are valuable organisations. It is easy to portray them as special interests intent on undermining democracy and the interests of the public, but they represent and articulate legitimate viewpoints which need to be expressed. Modern government could not exist without them, for they provide necessary knowledge and expertise to policymakers, and monitor the effectiveness of existing policies and ideas for alternative ones. They may at times make unreasonable demands, but it is in the interests of those who govern to try and work with them rather than against them. They are an inevitable feature of any democracy and their growth is unlikely to be reversed.

political knowledge and expertise to clients in return for considerable financial reward. They are hired for their inside knowledge of the workings of government and their contacts. Many major pressure groups either have a specialist lobbying department or employ the services of one of the professionals. Such lobbying has become a vast industry in America, and it is accepted as natural for a member of Congress to have a close connection with some outside interest. In Britain, the practice is regarded with greater suspicion, especially if it is associated with pecuniary advantage. Rules have been introduced to regulate the practice.

Direct action has become more acceptable

A number of groups have seen more point in using direct action as an additional means of persuading government into following their ideas. By so

Pressure groups in Britain and the United States: a summary		
	Britain	*The United States*
Size and character of country	Small, compact and fairly homogeneous, though growing per cent of ethnic minorities and non-Christians.	Vast country of regional variations and diverse ethnic and religious backgrounds. Very pluralist society with influential groups such as Italian community and Jewish lobby. etc.
Nature of constitution	Uncodified, rights of groups not guaranteed – e.g. removal of rights of protestors to freedom of assembly by Criminal Justice Act, 1994.	Written constitution, with group rights more secure. Legislation to take away rights of protestors would have fallen foul of the 1st Amendment.
Level of centralisation in a unitary and federal country	Leading groups target Whitehall/Westminster where key decisions are made, though devolution has created additional targets in other parts of the UK; local action groups lobby councils.	Much activity in the states – e.g. key decisions on welfare are made in state capitals; also, much local lobbying.
Targets or 'access points'	Interest groups (insiders) tend to concentrate on Executive, but Parliament and public are other targets. More recently, EU and other pressure groups.	Separation of Powers encourages groups to lobby three areas of government and public at and between elections, states and other groups

doing, they achieve publicity because the television cameras are likely to be present at some mass protest or demonstration. Of course, noise and publicity are not the same as influence, and it is still true that for some organisations resorting to such forms of demonstration is an indication of weakness rather than strength. However, many local action and promotional groups have used direct action as an additional tool, in their bid to block moves to build a housing estate on green-belt land, or stop the felling of some ancient tree in the name of progress. Mothers and Children Against Toxic Waste (MACATW) is a Welsh example of the genre. It sought to prevent the burning of toxic waste by a chemical processing plant. In America, the activities of anti-abortionists have been widely reported; Operation Rescue has moved on from blockading clinics to engage in more violent forms of protest.

	Britain	The United States
Party system	(a) Two-party system, but three- or four-party politics, offers opportunities for some groups to work with and through parties – e.g. Welsh-language groups and Plaid Cymru. (b) Strict party discipline discourages main groups from seeking influence at Westminster, though unions have Labour links.	(a) Fairly strict two-party system encourages activists to form groups rather than find parties to express their viewpoint. (b) Looser party discipline, so more point in groups seeking to persuade congress members and committees.
Funding of election campaigns	Conducted mainly through parties, Conservatives having links with some sections of industry (though not what they were) and centred electioneering.Labour having union financial backing (though less than in the past).	PACs, the financial and political arm of pressure groups have a central role in more candidate-
Open/closed system of government	Much interest group activity behind closed doors (e.g. NFU, as powerful insider group) and less open to public scrutiny. A generally closed system of government which keeps activities of Executive as secret as possible.	More open government. Media have protection of 1st Amendment, and effective Freedom of Information legislation provides access to documentation. Pressure group activity more open to public examination.

Hijackers and terrorists among other have shown how effective techniques of law-breaking can be, but few groups are willing to resort to such extremist tactics in order to attain their desired objectives. However, many groups are willing to employ forms of direct action, most of which are illegal.

Conclusion

The influence and effectiveness of pressure groups varies according to the country and its internal circumstances, as well as to the time and the nature of the cause. Where governments are sympathetic to what is being proposed, there is more likelihood of success, the more so if the group concerned can exercise some political leverage. Generally speaking, money and resources are an advantage, and those key groups in the economy, such as the large producer groups on either side of manufacturing industry, are better placed to press their case than are consumers or much smaller promotional bodies.

Again, groups which can speak for the majority of those who work in an industry or profession are in a powerful position, as are those which can demonstrate that they are democratically constituted and genuinely speak on behalf of those who form their membership. They will be all the more influential, however, if they can show that the interests or causes which they represent are ones which are relevant to the wider national good

Generally speaking, there is greater scope for group action in more advanced nations and in those which allow many access points at which groups can employ pressure. Britain and America meet both of these requirements. But, as a whole, groups are more powerful in the United States, both for institutional reasons as well as factors associated with the political culture and the greater openness of America society. In addition, American groups have the protection of the Constitution, which safeguards their rights of assembly and to petition government.

Britain has followed America in the development and rapid growth of group activity. Both are pluralist democracies in which there is a multiplicity of groups. There is some overlap in the methods they employ and since the 1980s there have been significant changes in the pressure groups scene, among them:
- the decline of organised labour;
- more direct lobbying by big business organisations;
- increased activity by environmental groups;
- the greater use of professional lobbyists;
- the rise of single issue groups;
- the growth in the use of direct action (encouraged by media interest).

However, there are significant differences, in part deriving from the size and composition of the two countries, their constitutional arrangements and the relative openness/secretiveness of government. These are set out in the summary box on pp. 238–9.

REFERENCES

1 A. de Tocqueville, *Democracy in America* (trans), Doubleday, 1969.
2 A. Heywood, *Politics*, Macmillan, 1997.
3 G. Wilson, *Interest Groups*, Blackwell, 1991.
4 T. Doyle and D. McEachern, *Environment and Politics*, Routledge, 1998.
5 As note 5 above.
6 I. Budge, K. Newton *et al.*, *The Politics of the New Europe*, Longman, 1997.
7 P. Johnson, 'Interest Group Recruiting: Finding Members and Keeping Them', in A. Cigler and B. Loomis (eds), *Interest Group Politics*, Congressional Quarterly Press, 1998.
8 A. Davies, *Introducing Comparative Government*, PA/SHU Press, 1997.
9 W. Grant, *Pressure Groups, Politics and Democracy in Britain*, Harvester Wheatsheaf, 1995.
10 R. Salisbury *et al.*, 'Who works with whom? Patterns of Interest Group Alliance and Opposition', Paper to American Political Science Association in Washington, 1986.
11 R. Salisbury, 'The Paradox of Interest Groups in Washington DC: More Groups and Less Clout', in A. King (ed.) *The New American Political System*, American Enterprise Institute, 1990.
12 R. Hague and M. Harrop, *Comparative Government and Politics: An Introduction*, Palgrave, 2001.
13 J. Richardson, 'American Interest Groups' in J. Richardson *et al.*, *Pressure Groups*, Oxford University Press, 1993.
14 R. Baggott, *Pressure Groups Ttoday*, Manchester University Press, 1995.
15 S. Finer, *Anonymous Empire*, Pall Mall, 1967.

USEFUL WEB SITES

NB Individual pressure groups on both sides of the Atlantic have their own sites dealing with the specific issues of interest to users. They cover such things as a group's history, objectives and organisation. A few examples are listed.

For the UK

www.demos.co.uk Demos.

www.adamsmith.org.uk Adam Smith Institute.

www.cbi.org.uk Confederation of British Industry.

www.tuc.org.uk Trades Union Congress.

www.etuc.org European Trade Union Confederation.

www.countryside-alliance.org Countryside Alliance.

www.greenpeace.org.uk Greenpeace.

For the USA

http://turnleft.com Turn Left.

www.opensecrets.org Center for Responsive Politics. A useful American site, which contains information about PACs and lobbying activities.

www.handguncontrol.org Brady Campaign to Prevent Gun Violence.

www.nra.org National Rifle Association.

www.now.org National Organisation for Women.

www.sierraclub.org Sierra Club.

SAMPLE QUESTIONS

1 'In Britain and America, the producer lobby is far more powerful than that representing consumers'. Is this true and, if so, does it matter?

2 Why and in what respects are American pressure groups more significant than groups in Britain?

3 To what extent and for what reasons do British and American pressure groups differ in the tactics and strategies they adopt?

4 Discuss the view that the activities of pressure groups constitute a threat to the operations of liberal democratic systems of government.

The mass media

10

In advanced Western democracies, the media perform a major role. Freedom of expression is well established in the West and journalists are vigorous players on the political scene. They are sometimes portrayed as the 'fourth branch of government' or the 'fourth estate', rivalling the three official branches of political power. Television and the press can't actually do what the other three branches do, but the way in which they help to shape attitudes makes them very significant in the political process. We live in a media-saturated society and, in the eyes of some analysts, the media now wield excessive political influence.

In this chapter, our primary concern is with the impact on political life of the two major mass media: the press and television.

POINTS TO CONSIDER

➤ What is meant by the term 'cross-media ownership' and what problems can arise as a result of its occurrence?

➤ How do the media set the agenda for political discussion?

➤ How and why do politicians attempt to 'sell' themselves via television?

➤ What is the role of political consultants?

➤ What is meant by the 'Americanisation' of British electioneering?

➤ What are the main differences in the way television covers political issues and personalities on either side of the Atlantic?

By the mass media, we mean those means of communication which permit messages to be conveyed to the public. Media such as television, radio, newspapers, books, magazines, posters, the cinema and, more recently, videos and computers provide important links connecting people to one another. They allow information to be passed from one person to a vast audience at approximately the same time. Sending a fax or e-mail to a friend is a personal form of communication, but if the message is sent simultaneously to large numbers of people it becomes part of the mass media. The mass media can reach a large and potentially unlimited number of people at the same time.

The most important forms of the media are newspapers and broadcasting by radio and television, but over the last generation television has surpassed any other medium as the source from which the majority of people derive their information (see table below), for it provides an easily accessible, easily digested and credible medium available in almost every household. Today, how voters view politics and politicians is much influenced by television. Politicians recognise this and act accordingly, often seeking to influence the television at least as much as they are influenced by it.

But other forms of communication exist, including a number of ways by which local communities can exercise some political muscle. In the United States, these may range from the familiar to the uncommon. In New Jersey, those who opposed a tax increase organised a mass phone-in to a radio station to attract attention to their grievance, as part of a general revolt against their growing burden of taxation. By contrast, landlords in California who objected to the introduction of rent control decided to circulate video tapes which depicted pro-control members of the Santa Monica city council in an unflattering light. In 1997, the Referendum Party sent a video to every British household, as a means of conveying its anti-European message.

Sources of political information in Britain and the United States

Source	% in Britain	% in United States
Television	62	63
Newspapers	23	22
Radio	14	12
Other	1	3

Source: Adapted from contents of tables in E. Gerber, 'Divided We Watch', *Brills Content* (Feb. 2001) and IBA/ITC research findings.

Organisation, ownership and control in Britain and America

Britain has a centralised communications system, a factor related to geography and population distribution. By European standards, the population is urbanised, the majority living in the area between London and

Manchester. Regional media declined as the twentieth century progressed. The regional press has become significantly smaller since 1918, and although since the early days BBC and ITV have always had a regional element, BBC2 and Channels Four and Five are solely national ones. The political system too has always been highly centralised, encouraging the media to emphasise national concerns at the expense of regional ones.

Another feature of the British media is the balance which has been struck between the values of commercialism and public service. Commercialism is represented by the private ownership of the press and of ITV, and public

---

Public service broadcasting

From the time of its establishment as a public corporation, the BBC has always been viewed as a vital national resource which must operate in the public interest. As an institution, it was committed to the broad social and political objectives of informing, educating and entertaining, rather than the maximisation of profit. When commercial television came along, it posed a threat to these notions of public service broadcasting, and television could have gone downmarket in a bid for viewers. To a considerable extent, the danger was avoided because the 1954 Act that established ITV set out guidelines concerning the amount of news and current affairs programming it should have and the need for a high degree of impartiality. There were significant differences in the institutional ethos and funding of the two stations, but ITV was in important respects fashioned in the BBC's image.

There developed a great convergence between public and commercial broadcasting in Britain in which the two sides influenced each other. Both shared a belief in the importance of news and current affairs programming, and recognised the importance of informing the nation, and they became two halves of the same system which, in Wedell's words, 'derived from a single root and ... these branches, instead of diverging over the years ... stabilised their concentration more or less in parallel. There was a circumscribed form of competition as BBC and ITV producers vied for their reputations, critical renown and audience approval.[1]

The concept of public service broadcasting which both channels embraced was characterised by several shared beliefs, namely that:
- everyone should have access to the same service;
- all interests and tastes should be catered for, including minority ones;
- both national identity and a sense of community should be recognised;
- the television service should be free from the influence of vested interests or of government;
- competition should be in the field of quality programming, rather than the pursuit of the highest ratings;
- there should be no competition for revenue, with one channel being funded by the body of users and the other by advertising.

These features underpinned the duopoly of British broadcasting, and the domination of the duopoly went unchallenged until the 1980s. As that decade progressed, Margaret Thatcher began to lament the lack of competition in British television, and was keen to encourage technological innovations which were to change the character of broadcasting.

service by the BBC. There is a public-service requirement to which commercial television broadcasters are expected to respond.

Much of the development in the British media has been influenced by what has happened in the USA. Ideas and innovations have often come from across the Atlantic, and many press moguls on the British stage have spent much of their life in North America – the Astor family, the Canadians Roy Thomson and Conrad Black, and the Australian-American Rupert Murdoch. Many American communications companies are active in Britain, with several cable concerns and some large telephone companies having bases here.

In Britain, newspapers have declined in the postwar era, sales records having been established in the 1940s and 1950s. Tunstall points out that 50m Britons purchased 30m newspapers on a typical Sunday in 1955, whereas in 1995 58m bought only 16m – itself a figure higher than that for today.[2] Most of the papers published daily and on Sundays in the mid-1990s had changed ownership at least once in the previous two decades. The trend in recent years has been to a concentration of ownership, with major actors on the newspaper/magazine scene being groups such as News International, the Mirror and Pearson Groups, and Trinity Publishing.

The postwar reduction in the number of newspapers and the tendency towards ownership being concentrated in too few hands meant that for many years there was a preponderance of right-wing views. In spite of this trend, Labour has shown that it can win elections handsomely, partly because Tony Blair has been so skilful in his wooing of newspaper proprietors such as Rupert Murdoch. Since 1997, it has sometimes seemed that keeping the owner of News International on board has been more important than retaining the support of traditional Labour loyalists, so that electoral success has been achieved at a cost. Another effect of the trend to a concentration of ownership has been to reduce the availability of alternative ideas. Left-wing critics dislike the way in which the process of disseminating political news and other current affairs information is reliant upon a few newspaper owners. They argue the case for choice in a democracy.

The relaxation of the regulations on cross-media ownership in recent years has meant that several media companies have emerged with wide interests in several areas of the communications industry. For example:

- **News International** owns several newspaper titles (*The Times*, the *Sunday Times*, *The News of the World* and *The Sun*), 40 per cent of BSkyB, Harper-Collins (the book publisher), a share in Talk Radio, apart from its world-wide interests in Australia, America and Asia.
- **Pearson** owns the *Financial Times*, North of England Newspapers, Westminster Press, Thames TV, an interest in Essex Radio, and publishing chains such as Longman, Penguin and Viking.

The two older technologies, newspapers and the radio, continue to be significant among the American media. Newspapers are the oldest form of mass communication in the US, with some 80 per cent of adult Americans now reading a paper on a regular basis. America has traditionally lacked a strong national press, which is not surprising given the divergent interests of people in different parts of the country, and the difficulties of transporting morning editions quickly around the country. The middle-market *USA Today* has helped to fill the gap, but the likelihood is that over the next few years more national papers will be created, given the new technology available. In the meantime, however, in most American cities there is only one regular newspaper available, although countrywide there are some 1800 titles. Small-town dailies thrive on presenting stories of local interest, but may also provide a sketchy coverage of national events.

Americans have always been deeply attached to their free press. Newspapers are often criticised for their bias, on the Right there being complaints that they are dominated by a liberal elite and on the Left that they are unduly influenced by rich and powerful moguls. They may be sometimes attacked as unduly sensationalist in their coverage of events and too obsessed with the trivia of the personal lives of those who aspire to lead them. But many voters trust their journalists more than their politicians and have a strong suspicion that exposés of corruption and scandal are more than likely to be justified. In episodes such as Watergate and the Iran–Contra affair (see pp. 12–13), they had reason to be grateful for the investigative instincts of persistent newshounds.

Unlike Britain, there is no concept of public service broadcasting in America, on either radio or television. Radio is still extensively used in the United States. It had always remained popular as an outlet for political advertising in some of the smaller states, but has recently experienced a surprising revival in the television age. The popularity of chat shows and particularly phone-in programmes of the *Talk Radio* variety has aroused considerable interest, as have the new stations which cater for minority groups and tastes. Radio talk shows have been described as the equivalent of 'a 1990s American town meeting',[3] a chance for the voters to listen to and call the candidates. These may have vast audiences, and act as a lively medium for the exchange of views between often-conservative presenters and equally (if not more) right-wing listeners. Individuals can vent their feelings, however blatant, and listen to those of others.

Television in the USA is still dominated by three major commercial TV networks – CBS, NBC and ABC – although their hold has weakened in recent years. These networks sell programmes to local broadcast stations known as affiliates, and in 1995 the three long-established ones each had more than 200 of these, Fox Broadcasting some 150 or so. What has happened in the last decade, is that the hold of the three networks has been challenged not only by Fox but also by the development of new technologies which are widening the

---

The debate about ownership and control of the media

In Britain, the rest of Europe and America there has been a trend towards concentration of ownership, and concerns about whether this is harmful to democracy. Powerful tycoons head vast corporations often owned and dominated by a few individuals and families, many of whom also have extensive publishing and broadcasting empires including television and the wider entertainment industry.

Australia has the greatest concentration of media ownership in the Western world, control being dominated by Rupert Murdoch and Kerry Packer who respectively control the press and television (plus the bulk of the nation's magazines). France has the Hersant and Hachette information empires, Germany has the Springer and Gruner organisations, and in Italy Berlusconi, Agnelli, Ferruzzi and De Benedetti (who made their money in real estate, automobiles, food and chemicals, and industry and finance, respectively), have all bought substantial interests in the old and new media fields. All of these moguls have found that ownership of the media business in the 1980s and 1990s is a very lucrative business. Beyond making money, however, they wish to influence public opinion and the political arena.

By their own testimony, the multi-millionaires who can afford to own newspapers are not just in the business of making a fast profit; indeed, in the case of *The Times*, Rupert Murdoch has been content to suffer a loss for much of its existence. His purpose, and that of other corporate giants, is to shape the political environment in which they operate. In the longer term, the rewards of Berlusconi, Murdoch and others in their own country and around the world are considerable. They can propagate their views and hope to influence decision-making in areas which matter to them, such as the future of their businesses.

In the United States there are similar tendencies. The number of cities where there are competing newspaper firms has steadily declined. More than 70 per cent of local newspapers are now controlled by large publishing chains in which the owners lay down the editorial policy which editors are expected to follow. In their defence, these American corporations do help to 'nationalise' coverage by providing information on what is happening in Washington and abroad, whereas local ownership tends to emphasise local preoccupations. This could be all the more important as America lacks a public broadcasting service such as that provided by the BBC in Britain.

Private ownership of newspapers, rather than any form of state control or interference, is widely seen as a guarantee of freedom of choice and a bulwark against state tyranny. But some commentators wonder if it is healthy if a few proprietors can dominate the dissemination of ideas. After all, moguls of the past have been open about their motives. Lord Beaverbrook made it clear that he ran the *Daily Express* 'for the purpose of propaganda, and with no other motive'. Lord Northcliffe referred to his wish to be able to tell the people 'whom to love, whom to hate, and what to think'.

A former journalist and Labour MP, Robin Corbett has explained the dangers of Murdochian

choice available to viewers. Many Americans now get their television signals not over the air but via cables. Several cable-only channels have emerged, such as CNN and C-Span.

dominance in the House of Commons. Having referred to Murdoch's 'awesome power', he went on to say that it

> threatens our democracy. It is not simply because Mr Murdoch interferes with editorial policy, which he does, but because his staff from the moment they are employed know what is expected of them and they know what to write and how to write – and if they do not they will be out the front door before they can pick up their hat and coat.[4]

As the potential profitability of television became apparent, news and radio proprietors have been keen to buy into television so that a pattern of cross-media ownership was established. In the eyes of their critics, such combines can have very detrimental effects. In particular, they:

- determine entry into the media market, promoting their own interests by eliminating the prospect of rivalry;
- erode diversity of choice, resulting in a more homogeneous presentation of issues so that the public has less varied information;
- reduce the availability of countervailing power centres to governmental policy. (If the powerful proprietors are sympathetic to those in office, then there is less likely to be any serious dissent or critical analysis, and there may be 'no-go' areas for investigative reporting – in the way that Rupert Murdoch is alleged to be reluctant to criticise the Chinese Communist regime for fear of jeopardising his prospects of establishing a foothold in that country);
- use their outlets to act as a megaphone for the proprietors' own social and political ambitions.

The media sector is a fast-changing one, and it is difficult to establish a regulatory framework which can keep apace with technological advances, cross-media alliances and global networks. Both Britain and America have tried to limit cross-media ownership, prohibiting newspapers from dominating the television industry as well. But they have recognised that the question of cross-media ownership is a complex and controversial area of policy. It seems self-evident that the existence of a diversity of media organisations must be to the benefit of the public, as this should ensure that the opinions and perspective of different groups within society get a hearing. Yet to impose strict curbs on ownership might be to affect adversely the economic prosperity of the media sector, one of the fastest-growing sectors of the modern economy. The European Publishers Council (EPC) has reported on the issue, its review noting that

> cross-media activity is not only inevitable, but essential if newspapers and magazine publishers are not to lose competitive advantage and so atrophy ... Large-scale deregulation of national cross-media ownership restrictions is a prerequisite for economic growth in order that European media companies can compete in the world market.[5]

Political coverage in the media in Britain and America

Setting the agenda

Journalists are necessarily selective in what they show, but by their choice they convey what they regard as important. They give status to events and people, for an interview on national television can help to turn someone into a national figure. They have the power to enhance or undermine the standing of political leaders. In the USA in the 1930s, they chose to conceal the fact that President Franklin Roosevelt was in a wheelchair and had a mistress, whereas more recently they were happy to report extensively on President Clinton's sexual preferences and habits. Today, all political leaders have to live with the probing eye of investigative journalists who are keen to expose examples of wrong-doing. This was and is of course in the nature of their work, but the character of their coverage has become more searching and damaging to those in authority. Journalists realise that scandals – sexual or financial – often make compelling viewing, and in the inter-channel battle for viewers this is an important consideration. Moreover, since the abuses of presidential power which occurred in Watergate and Vietnam, they are less willing to accept what politicians do and say without challenge. In their investigations and exposures, journalists are reflecting and perhaps contributing to declining levels of public confidence in those who rule over us.

> **agenda-setting**
> The media function of directing people's attention to particular issues for their consideration; giving some issues special, sometimes disproportionate, coverage.

Agenda-setting is a key function of the media. Editors and journalists create an agenda of national priorities, deciding what is to be regarded as serious, what counts for little and what can be ignored. If an issue appears on the journalists' agenda, it is likely to be more widely discussed by individuals and groups in society. The media may not have the power to tell people what they should think, but they can tell them what they should be thinking about. By emphasising the problems of inner cities in Britain, or of environmental degradation and of national defence in America, they have an effect on people's perceptions of how important these issues really are. As Gary Wasserman has written:

> How the problems are presented will influence which explanations of them are more acceptable than others, and which policies are appropriate as responses. Whether inner-city crime is tied to the need for more police or with inadequate drug programmes, will help shape public debate. Likewise, if unemployment in California is tied to illegal immigration rather than the lack of vocational training, the solution may be frontier barriers rather than aid to education.[6]

Journalists have their own criteria for deciding what is worth reporting as a good 'news' story. Much news is bad news, a point reflected in the phrase used by some Conservative MPs several years ago when speaking of the radio programme, 'The World at One'; they re-labelled it as 'The world is glum'. Other news concerns examples of conflict in society, whether it be racial attacks/violence in Britain, religious and other divisions in Northern Ireland, or ethnic cleansing in former Yugoslavia. Again, stories often are about famous people and the lives (preferably the scandalous lives) they lead. All of these are better from the point of view of a television producer if they are accompanied by 'good visuals'.

The mass media, ever on the look-out for a good story, find the political arena an almost limitless source of material. The demand for news is ever-increasing, and both broadcasters and politicians have an interest in what is presented and how stories are handled. Political stories can be welcome to politicians as a vehicle for publicity and promotion of their ideas, but if they are hostile they may be viewed with alarm. For the broadcasting media, they are the very essence of lively journalism.

The nature and quality of coverage

Political exposure on television comes via several outlets. Politicians appear on a range of programmes from news bulletins to current affairs episodes, from the broadcasting of political events to special election features. There are also newer types of coverage. The Americans speak of 'infotainment': programmes which employ the techniques of entertainment to present more serious issues. Among them are chat shows. which have a markedly less political agenda but which still provide an opportunity to project personality and get the message across in a less demanding atmosphere.

In recent years, the trend has been for even the more overtly political programmes to be presented in a way which grabs the attention. Rather than the early methods of 'talking heads', round-table discussions between weighty interviewees and a generally serious treatment of heavy issues, the emphasis is on featuring stories which are 'made for television', with good pictorial back-up. Such developments feed the fears of those who feel that television tends to trivialise and sensationalise politics. Producers are always on the look-out for opportunities to stress the confrontational approach, with plenty of personality clashes and scenes of groups and individuals locked in disagreement and conflict. As elections approach, these tendencies became ever more apparent.

In addition, politicians can communicate via the press. They like to receive as much coverage of their meetings, speeches and performances in the legislature as possible, and they are often adept at sending communications to editors outlining their lists of engagements as well as summaries of their contributions to public debate. They may also write newspaper columns. Once elected, the US Presidents may make use of the televised Presidential Press Conference.

Political coverage at election time (see also the effects of television on elections and electioneering, pp. 256–9)

Political interviews

There is a tradition in Britain of the extended political interview, often with a studio audience. They are less used in most other democracies and are not common in America. Interviews are useful as a means of establishing facts, probing motives and holding politicians to account. They also help the politician to develop his or her public persona, so that in Bruce's words, 'they are about performance'.[7]

Debates

Britain has not yet staged a debate between the party leaders. (The nearest we have is the studio discussion in which a speaker from either side of the political divide is chosen to put forward the party's viewpoint.) Leaders of the Opposition tend to urge such contests, sensing an opportunity to embarrass an incumbent Prime Minister. Routinely, the people in Downing Street or their advisers, reject them, perhaps because – as with the political interview – once in the studio and under starter's orders, politicians are effectively on their own. As Bruce explains: 'Any incumbent who accepts the challenge of their opponent in this form needs their head examined. The latter has very little to lose and the former very little to gain'.[8]

In America, debates have become the pre-eminent media event of the campaign, attracting vast audiences of 80–90 million. Depending on the format adopted they can be useful in clarifying the policies of those participating, and they allow the viewer to make a choice between the merits of rival candidates and to assess their effectiveness and sincerity when under pressure. American debates have been of varying quality, and the rules of engagement have differed from election to election. Some have almost certainly made a difference to the outcome (e.g. Kennedy v Nixon, in 1960), so that it is crucial for candidates to avoid mistakes. Errors have been made and some have been costly. President Ford committed an infamous gaffe and exposed his ignorance in 1976 when – at a time when the Cold War was still very much a part of the global scene – he said that Poland was not then under Soviet domination. By contrast, other candidates have used debates to their advantage. Whereas George Bush froze in front of the cameras in 1992 and Dole in 1996 similarly lumbered in discomfort, their opponent, Bill Clinton, was at home, using body language and eye contact to engage the viewer. George W. Bush also benefited from the debates, his relaxed manner contrasting markedly with the more aggressive style adopted by Gore. It was widely anticipated that he might suffer at the hands of the experienced Democrat who was better versed on policy issues. But in the event, simply by his avoidance of potentially costly mistakes, he benefited from the contests.

Party broadcasts

British politicians have a means of communicating with the electorate which is unknown in America, the Party Political Broadcast (PPB). At election time, Party Election Broadcasts (PEBs) are allocated to all parties who put up at least 70 candidates, the exact number depending on the number of votes received at the last election. The early ones were very amateurish, but after 1959 a new professionalism crept in. People who worked on PEBs were more skilled in the media, and occasionally 'stars' were brought in to lend support and add a touch of glamour. In the 1980s and 1990s, PPBs and PEBs developed into something more like their present form, often using music and landscapes effectively as in the 1987 **Kinnock – The Movie** broadcast, directed by an established professional film director, Hugh Hudson, who had been responsible for the highly successful film *Chariots of Fire*.

> **Kinnock – The Movie**
>
> Neil and Glenys Kinnock were portrayed strolling hand-in-hand over the Welsh hills towards a headland, to the accompaniment of Brahms First Symphony and soaring seagulls overhead. The broadcast had a strong script, depicting Kinnock in a range of favourable settings which showed his 'strength' and also his commitment to 'decent' community values. It was a high-spot of the 1987 campaign.

The trend has been for broadcasts to get shorter, more akin to American political advertisements. The Conservatives have often used less than their allocated time in recent years, in the knowledge that a brief slot can make catchy and memorable points. In 2001, none ran to more than five minutes; some were less than three. Labour's broadcasts were more celebratory in tone, with broadcasts about the 'real heroes who are building the fortune of Britain' (nurses, teachers and police officers, among them) in the 'new Britain', coupled with dire warnings of what might happen to the public services should their opponents return to power. Conservative ones were very negative in tone, often employing dark, menacing images. A part of the first broadcast dealt with crime, its approach being reminiscent of an American TV advert used by an 'independent' Bush-supporting PAC in 1988 against Michael Dukakis. Others depicted scary visions of further life under Labour.

At best, such broadcasts are polished pieces of film, and interested voters may be influenced by those that are well done. The professionalism, emotionalism and negativity of many others is very reminiscent of American techniques. Some evidence suggests that viewers often switch off or are bored by broadcasts, especially those between election campaigns.

Political advertisements

Whereas election broadcasts in Britain are strictly controlled, there are no such restrictions in America. A candidate may spend as much as he or she wished to on paid television time. Adverts place greater emphasis on candidates themselves rather than their party label. Those who make them are concerned to portray their candidate in a flattering light and to stress the demerits of their opponents.

American political adverts are overwhelmingly negative, for research has suggested that this is the most effective approach. Consumers can take in only so much information at any one time and it is easier to implant a negative message than a positive one in a brief broadcast. This is why it tends to go for the jugular and expose deficiencies in the moral character of an opponent. Often, they are used to attack an opponent's financial wheeling and dealing or to remind voters of personal weaknesses, perhaps in a back-handed way. In Tennessee, a candidate was congratulated for 'kicking [his] chemical dependency'.

Sometimes, adverts are longer portrayals, dwelling on the personal assets of the candidate. Television is good at handling personalities and telling stories, features which were combined in the 'Ron and Nancy' weepie in 1984 and the 'Man from Hope' film about Bill Clinton and his family eight years later. The former is thought to have provided the model for the 'Kinnock – The Movie' election broadcast used so effectively by Labour in 1987.

Television as a means of communication

The quality of news and current affairs programming matters for the public and the politicians. Ideally, coverage will be fair, balanced and interesting, straightforward and accessible for those who want a brief review and clear and comprehensive for those seeking a more detailed understanding. For many people, watching a news bulletin or reading a tabloid newspaper gives them as much information as they require. Others want more searching analysis and reflective comment to enable them to understand the background story behind the news.

Television has weaknesses as a source of political education, some of which relate to the need for balance and impartiality. In interviews with leading TV personalities it is sometimes difficult for politicians to get their views across for their replies can be cut off prematurely or they may not be given a chance to provide an adequate answer. Sometimes a sharp intervention by the chairman of a discussion is necessary to get a response from professional politicians who are skilled at being evasive, but on occasion the interview can be dominated by the personality of the interviewer more than by the answer being attempted.

Furthermore, there is a need for speed and brevity on television, and great issues are sometimes not handled at length, arguments are left unexplored and to keep programmes alive and entertaining they can be superficial and trivial. In-depth analysis – how events came to be – is often lacking. Yet at best discussion can be profound, elucidating the arguments on key issues and exploring the backgrounds of incidents and decisions.

Over the last decade, there has been some disquiet about the standard of news and current affairs coverage on television. Several allegations have been made, notably that:

- Television news was often reduced to the role of running other people's stories. Major issues often derived more from what was gathered from the newspapers than from original research undertaken by a television news operation. Good investigation by TV journalists was increasingly a rarity.
- The content and presentation of too many stories were dictated by the ploys of spin doctors and media experts who know how to manage the news. What resulted was an obsession with sound-bites and picture opportunities, whilst issues were neglected. As President Jimmy Carter once lamented: 'The peripheral aspects become the headlines, but the basic essence of what you stand for and what you hope to accomplish is never reported'.
- Though there were more and more bulletins on different stations and at different times of the day, most national coverage repeated the same stories about the same issues and the same people. The manner of presentation might vary and the information was sometimes regurgitated with a slightly differing slant – depending on the news editor involved – but this did not amount to genuine choice. The range of topics which made the agenda was too narrow.

An American insight

Walter Cronkite, a distinguished American newsman, has reviewed his experiences of television journalism in his autobiography, *A Reporter's Life*. Having praised the way in which television can 'lift the floor of knowledge' for those who know very little about politics, he argues that it can 'lower the ceiling' for the majority. He particularly regrets the trend towards sound-bite journalism:

> The sheer volume of television news is ridiculously small. The number of words spoken in a half-hour broadcast rarely equals the number of words on two-thirds of a standard newspaper page. That is not enough to cover the whole day's major events. Compression of facts, foreshortened arguments, the elimination of extenuating explanation – all are dictated by TV's restrictive frame and all distort, to some degree, the news on television . . .

> The TV correspondent as well as his or her subjects is a victim of this compression. With inadequate time to present a coherent report, the correspondent seems to craft a final summary sentence that might make some sense of the preceding gibberish. This is hard to do without coming to a single point of view – and a one line editorial is born . . . Sound-bite journalism simply isn't good enough to serve the people in our national elections.

An extract published in *The Guardian*, 27 January 1997.

The effects of the media

The effects of television on politics and the electoral process cover three main aspects: the effects on elections and electioneering, the effects on political leaders and candidates, and the effects on the opinions of the electorate.

Elections and electioneering

Today, the media, especially television, largely determine the form of election campaigns. They have replaced political meetings in importance, to the extent that today any large meetings are relayed on television and geared to its needs. Each news bulletin accords coverage of the main politicians, so that the main meetings are stage-managed proceedings timed for maximum television coverage, and sound-bites are delivered to grab the headlines.

Bowler and Farrell have illustrated the extent to which these trends are common to all democracies. Television is the main tool for campaigning, to the extent that 'free elections in a modern democracy would easily collapse if the mass media . . . were to ignore election campaigning'. Television has had its effect at the local level. The roots of party activity are atrophying, and canvassing and pamphleteering are less in evidence. As the same writers point out: 'Local electioneering has been overtaken by the nationalisation of the campaign and the growth of the mass media'.[9]

The media has another role in connection with the conduct of elections. Increasingly, they help to set the agenda for the campaign. As we have seen, journalists – or, more particularly, their editors – determine the issues they consider to be worthy of investigation and follow-up reporting and commentary. Some issues are kept in the forefront of the public mind (in Britain, sleaze in 1997), whereas other – perhaps more meaty ones – may be neglected.

The style of campaigning is much influenced by television. In America, electioneering is more candidate-centred (see pp. 289–90), so that candidates rather than parties seek to gain popular approval and support. In Britain, party counts for more, but there is still an infatuation with personalities. Although party managers may still be interviewed and seek to use the medium to promote the party cause, it is the candidate who is the focus of media attention. They and their team of consultants are constantly on the look out for opportunities to ensure that they gain favourable coverage and are vigilant in watching out for any signs of bias against them. They attempt **'management' of the news**.

> **news management**
> The techniques used by politicians and their advisers to control the information given to the media.

Managing the media involves ensuring that journalist get the right stories (information slanted to their particular viewpoint) backed up with good pictures. It can range from crude political arm-twisting to more subtle means. Advisers dream up sound-bites and photo-opportunities, and use their spin-doctors to put across an appropriate line (see box on p. 259). They try to book interviews with 'softer' interviewers, rather than undergo a potentially damaging interrogation. They seek to control the agenda, sticking to themes on which they are strong and avoiding (or downplaying) embarrassing issues.

Political consultancy is an area that has mushroomed. According to Rees, there are at least some 10,000 political consultants in the United States. He quotes one Democrat consultant as saying: 'In America today, without good professional help, if you're running against a person who has professional help, you have virtually no chance of being elected'.[10] These media advisers understand the way in which television works and what their candidate needs to do to create the right impression. They know that television is not just another channel of communication. It has 'changed the very way it has become necessary to communicate, and thus the very way it has become necessary to formulate political discourse'. Television has made the 'look' of a politician vital. When we think of Thatcher, Major and Blair or Reagan, Clinton and George W. Bush, it is their image, how they look on television, which is the main memory. Television is a medium in which attractive people flourish. Conventional good looks are an advantage; fatness or baldness quite the opposite.

Politicians need to be acceptable to the ear, as well as to the eye. Television has actually changed what is said, as well as how it is said. The form of debate is influenced by the professional persuaders. As we have seen, politicians increasingly talk in memorable sound-bites. The emphasis of their discourse is on broad themes, the phrases being simple and often repeated. Frequently their language is couched in emotional terms. If the message can be illustrated by a suitable picture, so much the better.

Party leaders and candidates

Today, the tendency of journalists in the media is to presidentialise our election coverage and do less than justice to the issues involved, for, as Negrine observes, there is an 'infatuation with personalities and, in particular, political leaders'.[11] Indeed, Foley notes that outside of an election period party leaders account for one-third of the time allocated to politicians in news coverage; during elections, the figures rises to half.[12] This being the case, parties feel that they must choose politicians who are 'good on television'. Unsurprisingly, politicians are highly sensitive to the way in which their behaviour and actions are reported. They realise that television, in particular, can do them great damage. It also provides them with a remarkable opportunity to influence opinion.

THE TERMINOLOGY OF MODERN ELECTIONS

Photo-opportunities

Carefully stage-managed episodes in which the leading figure is set against a particular background, perhaps to demonstrate concern for the area or its industry. Ronald Reagan favoured the image of the all-American cowboy, riding on horseback into the sunset, thereby conjuring in the mind of the electors an image of the great outdoors as part of the wholesome American dream. Tony Blair has sometimes been photographed with footballers and their managers, as when he had a heading encounter with Kevin Keegan or met members of the England team prior to the World Cup finals in Korea and Japan. Such occasions have a humanising effect, suggesting that the candidate is a 'regular guy', someone just like 'ordinary people'.

Sound-bites

Short sayings, full of concentrated meaning, which consists of a few easily remembered words, and yet convey a particular message. A well-known Reagan sound-bite was 'You ain't seen nothin' yet'. George Bush told voters to 'Read my lips. No new taxes', a slogan which backfired when, as President, he found himself supporting higher taxation. The Rev. Jesse Jackson (a charismatic, African-American and liberal Democratic politician) is a master of 'soundbitese'. Recognising that he will get perhaps 15 seconds on a news bulletin, he can summarise his argument in an exciting epigram. His rhyming sound-bite 'we're going to have demonstrations without hesitation and jail without bail' was a more memorable and catchy way of saying that 'we are not going to spend a long time deciding whether to have a demonstration. We are willing to go to jail for our cause and will not accept bail'. In Britain, the best-known sound-bite was that used by Tony Blair before, during and after the 1997 election: 'Tough on crime, tough on the causes of crime'.

Politicians on either side of the Atlantic have been forced to acquire new techniques of communication. When politicians addressed large crowds 'on the stump', the quality of oratory was all-important. Dramatic, expansive gestures were in vogue. Television requires a different, quieter tone. As Hague and Harrop explain: '[In the age of broadcasting] the task is to converse rather than to deliver a speech; to talk to the millions as though they were individuals'.[13] Some politicians have excelled in developing their technique, among them Franklin Roosevelt, whose folksy 'fireside chats' from the White House gave the American people renewed hope in the days of the Great Depression and after.

America has led the way in selling its public figures. Three of them have been 'naturals' for television, just as Franklin Roosevelt was for radio. John F. Kennedy portrayed an image of youth and glamour, and lifted the horizons of many Americans as he offered them a vision of 'new frontiers'. Ronald Reagan,

The use of soundbites by politicians is a recognition of the importance of the television in political affairs. In the limited time available for political coverage, they need to make maximum impact. Moreover, they know that the attention span of the voters – used as they are to the impact of pictures in this visual medium – is in many cases limited. Their response is to employ a brief, catchy statement which reduces complex issues into an easily memorable slogan. When Michael Howard (the Conservative Home Secretary in the Major government), wanted to convey the idea that ministers were taking a tough line in dealing with crime, by using imprisonment as a main means of deterrence and punishment, his easy catchphrase was 'Prison works'.

Spin-doctors

Spin-doctors are part of the media team, their task being to change the way the public perceive some happening, or to alter their expectations of what might occur. They try to put a favourable gloss on information and events. Spin has become an accepted feature of campaigns in the USA. The term derives from the spin given to a ball in various sports, to make it go in a direction which confuses the opponent.

Spin-doctors for candidates and parties may 'talk down' their own chances of success or build up those of an opponent. The idea of spin came from the United States and takes many forms, ranging from damage limitation (the management of things already out of control, in such a way as to prevent any further deterioration) to tornado spin (the attempt to create interest in something which is not inherently fascinating). Labour's use of spinning has been much criticised since 1997, because its alleged tendency to be 'economical with the *actualite*' encourages people to disbelieve what governmental spokespersons are saying.

a trained actor, looked good and sounded sincere. Known as 'the great communicator', he had the gift of making people trust in him. Using a teleprompter (the first political leader to do so), he was able to speak directly to his audience, in tones to which they could warm. His advisers presented him as the embodiment of the American Dream; he was an individualist who spoke in language which appealed to their hearts.

Bill Clinton was effective in speaking directly to the viewers, and was on occasion able to use television to launch his come-back after going through a bad patch. His style was in any case suited to the modern era, but he was also well-served by his script-writers. They were said to spend much time in his company, and as a result were able to incorporate words and phrases which he used in his private conversation. By so doing, they were able to convey the character of the person, in this case one who does not favour ornate rhetoric but likes to tell his story in a relaxed, conversational style.

In Britain, Harold Macmillan and Harold Wilson were able television performers, each having something of the actor in their personality and possessing characteristics that could make them seem amiable and interesting. Peter Hennessy has pointed out that Wilson was at first an uninspired communicator, prone to jerky movements with his right arm. But then he got a pipe and solved his problem. He 'changed the nature of the discourse, making it relaxed and conversational, but recognised that it is the well-fashioned phrase and sentence which will glow and be remembered'.[14] In Tony Blair, Labour found another man appropriate for the television age. He has revealed his mastery of the medium in a variety of circumstances, as in the tribute he paid on the death of Princess Diana, his appearance with Des O'Connor, and his sofa conversation with Richard and Judy on ITV.

Appearance as well as voice is important. Macmillan saw the need to change his image from that of a tweedy old Tory to an elegant Edwardian gent; Wilson carried a spare, carefully pressed suit; and of Margaret Thatcher it was observed that 'every part of her had been transformed, her teeth, her nose I suspect and her eyebrows'. The same writer, Peter Mandelson (a former TV producer who became a media/image adviser for the Labour Party, prior to becoming an MP and Cabinet minister), has noted that:

> TV does more to make or break a politician than any other medium. It is the voter's key source for forming impressions of politicians. They are looking for good judgement, for warmth, for an understanding of people's concerns. That can only be demonstrated on television.[15]

'Getting it right' does matter, as Sir Alec Douglas-Home (a former Tory Prime Minister) recognised before his death. Having been undermined by the medium – which made him look rather drawn and ill-at-ease, with his glasses too far down his nose and his face and head very skull-shaped – he admitted that he 'was bored by the whole business of presentation as far as television was concerned because I think television is bound to be superficial. I was wrong'. Other political leaders – from Ted Heath to Gerald Ford and Michael Foot to the elder George Bush – have learned that television is a two-edged sword. For the telegenic politician it presents an enormous opportunity, but for those who do not look or sound good it can be damaging. On the one hand, it exposes their limitations; on the other, it may enhance the stature of those around them, who may be potential rivals.

The effects of television on the opinions of the voters

Given the time many people spend viewing and their constant exposure to a mass of information in news bulletins and current affairs/discussion programmes, it would be surprising if there was no effect on the attitudes and judgements of the electorate. At the very least, electors would be expected to know more about topics on which they already had some knowledge, and to become informed about ones with which they were previously unfamiliar. At election time, one would expect them to have a heightened awareness of key issues. Indeed, some people tend to become mini-pundits on the issues of the day, having watched a programme the night before. One might expect increased interest, as well.

The real – as opposed to the imagined – effects of the mass media on popular attitudes are difficult to assess. They may be very different on different people. Viewers may spend hours watching the television or reading a newspaper, but this does not necessarily tell us that either or both are their main sources of information. There are many possible ways of obtaining knowledge, and it is impossible to separate that which has been derived from the media from conversations at the workplace or that which has been accumulated from elsewhere. Life is a continuing learning experience, in which knowledge and attitudes are liable to be influenced at many points in a person's lifetime.

The task of determining media influence is the greater because there are so many different forms of media, and to distinguish between the effects caused by one medium rather than another is near impossible. In developing their political attitudes, people might be influenced by television, radio, newspapers or quality journals, amongst other sources. It may more simply be an eye-catching poster which makes the greatest impression on them.

There have been four main theories concerning the study of the effects of the media on people's attitudes and conduct.

1 The hypodermic theory

Back in the 1930s, it was easy to think in terms of the importance of propaganda. The experience of the dictatorships, particularly Nazi Germany, led people to assume that the media must have a considerable impact, for Goebbels and others like him were making so much use of persuasive techniques. Against this background, some political scientists suggested that the message carried by the media was like a 'magic bullet' or hypodermic syringe which, on contact with the audience, affected it in a uniform way. People soaked up the information they were given, rather as a sponge absorbs water.

The survey evidence to substantiate such findings was lacking. In any case, the effect of propaganda in a totalitarian regime was likely to be infinitely greater than in a liberal democracy such as America in which people could think, act and react under less threatening conditions.

2 The reinforcement theory

When researchers such as Paul Lazarsfeld looked for similar evidence of the impact of the media in postwar America, they were unable to find it. Using more modern and scientific techniques of investigation, Lazarsfeld found that there was no evidence to substantiate the idea of a significant effect. He first examined radio, and found no evidence of a decisive influence; indeed, 'it was the change of opinion which determined whether people listened, rather than their listening determining their change of opinion'.

Using the 1948 presidential election as a case-study, Lazarsfeld's findings showed that few people changed their vote in the campaign, and that those who did so were as likely to cite discussions with relatives, friends and colleagues at work as the major reason rather than television or newspapers.[16] This led Lazarsfeld to expound the **minimum effects** model of media influence, which recognised that knowledge may increase and attitudes may become clearer in a campaign, but that voting behaviour itself was little influenced by television. The reason for this was the **selective exposure theory**, according to which listeners and viewers filtered out and suppressed unwelcome messages while paying particular attention to those they liked. The idea was that television acts primarily as a means of reinforcement rather than fundamental change. People exposed themselves to communications with which they were likely to agree, and tended to remember only information which coincided with their own outlook.

3 The agenda-setting theory

Coverage of the effects of the media moved on from the 'reinforcement' phase to the 'agenda-setting' one, according to which the media achieve their aim of influencing people by more subtle means. They can't directly tell people what to think, but they can tell them what to think about. They influence the public by determining what is shown or read, and many of the viewers/readers come to accept what is offered as a representation of the main things that are really happening.

Television does help to set the agenda for discussion. Journalists (or more particularly their editors) and producers of television and radio programmes decide on what they consider to be the key issues worthy of investigation, follow-up reporting and commentary. If they choose to highlight the character of a candidate, the budget deficit or the problems of the ghettos, then these may well become influential factors in shaping the image which people have of personalities or events.

4 The independent effect theory

A fourth model is in vogue today. The 'independent effect theory' is now sometimes advocated by sociologists on both sides of the Atlantic. This suggests that the media do have an effect on public attitudes, even if those effects are difficult to monitor and are variable in their impact. The effects may be negative – e.g. by ignoring certain candidates, the media make people believe that they are not important or do not exist – and may have small-scale and short-term influence, but it is naive to write off the power of the media.

We now have much greater experience of the media, and in particular are more familiar with the age of television. Hence, it seems to be only common sense to assume that the influence of the media must be greater than has been allowed for in the recent past. In particular, what has changed in the last generation is that the traditional identification of many Americans with a particular party has become less firm. It is now a commonplace to speak of declining voter-partisanship. If people are more receptive to a change of mind, it seems reasonable to suggest that the media, especially television, may have a greater effect than ever before on their attitudes and voting. There are more votes 'up for grabs'.

During a presidential or congressional election campaign, the elector today faces a huge amount of material from the mass media, including news bulletins, discussion programmes, talk shows and debates between the candidates. With political advertising on television, as well as posters, pamphlets and press advertisements, there certainly is a barrage of information available. It is hard to believe that such saturation does not have an impact. At the very least, people ought to be more fully informed than ever before, even if their attitudes are not altered – but this too may happen over a period of time.

The parties' professional advisers clearly think that television has a significant impact. They place much emphasis on ensuring that the campaign is appropriate for the medium, carefully packaging the product, and portraying their candidate in his or her best light. But the truth is that no one really knows what the effects are and different research points to different conclusions. People react in several ways. Some are partisans who seek to back up their beliefs with examples derived from the programmes they view; others are monitors genuinely seeking information with which to make up their minds. There are also those who are merely passive spectators watching out of apathy or without great commitment. In other words, it is misleading to speak of the impact of the media as though this was the same impact on all groups in the population. The effects of TV exposure may be entirely different on such categories as the young and the old, the employed and the unemployed. There are many effects on many different people.

Televised politics in Britain and the USA compared: the Americanisation of British politics?

Britain has in many ways learnt from the American experience. Election campaigners have visited the United States and sometimes participated in elections there. Inevitably, their findings have been relayed to their colleagues back home. In addition, people in Britain see pictures of presidential electioneering, and there has often been discussion in the media of the techniques employed. As a result, America has been a useful source of innovation in British campaign techniques. Just as the Conservatives under Margaret Thatcher absorbed a lot from the Reagan experience in the mid–late 1980s, so too the Labour Party was keen to derive insights from the success of the Democrat, Bill Clinton, in 1992 and again in 1996.

In recent years, there has been an increasing British obsession with walkabouts, photo-opportunities and other **pseudo-events** created for the media. In the 1980s and 1990s, there have been several examples of the Americanisation of politics at work, not least in the style of some party broadcasts (Kinnock – The Movie, **Jennifer's Ear** and others), and in the **Sheffield Rally**, a triumphalist occasion very reminiscent of the American convention.

Yet there are differences and some safeguards. In Britain, we are electing a party rather than just one person, and politics is not about personality alone. The in-depth interview provides a kind of antidote to the dangers of shallow but media-friendly leaders being chosen, for their personal qualities come under heavy scrutiny and in the in-depth Sunday lunchtime type of programme policy deficiencies can be much exposed. We also can now see our representatives in action in the House of Commons, and Question Time at least is an institution which shows those in power being forced to defend their position, even if it does little to inform people of the issues. The interviews conducted in the election in *Election Call* are a reminder of how leading figures can be put on the spot by skilful members of the public who can unsettle their composure.

But most people do not watch such encounters, and the likelihood is that those people who use television the most to obtain their information may be the very people who are least discerning and able to come to a reasonable conclusion

pseudo-events
Events such as press conferences or photo-opportunities which would not take place were it not for the TV coverage they attract. Their use illustrates the importance of 'news management' by political consultants, to ensure that the best impression of the party or candidate is provided.

Jennifer's Ear
A 1992 Labour broadcast, the story of two girls and their similar problem of 'glue ear'. The parents of one girl could afford private treatment. The other girl, Jennifer, was reliant on the National Health Service to remedy the affliction. The issue at stake – the funding of the health service – was later lost in a series of revelations, explanations and denials. But the approach of the programme was very American, professionally accomplished and strong on emotion and with the added-extra ingredient of a sickly child. Ultimately it backfired, and failed in its purpose.

Sheffield Rally
A slick, visually striking, stage-managed, glitz and glamour Labour election gathering (1992), which treated its characters more as movie stars than as politicians striving for office. Some people did not like the display of fervour which had overtones of Hitler's Nuremberg rallies in prewar Germany.

based on knowledge. They probably don't read other sources and therefore what they see and hear has a potent effect on the least sophisticated electors.

Party broadcasts instead of political advertisements, free air-time, vigilant journalists, and politicians more prepared to answer questions about their proposals, help to differentiate us from US experience in certain respects, and are some kind of protection against our adopting the worst aspects of American electioneering methods into Britain. Yet as we have seen, the party broadcasts themselves have to some degree 'gone American' in style and form.

It may be that on this side of the Atlantic we are less susceptible to the excesses of emotionalism and negative campaigning that beset American politics. In 1992, in different ways, Jennifer's Ear and the Sheffield Rally could be said to have backfired. In the long term, they may even be seen as the time when British politics diverted from the path pursued on the American scene, or at least held back from its worst excesses.

A note on the Internet

In the last few years, the Internet has been one of the most discussed means of communication. Partly this is because it allows the diffusion of several kinds of data, images, speeches, text and video. The level of interest also reflects the speed with which the Internet has been adopted across the world. Nearly half of the world's users are in the United States, where regular use has been considerably higher than in Britain: 54 per cent as against 43 per cent. One study has calculated the number of years from inception for new media to reach 50m households in the USA: radio 38, television 13, cable 10, and internet 5 (estimate for 1995–2000). (Quoted by Hague and Harrop[17].)

Enthusiasts for the Internet often claim that eventually it will become a key source of political information, as voters seek out news and comment on personalities and issues. Candidates and parties have responded to the challenge it presents, spending vast sums on creating web sites and e-mail address lists. The impact of such activity is as yet hard to assess. The proportion of the electorate with regular access to the Internet who use it for political purposes is small but growing, more concentrated among younger and more educated voters. There is little indication that it has as yet had much impact on undecided voters.

The Internet was used by candidates and their campaign managers in the 2000 and 2001 national elections. In America, Republican John McCain employed it as an effective means of raising money, Bush used it as the place to announce his financial backers, and in some battleground states supporters of Gore and Nader used it as a vehicle via which they could attempt to engage in mutually beneficial tactical voting.

At this stage, the Internet poses no serious threat to the more established media. Indeed, newspaper and television companies are the main providers of political information on web sites. It is, however, becoming more important as a campaigning tool and in both America and Britain major candidates and parties see it as a suitable place to outline their background, present policy positions and provide instructions for making on-line contributions.

Conclusion

The influence of the media is all-embracing. They are a tool of communications and a profitable economic resource. They also have significant political influence. Via news reports, entertainment and advertisements, they help to shape political attitudes. What is and what is not broadcast and printed helps to establish political figures, sets out priorities and focuses attention on issues. The media make politics intelligible to ordinary people.

The media in turn are affected by the corporations which own them, the advertisers who pay for their messages and the public which looks, reads and listens to what they have to offer. Technology has increased the number and variety of outlets, and led to the merger of many of them, which are now part of giant media corporations. Political leaders grant or withhold licences, stage pseudo-events and make available or withhold information to them as suits their purposes.

The mass media in Britain and the United States: a summary		
	Britain	*United States*
Main sources of political Information	Television, newspapers and radio.	Television, newspapers and radio.
Organisation, ownership and control – (a) television, (b) newspapers	(a) Mix of commercial and public service broadcasting, (b) Commercial – more national than local.	(a) Commercial, (b) Commercial – more local than national.
Political coverage at election time – differences	Extended political interviews, party broadcasts.	Presidential debates, advertising.
Political coverage at election time – similarities	Use of political consultants, sound-bites, photo-opportunities, pseudo-events, spin, increasing impact of Internet.	Use of political consultants, sound-bites, photo-opportunities, pseudo-events, spin, increasing impact of Internet.
Impact of media on voters	Minimum effects theory (reinforcement) giving way to independent effects theory.	Minimum effects theory (reinforcement) giving way to independent effects theory.

REFERENCES

1 E. Wedell, *Broadcasting and Public Policy*, Joseph Books, 1998.
2 J. Tunstall, *The Media in Western Europe*, Euromedia Research Group/Sage, 1997.
3 G. Edwards *et al.*, *Government in America*, Harper Collins, 1996.
4 R. Corbett, speech in House of Commons, 6 July 1997.
5 European Publishers Council report, *The Emergence of a Multimedia Industry in Europe*, 1995.
6 G. Wasserman, *The Basics of American Politics*, Longman, 1997.
7 B. Bruce, *Images of Power*, Kogan Page, 1992.
8 As note 7 above.
9 S. Bowler and D. Farrell, *Electoral Strategies and Political Marketing*, Macmillan, 1992.
10 L. Rees, *Selling Politics*, BBC Books, 1992.
11 R. Negrine, *Politics and the Mass Media in Britain*, Routledge, 1994.
12 M. Foley, *The Rise of the British Presidency*, Manchester University Press, 1993.
13 R. Hague and M. Harrop, *Comparative Government and Politics: An Introduction*, Palgrave, 2001.
14 P. Hennessy, *The Prime Minister*, Allen Lane, 2000.
15 P. Mandelson, as quoted in Rees (see note 10 above).
16 P. Lazarsfeld, *The People's Choice*, Columbia University Press, 1968.
17 As note 13 above.

USEFUL WEB SITES

The BBC, CNN and New York Times among other organs of mass communication have valuable sites, which are regularly updated:

www.news.bbc.co.uk

www.cnn.com/WORLD

www.nytimes.com

SAMPLE QUESTIONS

1 Why does Britain have and America lack a main channel dedicated to the idea of public service broadcasting?

2 Does the increasing concentration of media control in the hands of a few giant corporations threaten the accuracy and diversity of information available to the citizenry?

3 How do the British and American media shape the ideas and information that people on either side of the Atlantic have about politics and politicians?

4 How has television influenced the way in which politics are covered on either side of the Atlantic?

5 Today, election campaigns are geared to the needs of television'. Discuss.

6 'The media have little affect on political attitudes, other than to reinforce what people already believe'. Does British and American experience bear this out?

7 'The media have the capacity to determine what people feel and what they think and talk about? How responsibly do the main media of the day in Britain and America fulfil their responsibilities?

8 What role should the media play in a democratic society and what can done to ensure that they play this role?

Voting and elections

11

Elections are the main mechanism for expressing the public's collective desires about who should be in government and what the government should do. Elections in Britain are not as frequent or extensive as they are in the United States. There are no direct elections for the Executive as there are in a presidential system. Neither are there primary elections within the parties to decide on the choice of candidate.

In this chapter, we examine a number of issues about the functioning of elections in two democracies, looking at the electoral system, the nature and costs of the campaign, and the way in which voters behave and the influences upon their voting. In addition, we consider the use made – particularly in America – of various forms of direct democracy.

POINTS TO CONSIDER

➤ Are the benefits of the First Past The Post method of voting outweighed by the disadvantages?

➤ Who would gain from the introduction of some variant of proportional representation in Britain and the United States? What is the likelihood of the introduction of such a method of voting?

➤ Does a low turnout signify broad contentment, or apathy?

➤ 'In British general elections and American presidential elections, turnout has declined in recent decades'. Are there common factors which explain the decline?

➤ Why has turnout been falling in most countries in recent years?

➤ Compare the level of popular involvement in British and American elections.

➤ 'Americans participate more in the workings of their democracy than do British people.' Is this true?

➤ Which are the more important in voting behaviour today, long-term or short-term factors?

➤ To what extent has partisan dealignment occurred in recent decades on both sides of the Atlantic?

➤ Has class voting in Britain and the United States declined in recent years?

➤ Why is television so infatuated with personalities?

➤ In what ways does television set the agenda for election campaigns?

➤ Has there been an Americanisation of British electioneering methods and, if so, does it matter?

➤ Why has it been necessary to introduce legislation in Britain and the United States to control the raising and spending of public money in national elections?

➤ Why has 'soft money' become an issue in British and American politics?

➤ Does British and American experience suggest that money buys elections?

➤ Is state funding of parties and/or candidates a good idea?

➤ Why has direct democracy become more popular in recent years?

➤ Does American experience of direct democracy have anything to teach us on this side of the Atlantic?

All Western countries hold regular elections. Voting is the primary symbol of citizenship in a democratic society; indeed, 'one person, one vote' is one of the core principles of democracy. In established democracies, elections are generally free and fair, although doubts about the legitimacy of the outcome can arise, as in America 2000. Elections are the major way by which those who rule are made answerable to the mass of people.

Some countries hold many types of election, others few. In the United Kingdom, electors can vote in local and European elections, as well as in a general one every four or five years; the Irish, Welsh and the Scots also get the opportunity to vote for their devolved legislatures, and have had more opportunity than the English to vote in national referendums. In the United States, elections are much more common so that Americans elect people for offices which in most states would be filled by appointment. At every tier of political life, from President to Congressman on the national level, from Governor to Representative at the state level and from City Mayor to town councillor at the local level, the incumbent is chosen by election. School board contests are particularly hotly disputed. In some states, even such offices as the Municipal Judge and the Registrar of Wills, and in parts of the South the local undertaker and even dog catcher are contested. Most of these are local contests which rarely make the news outside the immediate vicinity.

It has been estimated that there are a million elected offices in the USA. Americans clearly have a great enthusiasm for the ballot box, even if they do not avail themselves of the opportunities it provides. The popularity of elections owes much to the general growth of the democratic principle since the days of the Founding Fathers. Americans have long believed that the greater the degree of popular involvement, the better the outcome is likely to be in terms of the quality of output. But beyond this is another consideration, the preference for limited government. Americans have always feared a concentration of power in too few hands. Even when they elect officials, they do not in most cases allow them to serve for too long. It is felt desirable to subject them to continuous accountability

In consequence, the task before an American voter is greater than that for his or her British equivalent. Whereas a British election ballot paper is a straight-forward affair, usually involving putting a cross on a piece of paper, an American one is rather different. The American voter may be casting a vote for the Presidency, the Senate and the House of Representatives at national level, and for a group of state and local offices which may be contested at the same time. In addition, there will probably be a number of propositions arising from state constitutional requirements or citizens' initiatives, calling for a response. In preparation for the propositions, a booklet or two may be provided containing closely printed pages outlining the proposals and the arguments advanced by proponents and opponents.

Britain has never had the same emphasis on electoral participation. The tradi-tional view is that voters should have their chance to vote every few years and in between allow the government to get on with the job. Until the last few decades, there has not been the same degree of distrust of politicians or wariness about letting appointed people exercise responsibility.

In several countries, elections are used by those in power to give the illusion of popular participation. They can range from being a meaningless exercise in which there is no genuine voter choice to a downright fraud, because of the tampering with votes or the lack of freedom in which polling is carried out. For example, in Bosnia, in the autumn of 1996, there were more ballot papers counted than there were members of the electorate. However, the object of elections is the same, to confer legitimacy on the government. In Britain, we may only get a vote every few years, but at least there is a genuine opportunity to express an opinion on those who have presided over our fortunes and to indicate whether it is, in our view, 'time for a change'.

A democratic general election is distinguished by several characteristics. These include such features as:
- a universal franchise;
- a secret ballot;
- a time limit on office;
- the freedom to form parties;
- contests in every constituency;
- campaigns regulated by strict and fair rules.

Of course, entitlement to vote is not the same as the effective ability to vote, and in a democracy it is important to ensure that there is an effective procedure by which people can be registered. In several countries there are permanent registers, amended at periodic intervals, as in Britain and most of Europe. Elsewhere, registers have to be created from scratch, so that in most American states it is necessary for the would-be voter to register his or her vote before polling day. This reflects the American emphasis on the mobilising effect of elections. Such an approach tends to be less efficient in ensuring eligibility, and in the USA the Motor Voter Act of 1993 was designed to make registration easier and thereby hopefully raise turnout by a few percentage points. It is significant that in the southern states, which have traditionally erected barriers to voting, there have always been lower turnouts than other parts of America.

Whatever the system, it is likely that some voters – perhaps 5-10 per cent or more – will not be registered. Of those who are registered, others will be unable to cast their vote because of illness, absence or other pressing circumstances. Some people are just unwilling to make the effort, especially if obtaining a postal vote is a complex process. Hence the remedy introduced in several countries: compulsory voting. Australia, Austria, Belgium and some Latin American states are among those which have resorted to this method, but in most cases its effectiveness is limited by the low level of fines and the difficulties in collecting those which are due.

Types of election

Some writers distinguish between different types of election, especially between the **maintaining** ones in which the party in power continues to hold the reins, and **realigning** ones in which voters opt for a change of direction and the underlying strength of the main parties is significantly changed. Sometimes, of course, voting for a different party does not fundamentally shift policy onto a new course, but in most countries it is possible to think of landmark dates when electors signalled their wish to opt for something different.

In postwar Britain, there have been elections which have produced (or promised to produce) a critical realignment, and these have included 1945, 1964, 1979 and 1997. In 2001, voters opted for 'more of the same', a maintaining election. Some presidential elections in the United States have led to a significant change of emphasis or direction, as with the election of Franklin Delano Roosevelt in 1932, the election of Kennedy in 1960, Reagan in 1980 and Clinton in 1992. The 1984, 1988 and 1996 elections were maintaining ones.

Electoral systems

The choice of electoral system to elect a particular assembly is a question of great importance in our democracy. To a significant degree electoral systems define how the body politic operates. As Farrell points out: 'they are the cogs which keep the wheels of democracy properly functioning'.[1] The choice of system raises issues about the nature of representative government and the purpose of elections. Indeed, the interim report of Labour's Plant Committee observed that: 'There can be nothing more fundamental in a democracy than proposals to change an electoral system'.[2]

In making that selection, much depends on what the electoral system is supposed to achieve. Obviously, it is desirable that it produces an outcome which is intelligible and acceptable to as many people as possible, so that when they vote they feel comfortable with the arrangements made and accept that the outcome on polling day is fair and legitimate. Beyond that, there are other possible functions which those interested might expect any system to fulfil, the accurate representation of the popular will and/or the production of effective, strong governments among them.

Fundamental to the issue is the question 'What is the point of voting?' Is it primarily to choose a government, or is it to choose membership of the legislature? Is the emphasis placed upon electing a strong administration which has broad (if not mathematically exact) support in the community, or is it to elect an assembly which accurately reflects prevailing opinion? On the continent the emphasis is upon choosing a representative assembly, and then from its midst finding a government which commands sufficient support – usually, a coalition government. In Britain, which has tended to pride itself upon its tradition of strong, single-party government, importance is attached to ensuring that there is an effective administration in place.

The question of ultimate purpose is an important one, for the answer which is given will help to determine the most appropriate electoral system. Broadly, variants of proportional representation might well produce a more representative parliament whose composition fairly reflects all or most shades of popular opinion. They are less likely to yield a 'strong' government.

Of course governments can still be effective if they are coalitions, and the virtues of strong administrations can be over-played. Different writers reach different conclusions about what constitutes strength. For Philip Norton, a defender of the First Past The Post (FPTP) method of voting, a strong government is one which dominates the House of Commons. For Vernon Bogdanor, a government cannot be strong unless it represents the majority of the voters, on which test all postwar British governments have failed.

Types of electoral system

There are two broad categories of electoral system. It is, however, possible to combine elements of the two categories, and within both groups there are many potential variations. The two categories are:

1 **Majoritarian systems**, which are designed to leave one party with a parliamentary majority. In this category, we may include:
   - **First Past The Post (FPTP)**;
   - **the alternative vote (AV)**;
   - **the double ballot**.

2 **Proportional systems.** There are many different forms of proportional representation, all of which are designed to ensure that the number of seats allocated in the legislature is broadly in line with the number of votes won by each party in the election. Two main sub-divisions are:
   - **list systems**. Lists may be of the open variety in which the voter can express a preference between individual candidates in a party list, and the closed variety in which he or she votes for a list but is unable to influence the ranking of the candidates;
   - **single transferable vote (STV)**.

3 **Mixed systems**. These represent a compromise between majoritarian and proportional systems. For example, the **Additional Member System (AMS)** preserves elements of the FPTP mechanism yet also provides a substantial element of proportionality.

The situation in Britain and the United States

The traditional Anglo-American method is the FPTP system, by which the candidate/party with the most votes in each constituency wins the contest.

SYSTEMS IN USE IN BRITAIN AND THE UNITED STATES: A SUMMARY

UK

- General and local elections: FPTP
- European elections: closed list
- Scottish and Welsh devolved assembly elections: AMS mixed
- London mayorality: Supplementary Vote (a cross between the French Assembly double ballot and the AV)
- Northern Ireland: FPTP for Westminster elections, but STV for local, assembly and European elections

USA

National and state elections, and most local ones also, use the single member, FPTP system. In some states, a candidate in a given election must win a majority of the votes cast: Georgia requires such a run-off in the election of senators, as it does – along with Arizona – for the election of governors.

The successful candidate/party does not need to have an absolute majority of votes, but rather a plurality: the largest number of votes. This system is used in several other countries such as Canada, Chile, India and Thailand. Often it is referred to as the Simple Majority or Simple Plurality System, or more colloquially as 'winner takes all'. The latter is an appropriate nomenclature, for under this method all a person needs in order to be victorious in his or her constituency is to win more votes than any rival candidate.

The effects of using FPTP in Britain and the United States

FPTP is widely associated with two-party systems. In Britain, the system is very harsh on small parties, which are usually clearly under-represented. The Liberal Party came off particularly badly in February 1974, its 19.3 per cent of the vote yielding only 2.2 per cent of the seats. However, on occasion third parties have surmounted the obstacles it poses and managed to perform well. Helped by the concentration of its attack ('targeted' seats) and tactical voting, the Liberal Democrats did well in 1997 and 2001, significantly increasing the number of seats won.

In America, the 'winner takes all' system has worked against the development of minor parties, which usually obtain scant reward for their efforts. Plurality systems convert seats into votes in a way that damages the interests of small parties, particularly if their limited support is spread across many constituencies. The effects of the system are evident in the fortunes of the American Socialist Party. Even during its peak years of electoral support (1912–20), when it won 3–6 per cent of the national vote in presidential elections, it was barely represented in Congress. At its high point of 1912 (6 per cent), it failed to elect a single representative to Congress. The evidence suggests that it makes more sense for an existing or would-be third party to form an alliance with a major one than to struggle on its own with little hope.

In choosing legislatures, plurality systems usually deliver parliamentary majorities. In Britain, FPTP yields a majority government most of the time, only failing to do so in Britain in the mid–late 1970s. Single-party majority administrations are said by their supporters to be capable of providing effective leadership for the nation. This is widely viewed as more important than achieving a proportional result. In Britain, we know who is to form the government immediately after the election is over. There is no need for private deals to be done by politicians who bargain in smoke-filled rooms, away from the public gaze; it is the voters directly who choose which party is in office.

The American situation is distinctive, for under its presidential system no government is being formed out of either chamber in Congress. When electing Presidents, there is only one prize available. The presidency cannot be shared, so that a proportional system would not work. In presidential elections the party with a plurality in a state receives all the electoral votes of that state, other than in Maine. In 2000, there was much disquiet about the outcome of the presidential election in America, in which George W. Bush defeated Al Gore. For the fourth time in American history, more people voted against the eventual winner than for him.

Some arguments surrounding the debate over FPTP v PR

For FPTP

1 The FPTP system is easy to understand, especially for the voter who marks an X on the ballot paper. It has the alleged merits of simplicity and familiarity and, as such, is widely accepted.
2 In parliamentary systems it usually leads to the formation of strong, stable, single-party governments with an overall majority; coalition government other than in times of emergency is virtually unknown.
3 There is a clear link between the elected representative and a constituency.

David Farrell has neatly summarised these three main themes in defence of the British system, as 'simplicity, stability and constituency representation'.[3] The enquiry led by Lord Jenkins found another 'by no means negligible' merit of the present system: the commissioners made the point that it enables the electorate sharply and cleanly to rid itself of an unwanted government in other words, it is easy to punish those responsible for their errors directly.[4] Pinto-Duschinsky made a similar point, by saying that voters should be able 'to hire and fire the executive'.[5] Voters can throw the rascals out, whereas under PR leading parties can stay in power interminably, with perhaps some reshuffling of offices. This is the essence of democracy, which depends not on mathematical fairness but on the opportunity to control who exercises power.

Apart from the positive case for FPTP, there is also the negative one which points to the disadvantages associated with PR. Among specific criticisms often made, it is suggested that:
1 PR may lead to economic, political and social collapse, as in Germany between the wars, where extremist parties were able to gain a foothold and then dramatically advance.
2 PR involves a proliferation of minor parties, and this results in instability and perpetual changes of government arising from shifting coalitions. In Israel and the Irish Republic, individuals and small parties have been able to gain representation, making it more difficult to form stable administrations. Many other countries which have PR also have more parties in the legislature than do Britain or the United States.
3 In parliamentary systems, the abandonment of FPTP would greatly increase the likelihood of perpetual coalition government. In that any 'third force' would gain a greater share of justice, this would be at the expense of the two main parties. As neither main British party has ever secured a majority of the votes cast in any election since World War Two, it is unlikely that single-party government would result.

For PR
The case for the use of a proportional scheme of voting is that it ensures that there is a

In elections to Congress, FPTP has the same effects as in Britain, only more so. There is an overwhelming preponderance of two main parties which totally dominate the Legislature. The association of FPTP and strong government is irrelevant, for the Executive is not chosen from the Legislature.

In Britain, because we have single-member constituencies, there is a close relationship between the MP and his or her constituency. One member alone

---

broad similarity between the number of votes obtained and the number of seats won by any political party. Unlike FPTP, a PR system:

1 Would not allow a government to exercise power on the basis of minority popular support; e.g., in Britain, Labour obtained power in 2001 with the support of only 40.7 per cent of those who voted, and with under 25 per cent of the backing of the whole electorate.

2 Would provide greater justice to small parties. In Britain, it has been the Liberals in their various guises who have suffered from FPTP, although in 1997 the Conservatives lost all representation in Scotland in spite of gaining 17 per cent of the vote. Socialist and other parties have fared badly in the United States.

3 Would in parliamentary systems yield governments with the backing of the majority of the electorate, which could claim legitimacy. They may be coalition governments, but the parties which voted for them would *in toto* have a broader appeal than is the case at present.

4 Would overcome a problem much emphasised by the Jenkins enquiry, namely that there are under FPTP 'electoral deserts', those areas more or less permanently committed to one party, in which the opposition can make little impact and get even less reward. Some two-thirds or more of the seats in the House of Commons and the House of Representatives rarely change party hands, so that supporters of the minority parties have little likelihood of ever securing the election of representatives who supports their views. Significant sections of the population are condemned to more or less permanent minority status.

Moreover, in parliamentary systems there is a positive case for coalition government. Among its alleged advantages, it is suggested that:

1 coalitions would provide the greater stability and continuity necessary for successful administration;

2 a third-party presence in government would tend to 'moderate' the tone and direction of governments, in such a way that their 'extremist' tendencies might be tempered;

3 governments would have more backing than those in Britain which have rested on the support of a minority of the people.

There is no perfect electoral system, appropriate to every country at every time. Indeed, it is quite possible to have different types of election within a particular country, as is now happening in Britain. FPTP may well be seen as inappropriate for elections to the European Parliament, to the new Scottish or Welsh assemblies or to an elected second chamber should one ever materialise. That does not necessarily mean that there has to be a change at Westminster for the way in which we vote in general elections.

has responsibility for an area which he/she can get to know well. The MP represents all who live in it, not just those who voted for one particular party; all citizens know who to approach if they have a problem or grievance needing resolution. This is very different from what happens under some more proportional systems, in which several elected members represent a broad geographical area. This relationship between individual legislators and their constituencies is highly valued by many commentators in Britain. In America, these local relationships are very significant, for elected representatives are judged according to their ability to 'bring home the pork'.

There is little pressure for reform in America. Proportional representation (PR) could only be used in limited circumstances. As we have seen, it could not be used for the presidency and as individual states only elect one senator at a time it would not work for these elections either. Six states return only one representative and would therefore be unable to employ multimember constituencies. PR could be used for congressional districts in larger states but their average size is already around 600,000, so that a multimember constituency of five representatives would be one of 3 million. Moreover, except in small states, the geographical areas which the successful candidates would have to represent would be a very large one, destroying much hope of keeping that sense of connection with a district and making electioneering particularly exhausting and expensive.

Proportional systems are often seen as especially suitable for countries where there are marked ethnic, linguistic or religious cleavages. Significantly, they have often been recommended for use in Northern Ireland when any new assembly is proposed. Indeed, STV is used in Euro-elections and in local government in the province, precisely because it allows for the recognition of minority rights. Israel is another country with basic ethnic and religious divisions make a proportional outcome desirable. Such conditions do not apply with the same force in Britain or the United States.

Turnout in elections

A good turnout of voters is often considered to be a healthy sign in any democracy, as this appears to indicate vitality and interest. In Britain, turnouts are lower than in several other European countries, and in Euro-elections the figures have often been particularly disappointing. In America, they have traditionally been considerably worse even than the relatively low British figure.

Differing theories concerning the level of turnout

Psephologists disagree as to whether a low turnout is a good sign or otherwise. Does it indicate broad satisfaction and contentment, or fear and alienation from the system? Often a low turnout is viewed as a sign that voters feel disillusioned with the parties, that they feel their vote will not make much difference because the parties are all 'much of a muchness'. They register this disappointment by staying at home. In 1970 there was a turnout of only 72 per cent in Britain, and this was widely interpreted as being a reflection of the widespread feeling among supporters of the Labour Party that the Wilson governments had failed to inspire them or 'deliver the goods'. When, in February 1974, the figure rose significantly to 79 per cent at the time of a miners' strike and a three day week this could be seen as a sign of excitement, for there was a really live issue on which passions were aroused.

Yet by another analysis, high turnouts can be interpreted as a sign of fear and anxiety. Peter Pulzer has suggested that people normally vote in high numbers when they are disturbed by trends in society:

> High electoral participation, massive attendance at meetings, enthusiastic processions and heated discussions may . . . indicate fever, not robust good health. Between 1928 and 1932 participation in German parliamentary elections rose from 75 per cent to 83 per cent, while the Nazi Party's share of the vote rose from 2 per cent to 37 per cent. Increased turnout did not reflect greater civic consciousness, but panic. It represented the mobilisation of the normally a-political . . . apparently apathetic behaviour can . . . reflect widespread acceptance of the way in which disputes are handled.[6]

Such a view challenges traditional notions. It would suggest that the impressive British turnout in February 1974 was a sign of voter anxiety about the state of the country, to the extent that many who might normally not have voted were mobilised by their anxiety about the disruption caused by social strife and the fear that the country was becoming especially difficult to govern.

More usually, it is suggested that the more or less continuous decline in turnout since 1951 suggests that the democratic enthusiasm of the postwar generation, when the two-party system was at its high water mark, has diminished, and that over a long period voters have wished a 'plague on both your houses'.

Some international comparisons

Turnout in the postwar era appears to be higher in the established democracies of Western Europe, and less so in countries which have gained their freedom more recently. In South Africa, the excitement produced by the first democratic elections inspired many people to queue up to vote. In the United States, where elections are so often held, there is no such enthusiasm. The figures for turnout in the most recently held election (prior to September 2002) in an assortment of countries are as follows (in percentages):

Austria	80.4
Denmark	89.3
Germany	80.2
India	60.0
Italy	81.2
Japan	62.5
Malta	95.4
New Zealand	74.5
Norway	74.7
South Africa	89.0
Sweden	81.4
United Kingdom	59.4
United States	51.2

Turnouts in Britain and the United States

The trend in national turnout (see table opposite) in British elections at first sight seems to be a broadly downward one, interrupted by occasional better results. It is commonplace to lament the disappointing figures for turnout in Britain, but David Denver provides a cautionary explanation.[7] He suggests that the true figures differ sharply from the real ones usually given. His research emphasises the importance of the accuracy of the Electoral Register, which – even when it is compiled – is not 100 per cent accurate. When it comes into force, it is four months out-of-date already. It continues to decline in accuracy until the next one is drawn up. When allowance is made for this factor, the impression is very different from that presented by a straight reading of the usually quoted figures. Thus the 78.7 per cent of 1959 becomes 85.0 per cent, the 72.0 per cent of 1970 becomes 75.2 per cent, and the 78.1 per cent of February 1974 becomes 78.8 per cent – the latter result perhaps being more a reflection of an up-to-date register than the public anxiety which Pulzer suggests (see p. 279). In 1992, the 'true figure' was 79.7 per cent, rather than 77.7 per cent. However, in 1997 the figure was low again, and 2001 was the worst since 1918.

Turnouts in elections for local councils, the devolved assemblies and the European Parliament are also low. Indeed, for local and European elections approximately only half the number vote as do so in a general election. The results in 1999 illustrated the poor response of the electors to what happens in the local council chambers, for only 29 per cent voted – the lowest figure recorded in living memory, and some 8 per cent down on that for four years earlier when the same seats were fought. In some urban wards in areas such as Sunderland and Wigan, only 12 per cent turned out to make their choice.

In the same year, the first elections to the new devolved bodies, the turnout in Wales was a meagre 40 per cent, in Scotland 57 per cent. The prospect of an assembly which had inspired the Scots in the referendum of 1997 no longer seemed to be so alluring, as 4 per cent less voted than on the second occasion. In the European elections, turnout was 23.6 per cent.

Turnouts in British general and American presidential elections, 1945–2001

General elections		Presidential elections	
1945	72.7	1944	54.8
1950	84.0	1948	51.6
1951	82.5	1952	61.6
1955	76.8	1956	59.3
1959	78.7	1960	63.8
1964	77.1	1964	62.1
1966	75.8	1968	61.0
1970	72.0	1972	55.7
Feb. 1974	78.1	1976	54.4
Oct. 1974	72.8	1980	52.0
1979	76.0	1984	53.0
1983	72.7	1988	50.0
1987	75.3	1992	53.0
1992	77.7	1996	49.0
1997	71.4	2000	51.2
2001	59.4		

In America, too, there has been a downward pattern, but starting from a much lower base. The 1960 presidential contest had a better turnout than was usually the case, but since then the percentage voting has declined more or less continuously, as the figures above illustrate. Whereas Britain normally achieves a 70–75 per cent turnout in general elections, 50–55 per cent is now more usual in America. However, the comparison is not an entirely appropriate one, for British figures relate to the number registered who vote whereas American ones are based upon the number of Americans over the minimum voting age who actually do so. According to V. O. Key, the difference may be worth as many as six or seven percentage points.[8]

The presidential campaign certainly gets massive television exposure, for it dominates the media from the time of the first primaries through to November. This might have been expected to generate interest and excitement, but yet in the media age we are faced by decline. Among the explanations offered for the downward trend are the following:

- Difficulties of registration, especially in some states a situation now improved by the 'motor voter' bill.
- Apathy: the feeling that politicians are all the same, and that voting makes no fundamental difference. This might be particularly the case in a country that has never had a significant left-wing party so that there has never been a major dispute over the distribution of income and the scope of government.

- The lack of inspiring leaders among presidential candidates. In 1996, some Americans unimpressed by Clinton's behaviour nonetheless found the alternative of Bob Dole not to their liking. Neither was the choice in 2000 impressive enough to encourage them to vote.
- The nature of electioneering: negative campaigning may be a 'turn-off'. In the 1994 elections, it was suggested that one of the most toxic campaigns in living memory had left many people 'switched off' from politicians. American voters appear to have become more disengaged from political strategy, as the style of advertising increasingly antagonises them.
- The composition of the electorate: some significant groups are less willing to turn out, e.g., blacks and the unemployed. Maidment and McGrew elaborated: 'Those categories of voters who have low turnout rates, such as those aged under 24, members of ethnic minorities and those who do not identify with parties, are a growing percentage of the electorate, which explains the steady decline in the rate of turnout.'[9]

Turnout is even worse in congressional elections in the years when there is no presidential contest: It is usually under 40 per cent, but in the 1998 mid-term contests it was 36 per cent, 3 per cent down from 1994. Voters were seemingly turned off by the Lewinsky affair, by Clinton's behaviour and the way in which the Republicans relentlessly pursued the issue. There is disillusion with Washington politicians and the political system in general. This cynicism is said by many journalists to have been a factor in the falling turnouts of the last generation.

Turnout varies from state to state, in large part a reflection of the different registration procedures employed across the country. In the North-west and in the Upper Great Plains, it has always been easier to register. In sparsely populated North Dakota, there is no registration at all, and Maine, Minnesota, Oregon and Wisconsin allow registration on polling day. These five states regularly feature in the list of those with the highest turnouts.

Some reflections on trends in turnout

As the right to vote has been extended across the world's democracies, so in some countries a smaller proportion of the potential voters have chosen to exercise that right than did so in the past. The pattern initially affected local elections more than national ones, but in recent years contests at the national level have produced some low figures – even in countries which previously had higher turnouts. In the USA, 80 per cent voted in the 1896 presidential election, whereas barely more than half did so in 1996. In the United Kingdom, the figures remain similar to those recorded in the interwar era, but rather less than those attained in the 1950s, when there was a surge of enthusiasm for the political process.

The average turnout in postwar elections in Britain has been 75.2 per cent and in the United States 55.5 per cent, a difference of 19.7 per cent. The gap narrowed in the last elections (2000 and 2001, 8.2 per cent). Both countries have poor turnouts in comparison with other democracies. One explanation that has been advanced is that whilst the British and Americans vote on a weekday (Thursday and Tuesday, respectively), continental countries with high turnouts normally opt for a Sunday, when it is easier for working people to get to the polls.

Despite living in a culture which has traditionally encouraged participation from its citizenry, America has woefully low rates of turnout. However, the US government at all levels asks Americans to vote frequently and for a wide range of elective offices, whereas the typical European voter does so much less frequently. Possibly it is no coincidence that the one European country which also has a poor turnout rate – Switzerland (46 per cent in 1991) – also calls upon its peoples to vote two or three times a year in referendums.

It is easy to assume that higher levels of voting are a sign of the health of a democracy, on the basis that those who get elected represent a broader segment of the population. But it is possible to argue that non-voting may amount to general satisfaction with the conduct of public affairs – most people are relatively content. This 'contentment' theory finds little support from Hames and Rae, who point out that 'if this were true, then the happiest Americans would be the poor, racial minorities and young people who have the lowest level of turnout, whereas affluent elderly whites who are most likely to vote, are truly miserable'.[10]

Their idea assumes that different groups in society fail to vote for the same reasons. It could be that there are some groups which genuinely feel alienated from a system which they feel no longer represents their interests, and do not vote. Equally, many groups who do not feel so alienated may also feel that the issues do not warrant positive action to go out and exercise their democratic rights. In Britain, in 2001, there were doubtless many voters who felt disengaged from the political world, including many young voters who felt that the political battle seems increasingly irrelevant, sterile and out of date. Older people who did not vote may have failed to do so either because – as traditional Labour supporters – they felt disappointed or even disillusioned with a government that they felt had let them down, or because in the absence of a clear and convincing alternative it seemed wise to leave ministers to get on with the job of improving the public services, which they had barely started. They seemed to be on the right lines, but needed time to get things right.

Finally, there is one other thought. Turnouts were much higher in the early postwar years. There were then really serious issues on which politicians disagreed: matters of peace and war, and of the fairest means by which to

Popular participation in the political process

In established democracies across the world, levels of popular participation are generally low. Of those who do engage in any activity, it is usually only to cast a vote in a national election. As we have seen, turnouts are in decline. Figures for party membership tell a similar story.

Political participation covers a wide range of activities, from becoming interested in and knowledgeable about politics to active engagement in activities that directly impact upon the political process. Most voters participate to only a limited degree, perhaps by discussing political issues with friends and family at election time, or following the coverage provided by television and newspapers. Some are more involved and write letters to officials or elected representatives, attend meetings, rallies or public hearings and join pressure groups. A few campaign in elections and seek political office. For many, voting is their only activity and, as we have seen, this is a declining activity on both sides of the Atlantic.

> **political participation**
> Individual or group involvement in activities intended to influence the structure, personnel and policies of government. Voting is the most common form of influence.

In the 1970s, Milbrath and Goel[11] analysed patterns of participation in democracies by categorising the American population as gladiators, who fight the political battle (5–7 per cent), spectators, who watch the contest but do little other than vote (60 per cent), and apathetics, who are detached from politics (around 33–35 per cent). They used the language of contests in Ancient Rome, when the few (gladiators) performed for the enjoyment of the many (spectators), whilst some were uninterested in even watching the show. Further studies have attempted to refine the distinctions, by pointing out that the large middle group contains people whose behaviour spans many possibilities. Some vote but do nothing else, others contact officials or representatives but are otherwise inactive and some do nothing but take part in protest marches. Whether or not a person engages in direct action doesn't necessarily tell us whether or not he or she votes. Activity is, in Harrop and Hague's phrase, 'multi-dimensional'.[12]

One recent study found 'a populace in the United States [that] is highly participatory in most forms of political activity (giving money to political organisations, contacting government officials, etc.) and even more so in non-political public affairs (from a vast variety of organisational memberships to charitable giving and volunteer action)'.[13] Over the two years previous to the study, 46 per cent had attended a meeting or hearing, 45 per cent contacted an elected official, 34 per cent contributed time or money to a political campaign and 27 per cent participated in a police-sponsored community-watch programme. In the age of the Internet, 34 per cent had visited a web site for government information.

Even of those who do nothing more active than cast a vote, they may engage in more passive activities. Ninety per cent of the electorate watch some coverage of the election campaigns, two-thirds read about the campaigns in a newspaper and a third talk to others and try to influence their opinions. At election time, many volunteers are willing to distribute buttons and stickers or decorate their cars, and many are willing to donate money – often via the Internet. Moreover, the spirit of volunteerism is alive and well, and many involve themselves in social and to a lesser extent political movements. Such research tends to support the idea that Americans are relatively willing to participate in public affairs, though few are willing to engage in active political work on behalf of a candidate or party.

A comparative study of five democracies (Germany, Great Britain, Japan, The Netherlands and the United States) found that Americans were more willing to engage in political activities than residents of the other countries.[14] They held a lead on issues such as signing political petitions, attending public meetings, contacting officials or politicians, and writing to newspapers. They also scored highly on volunteering and giving money to non-political public-affairs programmes.

America has a culture that values participation. When it comes to voting or standing for election, America provides more opportunities for participation than Britain. Apart from the frequency of elections for a vast array of public positions, many states hold initiatives and referendums (see pp. 296–7), some in New England also having town meetings. In Britain, only a very small minority of the population actively engage in political affairs and the indications are that the proportion is diminishing rather than increasing. Voting and party membership figures are sharply down in comparison with the early postwar years: levels of political knowledge are low, with many young people leaving school without the information, skills and attitudes which are necessary for citizens to contribute actively to democratic life. In a major study, Parry et al. concluded that 23.2 per cent of the population was involved in a variety of political activities beyond voting, 51 per cent limited their involvement to voting in elections and the remaining 25.8 per cent were almost inactive.[15] The political participation of the vast majority is either minimal or almost non-existent.

In Britain and America, the more active participants in the political process tend to be well-educated, middle-class, middle-income, middle-aged and white members of the electorate. Those who work in community organisations are more likely to engage in activities, as are those who have an allegiance to a political party. Lack of participation does not necessarily imply apathy, though it may indicate a feeling that the effort involved will have no impact on the outcome of events. Some people are too busy with work and family responsibilities to find time to follow events closely, attend meetings or join groups. In America, those traditionally reluctant to participate have sometimes in the past been deterred by threats of intimidation. Whereas many African-Americans in the South a few decades ago engaged in sit-ins, boycotts and acts of civil disobedience in a bid to obtain the full rights of citizenship, others were afraid that such forms of activity might endanger their livelihood.

The reluctance of young people to get involved may reflect the fact that they tend to lead more unsettled lives or experience changes in their lifestyles. They may be attending college, adjusting to work, starting a family or trying to carve out the means of financial self-support. Moreover, older people are sometimes more affected by the issues which often arouse civic activity. As parents, homeowners and taxpayers, they may find more reason to get involved because their own or family interests are much at stake.

Practising politicians and those who write about politics often urge greater commitment to and participation in public affairs, bemoaning the lack of interest which they portray as indicative of apathy. There is an opposing view, argued by Lipset and others which suggests that participation is low because the majority of people are broadly satisfied with the political system as it is and the way things are for them.[16] They do not feel inspired to engage more actively simply because they are suffering no real hardship and what happens at election time is unlikely to change their lifestyle seriously for the worse. Increased activity – should it ever recur – would perhaps indicate that the fundamental cohesion of society is under stress.

organise society. Today, many of the great issues have gone. We live in a post-materialist age in which the majority of people now live a much better life than their predecessors of fifty years ago. Increasingly what matters are quality of life issues such as minority rights and the environment, and pressure groups represent these as well as, or better than, political parties. The descendants of the committed voters of yesteryear are perhaps today's pressure-group campaigners, who feel that involvement in community issues makes more sense than the conventional world of party politics, in which the parties no longer represent any real clash of ideas.

Voting behaviour

The scientific study of voting habits (psephology) was one of the early areas of academic interest in the study of political behaviour. The subject lends itself to various forms of academic theorising, much of it based upon the findings of samples of opinion and various forms of statistical analysis. Early studies were *The American Voter* in the USA, and the Butler and Stokes' volume on *Political Change in Britain*. These and other works illustrated how voting was influenced by long- and short-term influences. In particular, they showed that voting was connected with long-term loyalty to a particular party (party identification) and was reinforced by membership of particular groups, based on class, membership or otherwise of trade unions, gender and religion. In America, the deep-seated association with party was often stressed, whereas in Western Europe more attention was paid to loyalty to some social grouping; as Hague and Harrop explain, their 'social identity anchored their party choice'.[17] Either way, be it identification with a party or with a group, the outcome was that voting behaviour was – in Punnett's phrase – 'habitual and ingrained'.[18]

Since those early days, theories of voting behaviour have undergone substantial change. Social changes have occurred in all developed countries, and these mean that old nostrums have had to be reconsidered in the light of experience. The old certainties have vanished, and voting is now less predictable than in the past. In an age of greater volatility, short-term influences are likely to be more significant, and parties cannot count on traditional loyalties to provide them with mass support.

As a broad generalisation applicable to most Western democracies, voting behaviour has departed from class and party alignments. The key factors usually identified today are issues (in particular, the state of the economy), competence in government and the personal appeal of individual leaders. As a result of the performance of the leader, the handling of events and the effectiveness of its campaigning, the party creates an image in the mind of the voter. A reputation for competence and credibility is essential; without them, it is hard to convince people that the party deserves their vote.

Voting is no longer a matter of lifelong commitment. Voters judge govern-ments more by the results of their labours, usually rewarding them for economic prosperity and punishing them when times are hard.

Determinants of voting behaviour: short- and long-term factors

Short-term influences relate to a particular election, and any conclusions based upon them lack more general validity. The most important of them are:
- the state of the economy;
- the personality and performance of political leaders;
- the nature of the campaign;
- the mass media;
- events in office, especially those leading up to the election.

Long-term influences upon voting include:
- party identification and loyalty;
- social class;
- other long-term factors relating to the social structure, which include age, gender, occupation, race and religion.

Broadly, the long-term factors have declined in their importance in British and American politics and the short-term ones have assumed an increased signifi-cance. The breakdown of traditional associations has been of considerable importance for the main parties which can no longer count on the support they once took for granted.

Traditional sources of party support in Britain and the United States

The two main parties in Britain and America still appeal more strongly to particular groups in the electorate. In spite of its losses in 1997 and particularly 2001, Labour still has a core of support among working-class voters of the industrial North, Central Scotland and the Welsh valleys, but it is also strong among many of those professionals who work in the public sector and among ethnic minorities. The Democrats still have the backing of many less well-rewarded Americans, among them poor whites, blacks, Hispanics and Jews, as well as that of the liberal intelligentsia in the northern towns and cities; they have also scored well among Catholics. The Conservatives have always gained the backing of a solid section of the middle classes (although that support is declining) and business interests, although many working people are attracted by the 'tough' attitudes it has long adopted on issues such as immigration and race relations, and law and order, and by its strongly patriotic stance. The Republicans have tended to draw their support from the better off, business and professional classes, and especially among rural, small-town and suburban Protestants.

Recent trends

Stability rather than change was once the established pattern in voting behaviour, and many voters were reluctant or unwilling to deviate from their regular habits. In recent years, partisan **dealignment** has occurred, and this means that there has been a weakening of the old loyalties.

> **dealignment**
> The process by which voters from a particular social class no longer support the party which has traditionally claimed to support the interests of that class.

Social class was once a key determinant of voting, with the working classes in any country tending to vote for the more progressive party and the better-off inclining to the political Right. Class identification has always been weaker in America than in Britain. Many Americans are unsure about the class to which they belong, and tend to regard the matter as relatively unimportant. Many describe themselves as members of the middle class, but those who might by commentators be defined as middle or upper class are often keen to point out that they are working Americans. This means that any analysis of American voting behaviour in class terms presents special difficulties. However, whatever the qualifications, class was still important until the 1980s, on both sides of the Atlantic.

Today, the importance of class has declined. There were always many voters in Britain, the rest of Western Europe and America who deviated from class voting, but that number substantially increased in the 1980s as right-wing administrations such as those of Margaret Thatcher and Ronald Reagan managed to increase their appeal – particularly among the more skilled working people who had aspirations to upgrade their lifestyles and prospects. With changes in the pattern of industry and a weakening of trade unions, class structures and allegiances were undermined. In most advanced countries, sections of the population have become better off and the manual working class has diminished in size.

In these circumstances, the personality of the candidate has assumed greater importance, the more so as party identification has become less firm and voters are able to learn and see so much more, via the mass media about those who would lead them. So too has the importance of issues and of the election campaign become more significant as there are today more votes 'up for grabs'.

The broad trends in voting behaviour in recent years are that:

- Party identification means less today than was once the case. The hold of the parties was eroded in the 1970s and 1980s, and especially in the latter decade Ronald Reagan was able to make decisive inroads into the more skilled white vote and among Democrat support in the South. Margaret Thatcher had the same appeal to C2s, who liked her policies of lower direct taxation and trade union reform. In both countries, many voters no longer feel the need to vote for their traditional party; they make their mind up according to the issues of the day and the candidates on offer.

- Voting has become more candidate-centred. In a television age, voters know much more about the candidates, and considerations of perceived competence, integrity and visual appeal matter more than ever before. In presidential debates, these qualities can be easily assessed by the electorate, but television presents many other opportunities for voters to learn more about the personalities and qualities of those who aspire to lead them.

- Policy issues may play a greater role than in the past. Even for educated and informed voters, it is not easy to know exactly what policies the parties stand for, and it was long thought that few people decided their vote according to what they thought the two parties believed about key issues. In *The American Voter*, the authors dismissed policy voting as something relevant to only a tiny percentage of Americans.[19] More recent studies have suggested that voters use policy positions to assess candidates; today, those who stand for office are regularly grilled about how they respond to particular issues and events.

- Parties of the Left have seen the need to widen the social basis of their appeal. Bill Clinton saw the need to attract the support of working Americans (see pp. 200–1), and Labour leaders from Neil Kinnock to Tony Blair have recognised the need to have a broader social base. Tony Blair has deliberately tried to pitch a claim to the voters of Middle England.

Election campaigning

Campaigns and campaigning are an integral part of the democratic process. The task of those who run campaigns is to ensure that the electorate is well-informed about the personalities and issues involved. In particular, campaign managers wish to see that there is a maximum turnout on the day. British election campaigns are much shorter than American ones. Even though there is much speculation and a pre-election atmosphere in the third or fourth year of the lifetime of a Parliament, the campaign proper lasts only three to four weeks. Campaigns for all elective offices in America are longer, but this is especially true of presidential ones.

Election campaigns have never been the same since the televising of politics began in the late 1950s. New styles of campaigning have developed, so that in recent years there have been innovative polling techniques, the wider use of focus groups, the introduction of professional advisers, and an emphasis on the training of candidates. This greater professionalism of campaigns has been fairly general in all political systems, as has the increasing emphasis on the qualities of the candidate rather than the party. In this world of more **candidate-centred campaigning**, professional consultants have acquired a new importance. For years major parties have brought in outside agencies to advise them, but now they maintain a core of their own image and marketing specialists, who are either employed permanently at headquarters or are easily available.

Skilful use of the media has become something of an art form in modern elections, and campaigns are often based around opportunities for media coverage, particularly on television. (see pp. 256–60 for further information on the use of the media and their impact on election campaigns). Like the cinema, television is a medium of entertainment, so parties, politicians (and in particular their advisers) have seen the need to attune perform-ances to its demands. Whereas the Victorian Prime Minister Gladstone set out to convince his audience by a reasoned statement of his views, the emphasis in political campaigning is now increasingly upon broad themes rather than policies, emotion rather than rational debate. There is a danger that sound-bites may replace genuine discussion.

candidate-centred campaigning

A campaign in which the emphasis is on the role and activity of the individual candidate, rather than on the party he or she represents. Consultants (see p. 257 and below) and volunteers coordinate campaign activities, develop strategies and raise funds, although parties are likely to be involved.

Media **consultants** are always on the look-out for opportunities to maximise free television coverage. Election advertising is expensive, whether the money is spent on American-style paid advertisements or on poster hoardings. So rallies and speeches addressed to large meetings are often scheduled to ensure that they gain as much exposure as possible on news bulletins. Today, meetings are often revivalist gatherings, staged occasions such as the Sheffield Rally (a triumphalist gathering in 1992, very reminiscent of the American convention), to which entrance is carefully controlled and in which everything is done to make it a media success.

In presidential states such as the United States, the marketing of politics has been particularly well developed. Electioneering has always been more candidate-centred, parties having been less entrenched in the political system. Not surpris-ingly, many new techniques of electioneering have been brought in to Britain from across the Atlantic, leading to accusations about the 'Americanisation of elections'. Britain has in many ways learnt from the American experience. In recent years, there has been an increasing British obsession with

consultants

Consultants have been increasingly used over the last three decades. Most of them specialise in some aspect of election campaigning such as fund-raising or polling, although others are involved in all aspects of the electoral process from advising on personal appearance, voice projection, the management of pseudo-events and even policy positions. They tend to work for one party, with whom they have political sympathies. In America, the influence of these communications experts is all-pervasive, and their numbers have grown dramatically. Their use has now spread to many democracies, including Britain. They are all in the business of 'selling politicians'.

walkabouts, photo-opportunities and other pseudo-events created for the media. As in other countries, parties have adjusted to the changes needed in the methods and to the changed environment in which they now operate.

British elections are still more party-centred than American ones, the party rather than the candidate being the focus of attention. It is the party which coordinates the campaign, raising and allocating the spending of funds and developing policies and strategies. However, party managers recognise that television is a medium which thrives on personalities, and they like to field politicians who flourish in media discussions and on chat-shows. Butler and Kavanagh recognised the importance of television in particular, in their summary of the impact of the media on the 1997 election:

> More than ever, election campaigns are managed and orchestrated. Each party attempts to shape the agenda so that the media reflects its views on favourite issues ... An election campaign is increasingly seen by those in charge as an exercise in marketing and many of the skills of selling goods and services to customers are now applied to the electorate.[20]

Party broadcasts instead of political advertisements, free air-time, vigilant journalists, and politicians more prepared to answer questions about their proposals, help to differentiate British from US experience in certain respects, and are some kind of protection against our adopting the worst aspects of American electioneering methods into Britain. But even the party broadcasts themselves have to some degree 'gone American' in style and form.

The role of money

The role of money in modern elections is very important. Indeed, some would say that it always has been. In nineteenth-century Britain, the old rotten and pocket boroughs were a byword for corruption, and a person's vote was highly prized. In 1895 in America, a Republican senator observed that 'there are two things that are important in politics. The first is money, and I can't remember what the second one is'. Today, financing campaigns is a particularly expensive proposition, especially in America where the charges for television advertising and the fees charged by pollsters and other election strategists are very high. The sources of campaign funding and the ways in which money is spent are hot political issues.

There are several reasons why individuals and organisations give money to political parties. It may derive from the benevolence of a benefactor, it may be given out of idealistic support for a particular individual, idea or set of party principles, or it may be offered in the hope of securing some goal of personal or group benefit. What is important is that, whatever the motive of the donor, elected representatives and parties – once holding public office – do not feel unduly beholden to those who have financed their campaign, at the expense of the general public who they are there to represent. This is the widespread fear about the role of finance in politics today, that money given is 'interested money' in that those who donate it are looking for favours from the people they back.

Controls over spending in Britain and America

In Britain, controls over electoral expenses have traditionally operated at the local rather than the national level. Each candidate is required to appoint an agent who has to authorise spending and file a statement showing the total sum spent and how the money was allocated. The formula used allows each candidate to spend between £5000–£6000. In comparison with what candidates can spend in America, this is a very small sum, a reflection of the shorter campaigns (no primaries are held) and the lack of paid political advertising; they also benefit from a free postal delivery to each voter. Most candidates spend considerably less than the permitted limit.

At the national level, there were no controls until those laid down for the 2001 general election. Again the amounts are considerably smaller than applies in America, for the reasons given above. Instead of paid time on radio and television, parties get an allocated number of free broadcasts and a great deal of free news coverage. Their spending is on newspaper advertising, posters and pamphlets, as well as on the personal appearances and news conferences of the party leaders.

In recent years, central expenditure has risen sharply because the parties have conducted more professional campaigns, and employ public-relations specialists – and other political consultants – to assist them in their task. By international standards, the amounts are not vast, but one feature which has aroused frequent comment in the past is the fact that the Conservatives could easily outspend their opponents. This happened in 1997, but not in 2001. For this election, the parties were subjected to a national cap on spending as one means of limiting their necessity to raise as much money (and therefore in the eyes of the Neill Committee weakening the case for state finance). The Political Parties, Elections and Referendums Act (2000) meant that the election campaign would cost no more than in 1997. There was a ceiling of £14.5m per party on national spending. In fact this figure was not reached by Labour or the Conservatives, who each spent less than four years earlier. Provisional figures by Butler and Kavanagh suggest that whereas Labour spending was around £12–13m, the Conservatives on this occasion spent only £9m.[21]

The new arrangements have not ended the controversy surrounding party finance. For the 2000 election, the parties sought and received large donations from wealthy businessmen such as Lords Hamlyn and Sainsbury, who both contributed generously (£2m each) to Labour funds. Lord Irvine caused some controversy by staging a fund-raising dinner for Labour-supporting lawyers, a move seen by some commentators as inappropriate because as Lord Chancellor he would be making future judicial appointments which might involve some of them.

The whole issue of spending on elections is of course related to the issues surrounding party funding and the desirability or otherwise of state aid. These are discussed under Party finance on pp. 207–11.

America

The role of money in American elections has long been controversial, as have been the sources of funding. The concern pre-dates Watergate, and was originally caused by anxiety about the large increase in campaign spending which resulted from the use of political advertisements on television. In the 1960s, some states were introducing limits on campaign finance. The first federal legislation was in 1971, but it was the illegal activities of the pro-Nixon Committee to Re-elect the President (CREEP), which provided for a tightening up of the law, that led to demands for a further tightening. As a result of the 1974 Federal Election Reform Act, much tighter controls were introduced.

Two main themes were tackled in the second measure: the importance of tough limits on contributions and the need for public funding of election campaigning. The new legislation tightened up the rules for disclosure of campaign income, and restricted the influence of wealthy individuals. Strict limits were imposed. Donations of more than $100 had to be disclosed. Individuals could pay up to $1000 towards a single campaign, with primaries and general elections being counted as separate entities; a maximum expenditure of $25,000 per year was permitted. There was no overall limit on the amount which PACs could provide in a single year or on the number of candidates they could support, but they were restricted to $5000 a candidate per campaign. PACs were thus placed at an advantage over other donors, so that, as Grant has pointed out, 'the law effectively increased candidates' reliance on them'.[22]

The law has been used to regulate the raising and spending of money, but there remains a significant difference in the actual provisions of the law and current practice. There are ways in which the regulations can be evaded, particularly by the collection of so-called '**soft money**'. An amendment to FECA in 1979 allowed parties to raise and spend money to be used on party-building and get-out-the-vote activities, a purpose which is not easy to distinguish from supporting party candidates. As the amount of spending on these activities has significantly increased of late, there are grounds for suspicion about the ways in which money is used.

Given the new technology and methods of electioneering, the costs of presidential elections have risen dramatically in recent years. An

soft money
Money contributed in ways and for purposes (such as registration and mass-mailing) which do not infringe the law, as opposed to 'hard money' contributions which are strictly regulated. Soft money is collected at state and local level, but is often used for national purposes.

individual is – in most cases – unlikely to be able to meet those costs on his or her own. The difficulty is all the greater if the candidate is not an incumbent congress member, for incumbents find it easier to raise money from affluent individuals and from PACs, which prefer to contribute to sitting tenants than to challengers. Figures from the Federal Election Commission suggest that in the 2000 contest, Al Gore spent $117.1 on his primary and general election campaigns, George Bush $168.4.

It is not just presidential elections which are hugely expensive. Congressional candidates can spend as much as they can raise and there are no limits on how much a candidate can spend from personal funds. Obviously, richer candidates benefit from this, which leads to the criticism that only wealthy people can succeed in American politics. In 1994, Michael Huffington spent $28m on trying, without success, to unseat the Democrat incumbent, who herself spent $8m. In 2000, Jon Corzine, running successfully in the New Jersey Democratic primary for the senatorial election, spent $33m, more than Huffington had spent on the entire Senate race. In both cases, much of the money was spent on advertising. It is the frequency with which advertisements are repeated which makes election campaigns so expensive, for what happens is that at present candidates with greater means available can outgun their opponents simply by reiterating the message over and over again.

Referendums and their value

Those who advocate a referendum – with or without an initiative – are concerned with the way in which decisions are taken. They want to see more direct public involvement, so that those in power act in accordance with the express wishes of the electorate. Referendums, initiatives and the recall are methods of direct democracy, enabling the voters to decide issues for themselves.

Forms of direct democracy: some definitions

The **referendum** has been defined by Magleby as a 'vote of the people on a proposed law, policy or public expenditure'.[23] In other words, it is a vote on a single issue, allowing people to respond in a simple 'yes'/'no' fashion to the question asked. In many countries, the vote will be on a constitutional matter, such as a change in the system of holding elections.

An **initiative** is a device via which an individual or group may propose legislation by securing the signatures of a required number of qualified voters (usually around 10 per cent in American states). In most countries that have referendums, there is also provision for the right of popular initiative as well.

A **recall** allows a specified number of voters to demand a vote on whether an elected official should be 'recalled' or removed from office. Fifteen American states have provision for the recall, but it has very rarely been employed.

The growth of interest in referendums world-wide

Referendums, usually then called plebiscites, were used by some twentieth-century dictators. They used the trappings of democracy to conceal their real intention, which was to boost their authority by creating the impression of legitimacy. This is why Prime Minister Attlee (1945–51) was disparaging about them, portraying them as 'devices alien to our traditions', the instruments of 'demagogues and dictators'. They have also featured in democratic regimes with authoritarian overtones, such as the Fifth French Republic in the days of Charles de Gaulle. However, such overtones have largely disappeared, and initiatives and referendums are now used with increasing regularity in countries and states which have impeccable democratic credentials.

In recent years referendums have been much more widely used in most parts of the world. Hague and Harrop have calculated that of the 728 referendums held in the world between 1900 and 1993, 65 per cent occurred after 1960.[24] A growing number of American states have used them to decide on contentious moral issues from the use of cannabis for treatment of the sick to the right to 'death with dignity' via euthanasia, on social issues such as the rights of minorities to health reform and on constitutional issues such as term limits for those who serve in positions of political power. Some member states of the European Union have used them to confirm their membership or to ratify some important constitutional development. In Switzerland, they are built into the regular machinery of government, and are held on a three-monthly basis.

In some countries, the outcome of referendums is binding, in others it is advisory. In Britain, with its commitment to the idea of parliamentary sovereignty, only Parliament can cast a decisive vote on any issue, but it is unlikely that a majority of legislators would make a habit of casting their parliamentary vote in defiance of the popular will as expressed in a referendum. The Swedes did so in 1955, when the people voted to continue to drive on the left and the government of the day ignored the outcome. (They were slow to follow the voters' wishes expressed in 1980 to decommission nuclear power stations; the process did not begin for twenty years.) British governments have accepted that to consult and then to ignore the verdict is worse than never to have sought an opinion. In 1975, Prime Minister Wilson accepted that a majority of even a single vote against so doing would be enough to take Britain out of the European Community. In other words, both governments and MPs accept that they should treat the popular verdict as mandatory, in the sense that it is morally and politically binding.

Referendums in Britain and the United States

Britain has until recently had very little experience of voting on a single issue, even though the case has often been canvassed in the twentieth century. The

Conservatives held a referendum on the border issue in Northern Ireland in 1973, and Labour allowed the Scots and the Welsh to vote on whether they wanted devolution in 1979. Yet the only occasion when all of the voters have been allowed to vote on a key national issues was four years earlier, when they were asked whether or not they wished the country to remain in the European Economic Community. There have been local votes on the future status of schools and the ownership of council estates, as well as in a few cases on the issue of whether to cut the level of Council Tax or to cut services provided. In Wales the issue of 'local option' (the Sunday opening of pubs) was decided in this way.

Since May 1997 referendums have already been used to resolve the issue of devolution, and the future shape of London's government. Also, in concurrent votes, the voters of the six counties and of the Irish Republic signified their approval of the Good Friday Agreement. Ministers have held out the possibility of a vote on electoral reform at some time in the near future, and should there be a decision for Britain to join the single currency then this too will be submitted to the people for popular backing.

Experience of national referendums in the United Kingdom 1973–2002

Year	Topic	Turnout and outcome
1973	Border poll in Northern Ireland: electorate askedif they wished to remain a part of the UKor join the Republic of Ireland.	61% Massive majority to remain in UK
1975	UK's membership of EEC: electorate asked if they wished to stay in the Community or withdraw from it.	64% Two-thirds majority to stay in (43% of whole electorate)
1979	Devolution to Scotland and Wales: each electorate was asked if it wanted a devolved assembly.	Scotland 62.8% Narrow majority in favour Wales 58.3% majority against
1997	Devolution to Scotland and Wales: each electorate was asked if it wanted a devolved assembly.	Scotland 60.1% Strong majority for Wales 50.1% Very narrow majority for
1998	Good Friday Agreement on Northern Ireland: voters north and south of border asked to endorse the package.	81% Overwhelming majority in favour

In America, there has never been a national referendum, but most of the states have provision for some form of direct legislation. In about one-third of them, it has become an accepted feature over the last two decades. In almost all cases, the facility has been available for much longer, and although some states have recently considered incorporating it into their constitutional arrangements only Mississippi has actually done so. It is in the western states that direct legislation is most widely used; few states in the South and North-east employ it, New England still using the town meeting (see p. 301) to resolve many issues.

American direct democracy has its roots in the Progressive era before World War One. Reformers wanted to open up and cleanse politics in state legisla-tures, which were often excessively beholden to powerful interests and sometimes downright corrupt. Initiatives and referendums fell out of fashion for several decades, but acquired renewed appeal in the 1970s, became more widespread in the 1980s, and in the 1990s became so popular that there were some 400 of them. Today, initiatives outnumber referendums by approxi-mately five to one. Recent topics on which the people have voted include term limits on how long a person can serve in a state legislature or on Capitol Hill, fiscal policy (especially concerning taxes), utilities policy, business policy, environmental policy and issues of minority rights such as the treatment of the disabled and of gays. An innovatory one was the Death with Dignity vote in Oregon by which voters backed euthanasia, a decision subsequently challenged in the courts.

California has shown the greatest enthusiasm for direct democracy. In 1978, Proposition 13 limited the extent of property taxes and by so doing gave an early indication of the strength of feeling of many Americans about the levels of taxation imposed upon them; in 1988 (Proposition 98), the voters decided to specify that at least 40 per cent of state expenditure must be spent on education, the effect being to protect school budgets, at the expense of higher education and welfare provision. Sixteen years on, Proposition 187 in the same state denied all but emergency services to illegal immigrants.

Activists in pressure groups have come to see the initiative in particular as a means of moving their concerns up the political agenda, and as part of their growing professionalism have brought in consultants to offer expertise in handling initiative campaigns. In other words, organising direct democracy has become a growth industry, and it has been encouraged by the media, who like to provide coverage of the causes and those who advocate them. Campaigners are often colourful characters, and the stories often have a human or self-interest aspect, of broad appeal.

The arguments surrounding the use of direct democracy

The case for

1 The basic case is that a democracy rests upon the people's will; a vote on a single issue is the most direct and accurate way of getting their verdict. Such an exercise in direct democracy has an intrinsic appeal, for the idea of 'letting the people have their say' appears to gel with the usual understanding of what

democratic government involves. America, with its use of the initiative, capitalises on this idea.

2 General elections in Britain and statewide elections in America have their limitations as a means of consultation, in that they only occur every few years so that for many people their political involvement occurs only very infrequently. They have no chance to register their changing opinions and are excluded from the process for much of the time. Referendums offer the possibility of more regular participation and help maintain interest in the political process. Also, general elections are usually won on a minority basis which casts doubt upon any claims that the government of the day is acting with popular backing in pursuing its policies. Moreover, elections are essentially an overall verdict on the performance of the government, and do not show the strength and extent of feeling on particular issues.

3 Referendums are also useful for the government in that they can strengthen its authority as it seeks to deal with difficult issues. France and Australia have provision to resolve a political impasse by using such direct questioning, and there are occasions when a government – faced with a difficult, divisive issue on which feelings cross party lines – may wish to reinforce its own stance and improve its negotiating position.

4 Referendums are a particularly useful expedient for those issues on which government seems to be divided; they help to resolve the impasse.

5 Referendums resolve questions in such a way that there is a final solution to an issue which will not go away. Critics of a particular policy are more likely to accept the result if they know that it is the public view.

6 Where the initiative is used, citizens have an opportunity to raise issues and criticisms which politicians might be reluctant to take up and which otherwise might not be aired.

7 Initiatives and the recall are means of overcoming the obstructionism of out-of-touch legislators and therefore make reform more likely.

The case against

Many of the points raised by critics have more force in Britain than in America. In Britain there has been much more unease about its use than has been the case in America which allows initiatives on moral and social issues, as well as political ones.

1 Britain is a representative, not a direct democracy. It does not require that people vote on every single item, rather that they elect MPs who being close to the centre of the argument and able to inform themselves fully on the issue, then vote on our behalf. If we then do not like how they exercise that choice,

we can deny them our vote at the next election. If elected representatives pass the question back to voters for their determination, then they shirk the responsibility which representative government clearly places upon them.

2 The questions asked can be very complicated for the electorate. Some issues are so complex, and require such knowledge and understanding, that a worthwhile judgement is difficult for the average voter to make. Making a general assessment of the performance of the government at an election is arguably much easier than deciding on the merits of a single European currency. Sometimes information is very technical and people may lack sufficient information to form a fair and balanced opinion on a topic.

3 The result of a referendum can get muddled up with other issues. Thus in 1979 opinion polls suggested that the majority of Scots favoured devolution, but there was a background of governmental unpopularity. It is significant that the Conservatives campaigned for a 'no' vote and argued that this was a vote against the Labour Government's plans and not against the principle of devolution; indeed, they promised to bring forward proposals of their own!

4 If the principle of giving people a referendum on constitutional issues is conceded, then it is not easy to resist the desire for one on social issues. It is hard to see the logic by which, in a parliamentary system, you can pick and choose your forays into populism and hope to retain respect. Many people would like a vote on capital punishment, and judging by opinion polls the verdict would be strongly in favour of its return, despite the fact that there is much evidence to show that it has virtually no deterrent effect. Surely ministers and MPs have a duty to give a lead on such issues? They have the chance to hear expert evidence – in this case that of criminologists and from other countries – and can educate the public accordingly. Sometimes, a government might quite properly defy public opinion in the long-term interest of society. Political leadership does not consist of slavishly following public opinion, but in shaping it.

5 In addition, there are certain technical problems with a referendum. The wording of the question can be a problem. It has often been said that 'he who frames the question determines the outcome'. In Chile, the notorious General Pinochet gained 75 per cent acquiescence for the proposition: 'In the face of international aggression unleashed against the government of the fatherland, I support President Pinochet in his defence of the dignity of Chile'.

6 Timing can be another difficulty. For instance, any vote on hanging held in the aftermath of some horrific killing could be unduly swayed by emotional considerations. There is a danger that the circumstances in which it takes place could affect the result. Moreover, the referendum only tells what the public

are thinking at a particular time, on a particular day. Logically, further votes are necessary to ensure that ministers are acting in line with the public mood.

7 The status of referendums is also a difficulty. If a referendum is advisory, as in our system it must be (for Parliament makes the law), could one really expect MPs to support reintroduction of the death penalty against their deeply held beliefs? Yet if MPs ignored the popular verdict, the situation would be that people would have been invited to declare their preference and the House of Commons would have exercised its undoubted right to decide differently. This would only further damage people's faith in the parliamentary system.

8 [Applicable more especially to America, with its widespread use of initiatives.] Proposals can be ill-thought-out and badly drafted, their ambiguities leading to lawsuits and court interpretation and eventually requiring the passage of corrective measures. Moreover, they encourage voters to think in terms of single-issue politics rather than debate the issues involved in the context of broad principles which might govern all policy areas. They work to the advantage of illiberal majorities, which can legitimise their discriminatory feelings against minorities; the losers are often minorities such as gays and immigrants.

9 [A general point, widely applicable.] Campaigns can be expensive, so that well-funded groups are at an advantage. In particular, wealthy business interests are likely to have far more money to deploy than environmental or social groups with which they may be in conflict. In Britain, the pro-Europeans in the 1975 referendum were backed by powerful pro-business vested interests. On one issue concerning increases in automobile insurance, 250 Californian insurance companies raised over $43m in contributions, but with over $8.6 billion in automobile insurange premiums at stake such efforts are not surprising.[25] In New Jersey, gambling interests spent heavily on advertisements that painted an unduly rosy picture of the benefits of introducing gambling into the state.

The case considered

The case is not clear-cut, and many who warm to the idea of votes on constitutional issues are reluctant to see the public vote on issues such as abortion, capital punishment and gay sex. Much clearly depends on the view taken of legislatures and of the collective wisdom of the electorate to determine difficult issues. Those of more liberal persuasion have often expressed some suspicion of initiatives and referendums, seeing them as an instrument of conservatism. In Switzerland, the voters have consistently voted to reject membership of the United Nations and elsewhere they have often been seen as a means of defending the status quo.

The motives of those who call for a vote might be doubted. It can be for the wrong reasons, such as the self-interest of big business companies. Or again, the demand for a referendum can be the political refuge of the politician whose purpose may be to dodge a damaging internal party division. Usually, referendums are advocated by those who think that their side can win. Often, support for direct democracy has little to do with the merits of democratic consultation and popular participation. Lord Jenkins, whose interest in the rights of voters and politicians has already been mentioned, summed up the point about the proper usage of referendums when he spoke in the debates on the passage of the Maastricht Bill in 1993. They should be used 'as part of a clearly thought out constitutional scheme and not just as a by-product or a tactical ploy by those who have tried and failed to defeat this Bill in every possible way'.

OTHER FORMS OF DIRECT DEMOCRACY

Town meetings

In the six states of New England, local governments rely on a very democratic form of governance, the town meeting. Every year, residents gather to vote on a range of issues such as the local budget, tax levies, marriage for gay couples and the purchase of a new pickup truck to clear the snow-bound streets. Having made their decisions, they then elect town officials from amongst their midst, whose task is to implement the decisions and conduct council business over the coming year.

As a means of discerning the majority will via debate and voting, the method has much to commend it, although this method of direct democracy is more suited to thinly populated areas than to giant metropolitan ones. Even in parts of New England, it is has run into diffi-culties in recent years. There are complaints of low attendance, with the same few dozen people appearing every year and 'calling the shots'. In Maine, 80 out of 7600 residents of Farmington turned out in 2000, in Skowhegan the figure was 60 out of 9,000. Voter apathy, changing working hours and a fast-forward lifestyle are seen as the enemies of popular involvement, which flourished in days when there were few other attractions than a travelling circus. Maine and other states has made greater use of citizen-initiated refer-endums over the last decade.

Teledemocracy

As yet, the hi-tech age has not significantly impacted on the democratic process, other than in the use of voting machines and punch cards to record votes. But in North Carolina the cable has long been used to broadcast discussion of civic issues to many towns and cities. A taped government meeting is relayed for an hour, followed by a second hour of panel discussion involving officials and appropriate experts. Citizens can then interact directly with the panel during a call-in. The idea has been extended to allow voters to call in and cast a vote for or against particular proposals. As computers become ever more widely available, the method can be easily used as a means of conducting direct democracy from the comfort of the armchair.

In America, direct democracy has not always worked as the original pioneers anticipated. Critics wonder whether complex issues can be reduced to 'simplistic sloganeering'. As Bowman and Kearney ask:

> Is the initiative process appropriate for resolving tough public problems? Seldom are issues so simple that a yes-or-no ballot question can adequately reflect appropriate options and alternatives. A legislative setting, in contrast, fosters the negotiation and compromise that produce workable solutions. Legislatures are deliberative bodies, not instant problem solvers.[26]

Conclusion

An astute American observer of the political scene, Walter Lippman, made the following observation on the process of elections:

> We call an election an expression of the popular will. But is it? We go into a polling booth and mark a cross on a piece of paper for one of two, or perhaps three or four names. Have we expressed our thoughts on the public policy of the United States? Presumably we have a number of thoughts on this and that with many buts and ifs and ors. Surely the cross on a piece of paper does not express them?[27]

British voters have even less chance to make their views known on policy than do Americans in many states. They at least can express their thoughts on a range of issues via the referendums and initiatives that are held with increasing frequency across the country. In other ways, too, Americans are more willing – as well as more able – to involve themselves in political life and express their inclinations.

In comparison with the situation in the United States, British elections are relatively short-lived, inexpensive affairs. Moreover, the task facing the American voter is considerably greater than that confronting his or her British counterpart, for there are so many posts to be filled and issues upon which to pass a verdict. The process may be eased by technology which allows voters to opt for a straight party ticket by pulling a lever on the voting machine, although today there is far more split-ticket voting than in the past.

Many millions of Americans do not use their vote, even if they are more willing than the British to engage in other forms of political participation. In Britain, too, it is proving increasingly difficult to persuade people to vote. Proponents of electoral reform might argue that the FPTP electoral system provides insufficient incentive for them to turn out on election day, particularly for supporters of small parties which gain little recognition in the legislature. In some areas of Britain and America, even supporters of one of the two main parties may see little point in voting, given the existence of 'electoral deserts' in which their party is never or very rarely victorious.

REFERENCES

1 D. Farrell, *Comparing Electoral Systems*, Harvester Wheatsheaf, 1997.
2 *Plant Report: A Working Party on Electoral Reform (Interim findings)*, Guardian Studies, 1991.
3 As note 1 above.
4 Report of the Jenkins Commission on Electoral Reform, 1998.
5 M. Pinto-Duschinsky, in *Representation* vol. 36 ii, McDougall Trust, 1999.
6 P. Pulzer, *Political Representation and Elections in Britain*, Allen & Unwin, 1968.
7 D. Denver, *Elections and Voting Behaviour in Britain*, Harvester Wheatsheaf, 1994.
8 V. Key, *The Responsible Electorate*, Random House, 1996.
9 D. Maidment and D. McGrew, *The American Political Process*, SageOpen University, 1992.
10 T. Hames and N. Rae, *Governing Britain*, Manchester University Press, 1996.
11 L. Milbrath and M. Goel, *Political Participation: How and Why Do People Get Involved in Politics?*, Rand McNally, 1977.
12 R. Hague and M. Harrop, *Comparative Government and Politics: An Introduction*, Palgrave, 2001.
13 M. Conway, *Political Participation in the United States*, Congressional Quarterly Press, 1991.
14 G. Almond and S. Verba, *Civic Culture: Attitudes and Development in Five Nations*, Sage Publications, 1989.
15 G. Parry, G. Moyser and N. Day, *Political Participation and Democracy in Britain*, Cambridge University Press, 1992.
16 S. Lipset, *Continental Divide: The Values and Institutions of the United States and Canada*, Routledge, 1990.
17 As note 13 above.
18 R. Punnett, *British Government and Politics*, Gower, 1971.
19 A. Campbell *et al.*, *The American Voter*, John Wiley, 1960.
20 D. Butler and D. Kavanagh, *The British General Election of 1997*, Macmillan, 1997.
21 D. Butler and D. Kavanagh, *The British General Election of 2001*, Macmillan, 2002.
22 A. Grant, 'Pressure Groups and PACs in the USA', in A. Grant (ed.), *Contemporary American Politics*, Dartmouth, 1995.
23 D. Magleby, 'Direct Legislation in the United States', in D. Butler (ed.) *Referendums Around the World*, Macmillan, 1994.
24 As note 13 above.
25 As quoted in A. Bowman and R. Kearney, *State and Local Government: The Essentials*, Houghton Mifflin, 1999.
26 As note 25 above.
27 W. Lippmann, *Public Opinion*, Macmillan, 1938.

USEFUL WEB SITES

For the UK

www.keele.ac.uk/depts/por/ptbase.htm Keele Guide to Political Thought and Ideology. Contains information about elections, voting and the electoral system.

www.charter88.org Charter 88. Information about use of different electoral system.

www.electoral-reform.org.uk Electoral Reform Society. Excellent source of election statistics and ideas on alternative voting systems (especially STV) and how other current schemes are functioning.

For the USA

www.fec.gov The Federal Election Commission. Provides election statistics and data on the financing of election campaigns.

http://pollingreport.com The Polling Report. Gives data on elections and campaigning events.

www.ifes.org/eguide/2002.htm

www.electionworld.org/election/calendar.htm Both give useful up-to-date information on recent election outcomes.

www.umich.edu/~nes The University of Michigan National Election Studies site offers information based on polling research about such matters as voter attitudes, split-ticket voting, party identification and turnout.

SAMPLE QUESTIONS

1 Discuss the view that the use of FPTP in Britain and America means that both countries will always have two-party systems.

2 Why is turnout lower in the United States than in Britain?

3 Compare the conduct of elections and the methods of electioneering in Britain and the United States.

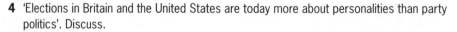

4 'Elections in Britain and the United States are today more about personalities than party politics'. Discuss.

5 'Vast amounts of money are spent on elections and electioneering in the USA, more than in any other democracy'. Are the elections better for all this expenditure?

6 Consider the role of money in British and American voting and elections.

In recent years, the leaders of many countries have described their systems of government as democratic. The emphasis they place on certain institutions of government and their interpretations of the role of the state and individual in society may vary, but the label carries definite prestige and esteem. Britain and America are usually seen as examples of model Western representative, liberal democracies in which the people choose representatives who govern on their behalf and according to the wishes of the majority. In newer democracies, some familiar features of liberal democracies are absent or undeveloped.

In this chapter, we explore the nature of democracy and differing forms that it takes across the world. However, the main emphasis is on the way it works on either side of the Atlantic. Basic similarities and differences are highlighted, with consideration given to alleged defects in its operation.

Democracy across the world

At first sight, democracy appears to be an immensely popular political creed. Dictators such as Hitler and Mussolini sometimes proclaimed their acceptance of and support for democratic ideas, even though their governing approach was highly authoritarian and intolerant of opposition. Leaders of countries whose governing arrangements were as far apart ideologically as the old USSR and the USA called themselves democratic. This is why Crick referred to it as 'the most promiscuous word in the world of public affairs. She is everybody's mistress and yet somehow retains her magic, even when a lover sees her favours being . . . illicitly shared by another'.[1]

The so-called People's Democracies which existed under communist rule in Central and Eastern Europe offered an alternative and widely divergent model of democracy to those familiar with the Western one as practised in Britain and America. Marxists liked the egalitarian implications of democracy, and welcomed the goal of social equality brought about through the common ownership of wealth. Communists everywhere would unite in condemnation of American society, where racial integration proceeded only slowly and private enterprise was strong, and portray it as undemocratic. Similarly, most Americans regarded the system of government in the USSR as undemocratic. As Heywood points out, democracy in the USA is more concerned with the form of government, which made it a political democracy, whereas the former USSR was more concerned with the purpose of government, and attached importance to the socialist goals on which the regime was based.[2]

The concept of democracy held by inhabitants of Britain, the USA, several European and Commonwealth countries is vastly different to the view held by communist countries. This indicates that there are widely differing conceptions about what constitutes a democratic state. For our purposes, we are concerned only with those countries that have the form of democracy, for most people would find it difficult to see any system which gives overwhelming power to the state and denies free expression in many areas of life as democratic.

The popularity of democracy

Well over half of the world's population and half of its countries live under democratic rule of some kind, even if we exclude the experiences of the People's Democracies. Democracy is no longer confined to Western countries or those connected to them as a result of past colonial ties. Former European communist states (for example, Poland), several Latin America ones (Mexico) and parts of Asia (Taiwan) – as well as South Africa – would all claim democratic credentials. Democracy has expanded far and wide. Today, the main areas unaffected by the surge of support for democratisation include significant areas of Asia (for example, China and Vietnam), much of Africa (Nigeria) and the Middle East (Saudi Arabia) and parts of Latin America (Ecuador).

The growing support for the democratic process inspired the American social analyst and political commentator Francis Fukuyama to write of *The End of History*[3]. He suggested that the conflict of ideas which had dominated political thinking for much of the era since the French Revolution was over. The causes of liberal democracy and the free market had triumphed, as 'the final form of human government'. Such a claim highlights the importance of having a clear understanding of what democracy entails.

The meaning of the term 'democracy'

The Ancient Greeks were the first people to develop democratic ideas, Athenian democracy being practised in a small city-state or *polis*. Pericles observed that: 'Our constitution is named a democracy, because it is in the hands not of the few but of the many'. This is the essence of any democracy. The word is based on two Greek terms, *demos kratos*, which literally mean 'people power', or 'rule by the people'. In the city-state, it was possible for all citizens to come together and make decisions, a state of direct democracy. Debate was free, open and wide-ranging, each citizen having a single vote. Until the nineteenth century, democracy was generally viewed in terms of some form of **direct** government through majority rule, an idea little changed since the time of the ancient philosophers.

In more advanced and more complex industrial states, sheer numbers made the direct and continuous participation of citizens in government impossible. Face-to-face popular rule, with the mass of people coming together to make decisions, could not work. A new form of democracy replaced the Athenian variety, known as indirect or **representative democracy**. This involved freely elected representatives of the people making decisions subject to popular control. In effect, the few govern on behalf of the many, so that democracy as it now operates is actually a form of oligarchy or elitism. What is crucial is that there should be effective popular control over the rulers or decision-makers. A system is democratic to the extent that those who have power are subject to the wishes of the electorate. The majority of people are vote-casters every few years at election time, but in between have little say.

> **direct democracy**
> Government in which citizens come together in one place to make laws and select rulers. The term often nowadays refers to populistic measures such as the initiative and referendum.

> **representative democracy**
> Government in which citizens elect people to rule on their behalf.

The criteria of a Western democratic system

Key elements of a modern democracy include the following

- **Popular control of policy makers.** This involves the right of choosing the policy makers at a general election. The voter has the right to vote in periodic elections, and in the lifetime of a government the opposition parties perform the role of criticising its policy and seeing that the rights of the individual are respected. Government must be subject to control by the governed, and this control is exercised through elected representatives. The existence of opposition, by individual MPs and parties is a litmus test; without a right to oppose, there can be no democracy.
- **Political equality.** Every adult must have the right to vote, each person having only one vote. In the words of the nineteenth-century radical Jeremy Bentham, 'each to count for one, and none for more than one'.
- **Political freedoms.** There must be a free choice, without coercion of the voters, at a secret ballot. If voting is to be effective, it must be free in the sense that opposition candidates can come forward. In other words, there must be a meaningful choice of candidates. There must also be rights to free speech, assembly, organisation, etc., and the existence and extent of such liberties as free expression is a crucial test for any would-be democracy.

• **Majority rule.** The right of the majority to have their way may seem just, but it needs to be accompanied by toleration of any minority, its views being recognised and respected.

From such a listing of characteristics, we can piece together the following definition: 'A democratic political system is one in which public policies are made, on a majority basis, by representatives subject to effective popular control at periodic elections which are conducted on the principle of political equality and under conditions of political freedom'. Abraham Lincoln put it more succinctly: 'government of the people, by the people and for the people'.

Dahl argued that a political democracy must include 'processes by which ordinary citizens exert a relatively high degree of control over leaders'.[4] But our expectations of a democratic state go beyond these processes. Those who run the government must be elected via an inclusive suffrage, and there must be avenues for political association and communication, and meaningful opportunities for recording the popular will. Democratic systems must also embody a number of other ideas – that every individual matters ('each to count for one and none for more than one'), that there must be equality of

---

OTHER FORMS OF DEMOCRACY

Participatory democracy

Despite the general acceptance in the West of representative and liberal democracy, some writers see this view of democracy as incomplete and say it concentrates on the government of the many by the few and involves the idea of the mass of the citizenry only in a very minimal way. Writers from Rousseau to J. S. Mill, G. D. H. Cole to Peter Hain have argued that individual and group participation should be a distinguishing feature of a democracy. They stress the educational and integrative effects of political involvement. Higgins and Richardson observed that when Aristotle described man as a political animal, he meant that man realised himself fully only when participating in self-government. The goal of participationists thus becomes not merely active participation in government, but a participatory society: 'Democracy is no longer seen as a means of good government but as an end in itself'.[5]

Authoritarian or 'façade' democracy

The version of democracy outlined so far is based primarily on the experience of Western Europe and North America. In other parts of the world, newer forms of democracy have been developed which cannot be included within the orbit of liberal democracy.

Whilst many in the West would find it hard to accept the idea of People's Democracy as being truly democratic (see pp. 305–6), there are several examples of what Hague and Harrop refers to as semi-democracies,[6] blending features of a Western-style democracy

opportunity, and that people should be able to act rationally and in a spirit of compromise where necessary, and show tolerance for the views of minorities. Democracy thrives where there is moderation, a spirit of compromise and tolerance, based on respect for the rights and feelings of others. In a democracy, government must rest on the basis of consent, with the broad agreement of the voters that the government has the right to govern, even if they do not like what it is doing. Consent is essential, for without it government rests solely on power or force.

Liberal democracy

Britain and the United States, along with the democracies of Western Europe, Australia, Canada and New Zealand, are often described as **liberal democracies**. This means that they are representative systems which also embody the concepts of diversity, choice and individual rights and freedoms, as opposed to collective equality or mass participation. Liberal democracies are noted for their adherence to the ideas of:
- Pluralism – the existence of diverse centres of economic and political power;

---

with more authoritarian impulses. They have been developed in countries whose conditions are very different to our own and are an attempt to graft on the familiar democratic features of elections to regimes whose tone has in the past often been severely repressive. Finer) dismissed them as 'façade democracies', but sometimes they are less pejoratively labelled 'limited democracies', 'authoritarian democracies' or 'semi-democracies'.[7] Good examples are provided by some of the Asian states such as Malaysia and Singapore, in both of which effective, stable government has been provided by regimes which are 'repressive–responsive'. Hague and Harrop quote Egypt, Singapore and Tunisia as having systems in which semi-competitive elections are held (there may be some attempt to manipulate the outcome), but in which opposition can also be kept under control by intimidation. Semi-democracies are illiberal democracies in which policies are pushed through with scant concern for their impact on particular groups or communities. Institutions such as the assembly and the judiciary are cowed by the dominant force. This enables semi-democratic regimes to rough up their opponents and harass dissidents, tactics which are often wrapped in a nationalist cloak.

These democracies are far removed from the Western-style ones as exemplified by Britain and the United States. The transition to power has been achieved by peaceful means via the process of elections, whether it be in parts of Africa and Latin America, and the bulk of Eastern Europe. However, in several cases it has been hard to construct a democracy on weak foundations. Given these countries' authoritarian legacies, liberal ideas and institutions are often insecurely established and respect for basic rights can easily be ignored. In Russia, a 'new' or 'fledgling' democracy, the media has been prone to attempted manipulation by government. In other countries, be they 'new' or 'semi' democracies, it has been difficult to ensure democratic control over the military and security services.

- Limited government – checks and constraints on the power of government;
- Open government – non-secretive government which can be seen to be fair and accountable;
- Independent judiciary – a just, impartial legal system.

> **liberal democracy**
>
> An indirect and representative form of democracy in which political office is gained through success in regular elections, conducted on the basis of formal political equality under a universal franchise. There is pluralistic tolerance of a wide range of groups and interests, with open expression of political dissent via the mass media and voluntary groups, as well as through competing parties. People enjoy extensive political rights and civil liberties. The system is based on acceptance of the market or capitalist organisation of economic life.

Britain and the United States

Americans admire democracy and believe that it is the most appropriate type of government for the United States. Their commitment to free and fair elections, popular control and widespread tolerance of differing political viewpoints is shared by British people, the vast majority of whom would have no difficulty in describing the British system of representative government as democratic. By the criteria in the section above, Britain and the USA do both qualify as liberal democratic states. Indeed, some would go further and say that they qualify as the foremost democratic states, so that Hacker felt inspired to describe them as 'the world's two leading democracies'.[8]

> **republic**
>
> A constitutional form of government in which decisions are made democratically by elected or appointed officials. This was how Plato used the term; those in power obtained and retained their position as a result of winning elections in which all free adults are allowed to take part: the people had the supreme power.
>
> Note that this is a meaning very different from the usual one familiar to British students – a constitutional form in which the head of state is an elected or nominated President, rather than a monarch.

The Founding Fathers favoured a representative democracy in which the people govern indirectly by electing key individuals such as the President, members of Congress, governors, mayors, state legislators and others, to make decisions on their behalf. As we have seen, in such a democracy, the people do not normally vote on or directly make specific policy decisions – they do so indirectly, through those they elect to represent their interests. The word 'democracy' is not used in the US Constitution and, although the opening sentence of the document refers to 'We the people', the people its framers had in mind certainly did not include the whole adult population. The Fathers preferred the term **republic** to describe the form of government they wished to create. 'Republic' lacked the connection with direct democracy, with its undesirable overtones of mass rule, demagogues and the mob.

As Hague and Harrop explain, the American Constitution 'contained the seeds of democracy, but it placed government under law before government of all the people'.[9] Because Madison and his colleagues were concerned about the danger of an undue concentration of power in too few hands, they established a system based on the Separation of Powers, including a series of in-built checks and balances {see pp. 36–8). They favoured limited government to stop any individual or group from using its power to damage the interests of other people. They disliked the idea of excessive governmental power, which could be a threat to individual freedom. They wanted to protect not just minorities but also the population as a whole from arbitrary or unjust rule. In the Constitution, therefore, 'power checks power, to the point where it is often difficult for the government to achieve anything at all ... American government was liberal before it was democratic. Many would argue that liberalism, not democracy, remains the guiding principle of American politics'.

The framers of the Constitution did not believe that governmental authority should rest directly in the hands of the people. They were seen as unfit to rule. In *The Federalist*, James Madison echoed the outlook of many of his co-framers of the American Constitution when he wrote:

> Such democracies [as the Greek and Roman] have ever been found incompatible with personal security of the rights of property; and have in general been as short in their lives, as they have been violent in their deaths.[10]

But if, at the time of writing the Constitution, the Americans were wary of the power of the mass of people, their ideas about democracy have evolved in the subsequent two hundred years. In the eighteenth century, the French philosopher Rousseau argued that the best form of government is one that reflects the general will of the people, which is the sum total of the interests that all citizens have in common. His writings were regarded as too radical by those meeting in Philadelphia, although they influenced the French revolutionaries of 1789. Today, the American idea of democracy is a belief in government where authority is based on consent and the will of the majority. If asked 'who should govern?', most Americans would respond 'the people'. The notion of 'popular sovereignty', that authority flows from the ruled to the rulers, is well established.

Many Americans have a dislike for and distrust of government, a classical republican fear of tyrannical rule. Sceptical of politicians, they have been increasingly attracted to the idea of deciding issues for themselves. A modern form of direct democracy is well established in many states, in the form of initiatives, referendums and the recall. In New England, with its surviving town meetings, it is more similar to the Athenian approach, with people meeting together to make decisions for themselves.

Along with representative government, the idea of 'limited government' is basic to the idea of liberal democracy. If the Americans give much weight to preventing the abuse of power, the British have placed greater emphasis on the representative element. In Britain, there are no such formal restraints on the power of government – a codified constitution, a bill of rights and a separation of powers – and the winning party in an election is able to act in a way which Hailsham described as an 'elective dictatorship'.[11] For the British, the concept of democracy has traditionally been about ensuring that, following the contest of parties in free elections, a group of politicians are elected to get on with the job of governing. If they fail to act in a way the electorate likes, they can be ejected at the next election. The idea of party competition is more deeply ingrained in the British system than in the American one.

As in America, what Hague and Harrop call 'the battle of principle' for democracy was won in the nineteenth century, but 'the implementation of democratic procedures' continued well into the twentieth. Women did not get the vote in either country until after World War One, and in Britain neither did six million men . In America, not until the 1960s did African-Americans so benefit. In Britain, reform of the House of Lords to trim its powers did not get underway until 1911, and the process of democratisation of the chamber is still unresolved today. The removal of the bulk of the hereditary element has been accomplished, but election of a segment of the membership has yet to be introduced. The Americans opted for direct election of their upper house via the passage of the 17th Amendment (1913) and also took steps to involve more people in the process of choosing candidates by the adoption of primary election contests.

There been no significant British interest in direct democracy until the last three decades, although from time to time the idea of a referendum had been floated. The first national referendum took place in 1975 and there have been others since, in parts of the United Kingdom. Whenever they have been discussed, whether for the Euro, the use of proportional representation at Westminster or the re-introduction of the death penalty, the counter-argument has usually been made forcefully – that Britain has a representative democracy in which those in power, who have had a chance to research or listen to the arguments, make often-complex decisions on our behalf.

Supporters of a participatory democracy argue that much more should be done to increase public input into policy decisions through procedures such as initiatives and referendums. Others believe that too much public input through direct participation can be damaging. In America, many local school districts have faced budgetary crises in recent years because local voters have constantly turned down requests to increase revenues. In Britain too, in some local referendums the voters have rejected Council Tax increases and better or maintained services.

The health of democracy on both sides of the Atlantic

Traditional features of the democratic way of life have long existed in both countries, including:
- ample opportunities for the free expression of opinions;
- elections by secret ballot from a choice of candidates;
- government resting on consent and being accountable to the people;
- opportunities for people to influence government;
- a spirit of tolerance prevailing between the majority and the minority;
- a reluctance to coerce recalcitrant minorities, and via free elections the means by which a legitimate and peaceful minority may seek to transform itself into a majority; power may change hands peacefully.

Both countries have long been regarded as model democracies. But democracy is more than observance of a particular form of government, based on the existence of free institutions. It is an ideal, something to aspire to. In other words, although the framework may exist, it needs to be maintained in a constant state of good repair, for otherwise erosions of the democratic structure can easily creep in and undermine the whole.

Anxieties about the state of democracy have been expressed in recent years. Some commentators on either side of the Atlantic believe that today the democratic system is not working as well as it should. In 1999, Kenneth Dolbeare wrote of 'the decay of American democracy' and asked whether the condition was a terminal one.[12] He saw the problem as one compounded by the sheer scale and power of the government in Washington, for this has meant that it is 'increasingly connected only to a steadily shrinking proportion of its affluent citizens'.

Dolbeare discerned several factors which contributed to the 'decay':
1 The decline of political parties;
2 The rise of television;
3 The dominance of money as a means of access to television and electioneering in general;
4 The rise of Political Action Committees;
5 Near-permanent incumbency in Congress;
6 A general abandonment of leadership to the latest opinion poll.

More seriously than any of the above factors, however, he sees the 'thirty-year trend toward abandoning political participation' as the most alarming indication of decay. In particular, this means a continuous decline in voter participation (a point well illustrated by recent presidential elections), a particular problem concerning those in the bottom one-third of the social pyramid. He notes the paradox which has emerged:

> The growing underclass has rising needs for education, jobs, training, health care etc., but these very services are being held to a minimum or even cut – and yet the voting participation of this same underclass is declining faster than that of any other population group.

Other writers have also noted that at the very time that Soviet control of Eastern Europe has broken down and given rise to the creation of 'new democracies', the American version of that same genre has shown severe signs of fatigue. Paul Taylor is an exponent of this viewpoint: 'As democracy flourishes around the globe, it is losing ground in the United States'.[13]

Similar criticisms have surfaced in Britain too. Indeed, other than points 4 and 5 above, Dolbeare's critique applies on this side of the Atlantic. There are alleged deficiencies in the workings of our democracy. Critics point to such things as the exceptional secrecy of British government, the election of strong governments which lack majority support among the electorate, the relative weakness of Parliament, the lack of opportunities for minorities and independents to gain recognition, and failings in the areas of civil liberties. In the early–mid-1990s, some commentators pointed to the poor British record in the European Court, in a series of cases concerning the failure of Britain to protect basic rights. Others noted the continuing failure to introduce an electoral system which more adequately reflected the way people voted in general elections and the lack of freedom of information legislation, among a number of other things.

The blemishes on democracy in the two countries

As in other democracies there are blemishes within the system in Britain and the USA. To take a few specific points:

Lack of knowledge, interest and belief in politicians on the part of the electorate

Many voters are ill-informed about political issues, or indeed any other issues affecting public affairs. A survey undertaken in 1988 found that 14 per cent of Americans could not even find their own country on a map of the world. Polls in the USA have shown that more Americans know their astrological sign than know the names of their representatives in Congress. The level of interest varies sharply between different groups on the community, but the findings of the 1992 *American National Election Study,* conducted by the University of Michigan, show that only 26 per cent were interested for 'most of the time', 41 per cent for 'some of the time' and 21 per cent 'only now and then'; 11 per cent were 'hardly at all' committed. In Britain, the same lack of political understanding and interest has often been highlighted, with many voters unable to name their MPs, MEPs and local councillors, and uninterested or not very interested in what goes on at Westminster. Crewe's survey of young people in Britain and the United States (1996) found that 80 per cent of British pupils engaged in very little or no discussion of public affairs at home, including issues of importance to their own communities.[14]

In both countries, there is a significant element of the population which forms an under-class, uninformed about, uninterested in and alienated from the political system. There is widespread scepticism about politicians and what they promise and deliver, and those who are alienated feel that politics has nothing to offer them. It seems irrelevant to their lives. This group is concentrated among the least well-off. There exist dramatic contrasts in lifestyles among the American and British peoples, with a significant element at the bottom in what Will Hutton calls a '40:30:30' society.[15] Dolbeare remarks that it is among the least-educated and lower-income groups that 'feelings of discouragement, lack of efficacy, and of never getting what one wants through politics despite one's best efforts, are particularly acute'. On top of the disadvantages of being poor, the underclass has no political outlet, certainly not one which they deem to be effective. Large numbers live below the 'poverty line', and the minority populations are heavily concentrated in this category.

Trust in government has declined, with fewer people thinking that politicians can be regarded as truthful, reliable and willing to act in the public interest. Parry's study in 1992 found that in comparison with other advanced industrial countries, Britain had a median position on the 'trust in government and politicians' scale, 'less trusting and more cynical than West Germany, Austria and Switzerland, but more trusting and less cynical than the USA and Italy'.[16] In his recent work, Putnam (writing in 2000) has echoed some of these concerns. More serious than a sense of apathy and alienation, he detects a really profound change of feeling. In his view, there is a decline in civil participation and public trust which together constitute 'a worrying decline in America's social capital'.[17] A degree of scepticism about those who govern may be healthy and desirable, but democracy is based on the consent of the governed and a lack of confidence in political leaders is a sign that the system is not serving the people well.

Low levels of political participation and of turnout in elections

If democracy thrives on popular involvement and participation, the number of people who are actively involved in the political process is very small. In Britain, we have only occasional referendums, few voters join political parties and even when there is a chance to register a vote an increasing number do not bother. Some recent turnouts in local and European elections point to significant levels of apathy, perhaps linked to the point of alienation already covered. More seriously, in 2001, turnout reached an all-time low of 59 per cent.

Traditionally, the number who vote in Britain is less than in most Western countries, but it has not fallen to such a low in any of the elections of the postwar era. In the USA, turnouts are again very low by European standards, and even since 'motor voting' the 1996 and 2000 elections have revealed that many Americans are disinclined to vote.

If low turnouts reflect an increasing distrust of politicians and a feeling that 'all of them are as bad as each other', then this may seem to be a healthy scepticism. But when large numbers of people feel disenchanted with the parties they represent, and have doubts about their personal ability and integrity, there is more cause for concern.

Moreover, the rates of political participation are unequal among the population. Almost every survey on the subject has pointed to the conclusion that citizens of higher socio-economic status participate more in politics. Those who believe in democracy should be concerned about both the low numbers who participate and the inequalities in participation. Those who endure the greatest inequality are more likely to resort to unconventional, even dramatic, means of protest as their only form of participation. In the words of Edwards *et al.*, 'those who participate are easy to listen to; non-participants are easy to ignore. In a democracy, citizenship carries the promise – and the responsibility – of self-government'.[18]

The electoral system

First Past The Post may usually provide a clear winner, but some would suggest that the grossly disproportionate power given to the two major parties (Conservative and Labour, Republican and Democrat) at the expense of small ones is not only unfair but undemocratic. In both cases, government does not rest on majority support, so that in Britain the Blair government has since 2001 governed on the basis of 24.2 per cent support of the total UK electorate, and in the USA (for the fourth time in its history) a President has been elected without the backing of the majority of those who actually voted; 48.1 per cent voted for George W. Bush, as against 48.3 per cent for his rival. In the eyes of critics of FPTP, such figures cast doubt upon the legitimacy of the governing administration.

Under the FPTP system, there are no prizes for coming second. Unless a party wins, it gets no reward for the votes it receives. No matter how close the vote, only one US representative is elected from each congressional district. Third or minor parties may accumulate plenty of votes across the state, but their support is not sufficiently concentrated to enable them to gain representation. In presidential elections, there can only be one President, but in congressional, state – and many local – contests as well, third parties find it difficult to make headway, not least because the electoral system does them no favours. FPTP encourages the belief that a vote for third or minor parties is a 'wasted' one which cannot affect the outcome. The British Liberal Party suffered from this belief for many years in the postwar era, which is why one of its election posters proclaimed: 'If you think like a Liberal, vote like a Liberal'. Even now, potential Liberal Democrat voters may vote for one of the main parties, thinking that the outcome is inevitable in their constituency. Major parties, which are often broad coalitions (especially in the United States), generally try to advance moderate middle-of-the-road positions which may appeal widely.

Electoral reformers on either side of the Atlantic would argue for a more proportional voting system via which the seats in the legislature are allocated according to each party's percentage of the vote. The cause has made little headway in the United States, but in Britain some elections (for the European Parliament and the devolved assemblies) are now contested under a 'fair voting' system, under which third and other parties have secured representation.

The media

At their best, the media expose wrong-doing and keep us informed about political matters, but often they fall well below the level that many people expect. In both countries, there is a free press, relative to that of former communist countries and present dictatorships. But the trends towards concentration of ownership means that there is insufficient diversity of viewpoint. Some groups cannot easily gain access to television either, such as those who are seen as threatening to the democratic system – students, feminists and militant trade unionists. According to Keane 'the activities of the tabloid press have been a disgrace to liberal democracy for a number of years'[19] and, at worst, television confrontations trivialise political debate, opting for the entertaining rather than in-depth discussion; issues are now less important than broad themes. The same is true of the United States. Discussion of policy often gives way to an infatuation with personalities. Marketable sound-bites are often a substitute for rational argument and elections are all about photo opportunites and pseudo-events.

Successful politicians in the media age invariably talk in entertainment-orientated themes. This can make political philosophy seem fluid. In the words of Professor Postman: 'You cannot do political philosophy on television. Its form works against the content. It is television which has enabled the propagandist to put over the candidate's case without recourse to philosophy or specifics'.[20] As Laurence Rees put it: 'For any politician who lacks conviction but has charming personal habits and appearance, there has never been a better time to seek office . . . Television as a medium is full of attractive people – often attractive people trying to sell you cars, washing machines or soap powder'.[21]

Today, Presidents are popularly remembered primarily by their looks more than by their abilities. Once, it was their utterances and the quality of their performance which mattered, but today image is all-important, and as we recall Carter or Reagan we think of how they appeared on television. Although party labels count for more in Britain, it has been increasingly the case in recent years that the public thinks in terms of the Kinnock v Thatcher or Blair v Hague/Blair v Duncan Smith duel.

Austin Mitchell MP, a British parliamentarian used to appearing on television and handling the media, has been scathing about their performance. His comments were written about British experience, but they might equally have been applied across the Atlantic. He suggested that the public is saturated with:

> gossip . . . personalisation, all the trivia of a tabloid world, rather than being satiated on hard information or educated by explanation and analysis. The media's preoccupations are never sustained. Education is not seen as one of its responsibilities. The public neither gets, nor is helped, to understand alternative strategies . . . The media demand instant answers . . . Sensationalism sells newspapers and wins viewers. Explanation and understanding are boring. Politicians are pushed into vacuities and every action is criticised. The bland lead the blind . . . Media democracy is perpetual populism and the endless clamour for easy answers.[22]

Rights have been neglected

Britain lacks a written constitution and a formal Bill of Rights, although the situation has now been partially corrected by the passage of the Human Rights Act, incorporating the European Convention. But citizens do not have an up-to-date, clear, tailor-made statement of the rights we might claim. There have been many anxieties about the security of long-established civil liberties in recent years, most notably in the years of Thatcherite rule in which there was perceived to be a disregard for freedom because of the alleged threat to national security. In the Blair era as well, libertarians have been dismayed by the inroads into trial by jury and by the wide-ranging nature of the anti-terrorist legislation passed between 1998 and 2001, and again after the events of 11 September 2001.

In the USA, basic freedoms are set out in the Bill of Rights. The idea of equality was proclaimed in the Declaration of Independence's resounding cry: 'We hold these truths to be self-evident, that all men are created equal'; this is often seen as an American contribution to mankind. Certainly, privilege and rank count for less in America than in Western Europe, and an egalitarian fervour is in a way a part of the American dream – that each person can go out and make a fortune, by using his or her gifts and exhibiting a pioneering spirit. But the position of African-Americans until comparatively recently suggested that in practice not everyone benefited from the Jeffersonian dream. Whatever the constitutional theory, it was a long time before African-Americans achieved their due recognition. Not until 1965 were there voting rights secured.

Furthermore, in America there has been a history of intolerance towards groups on the political left. In the 'Golden Decade' of the 1920s, those suspected of adhering to a progressive creed were denounced as 'reds' or 'subversives'. The mood of intolerance was again apparent in the late 1940s into early 1950s in the McCarthyite era and it remains the case that those who dissent from the American way of life are often regarded with suspicion. More recently, some of those who dared question the American response to the terrorist threat and the USA Patriot Act have complained of harassment or had their patriotism imputed. This mood and the treatment of terrorist suspects at Guantanamo Bay led one *Guardian* columnist to write of the 'new McCarthyism'.[23]

In both countries, very special challenges have provided the justification for a governmental clamp-down on those held to pose a threat to national security. Some people who feel little or no sympathy for the actions taken by terrorists nonetheless question whether it is right to ignore the rights of those seen as dangerous. They believe that the Blair and more particularly Bush administrations have been so understandably keen to combat terrorism effectively that they have been willing to sacrifice traditional values of justice and liberty.

Money has become too important in politics

Money has become a controversial factor in British politics in recent years, with constant press stories dogging New Labour in office. From the Ecclestone Affair onwards, a series of issues have arisen which point to a conflict of interest. Legislation on party finance has been enacted to place a ceiling on the amount any party can spend during an election campaign and to make donations more transparent, but greater openness has only highlighted the 'generosity' of wealthy backers whose motives may not be disinterested. Large gifts from multi-millionaires continue to offer problems as well as support for the parties and their images.

America has had curbs on the level of individual contributions since the 1970s, but money continues to be a cause of great unease. Money is an all-important campaign prerequisite. Without it, candidates cannot get elected to public office, because they need television to help them advance their campaign and viewing time must be purchased. Many people assume that those who provide funding want something in return and whether the money comes in the form of soft or hard money, it causes unease. Some candidates dislike having to plead for campaign contributions, but know that without it their efforts will stall.

Electoral success should not be determined on the basis of wealth. It is unfair that richer parties or candidates can use their affluence to buy a greater chance of success. But on both sides of the Atlantic there is a feeling that an undue emphasis on money damages the fabric of democracy.

Neither British nor American democracy might seem very healthy, after reading this list. There are flaws in both countries, but several of the points made against the health of democracy could be challenged. Few countries can claim to have a perfect system. Perfection is something to which we can aspire. Meanwhile, democracy should not be taken for granted. At least British and US citizens live in countries which have evolved by peaceful change, rather than through violent upheaval. Both also have a long attachment to freedom. If the reality has fallen short of the democratic ideal in several respects, the commitment to democracy has always been apparent and to their credit many people in either country have always felt uneasy about lapses from that ideal.

Some key differences

Decentralisation: government beyond the centre

Britain has often been described as a highly centralised state, something which the Scots and the Welsh – as well as some English regions – have found hard to accept. In recent years, a measure of decentralisation of government has been introduced via devolution, thus bringing government closer to the people, a belated recognition of the Gladstonian principle set out more than a hundred years ago that 'keeping government local makes it more congenial'. But, as we have seen, devolved power is always subject to supervision by the sovereign body (Westminster) and can in theory be revoked by it.

By contrast, in a federal state power is constitutionally divided between the central government and the provincial or state government. Federalism is much less common than the unitary governments typical of most parliamentary democracies. In the United States, it was instituted to increase democracy and it does strengthen democratic government in many ways. It was designed to allay the fears of those who believed that a powerful and distant central government would tyrannise the states and limit their voice in government. It provides more levels of government and consequently more opportunities for participation in politics. It gives citizens easier access to government and therefore helps keep it responsive to the people. It enables the diversity of opinion around the country to be reflected in different public policies; among the states local democracy has long been in decline.

British local government has been regarded by many commentators as being in a parlous state in recent decades. Many have commented on the decline of the democratic element. It exercises few powers, far less than in the 1980s. Legislation has restricted the capacity of local councils to raise money and constrained their discretion in providing local services. Many citizens are unclear what it is they are voting for. Lack of publicity may even mean that they are not sure than an election is taking place. If they are aware, they are not clear what the point is in giving up time to go to the polling booth. Interest is exceptionally low in some inner-city areas, but across the whole country there is little enthusiasm for anything to do with local government.

In America, the very existence of so many governments to handle the range of public services is an indication that decentralisation means more than handing greater power back to the states in recent years. States too have been willing to decentralise their governing arrangements, firstly through the creation of county governments and later via cities and townships. Each of the units of local government can participate in some way in the system of intergovernmental relations. They exercise considerable influence through local members of Congress who are responsive to the needs of constituents back home. They also exercise influence through membership of intergovernmental lobbying groups, which make up an increasingly important set of actors in the federal system. Today, local voters choose their own representatives to serve on city councils, school boards and some special district boards. As small legislatures elected from among the community's inhabitants, these bodies are usually the policymaking institutions closest and most accessible to all citizens. In many ways, American local government encourages popular participation and promotes the value of individualism at the local governing level.

In reality, American state and local politics are not as perfectly democratic as the comments above might seem to suggest. As in Britain, politics at the local level are poorly covered by the media and as a result much of the work done gets little attention or recognition. Many voters are ill-informed about what is going on, which makes it more difficult for them to hold those who govern accountable. Furthermore, the number who actively participate or even vote is often very low.

Britain: a quango state

Some of the lost power has been handed over to the numerous quangos which still exist, despite the fact that politicians in opposition often criticise their existence, and especially their undemocratically chosen membership. They range from NHS trusts to Training and Enterprise Councils. The Tony Benn question about those who exercise power over the rest of us is: 'Can you get rid of them?'. We cannot determine the membership of quangos, which are often stuffed with party appointees.

In the USA, there is a passion for the elective principle. In a country which has stressed the idea of limited government, holders of key positions are expected to submit themselves for periodic re-election and for some offices there are 'term limits' which determine the length of time for which people can serve. Quangocracy has never been a serious democratic issue.

Open government and freedom of information

Open government is the principle that the processes of government should be available for public scrutiny and criticism, based on a free flow of information from those who exercise power and make decisions to elected representatives, the media and the general public. In any society, there will be some information which has to be kept secret on grounds of national security. However, in an open system, the presumption is in favour of the public's 'right to know'. Ultimately, those who would withhold access and information have to defend their position in the courts. It is often alleged that information kept secret in Britain goes far beyond what is necessary to preserve public safety and often mainly covers material the publication of which would cause political embarrassment. Secrecy is then a key element of British government and it is re-enforced by a range of bureaucratic, constitutional, cultural, historical and military factors. The recent British legislation on freedom of information will now only take effect from 2005. It has been widely criticised for its timidity, even though significant concessions were extracted from ministers during its passage in 1999–2000.

On the principle of openness and the right of access to information, the US performance still leaves Britain trailing. America has had a freedom of information act since 1966, as well as a series of laws and rules (the 'sunshine' acts) which opened up the vast majority of congressional meetings to public view. Whatever the doubts about the costs of its implementation or its effects on carrying out confidential investigations, most Americans and consumer groups welcome the fact that the legislation is strong and effective, giving Americans a 'right to know'.

The use of direct democracy

The use of methods of direct consultation with the people – such as the referendum, the initiative and the recall – are practical demonstrations of direct democracy in action in the United States. As we have seen on p. 00, there are deficiencies in the way referendums operate, but America has gone much further in countenancing their use not just to decide constitutional matters, but also a range of social and economic issues. More unusual and distinctly American is the use of the town meeting in small rural areas of New England. Originally, such meetings were vehicles through which the mainly Puritan religious leaders informed and led other members of the community, a means of seeking a consensus via a guided discussion. They were not opportunities for the expression of majority will on issues of the day and those who declined to agree to the general will were likely to be driven out of the area. However, such meetings have developed into a more acceptable democratic form and in those that continue to function citizens gather together to make decisions for their community.

Future possibilities

We have examined some of the problems associated with the operation of democracy in the late twentieth century. Some fears may be over-stated, and different writers and politicians have their own particular misgivings and complaints. There is agreement among many commentators on either side of the Atlantic that all is not currently well with the body politic, and that British and American democracy are today under strain.

As to the future, new forms of democratic involvement have become a possibility with the development of media technology. The scope for the use of e-mail as a means of transmitting opinions and exerting pressure on those in office is enormous. Such technology empowers voters, and provides new means for them to be more actively involved in political dialogue. It opens up the possibility that they will be able to pass information to one another, so that the overall level of knowledge of the American citizenry will be increased. Voters might wish to use these developments to their advantage, and those elected to public office will need to be more conscious of those whose vote placed them there. This does not mean that they have to be subservient to public pressure but certainly their performances will be more effectively monitored.

In the longer term, another possible development is that the computer-literate might conduct some form of referendum on the net, giving many people a greater opportunity to participate in the political process than ever before. There may be dangers in 'electronic populism' and 'mobocracy', but for others such as Kevin Kelly 'the Internet revives Thomas Jefferson's 200-year-old dream of thinking individuals self-actualising a democracy'.[24]

In Britain, the system of interactive communications is relatively in its infancy as far as many people are concerned. But as the network of users of information technology is extended over the coming years, British voters too will have more scope to state their problems and express their views to their elected representatives. MPs and congress members will need to listen carefully to public demands, but of course they need to remember that those who use the Internet are not representative of the whole electorate. Any elected member must appreciate that it is inevitably a segment of the population, which has the facility to play an interactive role in both democracies. They are elected to their respective legislatures to represent the whole constituency, not just those who possess an electronic voice.

Conclusion

A political democracy exists when:

- the people have a right to choose and dismiss their government in free elections;
- they are faced with a choice of candidates from more than one party and those parties are allowed to place their views before the electorate without impediment;
- all concerned in the process of government subscribe to the values which make democracy work – in particular, there is 'an implicit undertaking between the parties contending for power in the state not to persecute each other'.[25]

In Britain and the United States, there exist institutions which can regulate the clashes of interest that inevitably arise in any pluralistic society. Both countries can be described as examples of liberal democracies. There are other types of

The state of democracy in Britain and the USA: a summary		
	USA	UK
Use of direct democracy	Widespread and regular of referendums and initiatives at state level; no national use.	Infrequent use at national level, some local referendums. No initiatives.
Attitude to representative democracy	Method by which democracy mainly operates.	Strong commitment. More important than notion of limited government.
Attitude to liberal democracy and concentration of power	Strong belief in limited government, as part of a general distrust of governmental tyranny. Power diffused, so that 'power checks power' via checks and balances.	Less emphasis on limited government, and no codified constitution, separation of powers or federalism to act as check. Criticism of undue, excessive concentration of power in Executive. Government has exceptionally free hand to govern.
Attitude to centralisation of power	Decentralisation written into Constitution, via federalism. States have been given new lease of life in recent years.	Traditionally a unitary and highly centralised state. More interest in decentralisation in recent years, with devolution to Scotland, Wales and Northern Ireland.
Existence of quangos	Many political offices are elected. Little anxiety expressed about power exercised by unelected bodies.	Anxiety about number of quangos, power they exercise and the personnel involved (especially the basis on which they are chosen).

democracy, countries which are 'semi-democracies' perhaps on the road to the more complete form, or 'façade democracies' which have some features recognised in the West as democratic, notably the existence of a government chosen via popular election.

Democracy is widely seen as the ideal form of government, which is why the leaders of so many nations are keen to describe their governing arrangements as 'democratic'. It is a model to which many aspire, but in practice many democratic countries have some blemishes on their records. The workings of both British and American democracy have been subjected to searching criticism in recent years and in some respects found deficient. But the overwhelming majority of people on either side of the Atlantic favour the self-government and freedom that the system allows over any alternative, even if the outcome is imperfect.

	USA	UK
Open government/ freedom of information	Reputation for open government and strong freedom of information legislation. Easier to unearth and get to bottom of scandals.	Traditional obsession with secrecy in government. Recent Freedom of Information legislation denounced by critics as over-protective of government – in any case, not due to be implemented until 2005.
Rights, their existence and the denial of them	Rights clearly stated in Constitution. But poor record on civil liberties and rights of minority and disadvantaged groups. Women did not get vote until after 1918, African-Americans had to wait to the 1960s. 'Tough' treatment of criminals.	Rights never clearly defined, rested on 'three pillars' of Parliament, courts and climate of public opinion. New protection since 2000, via 1998 Human Rights Act – degree of protection available via the incorporated European Convention yet to be clearly established. Right to vote achieved very gradually.

Some common problems

Lack of knowledge, interest and belief in politics and politicians

Low level of political participation, including turnout in elections

The FPTP electoral system

The media

The neglect of rights, especially in difficult national security cases

The importance of money in elections

REFERENCES

1   B. Crick, *In Defence of Politics*, Penguin, 1964.
2   A. Heywood, *Politics*, Macmillan, 1997.
3   F. Fukuyama, 'The End of History?', *National Interest, summer* 1989
4   R. Dahl, *Democracy and its Critics*, Yale University Press, 1989.
5   G. Higgins and J. Richardson, *Political Participation*, Politics Association, 1976.
6   R. Hague and M. Harrop, *Comparative Government and Politics*, Palgrave, 2001
7   S. Finer, *The History of Government from the Earliest Times*, Oxford University Press, 1997.
8   A. Hacker, 'Britain's Political Style Is Not Like Ours', *New York Times Magazine*, September 1964.
9   As note 6 above.
10 J. Madison, A. Hamilton and J. Jay, *The Federalist Papers*, re-issued by Penguin, 1987.
11 Lord Hailsham, *The Elective Dictatorship*, BBC Publications, 1976.
12 K. Dolbeare, *Political Issues in America Today: 1990s Revisited*, Manchester University Press, 1999.
13 P. Taylor, 'Democracy and Why Bother Americans', *International Herald Tribune*, 7 July 1990.
14 I. Crewe, *Comparative Research on Attitudes of Young People*, 1996.
15 W. Hutton, *The State We're In*, Vintage, 1996.
16 G. Parry, G. Moyser and N. Day, *Political Participation and Democracy in Britain*, Cambridge University Press, 1992.
17 R. Putnam, *Bowling Alone: The Collapse and Revival of American Community*, Simon & Schuster, 2000.
18 G. Edwards, M. Wattenberg and R. Lineberry, *Government in America*, Addison-Wesley, 1998.
19 J. Keane, *The Media and Democracy*, Polity Press, 1991.
20 N. Postman, *Amusing Ourselves to Death*, Viking Penguin, 1985.
21 L. Rees, *Selling Politics*, BBC Books, 1992.
22 A. Mitchell, *The Media*, Wroxton Papers, 1990.
23 G. Monbiot, *The Guardian*, 16 October 2001.
24 K. Kelly, *Wired* magazine, as quoted in *The Guardian*, 22 February 1995.
25 As note 4 above.

USEFUL WEB SITES

On the UK

www.data-archive.ac.uk UK Data Archive (University of Essex). Evidence on British social attitudes and public opinion.

www.natcen.ac.uk National Centre for Social Research.

www.ons.gov.uk Office for National Statistics. Useful source of up-to-date information on social/economic features.

On the USA

Polling evidence on American attitudes is available at the General Social Survey and National Election Study sites:

www.icpsr.umich.edu/GSS

www.umich.edu/~nes

SAMPLE QUESTIONS

1 'Flawed democracies'. Discuss this verdict on the British and American political systems.

2 'Democratic in theory, but less impressive in practice'. Discuss the fairness of this assessment of the operation of the political system on either side of the Atlantic.

3 Consider the state of liberal democracy in Britain and the United States. In which of the two countries has government in recent years been more democratic?

Index